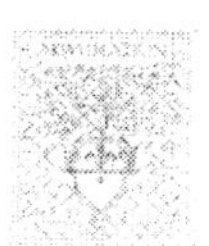

PRIOR'S FIE

RELIG

Annabel Walker

Julie Roseblade

6 July 2013

A COMPARATIVE STUDY OF RELIGIONS

A Comparative Study of Religions

Y. Masih

MOTILAL BANARSIDASS PUBLISHERS
PRIVATE LIMITED • DELHI

Reprint: Delhi: 1993, 2000, 2005, 2010
First Edition: Delhi, 1990

ISBN: 978-81-208-0743-3 (Cloth)
ISBN: 978-81-208-0815-7 (Paper)

MOTILAL BANARSIDASS
41 U.A. Bungalow Road, Jawahar Nagar, Delhi 110 007
8 Mahalaxmi Chamber, 22 Bhulabhai Desai Road, Mumbai 400 026
203 Royapettah High Road, Mylapore, Chennai 600 004
236, 9th Main III Block, Jayanagar, Bangalore 560 011
Sanas Plaza, 1302 Baji Rao Road, Pune 411 002
8 Camac Street, Kolkata 700 017
Ashok Rajpath, Patna 800 004
Chowk, Varanasi 221 001

Printed in India
By Jainendra Prakash Jain at Shri Jainendra Press,
A-45 Naraina, Phase-I, New Delhi 110 028
and Published by Narendra Prakash Jain for
Motilal Banarsidass Publishers Private Limited,
Bungalow Road, Delhi 110 007

PREFACE

A Comparative Study of Religions has been written by a scholar who has occupied himself with the subject of religion for over fifty years. But no finality can be claimed. The reason is that religion deals with what is transcendent in the sense that it deals with what man is going to be. Advaitism terms this futuristic end as becoming Brahman, Jainism as regaining one's pristine glory, theists as becoming gold fit for the heaven. However, Bergson and other evolutionists would say that religion is a collective and co-operative effort of men to become gods. This simply means the divinising of man what Aurobindo calls 'supermind'. The terms 'gods' and 'supermind' are vague and very very imprecise. They refer to a state beyond human ills, beyond human infatuation and beyond the befogging of human intellect. This is known in Jainism as *sarvajñatā*.

One thing is clear that fighting with other human beings in the name of religion is sub-human. As religious men we are fellow-travellers in the direction of the realm of *spirit*. Here the nomenclature of Hindus, Muslims, Christians etc., ceases to be meaningful. Ramakrishna meant this, but he was hearkening back to the past Sanatana Hindu Dharma. But here we are pressing Hinduism, Islam, Christianity and other religions for using all their resources for the birth of a New Man. Hence, the religion of man to which we are looking forward is not so much in the past as it is yet to be.

Of course, we have to go very far and we have not made any beginning yet. However, at present the advaitic principle of differenceless Brahman can serve the purpose of harmonizing all religions. Here we have adopted this principle. Secondly, the key-concepts of different religions have been shown to mingle into one another.

We are all beggars for spiritual alms and let us beg at all the doors the nourishment of our *ātmans*.

24th June, 1989 Y. MASIH

ABBREVIATIONS

B.G.	*Bhagavadgītā*
B.G.B.	*Bhagavadgitabhāṣya*
B.U.	*Bṛhadāraṇyaka Upanishad*
Chh. U.	*Chāndogya Upanishad*
Kath. U.	*Kaṭhopanishad*
M.	Mahendranath Gupta, *The Gospel of Ramakrishna*
N.V.	Nyāya-Vaiśeṣika
R.K.	Ramakrishna
Sayings	*Ramakrishna: His Life and Sayings*
S.B.E.	*Sacred Books of the East*
Svet.	*Svetāsvatara Upanishad*
T. Teachings	*Teachings of Sri Ramakrishna*
V.S.	*Vedāntasūtras with Shankarabhāṣya*

CONTENTS

Chapter I

INTRODUCTION

(The Nature and Function of a Study of Living Religions of the World)

The Necessity of a Comparative Study

Thinkers all over the world are first concerned with the self-understanding of man. Man wants to know about his own history. In the light of this history he determines his own destiny. Arnold Toynbee has done a monumental work in ten volumes regarding the world history of man through the ages. His findings are that religion stands in the centre

> "I have come back to a belief that religion holds the key to the mystery of existence; . . . "[1]

and further adds that the

> "Catholic minded Indian spirit is the way of salvation for human beings of all religions in an age in which we have to learn to live as a single family if we are not to destroy ourselves."[2]

Thus one good reason for a comparative study is that a thought-structure is reached which will stand against human conflict, religious wars and communal tension. Most probably this is a real fear in the mind of the moderners.

An Indian feels proud to learn that the comparative study of religions (Hinduism, Zoroastrianism, Islam, Judaism and Christianity) was started by Akbar in about 1575 A.D. This resulted in the eclectic religion of *Din Ilahi*. In this durbar of religions, a Sufi saint is said to have declared,

> Whatever be thy religion, associate with those who think differently from thee. If thou canst mix with them freely and

> are not angered at hearing their discourse, thou hast attained peace and art a master of creation.[3]

A comparative study of religions is supposed,

> to make us more catholic in our sympathies, more just and generous, in our attitude to foreign faiths, more magnanimous towards orthodox people......[4]

For understanding man from the earliest times up to the present, one has to study art, architecture, all kinds of remains, literature and beliefs. Religion is the most prominent feature which has found its expressions in human art, literature and his various activities, more in the ancient past than in the modern times. Hence, for understanding man, one has to study the architecture of temples, idols, hymns, songs, religious poetry of the *Gathas*, Zendavesta, Ṛgveda, the Bible, the Quoran, Adigrantha and so on. There is hardly any ancient work of art which was not sanctified and hallowed by religious inspiration. Some of the finest poetry in the world has been dedicated to religion. The Ramayana, Mahabharata, Dante's *Divine Comedy*, Milton's *Paradise Lost* and the *Paradise Regained* are some of the most glorious examples of religious poetry. Hence, in order to study man, one has to take religion seriously. One question, however, may be raised at this point.

The Doctrine of Religion *A Priori*

From the past tradition it is clear that man believed in religion *a priori.*[5] Plato held that all true knowledge is recollection. It is this pristine glory of the soul which makes men pursue what is good, true and beautiful. Following Plato, St. Augustine laid down: "O Lord thou hast made us for thyself, and our heart is restless till it rests in thee".

Islam also accepts the doctrine of religion *a priori.* According to Mahmud Shaltour[6] men are so psychologically constituted that they will confess to the existence of God, specially when they are free from distractions, or, when they are faced with hardships or misfortunes.

"And if thou (Muhammed) ask them:
Who created the heavens and the earth, they will surely answer: The Mighty, the Knower created them."

(Surah 50.9; 48.9)

It might be conceded that in the past man was religious, but at the present time in an age of science and technology religion appears to be an anachronism. A modern man has ceased to believe in heaven-hell, Virgin birth and many such stories of miracles. Thus, according to this view of debunking religion, it is held that religion is a time-bound phenomenon of man and with the deepening of the scientific spirit in man, it is bound to disappear. From a cursory survey of modern men...this conclusion appears to be plausible, for most modern men are getting away from religion. This is not only true in the communist countries, but is found in Europe and Britain as well. But is religion really a culture-bound phenomenon and likely to disappear with the slow but inevitable advance of a scientific world-view? However, this need not be a true view of religion and even of modern men.

Marxism, Freudianism and Dewey's type of humanism have very systematically tried to destroy the very foundation of traditional religions. But in their turn they have themselves assumed the form of some sort of religion. For example, communism in Russia and the Eastern Europe, is studied as seriously as once Christianity was studied in those countries. It is introduced from the infant classes up to the University education. Again, communism is preached throughout the whole world with the same commitment and self-involvement which characterized the preaching of the Christian gospel. In the same manner, Erich Fromm has shown that even Freudianism teaches a religion of human brotherhood, free from psychic complexes and dedicated to the alleviation of human sufferings. Above all Freudianism teaches a religion of resignation to the inevitable. How does this religion of resignation to the inevitable differ from Islamic and Indian teaching of resignation to the inevitableness? Islam teaches resignation to the sovereign will of Allah and the Indian bows down before the inevitable consequences of one's past *Karma*. Thus, the Freudian teaching about human brotherhood, free from inner compulsion and given to the resignation of the inevitable is not substantially different from other traditional teachings or other traditional forms of religions. Finally, it is a well-known fact that Dewey's teaching of humanism supporting the American type of democracy is itself a form of religion. Why other forms of democracy practised by the Communist Party of Russia be not regarded as democracy? John Dewey speaks of his Naturalism in the following eloquent speech:

> We who now live are parts of a humanity that extends into the remote past, a humanity that has interacted with nature. The things in civilization we most prize are not of ourselves. They exist by the grace of the doings and sufferings of the continuous human community in which we are a link. Ours is the responsibility of conserving, transmitting, rectifying and expanding the heritage of values we have received that those who come after us may receive it more solid and secure, more widely accessible and more generously shared than we have received it. Here are all the elements for a religious faith that shall not be confined to sect, class, or race. Such a faith has always been implicitly the common faith of mankind. It remains to make it explicit and militant.[7]

Thus, John Dewey too regards his naturalism as the *implicit faith* of all mankind. It is also a form of militant religion. Thus, religion cannot be banished from human beings. As such we hold on to the doctrine of *religion a priori*, according to which religion is implanted in man and cannot be eradicated without doing violence to his nature. We find the confirmation of this statement in the persistence of religion even in Russia where religion was suppressed with an iron hand. Religion is as natural in man as thinking and breathing. Banish religion through the door and it comes back to you from the window. One religion can give way to another form of religion, but man cannot live without religion. The doctrine of religion *a priori* follows from *holism* which is found in all living beings, from the lowest to the highest.

It was Aristotle who observed that there is a tendency in a hatched egg to become a chick. Much later Hans Driesch (1867-1940) found that an embryo has a holistic tendency within it to become a whole and complete animal of the species to which the embryo under study belongs. If some injury is done to the embryo, then all other parts come to compensate the injury by contributing the injured embryo to become complete and whole. Much later on Lashley working on the functioning of the brain in relation to the laws of learning, came to the conclusion about the equipotentiality of the brain. In other words, he found that the brain works as a whole. If a part of the brain is injured, then the other parts try to compensate the working of the injured part. In the same strain C.G. Jung found that the human psyche works as a whole, and, in due course, forces a man to become complete and whole. The holistic tendency in learning, perceiving etc., was demonstrated by the Gestaltists, W. Kohler, K. Koffka and others. However, the most interesting result concerning holism is found in a series of studies with regard to the working of personality. Kurt Goldstein, Andras Angyal, Abraham Maslow, Prescott Lecky, Carl Rogers and many others came to the conclusion that personality tends to become one unified whole. Each personality, either dimly or clearly has a picture of one's own ideal self which it wants to become. Under a strong drive in each man to become an ideal self, a picture of his ideal self is projected into gods, goddesses or God, by worshipping whom he gets the feel of his attaining what his whole being cries forth. Thus religion is an essential overtone of his striving towards his ideal self. Hence, as long as there is the formation of personality in each man, there will be a tendency to become a complete and whole self. And the ideal of an ideal self comes to be projected into a deity, by worshipping which each man gets the psychological satisfaction of his reaching and realizing his perfect self. Thus, religion is an inevitable conclusion of every man who consciously or unconsciously wants to reach his perfection. Hence, religion is as natural as breathing, thinking and becoming. The most important thing in religion is not only *to know*, but *to become* what concerns his most ultimate concern. In the field of religious philosophy Plato, St. Augustine and Paul Tillich are the stalwart thinkers who have held on to the doctrine of religion *a priori*. Our conclusion therefore is that any specific form of religion is certainly culture-bound, but religion in general is natural in man and is not likely to disappear in near future or at any time.

The doctrine of religion *a priori* has a deep lesson for man in relation to the evolutionary philosophies of emergentists, creative evolutionism of Bergson and ingressive philosophy of A.N. Whitehead. According to evolutionary philosophy in general, in spite of many failures, set-backs, backsliding, certainly there has been remarkable emergence of new beings and things out of the creative throw of nature. Out of gaseous form, matter did emerge. In the fulness of time matter did give birth to life. Once again, when the time was ripe, from living beings man did emerge. Whatever the early history of man could be, one thing is certain and no fiction that self-conscious man did emerge slowly, gradually and after a good deal of groping man is realizing today that man is the crown and roof of things in the whole evolutionary scheme of things. With this consciousness in him, he is also painfully realizing that he is very weak, frail and imperfect. He has to go very far. In this on-goings of the world, he is fully aware of the option of going further towards becoming a higher being, or, choosing the option of becoming a failure in the struggle of existence. The dilemma of becoming either a god or extinction is forced on him. The dilemma is posed for not an individual, but for the whole human race.

Looking back at the evolutionary scheme of things, there certainly have been cases of progress along with decline. There is something in the universe which pertains to advance. This push and pull for giving rise to higher emergence has been termed *nisus* by Samuel Alexander. Again, the tendency in each living creature to remain in the state in which it is found has also been termed by Alexander as *conatus*. By virtue of *conatus* in each man, man perseveres himself as a human being. But there is also a *nisus* which goads each man to become higher than what he is. It is due to the presence of *nisus* which drives a man to have his ideal self and to project this ideal self into what he considers to be his highest self in the person of his deity. By worshipping, praising and meditating on his deity he gets the feeling of his becoming a complete and whole being.

But it is not enough to become one's complete self by his individual self alone. He knows that in a society of other competing men and religions, his state of reaching perfection is always open to conflict. The perfection reached at the state of meditation (or, *samādhi*) is very short-lived. In the past, the Indian sages have clearly stated that individual liberation is not enough. An *arhat* has to work still and become a *bodhisattva* who has to work for the salvation of the human race. In the same strain, the Advaitins have been preaching for the goal of *sarvamukti* i.e., salvation for the whole humanity. At the very beginning of Christianity St. Paul has stated that the whole universe has to be won and changed into a new Jerusalem and man has to be transformed into a *New Being* (col. 1.20; Ephesians 1.20).

There has been the ushering in of great religions which appeared to be realizing the dream of infecting all men to be changed into higher beings. Christianity appeared to have realized this dream. At another time in the past the Upanishadic teachings had blazed the trail of becoming Brahman. In the same strain the *Siddhas* hoped to have become immortal by practising *tantra*. Aurobindo also taught the doctrine of becoming supermind. Again, we must not ignore the story of Islam which at one time appeared to have infected the whole civilized world to become gold fit for heaven. But, alas! man has to go far and yet very far.

In the preceding language of evolutionary scheme of things, the *nisus* in man came very near of creating a new Jerusalem and a new being. Today, religions differ and instead of combining the insight of each religion to change the whole universe, we find that many thinkers have become very critical of traditional religions. The end of a comparative study of religions is to enkindle the *nisus* within human beings so that new beings may emerge. Henri Bergson, in '*The two sources of morality and religion*' states his vision. According to Bergson, the vital living force has created man. But the universe cannot stop with the creation of man only. This man has to give birth to higher beings. According to him the essential function of the universe is the making of gods.[8] The created human beings have to turn into creators. This can be possible if the whole race gets infected in the task of transforming man into a creator or a god. Hence, a study of living religions might help to evoke in us a vision of higher beings and to pull us to put forth efforts in that direction. Why have religions so far failed us?

Dangers in the Study of Comparative Religion

With the rise of scientific world-view amongst philosophers, anthropologists and psychologists, investigators applied scientific methodology to ascertain the essentials of religions.

Sociologists regard religion as a social phenomenon. For them religion is a social activity which takes society as a reality. Durkheisn as such regards godfigure as a social truth and necessary for holding the society together as a moral community. For anthropologists too religion is concerned with beliefs and practices in a living community. Historians study religious beliefs in terms of events as influenced by such beliefs. For example, Christianity, Islam, Buddhism, Nazism have greatly influenced socio-political events in human history. Freud (1859-1939) and Feuerback (1804-1872) have declared religion as the projection of human psyche. Hence, statements about God are really statements about man. Again, many thinkers (e.g., G.W.F. Hegel 1770-1831), E.B. Tylor, J.G. Frazer, Robertson Smith have applied their minds to the evolutionary study of religions.

It is but natural to start with the simplest forms of religion, because the higher religions are far too complex to be studied at the beginning. Hence, anthropologists like J.G. Frazer and many others began to study primitive religions like Totemism (J.G. Frazer), Animism, (E.B. Tylor), Manaism (Marrett), Fetishism and so on. In this regard the ten volumes of '*Golden Bough*' by J.G. Frazer are monumental. But what has been his conclusion with regard to religion as a whole? The findings of Frazer are negative. Another attempt by Sigmund Freud spelled greater disaster, because his studies pretended to touch the depth of the human psyche in matters of religion. After a good deal of his preoccupation with the theistic form of religion, Freud declared religion to be a mass-neurosis of mankind and wholly infantile. (*The future of an Illusion*, 1927). The whole thing in religion, according to Freud:

is so patently infantile, so incongruous with reality, that to one whose attitude to humanity is friendly it is painful to think that the great majority of mortals will never be able to rise above this view of life.[9]

Why has a scientific study of religions failed? For the simple reason that religion is the whole of man, and science deals with what is partial. The language of science is factual and descriptive. In contrast, the language of religion is evocative, beckoning a seeker towards his own depth in the direction of new dimension of reality by changing the whole outlook of the seeker. It requires utmost *sympathy* for a student of comparative study of religion to enter into the shoes of another believer and feel the pinch which his shoes give to the believer of the faith other than his own. Perhaps it is difficult for a non-believer to develop that much of sympathy for entering into the feel and throb of believers. In has been held that non-believers are religion-blind. One has to get interested to see things as a believer sees the things for himself. In contrast, a scientist has to cultivate his attitude of utmost disinterestedness towards his facts and findings. In our language a scientist of religion can only know the *conatus* of a believer, but not his *nisus*. Hence, a non-believer scientist cannot help having a negative view of religion. The core of religion eludes his grasp. True, a believer, having some faith in a religion is better suited to approach other religions differing from his own than a non-believer. But even for a believer there are great pitfalls against which he has to guard himself.

A scientist is condemned to have only the husk and not the grain of religious belief. But even a believer has to be careful, otherwise, he would get only the diseased grain after winnowing religions. A great many times some theologians study religions and at the end of their study conclude their own religion as the best. This is specially the case with missionaries of different faiths. For example, Christian missionaries often studied other religions, viz. Islam, Hinduism, Buddhism, Jainism and invariably showed that Christianity was the best religion. This is very well illustrated in the case of John Muir who wrote a booklet called *mata-pariksha* (test of religions, 1839). In this *mata-pariksha*, he tried to show that Christianity was the only true religion. The result was that the Hindu Pundits not only defended their own faith, but became harsh and intolerant towards Christianity.[10] This type of comparative study pertains to the encouragement for fundamentalism in religions and paves the way for tension and conflict between religions. The same thing is found in relation to Radhakrishnan's defence of Hinduism '*Eastern Religion and Western Thoughts*, 1939' in relation to Dr. A. Schweitzer's attack on Hinduism in his book '*Indian Thought and Its Development*, 1935).

There is another related danger when a comparative study of religions is undertaken with a view to showing that of all religions one particular religion is the final fulfilment of all other religions. For example, J.N. Farquhar in 1913 wrote '*The Crown of Hinduism*' and showed that Christianity is the fulfilment of Hinduism. This approach did not satisfy the Christian thinkers nor the Hindus.[11] Such an approach is based on the ignorance of theologians with regard to the psychology of believers. Each believer in his faith feels his becoming complete, whole and perfect in terms of the holistic drive within him. Any attempt to show the absurdity, weakness or incompleteness in any religion will evoke tension and conflict.

Hence, by avoiding the dangers in a comparative study of religions, we can fulfil some of the tasks and aims of such a study.

Aims and Purpose of a Comparative Study of Religions

First only a believer in religion should undertake the task of studying religions belonging to different ages and peoples. Even a historical development of one's own religion will be a rewarding pursuit. For example, Rudolf Bultmann studied Christianity from its inception and has established for himself and for other fellow Christians the task of demythologizing Christianity. By demythologizing Christianity one would know the real message of Christianity for its modern adherents. Again, a comparative and historical study of prophetic religions will bring them much closer and would promote mutual understanding between them. In like manner a comparative study of all living religions with regard to some common salient features would show that after all the disagreement between them is much less than agreement. For example, the doctrine of eternal hell and the doctrine of innumerable rebirths are not as remote as people seem to think. And the same is true with regard to other key-concepts of religions.

Perhaps a word is needed to elucidate the phrase 'mutual understanding of different religious believers'. Mutual understanding of men belonging to different faiths means taking full cognizance of their conviction, commitment and existential decisions involved in their practice and beliefs. For reaching this kind of understanding a high degree of disciplined imagination is necessary by virtue of which one will be able to enter into sympathy with others by transporting themselves into their inside. This may be styled as *kathenotheistic* or *henotheistic* endeavour for placing oneself into the inside of different faiths. This requires us

> to step ourselves into the other fellows' shoes; and this again, as everyone realizes, also implies the capacity to take own shoes off first.[12]

This was successfully practised by Ramakrishna. His own testimony is:

> I had to practise each religion for a time—Hinduism, Islam, Christianity. Furthermore, I followed the paths of the Shaktas, Vaishnavas and Vedantists.[13]

A study of living religions would bring us nearer to the nature of religion. For example, Durkheism held that religion is a social affair of men. As against this A.N. Whitehead stated that religion is what a man does in his solitariness. It is true that for primitive races and for early form of Judaism and for Vedic Hinduism, religion is a matter of social affair. But against this for Christianity, later Judaism and Islam and Hinayana Buddhism salvation is for the individual with their moral and religious obligations to society. If Marxism be regarded as a religion, then for it social changes, leading to the withering of the state would lead to social millennium where everybody will get what he needs and would produce according to his abilities. Even Isaiah hopes for a millennium, "Wolves and lambs will eat together; lions will eat straw, as cattle do, ..." (65.25). It appears that society and the individual both must be transformed *pari passu*. The one-sided emphasis of *Sarvodaya* and *Sarvamukti* go together. Thus a study of different religions will give one a deeper insight into what religion is.

A study of different faiths will show us the common acceptable points found in them, which till now might have been only dimly noticed. For example, Alfred W. Martin (*Comparative Religion*, 1926) and Dr. Bhagvan Das find that all religions teach more or less the same moral code. Likewise, Rudolf Otto found that in every religion there is the same numinous feeling of awe, wonder and dread (*mysterium et fascinans*). Excepting the first five commandments given to Moses, all others are included in the *pañca mahavrata* of the Jains, which is the common property of all Indian religions. One very important moral code is reflected in the living religions of the world.

> 'Do as you would be done by' (Zoroastrianism, Christianity); 'One should seek for others the happiness one desires for oneself' (Buddhism).

This kind of cognizance of the common and shareable teachings of religions will inspire toleration and respect for religions other than one's own and perhaps may help us to evolve a kind of consensus of agreed beliefs and spiritual values. This is reflected in *Din Ilahi* of Akbar.

A study of various religions may serve to enrich and deepen one's insight into one's own religion. For example, a study of Hinduism created a new insight in Otto, and thereby he wrote '*The Idea of the Holy*'. In like manner, a study of advaitism led Paul Tillich to establish his fruitful theory of symbolism in religion. Hence, Radhakrishnan writes,

> Our aim should be not to make converts, Christians into Buddhists or Buddhists into Christians, but enable both Buddhists and Christians to rediscover the basic principles of their own religions and live up to them.[14]

Thus, a comparative study of religions teaches us to cultivate the virtue of appreciation and appropriation of the different insights of different religions.

A study of religions may cross-fertilize religions, leading to an amalgam of religious insight, or, might give rise to newer forms of religions. There is little doubt that in Dara Shikoh and in many sufis there was an amalgam of Hinduism and Islam. Their head was Upanishadic and their heart was Islamic.

A study of Christianity and the Upanishads gave rise to a new form of Hinduism known as Brahmo Samaj. Brahmo Samaj led to fruitful reformation in Hinduism like prevention of *sati*, condemnation of idolatry, anti-casteism and so on. In the same manner in the movement of Ramakrishna Ashrama Hinduism was sought to become a universal religion.

In the opinion of the author of this book, the most important task of comparative study of religions is to find out a principle of unity which will harmonize and balance the claims and counter claims of warring religions into one unity. Unity does not mean uniformity of religious conduct and belief, but a harmonious blending of religious variety into a symphony of spiritual striving and quest. In the opinion of the author such an absolute principle is found in Shankara's doctrine of differenceless Brahman which every form of religionists can accept without doing much violence to one's faith. The same point may be true of Kabir's teaching about *Purna Brahma* and certainly of Ramakrishna.[15]

For gaining insight into living religions certain common topics have been taken in each religion, for the purpose of relevant comparison. These topics are the doctrine of each religion with regard to God, world, soul, Heaven-hell, the day of judgment, ultimate destiny of each soul. Also some outstanding topics in some religions like the doctrine of atonement in Christianity, the doctrine of rebirth in Hinduism, prayers and meditation have been taken up. An attempt has been made with regard to the historical development of various religions, and a history of Indian religion. The purpose of this again is bringing the religions together, so far as their nature and origin are concerned.

There is little doubt that God looms large in the living religions of the world. God can neither be proved, nor disproved. Is this God-talk, then, nonsense? Or, is it a revelatory event of the universe in travail for giving birth to higher humanity? That there is God and He has been working in the Universe, and, most clearly in human history, and, even in individual lives, will remain an article of faith, and, perhaps nothing beyond this stand can ever be maintained. There is a perennial hope that man and his dearest hopes will not perish. There is the dawning awareness in man that 'God within man' has to be realized as his highest destiny. This realization of one's inner being is beyond all books, creeds and warring claims of different religions, even though religious scriptures and religious teachers are necessary in awakening Godward consciousness in man. May this book contribute a little towards the realization of 'God within man'.

The doctrine of 'God within man', or 'a lotus in the heart' is essentially Upanishadic and Vedantic, and, has been repeatedly emphasised by Ramanuja, Kabir and Guru Nanak and Ramakrishna. The teaching of realizing 'God within man' emphasizes that *knowing* has to be subordinated to the supreme task of becoming divine (*Brahmavid Brahmaiva Bhavati*). In other words, to know God has to point us the way towards becoming a thing of value, a pearl of great price, or, gold fit for the heaven. A knower of Buddha has ultimately to become a Buddha. This is the real meaning of *Appo Dipo Bhava**. Jesus too said, 'Be as perfect as your Father in heaven is'. This earth is a veritable vale of soul-making (Keats), or, as Bergson has said the world has undertaken the task of creating gods out of created beings.

*Be a light unto yourself and seek your salvation with diligence.

References

1. *The Observer*, October 24, 1954, p. 6, col. 4-5.
2. *Ibid*, col. 5.
3. A.W. Martin, *Comparative Religion*, pp. 2-3.
4. A.W. Martin, *Ibid*, p. 3.
5. Masih, Y., *Shankara's Universal Philosophy of Religion*, pp. 19-22.
6. *Islam*, ed. Kenneth W. Morgan, pp. 75-6.
7. John Dewey, *A Common Faith*, Yale 1960, p. 87.
8. *Two Sources of Morality and Religion*, London 1935, p. 375, *Vide* 201, 202.
9. S. Freud, *Civilization and its Discontents*, London 1930, p. 23.

10. Richard Fox Young, *Resistant Hinduism*, Vienna, 1981.
11. Robin Boyd, *Indian Christian Theology*, Madras, 1969, pp. 89-90.
12. R.J. ZWI Worblowsky, On the role of comparative Religion in Promoting mutual understanding, Hżbbert Journal, Vol. 58, p. 33.
13. *The Gospel of Ramakrishna*, Madras 1989, p. 129.
14. *Fragments of a Confession* in 'The Philosophy of Sarvepalli Radhakrishnan', p. 74.
15. *Bṛhadāraṇyaka Upanishad*, 5.1.

CHAPTER II

ZOROASTRIANISM OR PARSIISM

THE HISTORICAL IMPORTANCE OF ZOROASTRIANISM

Till very recently it was believed that Vedic Hinduism is really the oldest form of Indian religion. But, at the present time, it would not be correct to hold this view. Even at the time of Ṛgveda, there were at least the Dasas/Dasyus who racially differed much from the Aryans, and certainly much more in their religious theories and practices. The Dasas/Dasyus were *liṅga*-worshippers and had a god different from Indra. They did not have animal-sacrifice and had observances quite different from those of the Vedic Aryans. Most probably proto-Shiva of Mohenjo-daro was one of their deities.

It is not possible to know much at present about the Dasas/Dasyus. But certainly, we find Ajivikism, Jainism and Buddhism as three religions which did not share the Vedic Aryan religion called Brahminism which accepted the *Vedas* as the only religious scripture for it, and, keeping to the caste maintained the excellence and supremacy of the Brahmins over all other castes and people. The non-Vedic religions ef Ajivikism*, Jainism and Buddhism did not accept the Vedas as their holy books and did not have castes.

Later on Islam appeared on the Indian scene and also in middle East Asia, where Brahminism and Buddhism had considerable following. Previous to the advent of Islam many races other than the Aryans had entered India. They were all absorbed in the Indian people. With the conversion of Persians, Turks and Buddhists to Islam, a different kind of situation arose specially for the Buddhists. When they wanted to return to Hinduism, they were accepted only as the Shudras and at times as outcastes. Many of the so-called Shudras and outcastes took to Shaivism and Vaisṇavism where there was no caste and

*Ajivikism later on merged into Jainism.

which were really non-Aryan cults*. There is no evidence to show that Jainism and Buddhism ever subscribed to Vedic sacrifices, Vedic deities or caste. They are parallel and native religions of India and have contributed much to the growth of even classical Hinduism of the present time. At present there is a remnant of Buddhism, often called neo-Buddhists. But most of the Buddhists have taken the form of Kabirapanth, Natha-Sampradaya and the like. Sikhs really belong to a virile foreign race and now-a-days they do not call themselves 'Hindus'. Nonetheless their faith cannot be divorced from a wider definition of Hinduism. In the most distinctive sense, a person is a Hindu who subscribes to the four pillars of *Karma-Samsāra-Jñāna-mukti*. It is this definition which separates the Hindus from the other types of religions called Prophetic religions of Zoroastrianism, Judaism, Christianity and Islam.

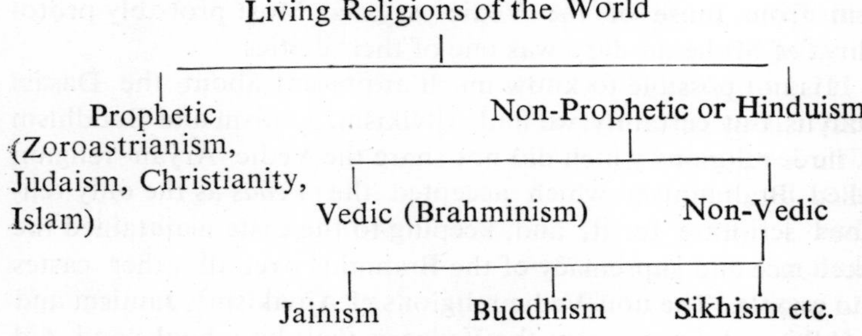

Zoroastrianism is most important in the sense that it gave birth to prophetic religions as well as to Brahminism.

Zoroastrianism and Prophetic Religions

Christianity came into the world as reformed Judaism, and, Islam has been regarded as a reformation movement of both Judaism and Christianity. But Judaism in its developed form owes much to the prophetic religion of Zoroastrianism.

Judaism is roughly found in two phases. First, it was a simple religion of Yahwe, who was essentially a nature-god of thunder and storm. He was regarded as a god and not the only God.

*Sir Jadunath Sircar, *India Through the Ages*, Calcutta 1928, pp. 56-57.

At most he was a tribal god who was appeased by the animal sacrifice of bulls and rams. Besides, the Jews believed in tribal morality in the sense that any transgression of the Mosaic law meant the transgression of the whole tribe. They also had a very indistinct notion about the soul in post-mortem existence. According to them the soul of the dead exists in some sort of a shadowy form in Shiloh. This kind of belief amongst the Jews prevailed when they were taken into exile in Babylonia. However, during the period of exile, the Jews imbibed a great deal of Zoroastrian religion which was the dominant faith of the people of Babylonia. The post-exilic beliefs of the Jews underwent a sea-change under the influence of Zoroastrianism.

In the post-exilic period, the Jews developed strict Monotheism, the doctrine of resurrection and the day of judgment, the teaching about angels, heaven and hell, hatred of idolatry and in the place of animal sacrifice, the Jewish prophets taught people to love mercy and to have a contrite heart for the remission of their sins. They also began to have a sense of individual responsibility for their acts, instead of tribal morality.

It is difficult to ascertain the time of the rise of Zoroastrianism, but it is surmised that it happened to have arisen about 2000 B.C. The Jews themselves were in exile in Babylonia between 712-600 B.C. But the Jews themselves trace their origin to Abraham who had left the idol worship of his ancestors in Mesopotamia and had moved towards the land of Canaan. Most probably in order to escape the persecution at the hands of the Muslims, some later Zoroastrian priests identified their chief prophet Zarathustra with Abraham.[1] This was untrue. But the teaching of strict monotheism is certainly Zoroastrian, to which we shall return just a little later. But it might be surmised that the Mesopotamian Abraham could have been influenced by the monotheistic movement amongst the Babylonians. Hence when the Jews were in exile in Babylonia they simply could recognise and regain their belief in pure monotheism which had no place for idol worship and animal sacrifice.

There is little doubt that Christianity arose as a reformist movement amongst the Jews. The Jews at the time of Jesus paid too much attention to rituals. For them the Sabbath had to be observed even at the cost of animal and human life. Besides, they still believed that God dwells in temples and is not essentially a spirit who can be found anywhere and at any time if a sinner returns to Him with a penitent heart. For Jesus, God is a Father and an object of love and trust. Jesus taught that God is to be found in fervent prayers, service to one's fellowmen. Above all He taught that it is better to die to bring home to the people that God is love who is looking out for a sinner to return to Him.

None of these things were really foreign to Judaism. But a few things offended the Jews. Jesus was regarded as God and the Son of God. This was against the teaching of monotheism for which God is One who is neither begotten nor does He beget. Besides, no man can be equal to God. Christians in their zeal tended to minimise the role of Moses who was the law giver of the Jews. The Christians also did not believe in the practice of circumcision and the animal sacrifice on the occasion of the feast of Passover. Hence, for the Jews, Christians did not keep to strict monotheism which was handed to them by Moses and which was purified and cherished by Ezra who was influenced greatly by the Zoroastrian concepts of strict monotheism.

At the time of the prophet Muhammad Arabia was under the Persian domination and was greatly influenced by the strict monotheism of Zoroaştrianism, Judaism and Christianity. Prophet Muhammad thought that the Jews were not strictly monotheists inasmuch as they often relapsed into idolatry. Besides, they venerated Moses and Ezra even more than God. In the same way the prophet regarded the Christians as blasphemous because they believed that Jesus was the begotten son of God. The prophet was greatly influenced by the strict monotheism of Zoroastrianism. Certainly there were Zoroastrians in Arabia and the name of Hanif is mentioned as one who kept the pure monotheism, which according to the prophet, was first preached by Abraham.

Thus, Islam regards 28 prophets who were sent by God to teach the people; nineteen of them have already been mentioned in the Old Testament and three more (Jesus, John the Baptist and Zachariah) have been taken from the New Testament. But the prophet Muhammad traces his pure monotheism to the preaching of Abraham and on the occasion of Id-ul-Zuha, the animal sacrifice by the Muslims is commemorated in the name of Abraham who proved his loyalty to God by being prepared to sacrifice to Him his only son, Isaac. Besides, the Prophet adopted five prayers a day as the Zoroastrians had practised in preference to three prayers a day, practised by the Jews.*

Hence, the prophetic religion was first introduced by the Parsis where Zarathustra was the prophet who preached the message of one God called Ahura Mazda. But this Ahura Mazda is really Asura Medha of the Aryans i.e., the living and wise God. Most probably Zoroastrian religion and the Iranians are far more directly related to the Indo-Aryans than to the Semitic Prophetic religions and people.

The Iranians and Indo-Aryans

The oldest Parsi scripture is known as *Gatha*. Later on it came to be written in Zend (commentary) and Avesta (the language in which it was later written). So it is now known as *Zendavesta*.

Zendavesta is divided in two parts.

1. The first part contains the Vendidad, the Visperad and the Yasna. Vendidad is a compilation of religious laws and stories; Visperad contains litanies pertaining to sacrifice, and, Yasna also has litanies and five hymns or *Gathas* in a special dialect.

2. The second part is known as Khorda Avesta or 'small Avesta' containing prayers.

When the language of Zendavesta could not be understood by the people, then the priests of Parsi religion translated it into Pahlavi which is the ancient form of Persian language. French, German and British scholars tried to decipher the language of *Gatha* and Zendavesta. Slowly and gradually it dawned upon them that the language of *Gatha* and Zendavesta has very great kinship with Sanskṛta language; when the grammar of Panini,

*The Parsis had five divisions of a day and they had five prayers for each division (Yes. XLIV.8). Five divisions are 6 A.M. to 10 A.M.; 10 A.M. to 3 P.M.; 3 P.M. to 6 P.M.; 6 P.M. to 12 P.M.; 12 P.M. to 6 A.M.

A great many Parsi ideas have entered into Islam through Talmudic Judaism. The doctrine of Resurrection, the Day of Judgment, the teaching of Heaven and Hell, the doctrine of angels and demonology, the trial of each person through passing of the bridge Sirat. Iconoclasm, militancy are also common features of Zoroastrianism and Islam.

Katyayana and Patañjali was applied then the Gatha and Zendavesta came to be understood by the westerners.[2] The lesson from this amazing fact is clear that once the Iranians of the *Gatha and Zendavesta* and the Indo-Aryans of the Vedas formed one single race, speaking language akin to Samskṛta. Indeed this is clear from the clay tablets found in Tell-el-Amarna in Egypt and Boghaz Keui in Asis Minor. On the tablets are mentioned Indra, Varuṇa, Mitra and Nasatya as witnesses of the treaty between the King Subiluliuma of the Hitties, and the Mitanni King Mattiwaza. These tablets date about 1600 B.C. These tablets clearly indicate that these are Vedic gods who were quite familiar in the region about 1600 B.C. and that the people living there and then had more or less a common religion. *Deva* and *Asura* (*Ahura*), *Yajna* and *Yasna*, *ṛta* and *asha* (Gatha) are one and the same religious terms. Other linguistic similarity in grammar and words is very great[3] which leaves one in no doubt that the Iranians of the Zendavesta and Indo-Aryans formed one and the same race. When they lived together, then what could be the reason of their separation?

This tall question cannot be easily answered with certainty. However, the scholars have attempted some sound conjectures which can be mentioned here. Martin Haug tells us that a part of the original stock of the Aryans turned into Agriculturist settlers. But another part of the Aryans remained a pastoral people These pastoral Aryans, who later became Indo-Aryans, often strayed into the Agriculturist Iranian Aryans, often looting their animal wealth and destroying their agricultural produce. In this recurring battles the Indo-Aryans enjoyed an upper hand. So they were hated and disliked by the Iranian Aryans. But, there appears to be a deeper reason of religious difference between them. It is difficult to say as to the time of some radical reformation in the Aryan religious cult. But at some remote time about 2000 B.C. the Agriculturist Iranians belonging to the Aryan tribe reached and preached the doctrine of strict monotheism with a good deal of stress on morality which means inner purity. In contrast, the pastoral Indo-Aryans were polytheists, ritualists and believed in the efficacy of animal sacrifice. Of course, for a pastoral people, as we also find amongst the early Jews, animal sacrifice was a natural expression of worship and adoration of their deity. However, the reformed Iranians did not favour animal sacrifice and idolatry. Thus there was a deep rift between the Persian Aryans and Indo-Aryans*. This is quite clear from the fact that Varuṇa was far more popular with the Iranians than Indra. It was this image of Varuṇa which was transformed into Ahura Mazda in Zoroastrianism. But Indra remained the warlord and the *Devanam Devah*.[4]

According to Martin Haug, in the Zendavesta, from the very beginning *deva* is a general name of an evil spirit and the Zoroastrianism is against the Devas (*vi-daevo*).[5] As against the devas, Zoroastrianism is the religion of *Asura* (Ahura) or Ahura Mazda. 'Mazda' is the same as 'medha' (in sanskṛta, meaning-wise). In the older portions of the Ṛgveda, '*asura*' is used in good sense. Indra (an asura god I. 54.3), *Varuṇa* (RV.I. 24.14), *Agni* (RV.IV.2.5; VII. 2.3), *Savitri* (RV.I.35.7) and *Rudra* (RV.5.42.V) are all called *asura* which means living, for *asu* means breath. But as time went on in the later Vedic literature *Devas* were taken to be creatures of light who were at war with the *Asuras*.

Thus, asuras became the demons in later Brahmin literature and in the Zoroastrian scripture *asuras* remained the object of worship and veneration. Hence, the Indo-Aryans became the deva-worshippers with Indra as the supreme war-lord whereas for the Iranians Ahura Mazda remained their one God who remained the father and friend of his worshippers. In due course there was a good deal of differences between the worshippers of Ahura Mazda and those of the Devas. The many gods of the Aryans were reduced to angels and some of the devas remained demons in Zoroastrianism. The Deva-worshippers continued to believe in the efficacy of animal sacrifice and even idolatry. As opposed to this deva-worship, the Zoroastrians became iconoclasts, disfavoured animal sacrifice and stressed the need of social morality. Thus in the Brahminical books the asuras are regarded as the enemies of the devas who disturbed the sacrifices offered to the devas.[6]

* This hypothesis of conflict has been discounted by James Darmesteter rather very vaguely (Introduction, SBE Vol. IV, 41, 42). James Darmesteter writes that a comparative study has pointed out the identity of Ahura Mazda, the supreme god of Iran, with Varuna, the Supreme God of the early Vedic age. (SBE, Vol. IV, Introduction XXIX)

From the above-mentioned points, it is conjectured that Indo-Aryans had to part company with their kinsmen called the Iranians or Zoroastrians.[7] But it is clear that the Parsi religion is as much related to the prophetic religions of the Semites as it is so in relation to the Vedic religion of the Brahmins. According to Dhalla, in the early days the two branches of Aryans sacrificed to the same gods and had the same ideas about their earthly life. They separated later on about 2000 B.C.[8]

On this score John Darmesteter writes:

> . . . . the long forgotten past and the origin of many gods and heroes, whom the Parsi worships and extols without knowing who they were and whence they came, were suddenly revealed by the Vedas.[9]

Again,

> The key to the Avesta is not the Pahlavi, but the Veda. The Avesta and the Veda are two echoes of one and the same voice, the reflex of one and the same thought: the Vedas therefore, are both the best lexicon and the best commentary to the Avesta.[10]

Basic Features of Parsiism

Some features of Zoroastrianism have been noted down by early historians. The earliest reference to Zoroaster has been given by Plato in Alcibiades. It is mentioned that Zoroaster was the son of Ahura Mazda. Then Herodotus B.C. 450, the father of historians, mentions that the Persians do not have idols, nor do they build temples. Further, he tells us, that the Persians believe Fire to be a god. Again, Strabo 60 B.C., the geographer, mentions that the Persians first invoke fire before they worship any deity. Plutarch (46 A.D.-120 A.D.) states that according to Persians evil is always mingled with good, and that the good god and the demon are engaged in a constant war. However, they believe that in the end, Ahriman will perish and disappear and all men will live in happiness.

In the light of what has been stated above, we can mention a few basic tenets of Zoroastrianism. One can easily see for himself that these features must have influenced Judaism, Christianity and Islam. Only the worship through fire reminds one of the Vedic god Agni.

It is presumed that Zarathustra simply reformed the pre-existing Parsiism belonging to the age of the Gathas. According to Martin Haug, Zarathustra maintained strict monotheism, that is, there are not many gods, but only One God. With the rise of speculative tendency, Zoroastrianism became dualistic, maintaining the conflict between two primeval forces. Reformed Parsiism has the following features:

1. Parsi God, Ahura Mazda is one and only God. As such Zoroastrian God is essentially monotheistic.

2. But God is essentially transcendent for He is much beyond and above His creatures. He is yet not so remote as a deistic God is, for He can be approached and worshipped by his devotees. He is immanent only in a metaphorical or secondary sense inasmuch as He enters into relation with His worshippers as their father, brother and friend.

3. As God is essentially transcendent to His creatures, so He can be found out through His intermediaries called angels, but above all by His prophet Zarathustra. Zarathustra meditated long in solitary seclusion on God and at last reached the conception of Ahura Mazda or the Wise Lord. At last Zarathustra got convinced that he was called upon to preach the message of God for all mankind. His preaching was concerned with a nobler religion than what was known then about spiritual life. Ahura Mazda was above all the gods and did not favour animal sacrifice. But he required genuine piety of the heart issuing in *humata* (good thoughts), *hukhta* (good words) and *hvarshta* (good deed). In other words, the wise Lord, Ahura Mazda demanded purity of thought, speech and action.

4. Zoroastrianism believes in the resurrection of dead, and, the day of judgment.

5. Every man will have to get across the bridge of Chinvat. Good souls who go across will go to heaven and evil ones who fail pass, into hell. Here one is reminded of the bridge of *al-Sirat* mentioned in the Quoran, through which every one has to pass through, either successfully to the Heaven or unsuccessfully to Hell.

6. However, the Parsis believe in Restoration, when ultimately

the whole universe will be restored to its purity.* The torment of hell is not eternal, for in the end man will be restored to a life of bliss after being chastised and purified by the hell-fire.

7. Later on, dualism entered into Zoroastrianism as its secondary tenet. It is secondary in the sense that it crept into Parsi religion later on, and, also in the sense that it will ultimately disappear in the period of Restoration.**

8. Even though dualism appeared in Zoroastrianism in a secondary way, it has a good deal of significance. The evil force is represented by Ahriman and his demons who instil evil thoughts in man and create evil in all other circumstances. As against the forces of evil, Ahura Mazda through His representative Spenta Mainyu and other good angels are there to fight evil so that the day of restoration be brought nearer.

9. Zoroastrianism with its doctrine of angels and demonology teaches that man is to become a co-sharer and co-worker in the conquest of evil by his goodness. This means that man can help the fight against evil by offering sacrifice of food and drinks to the gods for strengthening them and by cheering them through praise. This doctrine of becoming a co-worker with God was later on taught by William James. By the way through this grand plan of God, man has not only to serve God by his good thought, speech and action, but has to contribute materially for the welfare of man and beasts. Hence Zoroastrianism is a religion of inner purity and social benevolence.

Here one can easily notice that according to Islam, one not only purifies oneself through five prayers a day and Hajj, but has also to give money in *zakat* and *sadaqa*. Christians also believe in social charity and service.

10. Zoroastrianism as a reformist movement is characterized by a good deal of intolerance of idolatry, and over-zealous regard for monotheism.

* Here St. Paul seems to echo the same thought 'through the Son, then, God decided to bring the whole universe back to himself. God made peace through his Son's death on the cross and so brought back to himself all things, both on earth and in heaven'. (Colossians 1.20; Ephesians 1.10).

** Even evil is not independent of, and co-eval with God. "A separate evil spirit of equal power with Ahuramazda, and always opposed to him, is entirely foreign to Zarathustra's theology" (M. Haug, Ibid. p. 303).

This is also seen in post-exilic Judaism and in iconoclasm of Islam.

11. Animal sacrifice was not permitted by Zarathustra, though it was in vogue before his preaching.

12. But fire remained the symbol of Parsi religion, reminding us of its earlier religious practice of worshipping the gods through fire (*Agni*). It remained a symbol of light and purity.

Even in the Bible God is said to be the light of the world, and, Allah is said to be '*nur*'.

One consequence of this veneration of fire is that the Parsi does not dispose of the dead body by burning it. The reason for this is that for the Parsi, fire, water and earth are sacred and pure. On the other hand, the dead body is most impure. Hence, the impure dead body is not allowed to pollute fire (by burning), or, the earth (by burying) or by throwing the dead body into sea or rivers. For the Indo-Aryans, fire is god and also the mouth of the gods to consume the sacrifice. So for the Indo-Aryans too fire was most sacred.

13. Even though three castes of Brahmins, Kshatriyas and Vaishyas are known in the Gatha and Avesta, yet Zoroastrianism teaches equality and brotherhood of man. On this point too Christianity and Islam seem to echo and re-echo the voice of Zarathustra, the first known prophet of God.[11] Further, it is noted that Kshatriyahood is rated higher than the castes of Brahmins and Vaishyas, exactly as Lord Buddha is reported to have held. Of course, the doctrine of caste does not mention the shudras, and it is this fourth caste, which is deeply and widely decried in India.

But in one sense, as in the Vedas, priesthood was considered hereditary. The priest known as Dastur has to belong to a Dastur family, even when the son of a Dastur is not obliged to become a Dastur.[12]

14. Further, Zoroastrianism does not favour asceticism and prescribes the life of a house-holder.[13] It is to be noted that even the Vedic Brahmins put their great emphasis on the *Gṛhastha Ashrama*. As against Jainism and Buddhism the Vedic Brahmins did not favour *sannyasa* without undergoing the stage of a house-holder.

15. Again, there is no mention of the triad of Brahma, Vishnu

and Mahesha in the Gatha or Zendavesta. And this triad has not been mentioned in the earlier Vedic literature too.[14] This means that the doctrine of triad and the epics of the Mahabharata and the Ramayana are either later developments in Hinduism or of non-Aryan origin.

THE DOCTRINE OF GOD OR THE MONOTHEISM OF ZOROASTRIANISM

God of Zoroastrian religion is known as Ahura Mazda. 'Ahura' means 'The Lord', 'Mazda' means 'the Wise'. Hence, Ahura Mazda means 'the wise God'. At times even the single word 'Ahura' or 'Mazda' indicates the same 'The Wise Lord' of all that exists Ahura Mazda stands for a strict form of a monotheistic God. The earliest expression in the Gatha is:[15]

> 'Thee alone, I know to be the Supreme.
> Others all, I dismiss from my mind'—(Gatha 44.11)
>
> 'I know thee to be the supreme over all,
> —man, gods or beasts'—(Gatha 34.5).
>
> 'I know him, to be nobody except thee'—(Gatha 34.7)
> 'I have no other protector except thee'—(Gatha 29.1).

In 1843, the then learned Parsi priest Edal Daru described Ahura Mazda:[16]

> The one holy and glorious God, the Lord of the creation of both worlds, and the Creator of both worlds, I acknowledge thus. He has no form, and no equal; and the creation and support of all things is from the Lord.

Again,

> We are able to inquire into that Lord by the light of the understanding, and through means of learning. We constantly observe his influence, and behold his marvellous wonders. This is equivalent to our seeing that Lord himself.

Later on, M.N. Dhalla described Ahura Mazda as Transcendent, not in the philosophical sense, but in religious phrase, as a Being who is infinitely more sublime and greater than his creatures.[17] Again, he calls God transcendent, more or less, in the sense of Aristotle,

> 'He was, he is, and he will be the same transcendent being, moving all, yet moved by none'.[18]

Yet God has been described also as 'immanent in the religious sense that man can enter into close and loving relations with him as his father, brother and friend.[19] In the philosophical sense of 'transcendence' God remains beyond human speech, as the Upanishads, the Bible and later on St. Thomas Aquinas have maintained. In this sense God can be described only through analogies and that also most haltingly, most probably concealing more than revealing the ineffable nature of God. Keeping this meaning of 'transcendent', we can state the attributes of God only religiously, for the purpose of entering into fellowship with him, which fellowship is very real for the worshippers. Two things have to be kept in mind.

First, when mentioning the attributes of God, we have to keep in mind that the finite can describe the infinite through finite analogies and similes only.[20] Secondly, Zoroastrianism tries to put a member of intermediaries between Ahura Mazda and man in order to show that man can deal with God only indirectly with the help of his intermediaries and finally through his prophet Zarathustra. Here we are reminded of Plotinus who also described a number of Emanations of the Absolute there putting a distance between men and the Absolute. The same sort of arrangement is seen in the *pañcaratra*, where the supreme Brahma can be approached only through the lowest of its *avatara*. Keeping these two expedients in mind, the attributes of Ahura Mazda have been thus described.

Ahura Mazda is the first and the foremost Being. He is not begotten and none is like him. He is the most perfect Being, as Anselm and Descartes have called God. But from these metaphysical attributes, Ahura Mazda has been described as a loving father, brother and friend. He is responsive to the prayers of his worshippers. Ahura Mazda is also known as the creator of the whole universe, angels, animals and man. This creation takes place out of the creative and spontaneous free act of God.

'He created human beings and their spirits, breathed life in their bodies and endowed them with the freedom of will'.[21]

This Zoroastrian view of God has been retained in Judaism, Christianity and Islam.

Ahura Mazda is also said to be a law-giver to the whole mankind, for guiding man for what is right and conducive to his final weal and woe. We also find that Ahura Mazda is the dispenser of *ṛta* (of Varuṇa) which oftener is also called *Asha*. Like *ṛta*, *asha* is moral, natural and spiritual law. As he is the law-giver, so he will also judge the breaches and observances of his law on the day of judgment or the day of reckoning.

Spenta Mainyu

We have already seen that Ahura Mazda is transcendent, immutable and absolute unity. But the world in which we live is mutable and changeable. How can the two opposed things be reconciled? Here Zoroastrianism posits a reality in between the two. Here there is the conception of Spenta Mainyu who is the manifestation and projection of creative will and thought of Ahura Mazda. The two are co-eval and eternal. One is the unmanifest and Spenta Mainyu is its manifest form. Here one can easily discern the two forms of Brahma, *nirguṇa* and *saguṇa*. In other words, Ahura Mazda corresponds to the *nirguṇa* Brahma of Shankara and Spenta Mainyu corresponds to the notion of Ishvara in Shankara Advaita. Spenta Mainyu represents the good thought, will and creative act of Ahura Mazda *humata*, (good thought), *hukhta* (good words or speech) and, *hvarshta* (good deeds).

Ahura Mazda can be worshipped only through Spenta Mainyu who can be said to be the Vicegerent of God. Zarathustra also gives his blessings to his votaries who worship him through Spenta Mainyu. Spenta Mainyu is the creative, sustaining and administering Spirit of the whole universe.

Ahura Mazda's Angels

Ahura Mazda has six cardinal virtues of *Vohu Manah* (good mind), *Asha* (righteousness), *Khshathra* (God's Kingdom), *Armaiti* (Devotion, *Shraddha*), *Haurvatat* (perfection), and *Ameretat* (immortality). Soon these abstract and spiritual attributes of Ahura Mazda were personified and they became the holy angels or associates of God. Vohu Manah, Asha and Khshathra are male members in the divine hierarchy, and, Armaiti, Haurvatat and Ameretat are feminine names.

Vohu Manah has been personified into Vohu Mainyu (good spirit). But Vohu Mainyu should not be confused with Spenta Mainyu who is the supreme manifest spirit of Ahura Mazda. Vohu Manah furthers the kingdom of God.

Asha symbolizes nature's uniform and orderly workings and stands for the moral regeneration of man.

Khshatra signifies God's might and power. *Armaiti* symbolizes devotion to Ahura Mazda. Haurvatat (perfection) and Ameretat (immortality) are also personified attributes of Ahura Mazda.

Amongst all the attributes Vohu Manah and Asha are most important. The mighty power of Vohu Manah will become most manifest when all the people will have to pass through the bridge Chinvat. Vohu Manah will come to the aid of the righteous; whereas the evil-doers will be punished. It will be through fire that the righteous will be rewarded and the wicked will be visited by fire with a view to harming them.

Asha stands for righteousness which is the centre and soul of the ethical end of Zarathustra. It is the path of righteousness which Zarathustra sought and taught.

Angra Mainyu of Ahriman

Creation means finitization of the Infinite. Hence, imperfection is the inevitable result of creation. When Spenta Mainyu tried to create a good world, its counterpart in the form of Ahriman or Angra Mainyu introduced evil in the world. Drought, famine, pestilence, and all sorts of evil in the world are due to Ahriman and his associates.

From the very beginning, *devas* have been imagined as evil and in the long run Indra, the war-god after Indo-Aryans came to be regarded as the arch-devil.

It is also reported that like Lord Buddha and Jesus Christ, the first prophet of Zoroastrianism, namely, Zarathustra was also tempted by the devil called Ahriman. Again, Zarathustra succeeded in defeating the attempts of Ahriman.

Whatever be the account of the dualism of good evil in Zoroastrianism, it is fully religious. Unlike Indian religions of Jainism, Buddhism and Brahminism no philosophical explanation in terms of *Avidyā, Ajñāna* or *Māyā* is advanced by Zoroastrianism. Evil is accepted as a fact of life. Whatever the name of evil be given, Ahriman, according to Zoroastrianism, pollutes the whole creation and, lulls the conscience of men and lures their mind, speech and action for the evil. Thus, Ahriman creates an evil spirit in man, and, thoroughly distorts his real nature. It is this evil nature in men that has to be purified through prayers and rituals.

Fight against evil is a hard thing. Evil is a fact of real life, according to Zarathustra. He advises his followers to become a soldier to fight against the evil. Evil is as much within as without. Even in the soul of man there is a fight between the evil and good. God Ahura Mazda calls upon man to fight the evil in man and outside of him, against all the evil spirits of Ahriman and Ahriman himself. Hence, this struggle against all kinds of evil in nature and man has been ordained by Ahura Mazda himself. By fighting againt evil man becomes a co-worker and co-sharer of Ahura Mazda himself. Man becomes active in the conflict with evil through sacrifice. Sacrifice is more than worship. It is a form of assistance to Gods in their fight with evil. Gods, like men, need drink and food and encouragement by being cheered up through their praises.[22] This call to fight against evil has later on been emphasized by William James.

Evil no doubt is an evil, but it means a challenge for man so that by overcoming evil man may become fit for entering the heaven. As such evil is a necessary test and trial for man. It has been ordained by God so that man may rise higher than even angels. This is a conception which has been taken up in Islam by Iqbal. Man has been given free will either to choose evil or good. If he by his free will chooses the good, then he will rise higher than the angels. If not, then he will face hell and its torments.

Two things have been stated very clearly by the Zoroastrian, namely, the evil within man is a greater challenge than the evil outside of man. As such man can fight the evil through his good thought (*humata*), good speech (*hukhta*) and noble deeds (*hvar-*

shta). Secondly, one has to keep in mind that evil is not the final thing. Ultimately Ahriman and all his associates will be defeated and destroyed and a great renovation will be followed in the final reckoning of things. This means that evil is only a temporary phenomenon and goodness alone is the final thing. Thus, the dualism in Zoroastrianism is only relative and Ahura Mazda remains the only Reality. Thus dualism is swallowed up in the Absolute monotheism of Zoroastrianism.

The World

The one word 'Creation' explains many things about the world. The first thing is that the world has been created by the wisest and the best creator, Ahura Mazda. He has created this world for the enjoyment of his creatures. Nature in her multifarious phases delights man and gives him infinite enjoyments if he is prepared to live according to the rules given to him by his prophet, Zarathusthra.

Ahura Mazda has established a stable order in the whole universe. The sun and moon and everything in the universe work according to the laws called *Asha*. These laws speak of the providential care of Ahura Mazda for his creatures and creation. Stars do not go astray, the moon waxes and wanes, according to set laws. The whole universe betrays the working of the Logos, the divine *Asha*. Thus the world is good. There is not only Spenta Mainyu who has brought about this universe, but also Ahriman (Angra Mainyu) is there to create disorder. It is Ahriman who brings about pestilence, floods, droughts, earthquakes and so on.

Thus man has to know the laws of nature to guide him in his life. He has to fight against evil in nature. By fighting against evil, he becomes a co-worker with God. He has to realize that by siding with evil or by breaking the laws of nature, he will be punished. Hence, the world is there either for rewarding or punishing men.

On the whole, Zoroastrianism holds on to a cheerful view of life. For it life on this earth is a blessing and like the Indo-Aryans of the Ṛgvedic age, a Parsi prays for a happy, healthy and long life on this earth. Mazda is asked to bestow on his followers happiness and joys of a long life. As noted before, along with the creation by the best and most benevolent God, there is evil in the world. This evil has to be acccounted for and fought against. So we have to deal with it now.

EVIL

Along with Ahura Mazda and his materialized and co-eval power called Spenta Mainyu, there is Angra Mainyu (or Ahriman). In the early literature of Parsi religion, evil was considered to be a necessary consequence of creating a finite universe, for creation means finitizing the Infinite. Hence, M.N. Dhalla states:

> The materialization of the divine thought in creation spells imperfection and Spenta Mainyu is shadowed by his inseparable opposite. These two primeval spirits who are spoken of as twins, emerged from the divine bosom and by their innate choice appeared as the better and the bad in thought, word, and deed.[23]

Of course, later on Ahriman was taken to be an independent evil spirit for Ahura Mazda was thought of absolutely good and no evil spirit could ever arise from him.

Whether the later or earlier view be taken into account, for the Parsi evil is evil and real and should not be explained away as *Māyā*, or, an appearance only to a finite view in things. Bradley held that every evil is really good if it be perceived from a wider and deeper point of view. For example, cow-dung is bad when it soils the cloth; but is good if it used for cleaning the house or for fertilizing the land. For a Parsi evil is not only a foil to the good, as Leibnitz held, but has to be fought against and fully controlled through the wisdom granted to us by Spenta Mainyu.

Evil is most real. The catastrophes in nature are most palpable. Should man bow down before evil? No Parsiism teaches that evil is a challenge for man, and, he has to fight evil. He (man) is viewed as a militant soldier in the battle for conquering and mastering evil in nature. In order to strengthen one's resolve to fight evil, a Parsi has personified evil as the work of Angra Mainyu (or Ahriman). Not only Angra Mainyu creates natural calamities for men and animals, but he distorts the mind of man. Ahriman lures man towards evil deeds, lulls his conscience and makes the evil appear as good. Hence, man has to keep himself on his guard and discipline his mind, thought and acts. He has to pray to his God with full devotion so that he may triumph over the evil.

Therefore, for a Parsi, man's life is a constant struggle with evil. Man has to resist evil, whether in nature or in his mind or in society. A Parsi in the past held on to Zoroastrianism and was always involved in conflict with the State and other religions. Christians and Parsis fought for long in Persia and destroyed one another's holy places of worship. It is the Parsi who has sown the seed of fanaticism in all forms of prophetic religions.

In later thought, the Parsi regarded Ahriman as a power relatively independent of Ahura Mazda, for a good God could not be imagined to have created an evil power to injure his own creatures. But, whether we take earlier or later view of evil, it was never taken to be absolutely real. It was taken to be non-eternal. In the long run, Ahura Mazda will cause his worshippers to triumph over the activities of Ahriman. The people will become righteous and they will put Ahriman to flight. With the destruction of Ahriman, there will be the final conquest of evil by good. Thus, Ahriman is not eternal, is not omniscient and omnipotent. Evil, as such is secondary and the good Ahura Mazda alone is eternal and absolutely real. Thus, the dualism of Parsiism finally gives way to strict monotheism. Utlimately man has to triumph over evil through his *Humta* (good thought), Hukhta (good word) and *Hvarshta* (good deeds), which lie enshrined in the heart of reality.

The Doctrine of Man

Ahura Mazda has created this world and has endowed it with laws so that the world, with stars and skies, flora and fauna may be stable and wholly dependable. By knowing the laws of nature one can predict the future and thus can control nature and guide one's behaviour in relation to the world. In this good world, Ahura Mazda has also made man and his spirit, breathed life into his bodies and endowed him with freedom of will. Why free will?

Because, Ahriman and his associates have sown evil seeds in the world and cause many physical evils of flood and drought, earthquake and other calamities. Nay, the evil spirits prevent man's mind and corrupt his will. For this reason Ahura has granted free will to man so that he is free to choose the good for his salvation and final beatitude, or, may choose evil, working against the physical and moral laws and thus may choose punishment for himself after death and on the day of reckoning. Implied is the view that Ahura cannot make man always choose the good and shun evil. Islam has clarified this issue. According to it, God has made angels who always choose the good and avoid the evil. Because of this grant of free will, man may become much lower than the beast, but he has also the promise and potency of becoming a holy will. As a holy will man becomes higher than the angels and participates in the nature of God. This view of Islam is shared by Christianity also. However, Parsi religion holds man responsible for his acts.

If a man chooses to know the laws of nature and respects the moral injunctions of Ahura, as they have been revealed through Zarathustra, then he works for his salvation and as such becomes a co-sharer and co-worker with God. Ahura is good and he wants all his creation to reflect the good. Hence, in his choice of the good by defeating the evil in nature, in society and political realms, man sides with Ahura. With his praises of Spenta Mainyu and his good angels, he encourages them to fight the foes of Ahura and man. Thus, Ahura requires the praise, prayers and devoted worship of man.

Ahura has endowed man with his guardian angel who assists man in his choice of the good, and avoidance of the evil. But man has been created by Ahura as a militant and disciplined soldier to fight against evil in every sphere of his life. He has not only to choose good and resist the evil in nature, society and in himself, but he has also to help his fellowmen for the same purpose. Thus, man has been created not only to win his own salvation, but has to help his fellowmen to win their salvation. Thus, Parsi religion in spirit, advances the theory of

Sarvamukti of Advaitism and the doctrine of Bodhisattvas of the Buddhists.

A Parsi believes in a successful life of a house-holder and does not believe in a life of a recluse.[24] As a house-holder he prays for his health, vigour of his body, offspring and a long life on this earth. In higher moments he prays for the purity of his heart and mind. Thus, the end of life for a Parsi man is the same which was sought by his counterpart Indo-Aryans in their Vedic prayers.

Parsi religion is the first in Prophetic religions to emphasize the importance of this life. Only this life on the earth entitles a man for reward or punishment. It does not teach the doctrine of rebirth which was also absent in the Ṛgvedic age. This confirms the theory that the doctrine of transmigration is non-Aryan and was accepted by the non-Vedic and possible non-Aryan cults of Ajivikism, Jainism and Buddhism. The Indo-Aryans have borrowed the theory of rebirth after their coming in contact with the aboriginal inhabitants of India. Certainly Jainism and Buddhism and later on the non-Vedic Hindus, like Kabir-panthis, Gorakhnathis and the Sikhs have always accepted the doctrine of rebirth as a supreme postulate or article of their faith. Of course, in the present-day Hinduism, both Vedic and non-Vedic have made the doctrine of transmigration as the cardinal principle of their theology.

The seeds of caste are to be found in Yas XIX. 17, even though it talks of classes according to their functions:

> Through what classes, the priest, warrior, agriculturist, artisan, through the whole duty pertaining to the righteous man, to think rightly, to speak rightly, to appoint a spiritual guide, (and) to fulfil religious duties, through which works the earthly settlements advance in righteousness. (*Yasna* XIX. 17).

It is also worthy of note that only a Dastur can be a Parsi priest, though a son of a Dastur is not obliged to become a priest. However, there was no caste, apart from Dasturs. It is also worthy of note that Brahmin-caste as priests, has been there from the very beginning even from the Ṛgvedic times. But for

Viśvamitra nobody belonging to other castes has ever been declared as a Brahmin. Another thing to note is that there is no Shudra class in Parsi religion whose only function, according to Brahminism is to serve as a menial worker for all castes. Besides, 'class' is a functional concept; but caste is a matter of hereditary birth.

Life after Death: Like the Indo-Aryan people of the Ṛgvedic age, the Parsi believes in a life after death. According to Parsiism, man is an inter-mixture of body and soul. At the time of death the body perishes, but his soul survives death. In what form?

The Parsi is a religious man and he appears to have no speculative interest in the survival of the soul. The Hebrews believed in an embodied soul in Sheol. In India, after the Vedic people accepted the doctrine of transmigration, it was believed that a subtle embodied soul, called *Sukṣama Sharira* goes through many rebirths. It appears that for the Parsi the soul alone survives the death of the body and is either rewarded or punished in life after death.

One thing is certain that for a Parsi this world is a preparatory ground for the life to come. Naturally he is expected to live for the good life in the next. If he does not live for a good life, then he is punished for doing the evil. Secondly, a Parsi believes that this world is not a just world, for here at times the wicked thrives and a righteous man suffers. Hence, he believes that there must be a next life in which the virtuous will be rewarded and the evil-doers will be punished. This was philosophically supported by a famous philosopher called Kant, on exactly the same ground that now a Parsi accepts. In any case, for a Parsi this earthly life is only a prelude to a next larger and more enduring existence after death. According to Zoroastrianism man is an architect of his own destiny. He has to take the help of Ahura Mazda. He has to walk according to the laws of a good life as they have been preached by the prophet Zarathustra. Further, through prayers to Spenta Mainyu and his associates, he can derive spiritual strength in fighting against the powers of evil. He also believes that in a final reckoning of things evil will be utterly vanquished and destroyed, for Ahriman is not omniscient nor is he eternal. As such Parsiism is a robust faith for the triumph of the good over the evil. In the struggle with evil man is not only an architect of his own destiny, but as a good man he becomes a partner and sharer of God.

The Day of Judgment—Zoroastrianism believes that there will be a final day of reckoning on which man will be either rewarded for his goodness or will be punished for his evil acts. He also imagines that there will be a bridge called Chinvat. The righteous will pass through the narrow bridge without any fall, but the evil ones will fall and sink into hell for being tormented. At another times it is also said that the fire will test each man for his deeds. The righteous will experience the test of fire as soothing and comforting. As against this the wicked will weep and cry and will not be able to endure fire. But the final day of judgment is still in the future. What happens to a man just now when he dies?

It is hinted at that there is an intermediate place called purgatory where a man suffers for his evil deed, till he is fully reformed. But the righteous enters the kingdom of Ahura Mazda where there is no more sorrow and where there is a life of bliss and supreme felicity. But what happens after day of judgment?

It is suggested at times that the torment of hell wili be eternal. However, the dominant thought of Zoroastrianism is that there will be a period of great restoration or renovation in which even the wicked people will be fully reformed and they too will become perfectly righteous. Ahriman and his associates will be completely destroyed and there will be a life of holiness and bliss in the Kingdom of Ahura Mazda. Thus the period of restoration minimizes the torment of hell till eternity.

There is little doubt that Judaism, Christianity and Islam were greatly influenced by Zoroastrianism, especially in their acceptance of the day of judgment with its attendant doctrine of Heaven and Hell. It is surprising that few thinkers have adopted the doctrine of restoration. However, Dr. Md. Iqbal substitutes for the doctrine of heaven and hell, a life of unending progress.

On the whole the Parsis were less interested in speculation and were given to the practical task of religious beliefs and practice. But an Indian can always question the concept of eternal duration for a created being. For it anything created or produced can never be eternal. Again, soul alone is not responsible for its evil deeds. It is the body which is perishable, changeable and is infected with many desires. Why should soul be either punished or rewarded for the body with its evil tendencies? After all God has created the body with its imperfection. Does he not become responsible for the evil deeds of men?

Of course, no problem with regard to a transcendent Being can ever be solved, for a Transcendent Being is beyond human experience and thought. Perhaps a respectful silence is more appropriate. But reason has to be advanced even for maintaining silence. Alas! man has been condemned to know the unknowable, and, he has to suffer much because of his eating the fruit of the tree of knowledge. He has to construct a system of thought to satisfy his curiosity. But as soon as the house of thought has been built, it has to be pulled down because later thought must condemn it, as happened in the case of Nagarjuna and Bradley. Will this thought construction and its subsequent negation go on like the fruitless and never-ending task of Sisiphus? Or, does it show that we have not framed our questions and tasks in the right direction?

Parsi and Other Religions

Parsi is the first prophetic religion, and, Judaism and Islam were directly related to it. It cannot be historically speaking maintained with certainty that Abraham, the father of the Jewish race was really related to Parsiism. But there is a strong presumption that Abraham too was related to Parsiism. But apart from Abraham, a good number of Jews were taken as prisoners and were kept in Babylon. During this period of exile, the Jews developed strict monotheism, moral responsibilities for each individual for his acts, and fanatic iconoclasm. The most influential sect called Pharisees were greatly influenced by the Zoroastrian teaching of reward and punishment, heaven and hell, the doctrine of immortality and the day of judgment. The existence of devil, tempting man towards his destruction is really the picture of Ahriman. Most probably the Jews did believe in the existence of angels, but their this faith was greatly strengthened during the period of their exile.

Pre-exilic Judaism

1. Before exile, the Jews did not have pure monotheism. Their God, Yahwe was a tribal God and was one amongst other Gods.

2. Yahwe of the pre-exilic period was really a nature God, specially of thunder, storm and lightning.

3. Yahwe was pleased with the sweet savour of burnt offerings of animals.

4. The Jews had very vague notion of post-mortem existence of the dead in Sheol.

Post-exilic Belief of the Jews

1. The Jews believed in one and the only God who is a righteous judge and holy. Other Gods are false and unreal.

2. God is essentially moral and good. He is not pleased with animal-sacrifice, but prefers a humble and contrite heart.

3. Every individual is responsible for his acts, and, the good and evil of them will be visited on him alone. In pre-exilic period the Jews believed in tribal morality and tribal punishment if any individual of the tribe violated the command of God.

4. There is a life hereafter, there will also be a day of resurrection followed by the day of judgment.

5. As a result of the judgment, the righteous will be rewarded with their heavenly abode and the evil-doer will be punished by hell-fire, where there will be tears and gnashing of teeth. But the Jews did not accept the doctrine of Renovation.

6. As the Parsi believes that there will be intercessors, so the Jews also began to hope for a Messiah who will restore to them the lost kingdom of David.

7. Though the Jews did not accept the doctrine of Restoration, they entertained the hope that a day will come when the lion and the lamb will drink at the same fountain.

Difference

1. Judaism and Parsiism differ in their historical development. Yahwe of the Jews was at first the personification of the natural phenomenon of storm and thunder. In contrast, in Zoroastrianism Ahur Mazda was never the personification of any natural phenomenon.

2. Besides, in early Judaism, Yahwe was only a tribal god—a God amongst many other tribal Gods. In contrast, in Parsiism. there is strict and pure monotheism from the very beginning.

3. Both Judaism and Parsiism accept that God is transcendent. As such the transcendent God has to communicate himself to human beings through His intermediaries called 'prophets'. Theologically, Zoroastrianism posits Spenta Mainyu as the revelation of Ahura Mazda. This Spenta Mainyu is the direct link between the worshipper and Ahura Mazda. In contrast, Judaism strictly keeps to pure monotheism and regards the prophets as the chief intermediaries between the transcendent God and His worshippers. Moses and Ezra are considered to be the chief prophets. For Zoroastrianism, Zarathustra is the only prophet.

4. As time went on, the Parsi believer found the struggle between the good and evil very real and for him dualism appeared to be the most realistic doctrine. In contrast, once the Jews set their belief in monotheism, they never gave it up, even when they accepted the Devil as well.

5. True, both Judaism and Parsiism accept the existence of the day of judgment and the accompanying doctrine of Heaven and Hell. But for Zoroastrianism the existence of hell is non-eternal and at the end in the period of restoration hell along with Ahriman will finally disappear.

In the end it must be confessed that Judaism is indebted to Parsi religion for the acceptance of pure monotheism and pure morality. But prophetic religions as a whole cannot help becoming fanatics, for they accept the authenticity and unerring revelations made by the prophets. So both the Parsi and the Jews are really fanatic.

Zoroastrianism and Christianity

Zoroastrianism influenced Christainity indirectly through Judaism.

Both of them are fanatic religions and when Christianity came to Persia, both of them attacked each other and destroyed holy places of one another. Later on, in India, John Wilson and Parsi people were involved in bitter controversies. This is clear from John Wilson's book, '*The Parsi Religion*' (1843). But apart from the controversies, there is much in common between Zoroastrianism and Christianity.

1. Both Parsiism and Christianity are committed to strict monotheism.
2. Both of them accept the doctrine of the day of judgment, resurrection, Heaven-Hell.
3. Both of them accept strict morality and alleviation of human sufferings and the promotion of human well-being.
4. Both of them feel that man by himself cannot get rid of his own sins. Hence, they feel the need of an intercessor. This is far more prominent in Christianity than in Parsiism. Both of them are prophetic religions.

Along with resemblance in their fundamental tenets, there are important differences:

1. Both of them accept monotheism. But in Zoroastrianism there is dualism, which ultimately gives way to monotheism. In Christianity there is the doctrine of trinity, according to which Father, Son and Holy Ghost are three persons in One. This is a very difficult doctrine for any other religionist to accept. Along with this doctrine of Trinity, Christianity also accepts the doctrine of incarnation.
2. We will find that in Christianity a great need is felt for a redeemer who will teach the ways of God to men and would redeem them from their sins. Hence, Christianity accepts the doctrine of Incarnation, according to which God Himself became flesh and dwelt among human beings. He showed the way human beings should live to become fit for the kingdom of heaven. Hence, Christians talk about 'imitation of Christ'. However, the Parsi does not admit that God can become man. For the Jews, Muslims and Parsis this doctrine of Incarnation is blasphemy.
3. A Parsi believes that through moral activities and

penance for his lapses, he can defeat the evil and win the good. A Christian believes that man by his own efforts, however, laudable cannot save himself from his sins. He has to have firm faith in the redemptive death of Jesus, for Jesus died on the Cross to redeem man of his sins. Only he has to have a strong faith that the sacrificial death of Jesus has washed away all his past sins and now gives him spiritual strength to fight the evil in him, in nature and society so that he may remain righteous before God. This doctrine of atonement is hardly accepted by any other religion of the world. And there is no wonder that Parsis also do not accept this.

4. Both Parsiism and Christianity accept the doctrine of Heaven and Hell. But for the large part, the Christian believes that hell fire is eternal and once a person is cast in Hell, there is no more salvation for him. In contrast, a Parsi believes that life in Hell of an offender is non-eternal. After renovation even Hell will give way to the millennium of heavenly life.

5. In Christianity the life of an ascetic, devoted to the pursuit of Christian virtues, is regarded as a laudable life. But Parsiism does not favour either asceticism or monasticism. For Zoroastrianism, the life of the house-holder is best suited to fight the evil in man, nature and society.

6. According to Parsiism, Ahura Mazda created man as good and only after being tempted by Ahriman is likely to fall into evil. According to Christianity, God made man in His own image, but by his disobedience Adam sinned. And this origined sin is found in all subsequent generations of man.

Zoroastrianism and Islam

1. Historically speaking, Islam appears to have been greatly influenced by Parsiism. This should not be surprising, for the Babylonians had dominated over Arabia, and, in Babylon Zoroastrianism had a good deal of influence and following. Islam speaks more of the pure monotheism of Abraham than that of the Jews. Besides, one Hanif, probably a Babylonian, is regarded

as the holder of the true belief in monotheism. Both Islam and Parsiism are opposed to idolatry and encourage iconoclasm.

2. Both Zoroastrianism and Islam are prophetic religions, accept monotheism, hold on to the doctrine of resurrection, day of judgment, Heaven-Hell.

3. Again, both Islam and Parsiism accept five prayers every day. Here Islam follows Parsiism as against Judaism where three prayers a day are recommended.

4. Both Parsiism and Islam accept the reality of devil, angels and other spirits like Jins.

But in spite of resemblance between Zoroastrianism and Islam there are significant points of *Difference*.

1. In spite of both Zoroastrianism and Islam accepting the freedom of will in man, they differ in some detail. According to Parsiism, man is free and he is the architect of his own destiny. He is here on earth to fight against the evil as a co-sharer with God. As against this a Muslim believes that much in his earthly existence has been decreed by God and as such he has to resign himself to the sovereign will of Allah. In other words, a Muslim also accepts the working of fate along with the free will of man.

2. Zoroastrianism no doubt started with pure monotheism, but with the lapse of time it also accepted dualism. No doubt it believes that the Good will ultimately triumph over evil. But in this mundane existence, for Parsiism, evil is too palpable a fact to be explained away. As against this Islam keeps to strict monotheism. For it devil is really a rebel against God and is bound to be hurled into hell.

3. Both Parsiism and Islam accept that the righteous will inherit the Heaven and the evil-doer will be cast into Hell. But for Parsiism, Hell is non-eternal and on the day of renovation even Hell will cease to be. However, for Islam, as also for Christianity, Hell is eternal.

4. No doubt Zoroastrianism and Islam are both prophetic religions, but Zoroastrianism has only one main prophet, namely, Zarathustra. As against this Islam accepts 28 prophets of whom the last prophet Muhammad is the final prophet of Allah.

5. Zoroastrianism uses fire more or less as the Vedic worship

of *Agni*. But there is no such sanctity of fire in Islam. However, for Islam too God is taken to be light (*nur*).

6. Muslims bury their dead in the hope that on the day of resurrection they will rise from their graves. As against this the Parsi leaves the dead either on the tower of silence or any high hills to be consumed by vultures and other birds.

Parsiism and the Indo-Aryan Religion of the Ṛgveda

Considering the historical fact that once the Iranians and Indo-Aryans lived together and spoke the same language, there should be much in common with the *Gatha*, Zendavesta and the Ṛgveda.

1. As noted earlier the Indo-Aryans and Iranians worshipped together Indra-Varuna-Mitra-Aśvins. So on the whole they had the same kind of religion.
2. Both Parsiism and Ṛgvedic Religion regarded *svarga-prapti* as the highest destiny or *summum bonum*.
3. Both religions regarded the life of a house-holder as very important and did not encourage *sannyasa*.
4. Both religions will be regarded as life-and-world-affirmation. In both religions there are the prayers for worldly happiness, bountifulness of earthly goods, progeny and success over their enemies.

Later on the two religions differed in their emphasis:

1. Parsiism kept close to moral view of life. Opposed to it was Ṛgvedic religion which believed in the efficacy of animal-sacrifice.
2. Zoroastrianism held fast to monotheism. In contrast, Ṛgvedic religion remained polytheist, and, at most went as far as henotheism. And towards the close of Ṛgvedic age chose monism.
3. It is significant to note that in early Ṛgvedic religion, the deity is generally regarded as the personification of natural powers. This is specially true of Varuṇa, Maruta, Dawn etc. In contrast, Zoroastrianism with its teaching of Ahura Mazda will be considered as a spiritual religion and spiritual monotheism.
4. From the very beginning, Parsi religion did not worship *devas*, who were regarded as evil forces. In contrast, the Indo-Aryans worshipped the *devas* and regarded Indra as the king of *devas*. Parsi religion worshipped *Asura* which word became

'Ahura'. But the Indo-Aryans regarded the *asuras* as the enemies of the *devas.*

5. Zoroastrianism preached against idolatry and encouraged iconoclasm. But it appears that the Ṛgvedic religion was not opposed to image-worship, but there is not much evidence for image-worship in Ṛgvedic religion. However, it might not be in favour of iconoclasm.

6. True, the distinction of priestly class, warriors, traders and artisans is found even in the Zendavesta. Except for the priestly class, other professions are not regarded hereditary. They are the names of professional classes. There were no Shudras. However, the Indo-Aryans kept strictly to caste and never allowed any non-brahmins to become a Brahmin, except in the case of Viśvamitra.

But the case is quite different with Sanatana Hinduism and Zoroastrianism.

Parsiism and Modern Hinduism (Sanatana Hinduism)

Ṛgvedic Hinduism has vastly changed into its present form which is better known as Sanatana Hindu Dharma. This classical Hinduism has marked differences from Parsiism.

1. Parsiism does have classes, but not caste. Even when classes of priestly people, warriors, traders and artisans are mentioned, there is no mention of the Shudras. Shudras are not really artisans. Their sole *dharma* is to serve all other castes. This is an alien concept in Parsiism.

Secondly, even when four classes are mentioned, the warrior class is considered superior to the priestly class.[25] And this is so in the discourse of Buddha also.

2. Whilst in Parsi Religion, *Svarga-prapti* remains the *summum bonum* of life, in classical Hinduism *moksa* i.e., liberation from the endless chain of rebirths is considered the highest goal of human striving. The end of heavenly abode is considered temporary in relation to the eternal goal of *moksa.*

Naturally, Hinduism accepts the four-fold truth of *Karma-samsara-jñāna-mukti.*

3. Because Parsi religion accepts the doctrine of creation, so according to it, the world is good and one is enjoined upon

to further the human interest in having as much happiness as is possible. Hence, Parsiism is given to ameliorism.

Hinduism does not accept the doctrine of creation. Instead, in general (excepting *Mimamsa*) Hinduism believes in periodic creation and dissolution. Hence, there is the cycle of creation and dissolution. On the whole, this worldly existence is not considered good. Hence, in principle, Hinduism is pessimistic with regard to this worldly existence. Even Ramakrishna Paramahansa did not believe in ameliorism, even when Ramakrishna Ashram is engaged in improving the lot of the people.

4. Parsiism favours the life of a house-holder, because the house-holder is the mainstay of society. In contrast, Hinduism accepts the important place of a house-holder, but regards *sannyasa* (renunciation) as the highest station of life in this earthly existence.

5. Parsiism, under the prophetship of Zarathustra supported and preached iconoclasm. Hinduism, on the other hand, is given to image-worship. But for Hinduism image-worship is considered to be only an aid and not the end of worship.

6. Zoroastrianism has no place for animal-sacrifice. In Hinduism animal-sacrifice is no longer a popular creed. Only in Kali Puja or the worship of *Shakti*, animal-sacrifice is still practised.

7. Zoroastrianism was a fanatic religion and was backed by missionary enterprise. This is no longer true of Parsiism. Hinduism always believed in co-operative co-existence of religions. Only *Arya Samaj* of very recent origin believes in *Shuddhi* or conversion of people of other faiths into Hinduism.

8. One important point in Zoroastrianism is that there is no place of *Karmavada*, for the simple reason that there is no doctrine of rebirth in it. However, Hinduism has accepted the non-Aryan doctrine of rebirth and thereby it is committed to *Karmavada* i.e., the present life with its good and evil is the result of the past *Karma*. But it need not lapse into fatalism because it also accepts that man can destroy his own past *Karmas* either by the grace of God, or, by one's own efforts of penance, yoga and *jñāna*.

References

1. Martin Haug, *Essays on the Sacred language, writings and Religion of the Parsis*, London 1833, p. 16.
2. The whole story of this amazing discovery has been given by M. Haug, *Ibid.*, Introduction.
3. M. Haug, *Ibid.*, pp. 21, 67, 68-69, 70-72;
   J.M. Chatterjee, *The Gatha* (the end of the book);
   H.D. Griswold, *The Religion of the Ṛgveda*, Humphrey Milford 1923, p. 20,
4. J.M. Chatterjee '*The Ethical Conceptions of the Gatha.*
5. M. Haug, *Ibid.*, p. 268.
6. M. Haug, *Ibid.*, pp. 268-269.
7. For more detail, J.M. Chatterjee, *The Ethical Conceptions of the Gathas*, pp. 196-205; 498-499; H.D. Bhattacharya, *The foundations of living faiths*, Calcutta 1938, p. 423.
8. M.N. Dhalla, *History of Zoroastrianism*, New York 1938, p. 10.
   In the Avesta, the real name of the prophet is 'Zarathustra'. He is also known as Zartusht or Zardusht.
9. J. Darmesterer, SBE; Vol. IV, Intro. XVII; a detailed comparative account of the close relation between the Iranians and Indo-Aryans has been presented by J. Darmesteter in Introduction to SBE, Vol. IV.
10. J. Darmesteter, *Ibid.*, Intoduction p. XXVI.
11. J.M. Chatterjee, *The Ethical Conceptions of the Gatha*, pp. 281, 493, 511.
12. J. Darmesteter, SBE, Vol. IV, Introduction XLVI, XLVII.
13. J.M. Chatterjee. *Ibid.*, pp. 511-512.
14. M. Haug, *Ibid.*, p. 288.
15. J.M. Chatterjee, *Ibid.*, pp. 92-93. Ahura Mazda is later on also called Ormazd.
16. John Wilson. *The Parsi Religion*, Bombay 1843, p. 107.
17. M.N. Dhalla, *Ibid.*, p. 32.
18. M.N. Dhalla, *Ibid.*, p. 31.
19. M.N. Dhalla, *Ibid.*, p. 32.
20. M.N. Dhalla, *Ibid.*, p. 32.
21. M.N. Dhalla, *Ibid.*, p. 34.
22. J. Darmesteter, SBE, Vol. IV. Int. LXVIII.
23. M.N. Dhalla, *Ibid.*, p. 36; Yas XIX 9 and the Note of Martin Haug, *Ibid.*, p. 188.
24. J.M. Chatterjee, *The Ethical Conceptions*, pp. 511-512.
25. J.M. Chatterjee, *Ibid.*, p. 511.

CHAPTER III

JUDAISM

INTRODUCTION

The religion of the Jews is known as Judaism. The number of Jews is very small, but the Jews have made their presence felt wherever they have gone and settled. At present their number is quite large in the States, and, being industrialists, they control much of the policy of the United States of America.

There is little doubt that Christianity has come out of Judaism and the first apostles of Jesus were all Jews. In the beginning Christianity was preached among the Jews only, and, only later on St. Paul opened the gate of Christianity for all nations. Jesus himself felt that he was sent by God to reclaim the Jews only.

But apart from Christianity, Islam has been greatly influenced by Judaism most considerably. Thus Judaism is the parent religion of both Christianity and Islam.

The Jewish faith was first proclaimed by Moses and afterwards was elucidated by Ezra. Later on this faith was expressed in Thirteen Articles by Maimonides which are considered wholly authoritative.

Judaism is a robust religion which teaches strict obedience to the Laws, Statutes and Ordinances of God. Lord God of Israel is holy and just God and Judaism proclaims to follow Yahwe as diligently as is possible. Consequently Judaism teaches justice, righteousness and holiness in the life and conduct of the people. The ideal of holiness does not include a life of strict morality, but also a life of sanctity of human pursuit. As man is believed to have been made in the image of God, so by following the Laws, Statutes and Ordinances given by Moses one becomes a partner of God and fit for His fellowship.

The Jews believe that their ancestors came from Ur in Sumeria about 2200 B.C. Hence, Judaism is very ancient indeed. It is also mentioned in the Old Testament of the Bible (which is also accepted by the Jews) that their first ancestor Abraham was called by God from amongst the idolatrous people. He was promised that his descendants would rule over the earth and they will be as numberless as the sands of the ocean. Abraham begat Issac, and, Issac begat Jacob. Hence, the Jews are known as the people whose ancestors were Abraham, Isaac and Jacob. Nay more. The Jews regard themselves to be the chosen people on earth. This doctrine of being the chosen people accounts for much of their sufferings and triumphs. Why did God choose them from amongst the other races of the earth?

For the Jews it is a mystery that God should have chosen them. Certainly they do not claim any special merit in them, but they attribute this choice to the inscrutable will of God. The title being the chosen people might raise jealousy in the minds of people other than the Jews. But to be the chosen people of God carries not only a great mission for the whole mankind, but also a great responsibility and even much suffering for the Jews. First, 'the chosen people' means that Israel is to serve as a light for all nations of the world. Israel has not only to testify the Glory of God, but has to live most strictly according to the commandments of God.

The Jews have been chosen

> for the task of strictest obedience to His will, as an instrument in His hand for the redemption of mankind and as a teacher whom God Himself keeps from pride by applying to His chosen people the severest of judgment.[1]

Because the Jews are the chosen people, so they must be holy, just and righteous. The least disobedience to the will of God, as it has been revealed to them in Torah, the prophets and other writings, will be punished. For this reason the Jews have endured their suffering through the ages. They have treated themselves as 'the suffering servants' of God as their prophet Isaiah had taught them. Their temple at Jerusalem was first destroyed in 590 B.C. by Nebuchadnezzar and they were taken in exile to Babylon. For the second time their temple was destroyed by the Romans in 70 A.D. The Jews considered their calamities as the result of their sins.

Secondly, because the Jews are the chosen people, so they

alone serve as sacrifice so that mankind may be saved. The task of the chosen people is not only to redeem themselves but to lead mankind for its redemption too. This is how the Jews explain the great tragedies which befell them in Hitler's 'gas chamber'.

Thus, the chosen people have not only to receive the blessings, but also the punishment of God. This punishment is like the chastisement of God for reforming his erring child. Thus, the Jews have endured their calamities in their long history as 'the punishing rod of God, their Father'.

The Holy Book: The Old Testament of the existing Bible is really the book of the Jews, in which God has revealed His ways to His chosen people. This book has been divided into Law, Prophets and writings. The Law comprises the first five books of the Bible, namely, Genesis, Exodus, Leviticus, Numbers and Deuteronomy and together they are called Pentateuch. The Law was given to the Jews, by their greatest prophet Moses. This contains the basis of what is known as Torah. The distinctive point to note here is that for Judaism, God reveals Himself to His people. Thus Torah is the divine revelation to His people through His servant Moses, at Mt. Sinai.

In Torah there are 613 precepts covering the whole life of man, from his cradle to his grave. Torah is also a witness to God's promises to His people, who are the descendants of Abraham. The Jews are required to obey the commands of God for their own welfare in this world and in life to come hereafter.

The Prophets comprise the historical books, *Joshua, Judges* and *Kings* and the great prophets Isaiah, Jeremiah, Ezekiel and 12 other minor prophets mentioned in the Old Testament. The Writings includes the rest of the *Old Testament* like Job, Psalms, Proverbs and so on.

But apart from these sacred writings there is *Talmud* regarded as the great chain of tradition. It is said that the Law was handed over to Joshua, and Joshua handed it to the Elders, and the Elders passed it on to the Prophets, and the Prophets to the leaders of the Great Synagogue. The Talmud contains the teachings of rabbis, and Misnah, is the collection of rabbinic teachings which were collected by Judah the Prince. There are two Talmuds, known as Palestinian (composed during the 4th

Century) and Babylonian (composed about the 7th and 8th Centuries). Both traditions deal with commonproblems, but they differ in their various conclusions.

The Pentateuch contains 613 precepts and they have been compressed in the commandment 'to do justice, love mercy and walk humbly with God'. Even these three have been compressed into 'The righteous shall live by Faith'. Faith means the realization of that knowledge which induces belief in God.

Torah is supposed to have been directly given to the Jews by God through Moses. Torah is supposed to contain the sacred and avowed aim and aspirations of the Jews. In this sense Torah and the Israel are considered as one. Torah is eternal and the study of Torah is more important than the building of the Temple. As long as man studies Torah, no evil thought can assail him. In Torah a heavenly voice echoes forth from Mt. Horeb (Sinai). It is an 'Instrument' for instructing mankind in the ways of God and for purifying it from evil.

Apart from the Law, Prophets and writings, the Jews give due place to reason and tradition. In accordance with Saadia (882-942 A.D.) the Jews are said to know God by reason, faith and tradition.

The Jews did not indulge in philosophical speculation, but live in faith that God has chosen them due to the initial merit of Abraham and on account of their continuing faith in the courageous living of their ancestors through the whole history of their misfortune and joys. The reason why a Jew is a Jew, has been thus given. Edmond Fleg thus gives his reason for being a Jew.

"I am a Jew because I am born of Israel

I am a Jew because the faith of Israel requires of me all the devotion of my heart.

I am a Jew because in every place where suffering weeps, the Jew weeps.

I am a Jew because at every time when despair cries out, the Jew hopes.

I am a Jew because the word of Israel is the oldest and the newest.

I am a Jew because the promise of Israel is the universal promise.

> I am a Jew because, above the nations and Israel, Israel place Man and his Unity".[2]

A Jew is a Jew because he lives by the faith that the Israelites stood before the Mt. Sinai, heard the voice of the Lord through thunder and the sound of trumpets and saw the lightning and the quaking of the mountain. There is the indissoluble bond of the covenant between Israel and Yahwe.

DISTINCTIVE FEATURES OF JUDAISM

1. It has been noted before that Judaism is not a system of philosophical doctrines. It lives with God and knows about God what it finds in its encounter with God. A Jew discovers his God I-Thou relationship and hears His words, the echo of Torah in the deepest recess of his heart and responds to His call in humility. Hence, for Judaism, God is found in his encounter with God.

2. Hence, God is neither a matter of proof or disproof. God-talk is not nonsense either. He is *revealed* in Torah, Prophets and writings, but above all in the history of Jewish people. God is not a mere existence, but Yahwe is a God who *acts* in the life of His chosen people. The exodus of the Jews from Egypt, the conquest of the promised land of Canaan, the establishment of the kingdom of David are so many acts of Yahwe. Even the exile of the Jews into Babylon and the destruction of the temple in 590 B.C. and 70 A.D. are the acts of God for sinning against Him. Thus for the Jews God is a God who acts through history and as such progressively reveals Himself in His relation to the Jews and other nations. This awareness of historic memories shapes the morality and religious life of the Jews and prepares them for greater revelation in future. For them Messiah is yet to come. This awareness gives them an exalted idea of themselves over other nations, with a spiritual mission towards them. This is the meaning of their being a chosen people.

3. Judaism is a religion of God's covenant with his chosen people, the Israel. It was first a covenant with Abraham and God, for God made a solemn vow that He would multiply and preserve the seed of Abraham. When man sinned and Yahwe

had no other option but to destroy mankind through flood, yet because of His covenant He preserved the life of Noah and a sign in the form of rainbow vowing that Yahwe would not destroy man again. Yahwe married Israel and would not leave him when he strayed away, from Him. Thus, Judaism is a religion in which God makes a covenant between Himself and Israel, and addresses them 'Hear, Oh, Israel'.

4. Judaism is pure monotheism, because Lord, God is one, and none is besides Him. He is one because it is the One Lord and God who has betrothed His people Israel, and Isreal can have no other Lord besides Him with whom he is indissolubly bound up in holy marriage.

5. God is not only revealed in personal encounter, but He is also transcendent of all His creatures. He is above all human understanding for we know only this much that He is, but not *what* He is. There is no limit to what He is and can be known through His progressive revelation to Israel.

6. God no doubt is above human comprehension, but is omnipresent and takes care of His universe and creatures. He is the great providence and deliverer. Everything depends on God, but He depends on nothing that He has created.

7. Judaic God is holy and whatever that 'word' stands for God is not only moral and steadfast in all He does and promises, but He is also righteous and pure, and, no mortal can endure the sight of Him. He is not only a loving Father, but also a judge of men. No man can escape His punishment when he sins. God is to be feared, not because of impending punishment, but because of awe, inspiring dread and also fascination. He is so holy that no man can take His name in vain.

8. Because God is transcendent, so He can meet His people through the revelations He makes. This revelation has been progressively made through the ages by His prophets. In one sense, Judaism is most prophetic of all religions because the Prophets have brought the message of Yahwe throughout the whole history of the Jews. Moses was the greatest law-giver of the Jews, and, Ezra was the greatest reformer and interpreter of Torah. Isaiah, Jeremiah and Ezekiel brought messages of stricter individualistic morality, holiness of God, and a promise of a Messiah to come.

9. Judaism also believes that this world has been created by God out of nothing (*ex nihilo*). This makes God most supreme, but it also grants reality of the universe with all its order and regularity. The world has been created by God and He also created man to have dominion over the world. Hence, it is as much man-centred world, as it is God-dependent universe. This world is for the enjoyment of man.

10. Along with other prophetic religions, Judaism believes in the existence of angels and the devil. Certainly the devil is only a rebel out of God's angels, but his dominion cannot last long. He can be cast out by holy men amongst the Jews.

11. The idea of the immortality of the soul took hold of the Jews and now the Jews believe that the spirits of men survive their bodily death.

12. But along with the immortality of the soul, the Jew believes also in the day of judgment, and, the consequent belief in the existence of Heaven and Hell. Most probably this belief was borrowed by the Jews from Zoroastrianism.

13. Judaism believes in three prayers a day and keeps its history alive in the observance of Sabbath, Passover (the commemoration of the exodus from Egypt), the New Moon and Harvest festivals.

14. Like the Dasturs in Parsiism, and, Brahmins in Hinduism, there are the Levites who have to serve as priests of Yahwe for His people. Hence, priesthood is hereditary.

The Doctrine of God

Judaism keeps close to the doctrine 'God is one', and, in its defence countless Jews have laid down their lives. The first commandment of Moses is:

> Hear O Israel, the Lord our God, the Lord is One. You shall have no gods before Me. You shall not make to yourself a graven image, or the likeness of anything that is in heaven above or in the earth beneath or in the waters under the earth. You shall not bow down to them or serve them,......(*Exodus* 20:3-4).

God is the creator and ruler of the universe. Nothing exists which has not been created by Him. He is Omnipotent and Omniscient. Not only He has created everything, He takes care of them. He creates out of His free will and there is no limit on His will.

God is one in the sense that there is no plurality or even duality. He is unique and there is nothing like Him. 'One' does not mean numerical unity, for any human language cannot fully describe Him. Lord God is transcendent, which means

1. That He is hidden God,
2. He is beyond human comprehension,
3. He is above all His creation.

But God at the same time has been ascribed holy will and intellect. He has been described as just and merciful. Above all He is Holy which means moral purity and far and above everything unclean, physical or spiritual. As a matter of fact no attributes can be literally ascribed to Him. Words are used to describe God for the purpose of showing our reverence to Him and for our obedience to Him. For example, He is described as 'king' in the sense that all His wish is always fulfilled and His wish is command to be carried out. Saadia (882-942) in '*Book of Beliefs and Opinions*', and, Maimonides (1135-1206) in '*The Guide of the Perplexed*', describe God negatively. For example, Saadia holds that God is above every category of *relation*, for He was existing even when there was nothing. He is also above space and time, for He has created them and He has been there even when space and time were not. As a matter of fact the word 'creation' means creating things out of nothing. Hence God as a creator exists without any thing. Hence, He can have no relation with anything of the world.

Maimonides, the greatest of Jewish theologians expounds the doctrine of negative attributes with regard to God, for any attribute affirmed of God serves only to limit Him. For example, if it be said that God is good, then it means that He cannot be bad. We find that the echo of the statements of Maimonides is found in Spinoza (1632-1677). Here we also find the echo of Wittgenstein who was another famous Jewish philosopher. All words describing God, according to Maimonides are metaphorical. This really follows from the famous verse *Exodus* 3.14.

Moses wanted to know God and he asked God what name should he give to Him? Lord God said, 'I am that I am'. This simply means that it is sufficient for human beings to know that He *is*, but not *what He is*. In other words, no attributes can apply to God literally. St. Thomas Aquinas has developed the doctrine of *analogia entis*, and, later on Paul Tillich has advanced his theory of symbolical expressions in relation to God-talk arising from 'I am that I am'. In other words, to make God-talk possible we can use expressions about God with a view to getting an insight or intuition or glimpse of Him. In Indian thought this negative way of expression was systematically and dialectically advanced by Nagarjuna and Nagasena in Buddhism and by Shankara in Advaitism. The utterances of Kabir are also important in this context.

God is essentially moral. Does the good depend on God's will, or, God wills because He is bound by the good? The Jew never bothered about this point. He is convinced that the Lord is good and He demands goodness and righteousness from man. What does the Lord require of thee? Walk humbly, do justice and love mercy. The Lord Himself is merciful and gracious, slow to anger and abounding in love. Therefore, the Lord requires of man to seek justice, relieve the oppressed and take care of the widows and orphans.

If God were only just, then this world would not be possible, for every man has sinned and has to be punished. Hence His justice is tempered with mercy and forgiveness.

Above all God is Holy and so Holy that no man can set his eyes on Him, for surely then he would die. The reason is that man is unclean from within and without (*Isaiah* 6.5).

> Lord, who may enter your Temple?
>
> ....
>
> A person who obeys God in everything and always does what is right, whose words are true and sincere, and does not slander others.......... (*Psalm* 15).

Only by obedience and worship one can make oneself holy, and, specially by keeping the Sabbath, paying the tithes (tenth part of one's income) and carrying His commandments. God is near the godly, but far and remote from the ungodly. How can we have a strong faith in God?

Well, if one has been brought well by a believer, then his faith may be firm and unshaken. But then without the help of reasoning this faith, even unshaken is not quite healthy. Should we take recourse to reasoning alone? No, because there is always the possibility of a more convincing reasoning to the contrary. This is exactly what Ramanuja has held. Hence, the best thing for a Jew is that our belief in God should be based both on tradition and reasoning.

The Teaching About Man

There is a beautiful anecdote about the creation of man.[3] Before creating man, God consulted Torah which is divine wisdom. But the divine wisdom did not favour the creation of man, because of possible sinfulness. However, Lord God silenced the possible doubts about the sinfulness of man. Yes, man is found to fall into sins. But remedies are also provided for him.

1. First, the capacity of repentance has been given to man. If he repents, then God would not reject a contrite heart.
2. Besides, good and righteous acts are likely to atone for his sins.
3. Thirdly, there is the fear of hell, and the hope for heavens will help man from desisting from evil.
4. Lastly, there will come the Messiah who will bring salvation to all mankind.
5. Besides, man has been taught to pray. It is the tearful prayer which bridges the gulf between man and God.

The Judaic account of the creation of man grants that man will be prone towards sinfulness. But God created man in his own image to have dominion over the whole of His creation.[4] Thus man sharing the nature of God is a partner of God and to some extent shares divine glory. This is clear from the following *Psalm* 8.

When I look at the sky, which you have made,
at the moon and the stars, which you set in their
places......What is man, that you think of him;
mere man, that you care for him?
Yet you made him inferior only to yourself;
You crowned him with glory and honour.
You appointed him ruler over everything you made;
You placed him over all creation: (*Psalm* 8.3-6).

When man has been crowned with glory and honour, then it is his duty and the highest prerogative to love his God with all his heart, with all his soul, with all his strength. To love God means to carry out His commandments which the Lord God gave to the Jews through His servant Moses on the mount Sinai. These Ten Commandments have been thus listed (*Exodus* 20.3-17).

1. Thou shalt have no other gods before me.
2. Thou shalt not make unto thee any graven image.
3. Thou shalt not take the name of the Lord thy God in vain.
4. Remember the Sabbath day to keep it holy.
5. Honour thy father and thy mother, that the days may be long upon the land which the Lord thy God giveth thee.
6. Thou shalt not kill (*Ahimsa*).
7. Thou shalt not commit adultery (*Brahmacarya*).
8. Thou shalt not steal (*asteya*).
9. Thou shalt not bear false (*satya*) witness against thy neighbour.
10. Thou shalt not covet (*Aparigraha*).*

The whole purpose of creation is to establish a divine order and the establishment of the Kingdom of God on earth. Hence, it meant man's sharing the divine vision and divine purpose on earth. God, created man and blessed him, saying multiply and be fruitful.

---

*Thus the last five commandments are the same as *pañcha mahavrata* of the Jains, which has been accepted by the other Indian religions.

I am putting you in charge of the fish, the birds, and all wild animals, I have provided all kinds of grain and all kinds of fruit for you to eat..... (*Genesis* 1.28-29).

Hence, a Jew need not be an ascetic and need not look upon the world as a vale of sorrow. For the Jews life is holy for He has created it and so is the earth and all things in it. By doing justice, loving mercy and by walking humbly with one's God, one has to create the social and physical conditions of this earth, so that the divine purpose regarding this earth be fulfilled. Hence, man is the key to the hidden Shekhinah (presence of God) of this universe. Thus obedience to the ten commandments and other rules of conduct is not the slavery of God, but is the way of living in fellowship with God in I-Thou relationship.

A Jew has to live in holiness because he has to imitate and walk in the way of the Lord who is holy. He has also to do justice which means that he has to struggle against social injustice and oppression. Commandments 5-10 maintain family loyalty and discipline along with social stability. 'Not to kill' refers as much to living beings as to human beings, for life is inviolable. True, a Jew not only loves his God with all his heart, soul and strength, but the next important commandment is 'Love thy neighbour as thyself.' (*Leviticus* 19.18).

The most important rule of life is 'imitatio Dei' i.e., imitation of God. In personal life of strict morality, a Jew has to do justice, love mercy and walk humbly with God, repenting for his sins and asking forgiveness for his lapses in his prayers (three times a day) to his God. Thus a Jew has to live for himself, for others and for a life to come. Hence, for a sincere Jew there is no rest in this world, nor in the next, for he has to keep on striving till he sees God. In his social life, he is not asked to be an ascetic, but to add and multiply happiness. He is supposed to do everything with the full awareness that God is present everywhere and no deed is hidden from his God.

Man has been created free, either to obey or disobey God and His commandment. And God also knows the abuses of free will which a man is likely to make. If God knows everything, then why did God make man with free will? This is a question which Christianity along with Islam has to answer. And in due course, we shall find the answer. The possibility of the emergence of a holy will outweighs the sea of sins of many errant souls. Goodness cannot emerge without the price of sins of the many. But this thorny question has to be faced by any theist whatsoever. Why should Judaism alone be saddled with this almost insoluble problem?

Two other topics are worth mentioning. The first is about circumcision, and, the second pertains to marriage and family planning. Let us first attend to the first. We have already seen that Judaism is a covenantal religion in which God is said to have made a covenant between Abraham and his seeds. The physical side of the covenant is maintained through the rite of circumcision. God said to Abraham.

> You and your descendants must all agree to circumcise every male among you. From now on you must circumcise every baby boy when he is eight days old, including slaves born in your homes and slaves bought from foreigners. This will show that there is a covenant between you and me. (*Genesis* 17.10-12).

This rite of circumcision is considered very sacred and very great. Without circumcision God could not make His covenant with Abraham.

Again, a Jew has to live in society, and family is a real unit of society. Hence, after God made man, He did not think fit that man should live alone. Therefore, God created a companion for him out of his own rib and called her 'a woman' because she was taken out of man. She was the bone and flesh of man (*Genesis* 2.22-23).

> 'That is why a man leaves his father and mother and is united with his wife, and they become one' (*Gen.* 2.24).

Marriage for a Jew is a sacrament commanded by God and is not a mere contract. It is also obligatory for a married couple 'to be fruitful and multiply'. Only under certain pressing circumstances, the couple is allowed to use contraceptives or the like.

Judaism admits converts. They are precious to God. A Jew by birth is a Jew because of the long tradition of God's miracles in Egypt and His Ordinances drawn up at mount Sinai. But a convert who accepts a holy God without being brought up in tradition is thrice blessed before the Lord. Many Abyssinians are said to be 'black Jews'.

The World

The prophetic religions of Judaism, Christianity and Islam believe that this world has been created. Creation means that this world has been created by God out of nothing and by His will alone. God does not require any matter with which to mould this world. As such the world wholly depends on God, but God is in no way dependent on this world. This world does not add anything which God does not possess from all eternity.

Of course, God is not in Time or Space, for God has created them, and, God has existed even when there was no time or space. This also means that the world will disappear as soon as God wills its dissolution. This Judaic view of creation has to be contrasted with the Indian view concerning the world.

Mimamsakas and Jains believe that the world is eternal and did not have any beginning. On the other hand, excepting the Buddhists, other Indian schools take this world to be in cyclic order. There is the periodic creation and also periodic dissolution. This cycle is treated as eternal. Then again, *Nyaya-Vaiśeṣika* philosophers believe that certain elements are eternal. Hence, God is only an architect who periodically creates this world with the help of eternal elements and *Karman* of living beings. In advaitism Iśvara creates this world out of himself. Hence, He is the creator, both of matter and the order in the world. Thus, advaitic view of creation comes very near the Judaic and other Semitic theistic forms of religions. But even here there is a good deal of difference.

Ishvara, the creator himself is *mayic* and he creates the world out of his *māyā*. As such the world is not absolutely real. In contrast, Judaism accepts the full reality of the world. The world has been created by a good God for the benefit and enjoyment of man and other living beings. The Lord God said to Adam,

> I have provided all kinds of grain and all kinds of fruit for you to eat; but for all the wild animals and for all the birds I have provided grass and leafy plants for food (*Genesis* 1.30)

God has laid down the firm foundation of the earth and set the Sun, Moon and Stars in the sky. He has created all the seasons and has appointed time for rains and sunshine. In other words, the world is orderly and God has implanted laws in accordance with which the world goes on in an orderly manner. Not only the world is orderly but God wants His creature, the man to know the order so that he may plant the seeds and harvest in good time. Man has been asked to be fruitful and multiply. So he has to know the laws of nature and make provisions for his progeny. It also means that God wants man to become prosperous in the world and fulfil the divine purpose in the world. Man is required to make his social structure of the world in such a way that widows and orphans are well looked after, and the Levites are well provided with animals for sacrifice and wheat, wine and oil for the worship of the Lord and for the maintenance of His priests.

According to Judaism, the world is good and its laws have to be known and fully observed, both for self-preservation and social prosperity. Hence, the world is not a vale of miseries. Of course, there are periods of flood and drought by way of punishment. These natural calamities are there so that the disobedient Israelites may return from their sins. The Jews regard God as the sole omnipotent ruler of the world and even the movement of a fly all over the world is controlled by God (Isaiah 7.18). Hence, this is also true for natural calamities.

> "Shall there be evil in a city, and the Lord hath not done it?' (*Amos*. 3.6).

In the same way there was no rain for three years in Israel because of the idolatry of the people (*King* 17. 1-7).

Hence, the Jews believed that Nature works according to the laws, under the control of God's will. Therefore, the world and all the happenings in it are God-centred. It was later development in prophetic religions to search the laws of nature for predicting and controlling the futuristic events. But encouragement for knowing nature follows from the fact that the world is good and has been created by a good God for providing food, raiments and all other things for man and other living beings.

The creation doctrine has another important aspect for the Jews. The world has been created by God and it will last as long as He wishes. Man is required to feel responsible for his acts, for he will have to appear before the throne of God on the day of judgment where his work will be judged. For the good and righteous deeds, man will be rewarded by being given heavenly abode, and for his evil deeds he will be punished by being burnt in hell-fire. The life on this earth is the only life of which he can make most. No doubt, according to Judaism, after death, man goes down into a region known as Sheol. Here in Sheol he becomes so weak that he can neither praise God nor perform any deed. Here he has to remain till the day of judgment where he will be judged for his deeds. King Solomon said,

> Whatever your hand finds to do,
> do it with your might, for there is
> no work or thought or knowledge or
> wisdom in Sheol, where you are going —(*Ecclesiastes* 9.10).

Sheol, the abode of the dead was a place of forgetfulness, silence (*Psalm* 88.12; 94.17) and of weakness (*Isaiah* 14.9-10). Hence, this world has to be taken very seriously. Here many Indian thinkers in a different way have come to realize that human existence is very precious for one's future deliverance and ultimate deliverance from the cycle of miserable rebirths. But for the Jews the world is good and they believe in world-and-life affirmation.

Evil and Suffering

The Jews were not initially philosophical. They pondered over the question of evil in a spirit of spiritual meditation. The history of the Jews begins in sorrow. Adam and Eve sinned and they were banished from the Paradise of Eden. The first born son of Adam, namely, Cain killed his own brother Abel. Even when they were given the promised land of Caanan, the Jews enjoyed a very short spell of peace. Kings after Kings disobeyed God and were punished with famines, pestilence and defeats by the surrounding heathens. Twice their temple was destroyed. First in 590 B.C. when most of the Jews were taken into exile at Babylon and had to remain there for over 150 years. Second time the temple was destroyed in 70 A.D. Since then they had to live in foreign lands always under the threat of persecution. Lastly, Hitler destroyed a large number of Jews in gas chambers and sterilized a large number of them. But the remnants were saved to praise the Lord God Almighty. Hence, the problem of suffering posed a major centre of their thought.

The Jews never asked the question about God's goodness and His omnipotence. If God is good and abounding in mercy, then why is this suffering; and, if He is omnipotent, why doesn't He prevent evil? The pious Jew always remained content with the answer which Job offered at the time of his great personal calamity.

> I was born with nothing, and I will die with nothing. The Lord gave, and now he has taken away. May his name be praised (*Job* 1.21).

The Jews regarded God as the sole omnipotent ruler and nothing can happen without His will (*Exodus* 8.12-28; *Isaiah* 7.18; 45.7: 68.3-6.

> 'Shall there be evil in a city, and the Lord hath not done it?'
> (*Amos* 3.6).

Even the movement of a fly in the uttermost part of the world is willed by God. In the face of suffering can a devout Jew do? He has to bow down his head in submission to the sovereign Lord of the universe and resign himself to his lot. Most probably this is the only possible solution to the problem of suffering for the Jew.

At one time some Jews believed that man has been endowed with free will and his misuse in disobeying God is the cause of his suffering. But the book of Ecclesiastes refutes this doctrine.

> All things come alike to all,
> there is one event to the righteous,

> and to the wicked; to the good and to
> the clean and to the unclean;......A good
> man is no better off than a sinner,
> a man who takes an oath is no better off than
> one who does not. One fate comes to all alike,
> and this is as wrong as anything that happens in this world.
> (*Eccl.* 9.2-3).

This observation is not true only in general, but for the most particularly in the case of the righteous man, Job. The friend of Job suggests that Job's suffering is due to his sin. He asks,

> Remember, I pray thee, who ever perished, being innocent? Or where were the righteous cut off? (*Job* 4.7).

Job was fully convinced of his righteousness and so he brushes aside this explanation of his suffering. But what about the wicked?

> Wherefore do the wicked live, become old, yea, are mighty in power? Their seed is established in their sight with them, and their offspring before their eyes. Their houses are safe from fear, neither is the rod of God upon them. (*Job* 21.7-9)

The book of the Ecclesiastes is more sarcastic,

> After all, the same fate awaits man and animals alike. One dies just like the other. They are both the same kind of creature. A human being is no better off than an animal. (*Eccl.* 3.19).

But the Psalmist suggests that the wicked enjoy at most on this earth. There is something that a wicked man does not understand.

> ...the wicked may grow like weeds,
> those who do wrong may prosper;
> Yet they will be totally destroyed. (*Psalm* 92.7)

But who knows about life hereafter?

> How can anyone be sure that a man's spirit goes upwards

while an animal's spirit goes downward into the ground? (*Eccl.* 3.21).
There is no way for us to know
What will happen after we die. (*Eccl.* 3.22).

But even the book of Ecclesiastes teaches us to bow down before the inscrutable and the inevitable will of God.

> I know that everything God does will last for ever. You can't add anything to it or take anything away from it. And one thing God does is to make us fear him. (*Eccl.* 3.14).

Why did the pious Jew did not go beyond the advice of resignation to the will of God? One reason was that a Jew had no independent life. He was bound with tribal life with its joys and sorrows. The sin of one man in the tribe will be visited on his sons upto the seventh generation. But in post-exilic period, the Jew felt that each man will be judged, according to his own deeds.

> 'The soul that sinneth, it shall die' (*Ezekiel* 18.20)
>
> "Now, I the sovereign Lord, am telling you Israelites that I will judge each of you by what he has done" (*Ez.* 18.30).

Suffering for the Jew was not an evil. It is corrective, reformative and purificatory.

> Behold, happy is the man whom God correcteth: therefore despise not thou the chastening of the Almighty. (*Job* 5.17; also *Deut.* 8.5; 2 *Chronicles* 32.26).

Again,

> The Lord corrects those he loves, as a father corrects a son of whom he is proud (*Proverbs* 3.12).

Then again is the thought that suffering purifies a man, specially those who are righteous and walk in the ways of God. This is specially true in the case of Abraham and Joseph and above all in the case of Job.

There is another view of suffering, according to which suffering of a righteous man is intercessory and redemptive. It is this view of suffering which looms large in Christianity.

When the Israelites lapsed into idolatry, even after their miraculous exodus from Egypt, God became angry and wanted to destroy the Israelites. But Moses made an intercessory and redemptive prayer before God for sparing the Israelites. Moses said to the Israelites that he would go to God to obtain forgiveness for their sin of idolatry.

> Moses then returned to the Lord and said, 'These people have committed a terrible sin. They have made a god out of gold and worshipped it. Please forgive their sin; but if you won't, then remove my name from the book in which you have written the names of your people. (*Exodus* 32.31-32).

But the most graphic way in which suffering is said to be redemptive has been pictured with regard to 'the suffering servant' of God, in the book of Isaiah, Chap. 53.

> But he endured the sufferings that should have been ours, the pain that we should have borne.
>
> ....
>
> because of our sins he was wounded, beaten because of the evil we did. We are healed by the punishment he suffered. (*Isaiah* 53. 4-5).

There is little doubt that Christ himself was very much influenced by this picture of the suffering Messiah for his people. But even now the Jews look upon their national suffering as vicarious for healing all other nations of their sins. This is the deepest meaning of their being the chosen people of God.

But it is a mystery that God has chosen the Jewish people for redeeming the world. Through his suffering a righteous man bears witness to God. Can a mortal man be more righteous than his God, or, be pure before his creator? (Job 4.17). Job believed that God knows all and that He is benevolent beyond all degrees. He therefore bowed down his head in reverential silence before God and at last uttered:

> I know, Lord, that you are all-powerful;
> that you can do everything you want.
> You ask how I dare question your wisdom

> when I am so very ignorant.
> I talked about things I did not understand,
> about marvels too great for me to know. (*Job* 42.2-3).

Job was not declared guilty of any act, but man has to confess that the moral excellence of man accounts nothing before the boundless goodness and greatness of God. Hence the prayer of a pious Jew is:

> God do not tell me why I suffer, for I am unworthy to know why, but help me to believe that I suffer for your sake.

The important thing is to endure suffering without making complaint. Thus, Freud has taught us to resign ourselves to the inevitable without complaints and without any expectations. One question still remains, and, that is about sin.

Sin, according to Judaism, is disobedience of the commandments of God. Hence, sin means disunion with God, and straying away from the path of righteousness. Sin ultimately means that a distance is caused between God and sinner. Again, it is said that the wages of sin are death. God hates sin, but not the sinner. He desires rather the return of the sinner to God. How can he return?

By repentance only the divine image which is corrupted by sin can be restored to man. Of course, a prayer to God bridges the gulf between man and God, which gulf is created by man's sins.

> It is said that even the gates of heaven are shut to prayers, they are open to tears. What is needed is the tearful heart of the penitent.

Life after Death

The Jews were influenced by the Egyptians, Canaanite and later on by the Babylonians when the Jews were in exile. Last of all they might have been influenced by the Greeks. There is a significant difference between the Hebrew and the Greek views about the soul. For the Hebrew the soul is always embodied. For this reason Enoch and Elijah were said to have ascended into the Heavens with their earthly frame. In contrast, the Greek made a distinction between the soul and the body. He thought that the soul can live independently of the body. This is exactly what the Jainas and the Samkhya have held in India.

At first the Jew held that the soul of man was nothing but breath, as was also the view of some of the Upanishads. And the Biblical statement is:

> And the Lord God formed man of the dust of the ground, and breathed into his nostrils the breath of life, and man became a living soul. (*Genesis* 2.7).

Thus death simply means the passing out of this breath, and soul simply meant 'the breath of God in man's nostrils'. As man was a psycho-physical being, so with the perishing of the body, the soul was also taken to disappear. The Jew therefore was sceptical about post-mortem existence.

> "......for who shall bring him to see what shall be after him?" (*Eccl.* 3.22).

However, it is too painful to think that man will cease to exist after his death. After all the Jew had a vivid memory of the Egyptian practice of keeping mummies, which showed the Egyptian belief in life after death. Hence, the dead did matter to the Jew. He often practised necromancy, witch-craft and often through wizards established connection with the departed spirits (1 Sam. 28.3-25). Of course, the prophets decried this practice and discouraged witchcraft and sorcery (*Isaiah* 8.19-20). Yes, but the dead live in Sheol, corresponding to the Hades of the Greek.

The Hebrews believed in a three-storeyed universe of Heaven (the abode of God), the earth (the abode of man) and Sheol (the abode of the dead). Sheol was hardly the concern of God. Sheol was a place of forgetfulness.

> Shall thy wonders be known in the dark? and thy righteousness in the land of forgetfulness? (*Psalm* 88.12).

It was also a place of silence (*Psa.* 94.17) and weakness (*Isaiah* 14. 9-10). The world of the dead is getting ready to welcome the

King of Babylonia. The ghosts of those who were powerful on earth are stirring about. The ghosts of kings are rising from their thrones. They all call out to him 'Now you are as weak as we are'.

However, in Babylonia, coming in contact with Parsiism, the Jew changed a great deal in his religious view. First, God also became the Lord of Sheol.

> If I ascend up into heaven, thou art there:
> If I make my bed in hell, behold thou art there. (*Psalm* 139.8).

Again, in Babylon, the temple was gone and the congregational worship was destroyed. Jew stood alone before God and with his face towards Jerusalem prayed to Yahwe. He was awakened into a life of individuality and personal piety. Should a Daniel, an Isaiah, Ezra and a Nehemiah be allowed to perish, or, be allowed to languish in Sheol? No. The dead shall rise again.

> Those of our people who have died will live again!
> Their bodies will come back to life. All those sleeping in their graves will wake up and sing for joy
> ....
> So the Lord will revive those who have long been dead. (*Isaiah* 26.19).

No doubt, the Parsi of Babylonia believed in resurrection and the day of judgment. So the Jew living in Babylonia also shared this belief with the Parsi.

> Many of those who have already died will live again: some will enjoy eternal life, and some will suffer eternal disgrace." (*Daniel* 12.2).

This is the doctrine of Heaven and Hell in which a Jew believes even now.

There is little doubt then that the Jew was also deeply moved by the doctrine of renovation. As such he also began to entertain the thought of a coming Messiah who will bring salvation to all faithful Jews and will establish a Kingdom of universal peace.

where the lion and lamb will drink at the same fountain without any further fear (*Isaiah* 65.25).

To summarise the ancient Jewish belief was that a man after death goes into Sheol, from where he could hardly be recovered. The one sect of the Jews known as Sadducees believed that the dead do not rise from the grave. However, later on in the post-exilic period, under the influence of Zoroastrianism, the Jew believed in the resurrection of the dead, the day of judgment leading the pious into Heaven and the wicked into Hell.

The Ultimate Destiny

Not much is said about the ultimate destiny of the saints in heaven. It is enough that they enjoy the blessed fellowship of God, singing His praise and sharing his life of holiness and bliss. They will live like angels as spirits, requiring no food and no earthly pleasure of sex and drink. Hence, their life will be wrapped up in eternal Hallelujah.

It was also believed by Maimonides, that only the remnants will be saved and others, not living a life of discipline and obedience will be destroyed for ever.

Prayers

The temple was the place for prayers. But apart from this a Jew prayed three times a day, morning, after-noon and evening. He was obliged to pray for everything needed in his daily life. He had to pray so that God may grant to him a contrite and an understanding heart. Worship through prayers is a spiritual necessity for the Jew. But a man must pray with true inwardness, with freshness of feeling and regularly. A few words will suffice to illustrate the kind of prayers a Jew would make.

> Open my mouth, O Lord, and I will declare your praise
> Our Father, forgive us, for we have sinned;
> O lord, our God, hear our cry!

It has already been said that prayers bridge the gulf between man and his Creator. A repentant heart, with tearful words, is likely to obtain mercy and forgiveness of one's sins.

Festivals

A Jew had to keep the Sabbath holy. This is the fourth commandment and the Jew felt very strongly for it. It is to be noted that for the Jew Saturday is his Sabbath. The Jews were angry with Jesus, for very often he healed a great many people on the Sabbath.

Apart from the Sabbath, three times a year all males had to appear before the Lord.

> Celebrate three festivals a year to honour me. In the month of Abib, the month in which you left Egypt, celebrate the Festival of Unleavened Bread in the way that I commanded you. Do not eat any bread made with yeast during the seven days of the festival. Never come to worship me without bringing an offering.
>
> Celebrate the Harvest Festival when you begin to harvest your crops,
>
> Celebrate the Festival of Shelters in the autumn when you gather the fruit from your vineyards and orchards. (*Exodus* 23. 14-17).

The same instructions have been given in *Exo*. 34.18-26; *Deut*. 16. 1-17. The first festival is known as the festival of Passover. It was celebrated to commemorate the great miracle which God did in liberating the Jews from the slavery of the Egyptians.

The New Year is also celebrated to remind the people of God's creation and the origin of the Jewish history. Again, there is the important day of atonement. Atonement means 'wiping out', or, freeing oneself from the stain of sin. The Jew might not attend the service of the synagogue on other days, but he has to attend the synagogue service on the day of atonement. It is the time of repentance for sins of commission and omission, individual and communal, for acts done knowingly or unknowingly. In the past animal sacrifice was made by the Jew with his repentance. But later on fasting and repentance were emphasized at the cost of animal sacrifice.

Jewish Philosophy

Judaism is a matter of religious experience and does not indulge in philosophy. But in its long history it has developed important theology. Jewish philosopher Saadiah Gaon (882-942) was occupied with the problem of faith and knowledge. He has dealt with the proofs of God's existence. The most celebrated philosopher is Moshe ben Maimon (known as Maimonides) 1135-1204. He wrote as has been mentioned earlier, '*The Guide for the Perplexed*'. Here he has mentioned thirteen roots of Judaism:

1. Belief in God's Creation and His Providence.
2. Belief in His Oneness or unity.
3. Belief in God's incorporeality.
4. Belief in God's Eternity.
5. Belief in God's Omniscience.
6. Belief in the exclusive worship of God.
7. Belief in prophetic revelations.
8. Belief in the unique authority of Moses.
9. Belief in the acceptance of Torah given to Moses by God on Mt. Sinai.
10. Belief in the finality of the revealed instructions and laws contained in Torah.
11. Belief in the retribution of one's deeds both in this life and in life hereafter.
12. Belief in the coming of Messiah.
13. Belief in the resurrection of the dead and the day of judgment.

In due course, the Jews also developed religious mysticism which continues even now in the writings of Spinoza, Henri Bergson and Martin Buber.

Jewish mysticism rests on the belief in the direct vision of God. Here, in the mystic trance, things and objects are experienced which cannot be cognized otherwise. The tradition of Jewish mysticism is known as Kabbalah, where the doctrine of emanations (as in Plotinus) is most pronounced. In Indian religious philosophy, the doctrine of emanations is most articulate in the *Pancaratra.* In Kabbalan, Torah is not set aside but its secret and hidden meaning is sought and explained.

References

1. Edited by Arthur Hertzberg, Judaism, N.Y. 1966, XVI; See also XXI, XXII, p. 26.
2. Arthur Hertzberg, *Ibid.* pp. 23-24.
3. The same kind of anecdote is found in Islam.
4. The book of Genesis 1.27; 5.1; 9.6.

Chapter IV

CHRISTIANITY

Introduction

Christianity owes its name to Jesus Christ. Indeed the life, death and teaching of Jesus form the centre of Christianity. Jesus Christ was born perhaps in 4 B.C. in a small town of Bethlehem in the reign of Augustus Caesar. He was born out of holy wedlock, but his foster father Joseph came out of the line of King David who was considered to be the ideal King of the Jews. Thus Jesus was a Jew and he was soaked in the spiritual aspirations of the Jews which were centred round the vision of a forthcoming Messiah. This Messiah was variously conceived, but the predominant conception of a Messiah was that he would restore to the Jews the lost Kingdom of David. But Jesus had a quite different picture of a Messiah. This picture was painted by the prophet Isaiah in Chapter 53 as a 'suffering servant of God'. Jesus was not only influenced by the Old Testament, specially the Psalms, but also the Apocryphal books of Enoch and Daniel. The book supplied the key notion of 'son of man' which was very much used by Jesus in reference to himself.

Of course, the Christians derive their inspiration from the 39 books comprising the old Testament, but much more from the 27 books comprising the New Testament. The 'Bible' itself means a collection of books. This N.T. (New Testament) has four gospels which record the life, teaching, death and resurrection of Jesus. The first three gospels have more or less common contents and the fourth Gospel called Johannine has been written by St. John who gives a very intimate picture of his Master, regarded as the Messiah and the Son of God. But these terms like the 'son of man' or 'the son of God' have to be understood in terms of the religious language of some two thousand years ago. In simple words, the language of the Gospels and of the other books of the New Testament has been written in the mythological expressions of the time. Many diseases were supposed to be due to the working of the evil spirits. Even the Universe was a three-storeyed house of Heavens, the Earth and the Nether world called Sheol. In the same way, the expressions like 'the Virgin birth', 'the Son of God' and even resurrection, ascension and the second Advent of Jesus are to be understood as mythological constructions. What one has to know is to go beneath these archaic expressions in order to understand what the gospels intended to teach. These expressions were used as tools of preaching with a view to converting people.

> In his disciples' presence Jesus performed many other miracles which are not written down in this book. But these have been written in order that you may believe that Jesus is the Messiah, the Son of God, and that through your faith in him you may have life. (*St. John* 20. 30-31).

Thus Christianity is a missionary religion with a view to winning converts. Last words of Jesus just about the time of his ascension are:

> 'Go, then to all peoples everywhere and make them my disciples' (*Mt.* 28.19).

Judaism and the Gospel of Jesus

No doubt Jesus was a Jew, but he was very different from other Jews and his preaching was revolutionary for Judaism.

First, the Jews called themselves 'the chosen people of God', 'the descendants of Abraham, Isaac and Jacob', and, called other people 'pagans' or 'heathens'. Nay, by virtue of observing the Sabbath, the rite of circumcision and other external acts, the Jews were ritualistic and narrow minded, in spite of the fact that their prophets had given them enough indications of a universal religion and a religion of heart.

> "Through you I will make a covenant with all peoples:
> Through you I will bring light to the nations". (*Isaiah* 42.6).

Again,

> The Lord said to me,
> 'I have a greater task for you, my servant.
> Not only will you restore to greatness
> the people of Israel who have survived,
> but I will also make you a light to the nations'. (*Isaiah* 49.6).

In the same way the prophets had decried the ritual of sacrifice.

> The Lord says, 'I hate your religious festivals; I cannot stand them!......I will not accept the animals you have fattened to bring me as offerings'. Instead, let justice flow like a stream, and righteousness like a river that never goes dry. (*Amos* 5. 21-24).

In the same tone Micah writes that God does not want animal sacrifice.

> What he requires of us is this: to do what is just, to show constant love, and to live in humble fellowship with our God (*Micah* 5.8).

Jesus preached the universal brotherhood of man as sons of the same loving Father called God. He preached the equality of men before God because God does not judge persons.

St. Peter and St. Paul were Jews, but both of them went beyond the pale of narrow dimension of Judaism. For them Christianity was a universal religion, open to all nations. St. Peter saw that God is the Father of all nations. Peter began to speak: 'I now realize that it is true that God treats everyone on the same basis. Whoever worships him and does what is right is acceptable to him, no matter what race he belongs to" (*Acts* 10:34-35).

In the same way St. Paul regards himself as the apostle for the gentiles and writes, "I have complete confidence in the gospel: it is God's power to save all who believe, first the Jews and also the gentiles" (Romans 1.16).

For Jesus, God is God for all people alike who worship Him in the right way.

"God is Spirit, and only by the power of his spirit can people worship him as he really is". (*St. John* 4.24).

This is exactly what the medieval saints of India have stated, 'Hari belongs to him who worships Him'.

Again, against hyprocrisy and outward acts, Jesus taught the interiority of religion and morality. Jesus taught a religion of one's inner depth and heart. 'And your Father, who sees what you do in private, will reward you' (Mt. 6.18). He taught about the Kingdom of God which is within man (Luke 17.21). It is that kingdom which is not of this earth, for the humble and meek alone will inherit it (Mt. 5.5). Jesus protested against the hyprocrisy of the Pharisees who forgetting their own faults tried to find faults with others.

> Why do you look at the speck in your brother's eye, but pay no attention to the log in your own eye?
> You hypocrite! First take the log out of your own eye, and then you will be able to see clearly to take the speck out of your brother's eye. (*Luke* 6. 41-42).

In the same context a woman was caught in the act of committing adultery. She was brought before the Master to be stoned to death, according to the laws of Moses. Pharisees stood by to see what Jesus would say. Jesus said,

> 'Whichever one of you has committed no sin may throw the first stone at her' (*St. John* 8.7).

And none could do it, for they were are all convinced of their own sins. No doubt Jesus was a carpenter Jew and knew Judaism from its inside. However, his preaching and practice went much beyond the laws of Moses. Jesus explicitly stated that he had no mind to set aside the law of Moses, but wanted to fulfil it. How? By going beyond it, where it will not only be transcended but retained in a truer way. Jesus was quite conscious of what he had to teach.

1. The commandment of Moses was, 'Do not commit murder'. Jesus said, 'But now I tell you; whoever is angry with his brother will be brought to trial' (*Mt.* 5.22). How can there by any murder, if there be no anger in the heart?

2. "You have heard that it was said, 'Do not commit adultery'. But now I tell you: anyone who looks at a woman and wants to possess her is guilty of committing adultery with her in his heart' " (*Mt.* 5. 27-28).

3. "It was also said, 'Anyone who divorces his wife must give her a written notice of divorce'. But now I tell you: If a man divorces his wife, even though she has not been unfaithful, then he is guilty of making her commit adultery if she marries again; and the man who marries her commits adultery also" (*Mt.* 5. 31-32).

4. The Jews were told in the past not to break the vow made in the name of God. "But now I tell you: do not use any vow when you make a promise'. (*Mt.* 5.34).

5. Another very remarkable preaching of Jesus which also he practised even in the hour of his being hanged from the cross is: "You have heard that it was said, 'Love your friends, hate your enemies'. But now I tell you: 'love your enemies and pray for those who persecute you'. (*Mt.* 5. 43-44).

Thus Jesus taught the conquest of passion, inner purity of heart and conscience, equality of all men before the eye of God and love which fulfils all the laws of morality. Hence, Jesus taught a life of love, service to all fellowmen with the utmost sincerity of heart,......a truly universal way of life which is also the inmost meaning of the Hindu religious piety. Jesus could say what he did say as, for him God is love who makes no distinction between the sinner and pious, between the righteous and unrighteous.

> For he (God) makes his sun to shine on bad and good people alike, and gives rain to those who do good and to those who do evil. (*Mt.* 5. 44-45).

In his teaching Jesus was doing what he had been told '*imitatio Dei*'. Be as perfect as your Father in heaven is (Mt. 5.48; Luke 6.36). Jesus felt that he was imitating God so well that he could say, 'The Father and I are one' (Jn. 10.30). Then, again, 'whoever has seen me has seen the Father' (Jn. 14.9).

Special Features of Christianity

1. Christianity is monotheistic, meaning that there is one God

who has created the world and man. Some Christians hold that that God is both immanent and transcendent. They do not clearly explain the immanence of God, but they firmly hold to the transcendence of God. On this doctrine of transcendence of God the teaching of *analogia entis* and Paul Tilliah's theory of symbolism are based. By 'transcendence' is meant that nothing in the world can be definitive of God. Everything of creation falls short of the glory of God. In order to mediate between God and man, Christianity resorts to 'prophets' and 'Jesus as the Mediator between man and God'.

2. The most distinctive teachings about God is that He has been revealing Himself through His prophets and in the fulness of time Jesus has revealed God most clearly and finally the will and Person of God (Hebrew 1. 1-3). Hence, it is said that 'God is Jesus', for Jesus is the visible image of the invisible God.

Christianity also holds that God is Father and God is essentially redeeming Love. God as love searches man much more than man searches God.

3. There is the dogma of trinity, according to which Father, Son and Holy Ghost are three persons. But they are one. This doctrine of trinity in the western garb is not very intelligible, but as *saccidānanda* this is easier to understand. However, trinity is quite different from the triad of Brahma, Vishnu and Mahadeva, where all the three deities are quite distinct and separate with their distinctive functions.

4. The most distinctive teaching of Christianity is the expiatory and redeeming death of Jesus. In other words, Jesus died for redeeming the sins of the world.

5. Hence, a Christian has to have faith that Jesus died for his sins, and, that this faith alone wins forgiveness of sins of the sinners and he becomes at one with God. Hence, the adage is not by words, in obedience to the law of Moses, but by *faith* a sinner is saved from the hell-fire. This faith again is a free gift of God and is open to all men irrespective of race and colour. At times, this doctrine of faith as the gift of God turns into the doctrine of election and predestination.

6. This doctrine of predestination means that God has chosen some persons from the very beginning of the world for being saved and some for being damned. This doctrine of grace

by election is found in Ramanuja, who quotes the Upanishads in support of his view of 'election'.

The *prajñātman* chooses whom he will:

> This one, truly, indeed, causes him whom he wishes to lead up from these worlds, to perform good action. This one, also, indeed, causes him whom he wishes to lead downward, to perform bad action. (*Kaushitaki up* 3.8; also see *Kaṭhā* 2.23; *Muṇḍaka* 3.2.3).

7. According to Christianity, God created man in His own image. But through disobedience of Adam sin came to the world and this image of God has been corrupted by man. Hence, man has to live again in union with God. And this can be done through faith in the expiatory death of Jesus on the Cross.

8. In common with Judaism and Islam, Christianity believes in the resurrection of the dead, in the day of judgment and the doctrine of Heaven and Hell.

9. Most Christians believe in the immortality of the soul. But if this soul has been created by God, then how can it be immortal? Nothing which has been created is eternal. Jesus himself hints at it "Do not be afraid of those who kill the body but cannot kill the soul: rather be afraid of God, who can destroy both body and soul in hell" (Matt. 10.28). But the doctrine of immortality is not very clear in Christianity.

10. Christianity accepts the doctrine of creation which means that God has created the world out of nothing by His mere creative power. This doctrine of creation has to be distinguished from the Hindu doctrine of cyclic creation and dissolution.

11. Along with Judaism and Islam, Christianity accepts the doctrine of amelioration. This means that the world is real and should be improved for the good of the whole world. Hence, Christianity accepts the service of man for the uplift and alleviation of human suffering. Hence, Christianity accepts the World-and-life-affirmation.

12. In popular Christianity, the existence of angels, evil spirits and the devil is accepted. But the modern Christians do not believe in their existence.

The Doctrine About God

God is Jesus: Christianity is a theistic religion and belief in God is its important tenet. But instead of saying that God, according to Christianity is One, creator, sustainer, Judge, Loving Father and so on, at present Christians say 'God is Jesus'.[1] This means that Christians know nothing about God except through the life, teaching, death and the resurrection of Jesus. According to St. John, Jesus declared, 'Whoever has seen me has seen the Father' (Jn. 14.9). Then, again, 'The Father and I are one' (Jn. 10.30).

St. John himself writes in his gospel

> 'No one has ever seen God. The only Son, who is the same as God and is at the Father's side, he has made him known'. (*St. John* 1.18).

St. Paul also holds a similar view,

> 'He (Jesus) is the key that opens all the hidden treasures of God's wisdom and knowledge'. (*Colossians* 2.3).

St. Paul also maintains that Christ is the exact likeness of God (2 Corinthians 4.4; also See Hebrew 1.3). This is also supported by the statement which Jesus himself made, according to his beloved disciple St. John,

> 'I am the way, the truth, and the life; no one goes to the Father except by me' (*St. John* 14.6).

But whatever the Christians may hold about Jesus, he never said that he was God. On the other hand, Jesus clearly declared that God was greater than he (St. Jn. 14.28), and, that God alone knew about the last day of the world (Mt. 24.36; Mk. 13.32) and that God alone is the judge of men. At one time he also said that none but God alone is good and in that sense even Jesus is not the supreme good.

Hence when the Christians say that God is Jesus then it is only a metaphorical or honorific expression about Jesus in the same way in which we say that Jadu is a tiger or a lion. But perhaps the phrase 'God is Jesus' means much more than mere metaphor. It means that Jesus has shown what God as Love is, by means of his teaching, life and death. When Jesus was hanged from the Cross his seven utterances are remarkable. The first utterance was,

> 'Forgive them, Father! They don't know what they are doing' (*St. Luke* 23.34.)

It is much more than loving one's enemies. The prayer for his persecutors is for forgiving and redeeming them with a view to winning them for a good life. And it is recorded that a Roman soldier, standing at the foot of the Cross, and watching Jesus all the time declared, 'Truly he was the Son of God' (Mt. 27.54; Mk. 15.39; Lk. 23.47). This confession is wrung out from every one who sees the life, teaching and the death of Jesus. Hence, for the Christian God is father, forgiving, redeeming and reclaiming the sinners. And this picture of God is directly derived from Jesus. Thus, in terms of the prophetic religion which Christianity is, we can say that in the past God who *is*, spoke through the prophets, but revealed His Person through Jesus. Certainly Jesus was not God, but he was revelatory of the Person of God. Jesus was a man, a descendant in the line of King David. By sheer obedience to the Will of God, he could reflect the nature of God. By virtue of his life he evinced the power of God in working miracles and by forgiving the sins of men and women he showed that God is forgiving and redeeming Love. Thus in the words of St. Paul about Jesus,

> as to his humanity, he was born a descendant of David; as to his divine holiness, he was shown with great power to be the Son of God by being raised from death. (*Romans* 1.3-5).

God is Father: Of course, Jesus was a Jew and for him God is one and only God. He is the Creator, sustainer and the final judge of all things. But for Jesus God was essentially a Father who is much more real than our earthly father. Jesus assures all men that God the Father gives what they ask. God is found by men who seek Him and the gate of heavens is opened if they knock at it. He taught to trust God in all things. He tells us that our earthly father would not give stone if his children ask for bread, and would not give them snakes if they ask for fish.

> 'How much more, then, will your Father in heaven give good things to those who ask him: (*Mt.* 7.11; also *Luke*11.9-13).

Jesus had absolute trust in God and His Providence. He declared that God loves and cares for everything in the world. He declared that the very hairs of the head of each man are counted. If God provides the lilies which today is and tomorrow is cast in the oven, and, if He does not allow even a sparrow to fall, then, how much more care he would take for each man? (*Matt*. 6. 25-34; *Luke* 12.22-27).

Thus, God is much more than the Creator of men. He cares for them and Jesus teaches men that they should trust him for everything, provided they seek the Kingdom of God and His righteousness. Hence, the fatherhood of God was much more than the Jewish teaching in the abstract 'Love God with all thy Soul, with all thy heart and with all thy strength'. The Jewish teaching is taken up with far greater warmth of feeling and self-involvement and the intimacy of spirit. But the most distinctive statement of Christians is that God is love and what does that mean?

God is Love

First, God's love means the conquest of good over evil. Conquer hate by not resisting the evil.

> 'If anyone slaps you on the right cheek, let him slap your left cheek too'. (*Matt*. 5.39).

Again,

> 'Love your enemies and pray for those who persecute you'.

A Christian has to imitate God and become as perfect as the Father in heaven is, for God sends rains and sunshine to all, good and evil alike. Certainly God hates the sins of men, but by His love He teaches men to overcome even the worst of hate.

Because God's love overcomes evil, so God's love is *forgiving*. Peter asked Jesus, 'should he forgive his brother seven times?'.

Jesus replied seventy times seven (Matt. 18. 21-22). Jesus himself forgave the woman who was caught in the very act of committing adultery and said, 'Go, but do not sin again'. (St. John 8.11).

Forgiving love of God is best illustrated in the parable of the Prodigal son. According to the parable, a rich man had two sons. One day the younger son asked for his patrimony. On receiving his share, the younger son wasted his inheritance in evil conduct, and, at last became very poor, and began to starve. Kicked at by his friends, tormented by hunger, he was reminded of his father's home, his kindness and his love. So the prodigal son repented of his folly and resolved to kneel before his father and say,

> 'Father I have sinned against God and against you. I am no longer fit to be called your son' (*Luke* 15.18).

On the other hand, the father was on the look out for the return of his prodigal. One day he saw his prodigal son from afar and ran, threw his arms round his son and kissed him, saying

> 'this son of mine was dead, but now he is alive; he was lost, but now he has been found'. (*Luke* 15.24).

Jesus said that the Father is likewise on the look out for the return of a repentant sinner. No sin is too great to be forgiven. This love of God cannot be spurned, cannot be rebuked and rebuffed. Like the shadow this love follows man wherever he goes.

God's love is redemptive: Redemption means freedom from a bond of debt by the full payment of the promised amount. The full meaning of redemption will be explained in the context of atonement. Here it means that God annuls one's sins and takes him back into His protection and providence. The mark of redemption is that the sinner is transformed into a saint. For example, St. Peter denied his Master thrice. But Jesus forgave him and made him the leader of his followers. The result, Peter boldly witnessed the deeds, miracles and the good news about the love of God by describing the life, teaching, death and the resurrection of the Master. Finally, he died as a valiant soldier of the Cross.

The same transforming love is seen in the life of St. Paul. St. Paul persecuted the church and powerfully moved against it. But he saw the vision of Jesus, and, thenceforth followed him as the valiant soldier on the Cross. The testimony of St. Paul is:

> 'We are hunted down, but God never abandons us. We are knocked down, but we get up again and keep going' (II *Corinthian* 4.8-9).

Again,

> For I am certain that nothing can separate us from his love: neither death nor life, neither angels nor other heavenly rulers or powers, neither the present nor the future, neither the world above nor the world below—there is nothing in all creation that will ever be able to separate us from the love of God. (*Romans* 8.38).

Lastly, God's love means *service in humility*. Jesus illustrated this by the story of a Jew who fell among thieves. Nobody would bandage his wounds, not even a priest and a Levi. But a Samaritan who is hated by the Jews, took pity on the belaboured Jew. The Samaritan poured oil on his wounds and bandaged them, and, took him on his ass to an inn and paid for his treatment there. Jesus praised this love of service to a suffering man.

Again, in the event of the last supper, Jesus washed the feet of his own disciples and said, 'I have set an example for you. If a Master and your Teacher serves you because of his love for you, then you should also do likewise. The greatest amongst you is the servant of all' (Luke 22.26).

God's love means a life of sacrifice. 'For God loved them so much that he gave his only Son' for being sacrificed on the Cross for the ransom of the sins of the world. Then Jesus left his last commandment to his disciples:

> My commandment is this: love one another, just as I love

you. The greatest love a person can have for his friends is to give his life for them. (Jn 15.13).

And Jesus died on the cross so that the people may know the love of God for them.

Thus, God for Christianity means Jesus as the full revelation of what God is, God as Father, God as love that forgives, searches for the sinner, redeems him when he repents and turns to him, suffers on account of the sinful men and is willing to pay the highest sacrifice for redeeming them.

Trinity

Most probably a devout Christian need not know beyond the statements that God is Jesus, God is Father and God is love. But there are men who want to know the relationship between Jesus and God. Further, Jesus before his death promised that he would send them 'the Holy Spirit' who will teach them what else has to be known and talked about Jesus and God. Thus, there are three things, namely, God the Father, God the Son and God the Holy Ghost. Christian theologians in the west have held that these are three Persons in One. They distinguish trinity from the triad of Brahma, Vishnu and Mahesh. But quite obviously three *Persons*, as persons cannot be one, no matter how much closer they may be. Hence, theologians regard Trinity a great mystery. However, philosophers do not accept any unintelligible mystery. If Jesus and God are identical, then Jesus cannot be man. Hence, the crucifixion of Jesus was fake, for God cannot die. Besides, if Jesus and God are identical, then to whom was Jesus praying all the time in his life. True, Jesus has been called the 'visible likeness of the invisible God' (Col. 1.15). How can there be any comparison between 'Visible' and 'Invisible' beings? Quite obviously Jesus is just a picture that the devout men have drawn as to what God could be like. In the modern language of Paul Tillich, Jesus is the symbol of God.

But there is another difficulty. Was Jesus a human being only? In that case, the Christians will be dubbed as 'idolaters' inasmuch as a man Jesus a mere creature is worshipped in the place of God who is the creator of all men. Can we say then that he was both God and man—a perfect God and a perfect man? This will be self-contradictory inasmuch as it is tantamount to saying that a being is both finite and infinite. When Ram Mohan Roy had to face the doctrine of trinity, he denied that Holy Spirit is a person and held that God in the form of *Brahman* is impersonal. For him the holy spirit is the divine influence in the world guiding men towards righteousness. And 'Jesus' is a mediator who explains the will of God to men. Later on, Keshab Chandra Sen described Father (*Sat*), Son (*cit*) and Holy Spirit (*ānanda*). Again, Brahmabandhab Upadhyaya, a Christian thinker has written a beautiful poem describing trinity as saccidānanda.[2] In my opinion, Indian understanding of trinity as *saccidānanda* is less objectionable than the western formulation of it.

Thus, Jesus is not Brahman, nor is he God, the Absolute reality, the creator and destroyer of the world. The utterance of Jesus that 'I and my Father are one', or, 'He who has seen me has seen the Father' can be better understood as the more perfect revelation of God as Father and Love than was the case in the past or even after his death. He was just a revelatory event in history.

The World

The teaching about the first creation is bristled with difficulties, for there was no witness and there could be no witness as to the first act of creation. For example, the Nasadiya hymn, Ṛgveda X.129 expresses this.

> 1. Then was not non-existent nor existent: there was no realm of air, nor sky beyond it.
> 2. Who verily knows and who can here declare it, whence it was born and whence comes this creation? The Gods are later than this world's production. Who knows then whence it first came into being?

Then, again, we find that God thundered from the world-wind to Job,

> Were you there when I made the world?
> If you know so much, tell me about it.

> Who decided how large it would be?
> Who stretched the measuring-time over it? (*Job* 38.4-5)

Then what can man do? He resorts to a myth. According to the first book of the Bible called the Genesis, God by the mere fiat of His will created the world in six days. But what is the meaning of day and night. In the first three days of creation, there was no Sun and no Moon. Quite obviously then 'day and night', or 'Evening and Morning' did not mean our days and nights measured in terms of the movement of the Earth on its orbit. Hence, 'day and night' are mythical expression.

Secondly, the story of creation begins with the creation of man, and the description is in plural number.

> "Then God said, 'And now we will make human beings; they will be like us" (*Genesis* 1.26).

Then in Chapter 2 of Genesis the creation of Adam and Eve is given. But quite obviously there were other human beings besides Adam and Eve, for Cain, after being cursed by God for killing Abel, went to a land east of Eden and married there (Gen. 4.16). Thus, Adam and Eve were not the first created couple of human beings.

According to the myth of creation God created the Universe and man, out of Nothing. This was done to show that besides God nothing can be co-existent with God. But, according to the Bible 'The raging ocean that covered everything was engulfed in total darkness, and the power of God was moving over the water' (Gen. 1.2). Hence, there was something out of which God created the light, earth and all other things. According to the myth of creation, a great many questions simply become redundant. For example,

1. Why did God create at all?
2. Being Omniscient He knew well that man would disobey and would commit sin, then why did He create man with freedom of will and with the knowledge of good and bad?
3. Why did God choose a particular place and time for creating the World?

The problem (2) still racks the mind of theologians and they will be taken up later on. However, from the myth of creation, one cannot raise philosophical questions at all. The myth of creation simply shows how sin came into the world and how could the world be explained for answering religious questions of man. After all, even 'A Creator God' is only a myth.

The myth of creation is not a philosophical doctrine to explain, 'How can something come out of nothing?' But the creation myth of the Bible states that the world has been created by God and God takes care of what he has created. Not even a sparrow falls to the ground without the Father's will (Matt. 5.2; Luke 12.25). And God was happy with His creation (Gen. 1.31).

Nothing which has been created, can be said to be eternal. Nay, the world totally depends on the will of God, and, He uses flood, famine, drought to punish man if he disobeys Him. Actually it is mentioned in the Bible that excepting Noah and his family members, all other men were destroyed by flood because they had disobeyed God.

It tries to answer the questions about the creation of the world, space, and time, man and his final destiny.

Apart from the prophetic religions Jains, Buddhists and early *Mimāmsakas* have not advanced the myth of a creator God. Underlying the myth of a creator God or its absence, the question still remains, 'why should man worship at all?' Why should he not remain without God or any religion at all?

Such is also the case with famine and drought which were brought about by Elijah for punishing the rebellious Israelites who had started the worship of Baal. In the philosophical language, the world is contingent because it is dependent on God and has no basis of its own for existence. But it is real as long as it lasts, as is also the case of the empirical world of Shankara. The *Vyavaharika* world lasts, as long as the seeker does not have Brahma-*jañāna*. According to the Bible, God alone is the necessary ground for the existence of the world.

But the world has purpose. First, the world is there for the sake of all living beings and above all for man who has dominion over all things (Gen. 1.26). But it has the other function to know the world and by knowing it one may multiply and become prosperous (Gen. 1.28). Secondly, the world reflects the glory of God. Hence, by knowing the power and story of God, man should worship God, know His will and obey Him in all things.

> Ever since God created the world, his invisible qualities, both his eternal power and divine nature, have been clearly seen; they are perceived in the things that God has made. (*Romans* 1.20).

Then, again, the Psalm says, 'How clearly the sky reveals God's glory' (Ps. 19.1).

Because God is constant and His laws are everlasting, so man can delve deep into the secrets of nature, for knowing the secrets of nature means knowing the will and commandment of God. Hence, scientific pursuit was sanctioned by the sanctity of the statement of the Bible. Nature is God's creation, revealing the glory and nature of God for helping man to live and multiply. Thus in the European Christian world the pursuit of science was regarded sacred, nay, the very purpose of the creator for man, 'Be as wise, as the father in heaven is'.

Hence, the creation myth of the Bible encouraged the pursuit of science, for prediction and the future guidance of man. But for all its sacredness, the world is not the sole end for which man has to live. The world has only a secondary value. The most important thing for man is to know God and seek His righteousness and the kingdom of God. Jesus preached to his hearers:

> O men of little faith! why do you worry about food and raiment. Birds do not sow seeds, nor do they harvest. Yet God takes care of them. Why worry about raiments? Look at the lilies of the field. Even Solomon with all his riches was not dressed up like any one of these wild flowers. Seek ye first the Kingdom of God and His righteousness and all other things will be added to you. (*Matt*. 6.12-21; 24-34).

Then, again, the Bible teaches that the world is only a means for living in the world, but is not the final end of human striving.

> Do not store up riches for yourselves here on earth, where moths and rust destroy, and robbers break in and steal. Instead, store up riches for yourselves in heaven, where moths and rust cannot destroy. (*Matt* 6.19).

Thus, the world is man-centric, but man himself, the crown and roof of the whole creation has God as his centre and final goal. As such we have to turn to the doctrine of man, according to Christianity.

The Teaching About Man

According to the Bible God created man in His image so that he may resemble Him. He also gave him dominion over all created things. In other words, in the beginning man was essentially good and reigned over all things (Genesis 1.26) "So God created human beings making them to be like himself" (*Gen.* 1.27).

Now what does it mean that God created man in His own image or like Himself? Quite obviously God has no shape or form, or, as Jesus said, 'God is Spirit'. Then what does 'likeness of God, mean? We find that Adam and Eve in disobedience to the command of God ate the fruit of knowledge and discovered that they were naked and that they have done evil in the sight of God. Hence, the essential goodness of Adam and Eve was destroyed. By virtue of disobedience they discovered evil which they were likely to choose and do. Hence, 'likeness of God' means to have the free will to know and to have the choice either of the good or evil.

> "Then the Lord God said, 'Now the man has became like one of us and has knowledge of what is good and what is bad" (*Genesis* 3.22).

Therefore, the image of God means participation in divine holiness and goodness. The fall of Adam simply means the corruption of this image of God within him. Now Adam and men in general had also the power of choosing the bad, knowingly. This knowledge of the bad and the deliberate choice of the bad, mean the corruption of the original goodness and innocence of man. Hence, man is born now with freedom of will either to choose the bad or good, and, this choice of the bad is the original sin of man. In other words, strong and deep-seated tendency in man to disobey the commandments of God and the capacity to choose the evil, form the kernel of original sin. Even with this original sin there is also the capacity and a potentiality in man to overcome his original sin by surrendering his will to the will of God. For this reason man shares the glory of divine goodness. For this reason God cares for man.

> When I look at the sky, which you have made,
> at the moon and the stars, which you set in their places
> What is man, that you think of him: mere man that you (God) care for him? (*Psalm* 8.2-3).

Thus man is glorious in his potentialities. He can fall into sin. But he can also rise higher than the angels. An angel can do always what is right. He has no choice to be bad. He is always good. In contrast, man is free to choose either the good or bad. But by sanctifying his will, by surrendering it to God's will, he can reach a destiny which is higher than that of the angel. Ramanuja too was faced with the same problem and he has solved it through his doctrine of *Bhakti* and divine Grace. And Christian solution is also very akin to that of Ramanuja. The problem before Christianity is, 'How to become good, or, how to get the original image of God which has been corrupted by man's disobedience?

Man was made in the image of God, but through the disobedience of man, sin came into the world, and, sin separated man from God. The question now is, 'How can man be once again in union or fellowship with God?' This is the problem of sin and salvation. Here comes the most important feature of Christianity which people do not notice ordinarily.

Salvation of man: According to Christianity, Jesus died as a ransom for the sins of the world. Very often in the newspapers we come across the news that a sum of money has been demanded as ransom for the release of the kidnapped man. Hence, ransom sum is for the release of a person in captivity. In the same way human beings are in bondage of sin and Jesus by offering himself to be sacrificed for the sinner has released the whole world from the bondage of sin. This sacrificial death of Jesus on the cross has its linkage with the Jewish custom of animal sacrifice.

A lamb or a goat or one of the cattle could be sacrificed by a Jew for the remission of his sin. The animal would be without any defect.

The man shall put his hand on its (animal's) head, and it will be accepted as a sacrifice to take away his sins (*Leviticus* 1.3-5; also 3.5).

The animal sacrificed was deemed to carry the sins of the sacrificer. But, the Christian found that this animal-sacrifice was not enough. Even after the sacrifice was over the sacrificer found himself to be sinning again. Why? The laws of Moses were not easy to keep and men were found always violating them. They often found themselves in uneasy conscience.

For no one is put right in God's sight by doing what Law requires; what the Law does is to make man know that he has sinned. (*Romans* 3.20).

Hence, St. Paul and St. Peter argued that only a blameless, sinless man. sanctified and accepted by God alone can atone for the sin of man. This blameless lamb of God was the man Jesus.

The next day John (the Baptist) saw Jesus coming to him, and said, 'There is the Lamb of God, who takes away the sin of the world' (*St. John* 1.29).

Jesus also claimed to be sinless.

"Which one of you can prove that I am guilty of sin?' (*St. John* 8.46).

St. Peter too calls Jesus a blamless lamb of God.

"It was the costly sacrifice of Christ who was like a lamb without defect or flaw" (1 *Peter* 1.19; also see 2.22).

Second thing is that Jesus volunteered himself for being sacrificed for the remission of the sin of the world (Jn. 10-18).

No one takes my life awav from me. I give it up of my own free will. I have the right to give it up, and I have the right to take it back. (*St. John* 10.18).

Hence, St. Peter writes,

Christ himself carried our sins in his body to the cross, so

> that we might die to sin and live for righteousness. It is by his wounds that you have been healed. (1 *Peter* 2.24).

The words of St. Paul are:

> God puts people right through their faith in Jesus Christ... ....God offered him, so that by his death he should become the means by which people's sins are forgiven through their faith in him. (*Romans* 3.22, 25).

Hence, St. Paul preached that Christ was crucified so that through his vicarious, expiatory and intercessory death all the believing Christians may be saved. By their faith alone and not by obedience to the Law can man's sins be forgiven and his original image of God be restored to him.

Thus, salvation is not by obeying the Law, because no man can observe all the laws. Man is weak and he commits sins. By faith in the redeeming and expiatory death of Jesus, a sinner is forgiven his sins and he gets united with God.

Both Ramanuja and Christianity teach the doctrine of Faith, called *Bhakti* in Ramanuja. Both think that this faith is the free gift of God (*anugraha*). But for the Christian this faith lies in vicarious[3] and atoning death of Jesus, who served as a Lamb of God for the remission of the sin of the world. This unique view of salvation by faith and not by works, has its Judaic basis in vicarious and atoning animal-sacrifice.

Hence, for Christianity man was created by God so that the image of God in him may remain with him uncorrupted to the end of his life. Judaism accepts legalism as a means of salvation, and, Christianity takes recourse to faith in the redeeming death of Jesus for the salvation of the sinning man.

It is difficult for anyone, outside the pail of Christianity, to accept the doctrine of vicarious and expiatory death of Jesus on the cross.[4] His belief raises an important issue. However, for Christians even death in itself need not be regarded as an evil, for God Himself has ordained it as a means of salvation for the sin of the world. Certainly the question, pertaining to human suffering and evil is very important for any theist. So let us see how Christianity faces this question.

EVIL AND SUFFERING

The Old Testament declares that God is omnipotent and omniscient. Nothing happens in the world without Him.

> 'Does disaster strike a city unless the Lord sends it?' (*Amos* 3.6).

Here the advice was to follow the commandments of God. Suffering is due to sinning. Evil-doers are bound to be punished, if not in this world, then certainly in the next. Thus, God was to be praised for all things, whether disaster or prosperity.

However, Job was convinced that he had committed no sin, and, yet he was visited by unmerited suffering. In the final analysis Job was advised to accept the inevitable. God is good and omnipotent and yet disaster comes to the righteous man.

> "Shall mortal man be more just than God? Shall a man be more pure than his maker?" (*Job* 4.17).

Job comforted himself with the thought,

> "The Lord gave, and now he has taken away. May his name be praised?" (*Job* 1.21).

Resignation to the sovereign will of God may show piety, but not justification of evil. The book of Job leaves one with the feeling that man could be more moral than God who at times sends disaster to the good man for His mere sports. One thing is certain that the New Testament treats the question of suffering from the standpoint of Christian piety. Hence, the solution is not philosophical and not even theological. Certain viewpoints have been taken up with regard to suffering and they can be thus stated.

In general suffering awakens a man and serves him to think about God. This is clear from the story of the Prodigal Son. When the prodigal began to starve because of the famine in the land, then his thoughts turned towards his father. He repented his sins, and, he was finally reconciled with his father. This is also the view of Ramanuja.

Again, suffering is said to be corrective:

> Happy is the person whom God corrects!
> Do not resent it when he rebukes you (*Job* 5.17)
>
> The Lord corrects those he loves, as a father corrects a son of whom he is proud. (*Prov.* 3.12).

Further,

> In the case of our human fathers, they punished us and we respected them. How much more, then, should we submit to our spiritual father and love? (*Hebrew* 12.9)

At times a pious man suffers on account of others. This was the case with Moses. The Israelites went back to idolatry and God was angry with the people. So Moses had to intercede on their behalf:

> Please forgive their sin! but if you won't then remove my name from the book in which you have written the names of your people. (*Exodus* 32.32).

Suffering at times is not only intercessory but also redemptive. This is specially true about the suffering of Jesus on the Cross. This was described more than 600 years before the birth of Christ by Isaiah.

> .....he endured suffering and pain ......But he endured the suffering that should have been ours, the pain that we should have borne. (*Isaiah* 53. 3-5)

We have already referred to the vicarious and redemptive suffering of Jesus on the Cross. Hence, pain at times is for the manifestation of the glory of God. This is illustrated in the case of the man born blind, whom Jesus healed. His disciples asked Jesus, "why was this man born blind? Did he sin or his parents that he was born blind?"

Jesus replied, 'Neither he nor his parents sinned'. But he was born blind that, the power of God be made manifest'. (St. John 9.3). This was done when Jesus restored the sight to the man born blind. The suffering of Jesus is considered to be the glory of God, for through the faith in the redemptive death of Jesus, sinner is reconciled to God.

Suffering is also considered to be purificatory, for through suffering Abraham, Joseph, Job and finally Jesus reached their perfection. Hence, a Christain must suffer to participate in the suffering of Jesus on the cross, and thus perfect himself. Through his suffering Jesus learnt to be obedient and became perfect (*Hebrew* 5:8).

> My dear friends, do not be surprised at the painful test you are suffering...
>
> You are sharing Christ's sufferings......... (1 *Peter*: 4.13-15).

In the same way, St. Paul writes,

> For you have been given the privilege of serving Christ, not only by believing in him, but also by suffering for him. (*Philippians* 1:29).

Suffering is in the very lot of a Christian. The Master Himself was aware of this.

> Then Jesus said to his disciples, 'If anyone wants to come with me, he must forget self, carry his cross, and follow me' (*Matt*. 16.24; *Mk*. 8.34-35; *Luke* 9.23-24)

Thus, suffering is not an evil for a Christian. It is the means by which he participates in the Kingdom of God by sharing the sufferings of the Cross. Hence, the problem of suffering is not a philosophical issue for Christianity. However, it is so for theology and Christian Religious Philosophy.

The Doctrine of the Immortality of Souls

The Hebrew did not think of soul as a separate and an independent entity, apart from the body. This is really an Indian and Greek idea that a soul or spirit can exist apart from any bodily existence.

In the beginning this soul was considered as breath.[5]

> Then the Lord God took some soil from the ground and formed a man out of it; he breathed life-giving breath into his nostrils and the man began to live. (*Genesis* 2.7)

On death, this breath was supposed to return to God. But on the whole the Hebrew always imagined a soul to be embodied. For this reason Enoch, Elijah and Christ were held to have ascended into heavens with thier bodies. Even St. Paul who believed most sincerely in the resurrection of the body, hoped that the soul will not be without a body (2 *Corinthians* 5.3). He however held that the dead shall rise in their incorruptible body.

> "It is not the spiritual that comes first, but the physical, and then the spiritual" (1 *Corinthians* 15.46).

The early Christians believed in the resurrection of the dead, for the Gospels hold that Jesus resurrected the dead body of Jairus (Mark 5. 21-42), the only son of the widow of Nain (Luke 7. 11-17) and of Lazarus (St. John 11. 43-44). Jesus also believed in the existence of Paradise (Lk. 23.43; Lk. 16:19-31). Jesus also held that He Himself would rise from the dead on the third day of his crucifixion (Mk. 8.31; 9:31; 10:34; Math 12.40; 26:60-61; John 2:10). This was the proof and seal of his Messiahship. Hence, the most important thing for the then and subsequent Christians is that Jesus rose from the dead on the third day of his crucifixion. (Acts 13:33; 17:3, 31; 23:6). St. Paul mentions it thus:

> Christ died for our sins, as written in the Scriptures; that he was buried and that he was raised to life three days later, as written in the Scriptures: that he appeared to Peter and then to all twelve apostles. Then he appeared to more than five hundred of his followers at once, most of whom are still alive, although some have died. Then he appeared to James, and afterwards to all the apostles.
> Last of all he appeared also to me (1 *Cor.* 15. 3-8).

If Christ did not rise from death, then the dead will not rise to life. If so, then the Christian faith and life are still a delusion (1 *Cor.* 15-19). But for St. Paul,

> the truth is that Christ has been raised from death, as the guarantee that those who sleep in death will also be raised. (1 *Cor.* 15:20).

Anybody can see that the resurrection of Jesus is a matter of faith and the hope of immortality is only a religious belief. Two other minor points are worthy of some consideration.

As resurrection means rising of the body from death, so the Christian insist on making this body as sanctified as is possible. He has to treat this body as the temple of God. In Heavens, therefore, those raised to life live like angels. Of course, resurrection is reserved only for those who have sanctified their body.

> Jesus answered them, 'The men and women of this age marry, but the men and women who are worthy to rise from death and live in the age to come will not then marry. They will be like angels and cannot die. (*Luke* 20:34-36).

In the same way, St. Paul teaches that only the Christian believers will rise to meet the Lord.

> We believe that Jesus died and rose again, and so we believe that God will take back with Jesus who have died believing in him.
>
> ... ...
>
> Those who died believing in Christ will rise to life first: then we who are living at that time will be gathered up along with them...... (I *Thessalonians* 4:14-17).

Hence, life of value, goodness and righteousness alone will be conserved to the end.

About immortality it has to be noted that according to Luke 20:35, only worthy men and women will rise from death in the age to come. Secondly, no produced thing can be eternal. Jesus himself tells us that the soul can be destroyed by God if men persist in their evil ways:

> Do not be afraid of those who kill the body but cannot kill the soul: rather he afraid of God, who can destroy both body and soul in hell. (*Matthew* 10.28).

The Final Destiny

According to the Bible man was made in the image of God i.e., with the knowledge of good and bad and a free will to choose either. In due course, the final destiny for man is that he should surrender his will to God. But it is a difficult thing, for man participates in dual nature. He is a man of flesh and of nature, and, also has spiritual nature. And the carnal man and the spiritual nature in man very often come in conflict.

> For what our human nature wants is opposed to what the Spirit wants, and what the Spirit wants is opposed to what our human nature wants. These two are enemies. (*Gal.* 5:17).

The result?

'Man cannot do what he wants to do. He does what he does not want to do'.

> I know that good does not live in me—that is in my human nature. For even though the desire to do good is in me, I am not able to do it. (*Romans* 5.17).

The reason is that there is sin in man which he cannot overcome. How can a man get out of the impasse?

> And those who belong to Christ Jesus have put to death their human nature with all its passions and desires (*Gal.* 5.24)
> When we were still helpless, Christ died for the wicked—while we were still sinners that Christ died for us (*Romans* 5. 6-8).

One has to have faith that the death of Jesus has paid the price of sin for us. We are no longer sold out to sin, but being healed by faith in the redemptive death of Jesus we become children of God, and, by surrendering our will to God we live in union with God.

> It is through faith that all of you are God's sons in union with Christ Jesus. You are baptized into union with Christ, and now you are clothed, so to speak, with the life of Christ himself. (*Gal.* 3:26-27).

Hence, the message of the Cross is a free gift of God for the whole mankind.

> For it is by God's grace that you have been saved through faith. It is not the result of your own efforts, but God's gift, so that no one can boast about it. (*Ephesians* 2:8-9).

This is exactly the position of Ramanuja who lays emphasis on *Bhakti* for the deliverance of man. Of course, Christian *bhakti* is in the redemptive death of Jesus. Secondly, both Christianity and Ramanuja teach that the service of God is our greatest freedom.

'Our wills are ours so that we may make them thine'. Hence, the ultimate destiny of man is that he should overcome his physical passions and desires (*Gal.* 5.24) and make his will the will of God. How do we know that we now belong to God?

We must have the fruits of spirit and not of the carnal man.

> But the Spirit produces love, joy, peace, patience, kindness, goodness, faithfulness, humility, and self-control. (*Gal.* 5.23).

Secondly, a saved man can make no difference between one man and another, for they are all one in Jesus Christ. (*Gal.* 3.28; *Ephesians* 2:11-18). Further, faith without actions is dead (James 2.17, 26). And what kind of actions are expected of the redeemed man? The Lord will explain to the redeemed persons on the day of judgment.

> I was hungry and you fed me, thirsty and you gave me a drink; I was a stranger and you received me in your homes, naked and you clothed me; I was sick and you took care of me, in prison and visited me. (*Matt.* 25. 35-36).

How? The Lord will explain.

> I tell you, whenever you did this for one of the least important of these brothers of mine, you did it for me. (*Matt* 25:40).

Hence, faith in the redemptive death of Jesus issues forth in the alleviation of human suffering and service to fellowmen.

One more thing has to be kept in mind that like the doctrines of Bodhisattvas, *Sarvamukti*, Christianity also teaches the salvation for all. The whole universe has to be won for God.

> This plan (of salvation) which God will complete when the time is right, is to bring all creation together, everything in heaven and on earth with Christ as head. (*Ephesians* 1:10).

Again,

> "Through the Son, then, God decided to bring the whole universe back to himself" (*Colossians* 1:20).

But the two terms 'Redemption' and 'Salvation' require a few more words of explanation.

Salvation means 'saved from the impending hell-fire', or, 'the anger of God'. Similarly, 'redemption' means release from the bondage of sin. But both mean that in the end a sinner is changed into a new creature—a New Being in God. He regains the sonship of God, and, a reunion with God after the sin had separated the sinner from God.

> This is the new being which God, its creator, is constantly renewing in his own image, in order to bring you to a full knowledge of himself. As a result, there is no longer any distinction between Gentiles and Jews, circumcised and uncircumcised, barbarians, savages, slaves and free men, but Christ is all in all. (*Col..* 3:10-11).

This is how it happened in the lives of Peter, Paul and Zacchueus and a host of others. St. Peter who denied his master thrice, at the time of trial of Jesus, was made the corner-stone of the Christian Church. The master said to Peter: "Don't worry. From now on you'll be fishing for the Souls of men" (*Luke* 5.10). St. Paul, the persecutor of the church became the most important preacher of Christianity. Zacchaeus, the tax-collector became a new man by coming in contact with Jesus. Standing before Jesus, he said:

> Sir, from now on I will give half my wealth for the poor, and if I find I have overcharged anyone of his taxes, I will penalize myself by giving him back four times as much. (*Luke* 19:8).

This is the real meaning of conversion, i.e., transformation into a new and good life. This is also illustrated in the case of Tulsidas and Balmiki. Hence, salvation or redemption means that a ruined and tortured life is transformed into a New Being.

A new being in Jesus Christ means a daily struggle against the evil. A penitent heart and a sincere prayer to God in the name of Christ means victory over temptations and divine forgiveness of sins in the event of fall. Jesus himself has given the following prayer for everyday life.

The Lord's Prayer

Our Father who are in heaven,
Hallowed by thy name.
Thy Kingdom come
Thy will be done on earth, as it is in heaven.
Give us this day our daily bread.
And forgive us our trespasses, as we forgive them against us.
And lead us not in temptation, but deliver us from evil.
For thine is the Kingdom and the power, and the glory, for ever. (Amen).

Here also it was pointed out that unless we forgive others the wrongs they have done to us, our sins will not be forgiven by the heavenly Father (*Matt*. 6:14).

The Day of Judgment and the Doctrine of Heaven and Hell

There is little doubt, according to the Gospels, that Jesus believed in the day of judgment and in the existence of heaven and hell.

> When judgment day comes, many will say to me, 'Lord, Lord!' In your name we spoke God's message, by your name we drove out many demons and performed many miracles. (*Matt*. 7.22).

About the non-believing city of Capernaum, Jesus said, "You can be sure that on the judgment day God will show more mercy to Sodom than to you" (*Matt*. 11:24). Similarly, in many places in the Gospels, Jesus is said to have expressed his belief in the blissful life in Heaven and terribly painful life in Hell. This is clearly exemplified in the story of a rich man and the beggar Lazarus who used to sit at the doorsteps of the rich man. The poor man died and was carried away by the angels to sit beside Abraham at the feast in heaven. The rich man died and was buried, and in Hades, where he was in great pain; he looked up and saw Abraham, far away, with Lazarus at his side. So he called out, 'Father Abraham! Take pity on me, and send Lazarus to dip his finger in some water and cool my tongue, because I am in great pain in the fire" (*Luke* 16:22-24).

Jesus believed in hell-fire, where the sinner will cry and will be gnashing his teeth (*Math.* 8:12; 5:29-30; *Luke* 10-14; 18:9; 23:15, 33). But the following quotations will make this point clear:

> So if your hand makes you lose your faith, cut it off! It is better for you to enter life without a hand than to keep both hands and go off to hell. And if your eye makes you lose your faith, take it out! It is better for you to enter the Kingdom of God with only one eye than to keep both eyes and be thrown into hell. There the worms that eat them never die, and the fire that burns them is never put out. (*Matt.* 18:8-10; *Mark* 9:43-48).

Jesus promises paradise to the repentant thief who was hung by his side on the cross.

> "I promise you that today you will be in Paradise with me" (*Luke* 23:43).

But by 'Paradise' is meant angel-like existence, where no marriages are contracted (*Luke* 20:34-36) and where there is an eternal life of bliss.

Jesus said to Martha, the sister of the dead man Lazarus:

> I am the resurrection and the life whoever believes in me will live even though he dies: and whoever lives and believes in me will never die. (*St. John* 11:25-26).

Thus heavenly life is one of unending bliss in the faith in and service of God. This is what Ramanuja also held out. The individuality of the righteous man is retained to the end.

Hence, in Christianity creation is the first scene of which the day of judgment with Heaven and Hell is the last act.

The Apostle's Creed

Living with the Master everyday is one thing and the crystallized creed is another thing. Living with the Master is a living experience and that alone counts for the believers. In order to explain this experience creed is codified in the current language of the time. In the first five centuries, the position and nature of Jesus were hotly debated. If Jesus was just a man, then Christian worship of him is idolatrous; and, if he was God, then his crucifixion is unreal (since God cannot die). In order to tide over the difficulty the co-substantiality of Jesus and God was maintained. Hence, the creed formulated fifteen centuries before is still recited in the Christian Churches. However, it is to be noted that in the past, Jesus was regarded God, but in modern times, his manhood is emphasized much more. Most of the Indian Christians cling to the older belief in Jesus as God. The Apostle's creed runs thus:

> I believe in God the Father Almighty, Maker of heaven and earth; and in Jesus Christ, his only Son our Lord, who was conceived by the Holy Ghost, born of the Virgin Mary, suffered under Pontius Pilate, was crucified, died, and buried; he descended into hell; the third day he rose again from the dead; he ascended into heaven, and sitteth at the right hand of God the Father Almighty; from thence he shall come to judge the quick and the dead. I believe in the Holy Ghost; the holy Catholic church; the Communion of Saints; the forgiveness of sins; the resurrection of the body; and the life everlasting.

Christian Festivals

Christmas is observed all over the Christian world on the 25th December every year. This is usually supposed to be the birthday of Jesus. However, no date of the birth of Jesus Christ is known. This is observed as the day of rejoicing, for it is maintained that God gave a great present to mankind in the person of Jesus. Hence it is right and proper that Christians should also exchange presents, specialiy they have to remember the weak and the needy.

Good Friday and Easter

Perhaps Good Friday and Easter are not as well-known to the people outside the Church. Good Friday is observed on the most Moony Friday after the equinox. On this Friday Christ was supposed to have been crucified for the remission of the sins of the believers. Hence, this is called 'Good', because it means the door of Salvation for the believer.

Good Friday is preceded by the period of Lent of 40 days, in which most believers desist from meat and drink. They also donate their savings as 'Thanks-Offering'. Some devout Christians also observe fast for the whole period.

Easter is the Sunday, following Good Friday, on which day Christ was supposed to have risen from the grave. This also means the victory of goodness over evil, immortality over death.

Following the Judaic festival of *Shelters*, Christians in India, observe *Harvest Sunday*. On this Sunday, the Church goers bring the produce of their field, or, fruits of their trees. At times they bring to the Church even articles bought from the market. This is a beautiful festival, but it is not always observed all over the Christian world.

Branches of the Church

It appears that Christian Church remained undivided for a little over one thousand years. Then in 1054, the Church was divided into 'The Eastern Orthodox Church' and 'the Roman Catholic Church'. The reason of this rift was the claim of the bishops of Rome for being the supreme authority. The Eastern Greek Church rejected this claim and became independent of the Roman Catholic Church. The Eastern Orthodox Churches comprise Greek and Russian churches, Eastern European Churches and also of some other churches in the Mediterranian countries which once formed part of Byzantime Empire. The Supreme religious authority belongs to Ecumenical Council which alone is entrusted with the task of interpreting the 'holy tradition'.

Roman Catholic Church

It is the largest single branch which accepts the supreme authority and primacy of the Pope. However, in 1962-1965, Second Vatican Council stressed that due recognition has to be given to the authority of the corporate body of the bishops as an episcopal college.

Protestant Churches

Roman Catholic Church was further subdivided into Roman Catholic and Protestant Churches in 1517 by the great schism led by Martin Luther's reformation. There are a number of Protestant Churches, as a result of Luther's reformation.

The *Anglican Church* has kept close to Roman Catholicism in its belief and practices. It rejects the authority of the Pope and the doctrine of Mass. This enjoys the fellowship of many churches with the Archbishop of Canterbury as the First amongst equals, of the heads of the Churches.

Lutheran Church is the Chief Protestant Church of Germany and Scandinavia. It includes liturgy in Church Service, but sermon (the Biblical preaching) is given the main and central place in church worship. The Lutherans are numerous in Ranchi.

The Presbyterian Churches found by John Calvin are in mid-Europe and Scotland. Along with the Lutherans, they lay stress on the reading and studies of the Bible.

Congregational Church emphasizes the independence of the local church.

Baptist Churches insist on *adult baptism* for including a person in church membership. Once at Patna, Monghyr and Gaya, Baptist Churches were quite strong. They believed in the evangelism of the gospel of Jesus.

The Methodist Church was found by John Wesley. At present the membership of this church is very strong in America. In India there is also a 'Methodist Church of Asia'.

Pentecostal Churches are going strong in America and also in India. They stress the role of the Holy Spirit in guiding the church activities. In church worship, the members are noticed talking in foreign tongues as the gift of the Holy Spirit.

The Salvation Army churches reject the Sacraments (the Holy Communion), but emphasize the need of preaching the Gospel and social service.

The Quakers assemble in the church but believe in Silent worship and social service.

Christian Brethren hold on to the primacy of the Bible and evangelism.

The World Council of Churches was established in 1948 which lays emphasis on the loyalty to Jesus Christ as God and Saviour.

In India there is the Union of Churches of *North India* and of *South India*. It functions through dioceses presided over by elected bishops. A bishop has a good deal of administrative powers, but is not necessarily a sanctified person.

Christianity and Judaism

Christianity arose out of Judaism as its sect. But later on it was distinguished from Judaism in the following respects:

1. Judaism is based on Torah and it is based on the observation of Mosaic laws. As against this, Christianity lays stress on faith in Christ crucified for the ransom of the sin of the whole mankind.

Jesus himself was a Pharisee. But a Pharisee believed in the observation of Mosaic laws, specially the Sabbath. Jesus, however took his stand on the immediate institution of God in one's experience and conscience, which constituted for him the supreme spiritual authority.

2. Judaic God is a merciful Judge. As against this, for Christianity God is a forgiving love, out to reclaim a sinner. Hence, God as Judge remains subordinate to God as redeeming Love.

3. The Jews do not accept the Messiahship of Jesus. For them Messiah is yet to come.

4. The Jews believe in angels, prophets, but not in the incarnation of God. For the Jews, Jesus was not even a prophet, for he indulged in blasphemy, for he claimed to be one with God.

For Christians Jesus was the incarnation of God, and, much more than any prophet in the past.

5. For the Jews God is essentially transcendent. For Christians God is transcendent but He revealed Himself in the life, teaching and death of Jesus.

6. For the Jews, Abraham and Moses were the greatest prophets, specially Moses who talked with God face to face. However, Christians regard Christ to be higher than even Moses.

7. The Jews do not accept incarnation, nor do they regard Jesus as the Son of God. Hence, they do not subscribe to the doctrine of Trinity.

8. The Jews lay stress on the life of a house-holder. As against this Christianity admits the importance of asceticism. Jesus himself was more of an ascetic than a house-holder.

However, Judaism and Christianity have common beliefs with regard to monotheism, day of judgment, Heaven-Hell, Creatorship of God. Both of them also believe that God has progressively revealed Himself through the prophets. Further, God has created man out of dust and has granted him freedom of will either to choose good or evil.

References

1. There is nothing very strange in this epithet. Certainly for a number of Hindus 'God is Ram', or 'God is Krishna'. They can convert the proposition and say 'Krishna is God'. In modern Christian theology, it would be wrong to say, 'Jesus is God'.
2. Robin Boyd, *Indian Christian Theology*, p. 70.
3. The suffering and death of Christ held by orthodox Christians to be accepted by God in lieu of the punishment to which guilty man is liable.
4. It is a common belief in India that a saint can suffer for another person. It was suggested that Ramakrishna saffered from throat cancer, because he might have served just as a surrogate for another person. In this way of thinking, the vicarious suffering of Jesus can be explained. He took on himself the guilt for the whole world.
5. The importance of breath as life and as Brahma has been maintained even in the Upanishads (Chh. Up. 7.15; Kaushitaki 2.1; 3.2). "As for the intelligentical Self—Verily, that is the breathing spirit" (Kaush 3.2).

CHAPTER V

ISLAM

INTRODUCTION

Islam is a prophetic religion, and has issued out of both Judaism and Christianity. There is a place for asceticism in both Judaism and Christianity. But in contrast Islam is a middle-roader for it does not ignore worldly pursuits along with its concern for the other-wordly values. Islam accepts the 25 prophets of the Old Testament and 3 of the New. However, Islam accepts that prophet Muhammad is the final and last prophet who puts a seal on all that is most genuine message of God for the whole mankind.

Islam was founded by prophet Muhammad who was born in 570 A.D. and who died in 632 A.D. The prophet received his first revelation through the angel Jibrail (Gabriel) at the age of 40, whilst he was meditating in a cave of Mt. Hira. In the beginning of preaching Islam, the prophet met much opposition and had to face threat even to his life. His unflinching faith in Allah helped him to triumph over every difficulty and in the end he died in the midst of the suceess of his mission.

'Islam' means surrendering one's will to the will of God, throughout one's life. It means complete obedience to the laws of God as they have been revealed in Quoran and Hadith and later on in Shariah (Sharia). As such Islam includes faith, action and the realization of the divine end for man.

Faith means belief in Allah who is One, Omniscient and Omnipotent. He is neither begotten nor does He beget.* A Muslim believes that true existence is of God alone. Man and the entire creation exist only because God wills them to exist. God alone is the sole creator of everything that exists, and manifests His glory, power and attributes. Man has been created as a

*This is the very opposite of the Christian creed, according to which Jesus is the begotten son of God. Of course, this is only a myth and is not acceptable to all Christians now.

creature with free will so that by his surrender of free will to the divine will he may become worthy of God's fellowship (sura 51.56). This faith in God is realized by responding to the message of Allah through His prophet Muhammad.

Action: Mere faith, without its corresponding action is dead, as the New Testament says. This action of a Muslim has been fully exemplified in the life and teaching of the prophet and is embodied in the 'Five Pillars of Islam', which include:

1. Five prayers every day
2. Observing Ramadan fast
3. Hajj to Mecca
4. Giving of Zakat and
5. The utterance of *Kalima*:
   Lā ilāha illillāhu Muhammad ur-Rasulallāh (Sura 2:21-22)
   (There is One God who has created the heavens and earth, and Muhammad is His prophet).

Action implies that man is accountable for all he does before the judgment throne of Allah. This means the belief in life hereafter, and in the day of judgment, Heaven and Hell (Surah 6.160; 17: 13-14). Man therefore is believed to be endowed with free will to choose the good or evil. Hence, *Sharia* provides a Muslim with detailed rules for his guidance in this earthly life.

Realization: By expressing one's faith in *Kalima* and acting according to the five pillars of faith, a Muslim realizes his final destiny. Realization means the development of the divine spark in man by means of surrendering one's will into the divine will. This is possible by performing all actions with the full awareness that God is seeing Him he is also aware of this divine presence.

Let us proceed now with the five pillars of Islam which include inward faith and outward issuing of it in action strengthened by knowledge.

Five Pillars of Islamic Faith

By mere knowledge of Quoran, Hadith and *Sharia* one does not become a Muslim. A Muslim must have faith in the Quoran and the prophet with all his mind, with all his soul and with all his strength. A strong faith issues out in action. Faith is embodied in *Kalima* which has already been stated i.e., *Lā ilāha illillāhu Muhammad Ur-Rasulallāh.*

Adhan and Prayers: 'Adhan' means 'announcement', but really it means the call to prayer by a *muezzin*. This may be interpreted as the following:

> 'God is Most High. There is no god but God and Muhammad is His messenger'.

This *adhan* is so important that it is to be uttered into the ears of the new-born child.

A Muslim has to say his prayers five times each day. This means that a Muslim has to dedicate himself to Islamic faith from dawn to the time of his sleep. Naturally prayers strengthen a Muslim in his resolve to perform his actions enjoined on him by avoiding prohibited acts. Prayers aim at keeping the thoughts from wandering into the material world ignoring the divine rules of conduct.

Prayers are to be said by purifying one's body and mind, and, by having clean clothes. As such a Muslim has to wash the ordinarily exposed parts of his body, called *wudu*. Then he has to utter the name of Allah, the compassionate and merciful. He stands up as if he is standing before the throne of God begging for the forgiveness of his acts of commission and omission, and asking for the divine help for realizing the Islamic destiny of His worshipper. The prayer starts with the utterance 'bismillah' (God, the most merciful and compassionate). Each of the five prayers contains the *al-Fatiha*, the first sura of Quoran in which God is praised as the creator of Heaven and earth, and, strength from God is sought to walk in the straight paths of Islam.

In every prayer, a Muslim has to assume several postures known as *rak'a* symbolizing one's surrendering to God. These postures correspond to Yogic *asana*, though their purposes are quite different. There are five daily prayers. The first prayer is said at dawn before sun-rise. It consists of two kneelings, at the end of which the worshipper sits to salute the Lord. The second prayer is afternoon. Then there is the afternoon prayer between midafternoon and sunset. Both these prayers have four kneelings. The early evening prayer has three kneelings. The last evening prayer is just before sleep-time when the twilight disappears. It consists of four kneelings.

Prayers, five times a day, form the key to Heaven, for the worshipper. Even if a Muslim observes other rules of piety but does not offer prayers, he will not inherit the Heavens. Hence, the saying of prayers is an essential exercise of Islamic faith.

According to Dr. Iqbal, through prayers, a worshipper enters into a wider and higher dimension of life by leaving aside the narrower concern of this mundane world. He enters into the higher existence of spiritual life by shunning the life of material pursuits. In addition to private prayers, a special virtue is attached to collective prayers which are said each Friday and in larger gatherings at the time of *Eid al Fitr* and *Eid al-adha.* This is a fact of life that by participating in group mind in a congregation, the mental and spiritual powers of each participant are heightened. So the creative powers of the worshipper get additional impetus in the pursuit of a virtuous life.

Each Muslim, whether in private or in a mosque, prays with his face towards *Ka'ba*. This ensures unity amongst the Muslims. In the same way uniformity in words, their order and of postures ensure equality and brotherhood amongst all the faithful believers. Thus Islam does not favour caste and does not admit any priestly class (Surah 2: 179-183).

Observance of Ramadan Fast: Most of the living religions prescribe the keeping of fast for controlling bodily desires and mental fickleness. According to Islam keeping of fast during *Ramadan* helps in purifying the mind and removing one's sins (Sura 2: 179-183). The month of *Ramadan* is observed in the ninth month, according to the Muslim calendar. A Muslim has to keep fast for the whole month except childern, pregnant women, sick and very old men. A Muslim in order to observe fast does not take any food or water from dawn up to sun-set every day during the month of *Ramadan*. He is also desisted from smoking and having sexual intercourse during the state of fasting.

During the period of *Ramadan*, the doors of heaven open and those of hell are closed, and, the powers of the devil are weakened.

Keeping of fast is a very important mode of worship. He, the observer of fast, derives at least two very important kinds of satisfaction. First, he gets full satisfaction of food and drink at the end of the fasting day on account of his increased appetite. Secondly, there is the happiness of spiritual progress in his life. He gets the feeling of coming nearer to his God who strengthens him to observe the fast successfully. He also experiences self-control by not indulging in food and drink and by the control of lower passions. The saying of five prayers every day gives him spiritual strength in the pursuit of his daily life.

A Muslim who keeps fast for the full month of *Ramadan* not only gains his physical fitness, but also gains much spiritually. It is hoped that one who can control his senses during one month can also do so for the rest of the year. During this period a believer has to give *Zakat* and *Sadaqa*.

Ramadan reminds the Muslims that their lives have to be tempered and disciplined by sacrifice and self-control. Ultimately a Muslim has to surrender his will to the divine will, so that in the end not he but God lives in him. For this reason a Muslim observes the supreme festival of *Eid al-Fitr* at the end of *Ramadan*.

Zakat: Islam permits its believers to enjoy all the good things of life, whilst yet praying to God and observing Ramadan fast. But the prosperous Muslims have to render to society what belongs to society. In prayers, a Muslim recognizes his duty to God, but in *Zakat* he discharges his duty to society, specially to the poor and the needy. According to the Jewish custom a Jew had to pay tithe of his wealth i.e., 10% of his wealth either in cash or in kind. According to *Zakat* a Muslim has to pay 2½ to 5% of his income for the poor and needy. This may be termed as the religious service tax for the poor. *Zakat* is as important as the saying of five prayers every day. This giving is a religious obligation of the rich, and, at the same time is the claim of the poor on the rich. Most of the Arabs were shepherds, so they could pay their *Zakat* in terms of sheep and cattle.

Apart from *Zakat*, specially during the period of Ramadan,

Sadaqa was also an obligation for the Muslim. The difference between the two is that *Zakat* is religious obligation, but *Sadaqa* is voluntary.

Hajj: 'Hajj' means pilgrimage to Mecca. Whilst performing Hajj, a Muslim temporarily suspends all his worldly activities. He has to overcome all bad habits and has not to decorate himself. He has to put on very simple prescribed dress. A Haji is supposed to have all his bodily desires under control and has not to think of marriage.

In prayers, whether private or congregational, Muslims have to turn their face to Mecca. In the beginning the prophet Muhammad used to turn his face towards Jerusalem. But the Jews objected to his doing that as the prophet had accepted Jesus as a prophet, and, in the Quoran Jesus has been mentioned not less than twenty-five times. Hence, afterwards Mecca with *Ka'ba* in it became the direction in which all prayers had to be offered.

Mecca with *Ka'ba* is sacred to the Muslim, because this place is associated with the name of the prophet Abraham (Ibrahim, in Arabic). According to Islam, the prophet Abraham was the first recipient of pure monotheism. This monotheism was degraded by Judaism, because they mixed it with idolatry. Later on, the Christians added Trinity with the sonship of Jesus. Hence, the prophet had to win this monotheism by going back to the prophet Abraham.

The life of Abraham to commemorated for his singular obedience to the will of God. Listening to the voice of God, he left his ancestors and sojourned into a strange land. He was so faithful to his God that he was most willing to sacrifice his only son Isaac (Sura 37.81). Hence, the prophet Abraham is considered for commemoration. Mecca therefore is dedicated to the memory of the prophet Abraham. By the way Mecca with *Ka'ba* is supposed to have been built by Abraham and his son Ishmael. Mecca is also the birthplace of Prophet Muhammad and it contains the sacred well Zamzam. Hence, it is the psycho-spiritual centre of the Muslims all over the world, and regarded by them as the oldest shrine of the worship of one God.

The Hajj is performed during the second week of the twelfth month of the Islamic calendar. In commemoration of the intended sacrifice of Isaac by Abraham, there is the festival of *Eid al-*

Adha. This festival also means that in the place of human sacrifice, animal sacrifice has been instituted.

It is not necessary for every Muslim to perform Hajj. But a Muslim who has fulfilled all his earthly obligations, and without incurring any injury to his health or the members of his family can afford the cost, then he should perform Hajj. Before starting for the pilgrimage the intending pilgrim should ask God the forgiveness of his sins, should say his prayers and uttering *bismillah* should get ready for the pilgrimage.

Hajj is a call to all Muslims of the world. By the performance of Hajj at Mecca, the universal brotherhood of the Muslims is most palpably demonstrated. This also exemplifies Islamic equality of the rich and poor, of the black and white, irrespective of any race. Hence, there can be no caste in Islam. According to Islam, religion determines the nationality of the people. This conception of nationality is essentially Jewish. Islam has borrowed it from Judaism, and now the Sikhs have also adopted it. This has brought special confusion of politics and religion for the Indians.

Jihad: To the five pillars, the sixth pillar of *Jihad* may be added. *Jihad* means a striving and struggle in the path of God-realization. Hence it means readiness to give even one's life for the sake of Allah and His message. Therefore, it means readiness for a religious war. Surah 5.5 enjoins upon the Muslims to declare *Jihad* against the Christians and the Jews. Similarly, surah 5.9 permits the Muslims to declare *Jihad* against all atheists who do not accept Islam. Again, surah 2.190 enjoins the Muslims to declare *jihad* in self-defence. All those Muslims who die in this kind of religious wars, are regarded as martyrs who immediately pass into paradise (Surah 2.154; 3:169,195).

Muslim Creed: Creed means a system of religious beliefs. Muslims accept the following articles of their faith, namely, (1) Belief in God, (2) Belief in His holy angels, (3) Belief in His revelations in Holy scriptures, (4) Belief in His prophets, (5) Resurrection and the day of judgment, and (6) Belief in divine dispensation of things.

God: The cardinal belief of Islam is contained in the *Kalima* 'There is no god, but God, and Muhammad is His Prophet'. That God is one is known a *Tawhid*. He is eternal, without any beginning or end. He is neither begotten nor does He beget. He has no body nor form. But He is the creator of Heavens and Earth and all things in them. But He is transcendent to every thing that exists. He is above the throne and above all things and exalted by infinite degrees above everything. But He is also nearer to man than their veins and is witness to everything that happens. He is too high and too holy.

God is living, almighty, omniscient and never sleeps. Nothing possible can escape His grasp and vigilance. He is the judge of all men and their acts. But Allah is said to be compassionate and most merciful. The mercifulness of God is one of the grandest themes of the Quoran. Every sura, except the ninth opens with the words 'bismillah al-rahman, al-rahim' i.e., in the name of God, the merciful and compassionate. God is most merciful and forgiving and His love for man is more tender than that of the mother-bird (Surah III. 31) His forgiveness has been mentioned in Surah 27.11 and 33.73.

God is essentially unknowable because He is without form and body.[1] But He is known only through His grace. The possibility of seeing God in paradise by his faithful servants is also an article of faith for the Muslim.[2]

Islam does not accept the sonship of Jesus (Sura 17) and the doctrine of Trinity of the Christians. Hence Islam is not only against idolatry but also against the doctrine of incarnation. Islam is also against pantheism, for Allah is essentially transcendent. Islam looks upon the doctrine of identity of man and God as blasphemy. God no doubt is omniscient and omnipresent, but not immanent in all things and man.

Thus Islam accepts strict monotheism and the transcendence of God, but admits Gods omnipresence.

Angels: As God is transcendent, too high and too holy for human beings, so some intermediaries are necessary to mediate between men and God. Not even the prophet Muhammad could have direct contact with God, though the prophet had a vision of the Heaven in his state of *Miraj* (620 A.D.). Islam accepts the existence of angels who serve as intermediaries between God and man. Angels have been created out of light. They have no sex; they do not eat or drink. They have no free will. Their sole function is to sing praises of God and to carry out His command, day and night.

They always do the right and so they have not to stand before the judgment bar of God on the day of judgment. Some important angels are as follow: Jibrail (Gabriel) is the angel of revelations in relation to Prophet Muhammad; Mikail (Michael) is the champion of faith and a protector of the Jews; Azrael the angel of death who separates the soul from the body of the dead; Israfil who will sound the trumpet on the day of judgment.

Apart from the existence of angels, Islam also accepts the reality of *Iblis*, the devil who refused to carry out the command of God to bow down before Adam. As a result of this disobedience he was hurled down from the Heavens.

Islam also believes in the reality of Jinns. They are said to have been created from fire. They can be both good and evil.

It is clear that the doctrine of angels and Iblis has been taken from the Jewish and Christian belief.

The Quoran and Revelations: The Quoran contains the spoken words of Allah. The Arabic language in which the Quoran has been revealed is noted for its inimitably excellent language. It has only 114 chapters (Suras) and has not been chronologically arranged. The different pronouncements by the prophet at different intervals were recorded and were arranged in their present form by the orders of Caliph Uthman (645-656). It is worthy of note that the Prophet was an unlettered man. Therefore, the utterances in the Quoran are considered to be the genuine speech of God Himself.

The Quoran is the most sacred book of the Muslims, which they strive to learn by heart and refer to it for all teachings about God, Angels, the prophets, Resurrection and the day of reckoning and the doctrine of Heaven and Hell. The Quoran contains the final and definite revelation of God's will for the guidance of man. It is the foundation of the whole Islamic structure.

Though Islam admits that there were many prophets in the past, but the people have corrupted the true message of pure monotheism. Therefore, the Quoran contains the pure and the final message of Allah to all people and the Prophet Muhammad is the final seal of all the past prophetic utterances. The Jews no doubt received Taurait and Torah, but they are said to have corrupted the true monotheism given by Abraham by mixing it with idolatry. Christians too received God's revelation in *Injil*, but they have corrupted the message of pure monotheism by their doctrine of the sonship of Jesus and Trinity.

Apart from the Quoran, the Muslims accept Hadith too which contains the sayings and teachings of the Prophet Muhammad. As the Muslims think Islam to contain a complete way of life, so Muslim Law is also accepted as sacred. This is known as *Sharia.*

Sharia—means the path that leads to God's commandments. It is based on divine revelation and has been derived from four sources:

1. The Quoran is the most important source of divine commandments. It is also believed to be externally existing in Heaven in Arabic.
2. The *Sunna* (Hadith) comes next in this regard and it contains the speech, dialogue and practice of the prophet. It is really a sacred Muslim tradition which is believed to contain what the Prophet said, did or permitted.
3. *Ijma* simply means a consensus of the Muslim community, or, of its leading scholars.
4. *Qiyas* simply means analogical deductions.

Sharia has been classified under five heads:

1. What God has commanded.
2. What God has recommended, but has not ordered or made obligatory.
3. What God has left legally undecided or kept indifferently.
4. What God has depreciated, but not prohibited.
5. What God has prohibited or forbidden.

Sharia does not imply Governmental or ecclesiastical institutions. Rules and laws laid down hold individuals responsible for their deeds, before God.

The Muslim divines differ much about the Muslim personal law and in modern times western code of conduct has also been adopted.

Revelation: As human reason cannot know God, so revelation is necessary to serve as guide for the human beings. God has been revealing Himself from the very beginning to all nations, according to the Quoran:

> Unto each nation have We given sacred rites which they are to perform; so let them not dispute with thee of the matter, but summon thou unto thy Lord. (*Sura* 22:67).

Again,

> 'Allah will judge between you on the day of resurrection concerning that wherein ye used to differ' (*Sura* 22.69).

But the Quoran is said to have received the Word of God in the most complete form. The chief modes of God's revelation were in the following manner:

1. Through the mediation of an angel, often Gabriel, who communicated the message with a peculiar tinkling sound of a bell.
2. Through the mediation of an angel in human form.
3. By putting the message directly in the heart of the Prophet.
4. By the vision of an angel when the Prophet was asleep.
5. By direct communication by God to the Prophet either during waking or sleeping state.

The Quoran is said to be an eternal book which has been revealed to the Prophet part by part, during a course of twenty three years. As God is too high, too holy and too transcendent, so He can be known to mankind only through revelations, specially given to the prophets.

Belief in Prophets: Since God is taken to be a transcendent Being, He could commune with His chosen people only through the intermediaries. The Prophet Muhammad declared that there are 124000 prophets who have been sent to the various people at different times. In the Quoran itself 25 prophets have been named who were sent to the Jews (Sura 6:83-86) and later on three prophets were added from the New Testament. Abraham and Moses are most prominently mentioned and Jesus has been mentioned at least twenty five times in the Quoran. But the Prophet Muhammad has been called the last and final prophet of God to all mankind.

The prophet is a messenger of God to teach people about pure monotheism and law to guide the people (Sura 10:48; Sura

14:4). Prophets served the divine purpose of correcting the people and warning them against disobedience of His message and social law. Usually the prophets were God-intoxicated men who spoke things in their emotional outbursts and at times in poetic utterances, as in the use of prophet David and prophet Muhammad. The utterances were about God and warning against social injustice. They certainly were inspired men who were committed to God with a great deal of self-involvement.

The Day of Judgment: Islam holds that man has been given free will which he can choose rightly or wrongly. Each man is accountable for all his acts of commission and omission. On the day of judgment, each person will stand before God without hiding anything from him (Sura 34 and 39:67-73). A person who has disciplined himself by having Islamic faith and action will be rewarded by being sent to Heavens, or, otherwise he would be sent to Hell with its eternally burning flames. This concept of Heavens and Hell is also found in Judaism and Christianity. But Islamic concept differs in many details.

Again, Islam like the Jews accepts bodily existence of persons on the day of Judgment. This is quite different from the concept of pure spirits without the body in Platonic tradition and in the teachings of Samkhya, Jainism and Gita.

Islam believes that on the day of judgment, trumpet will be sounded by the angel Israfil and the dead will rise from their grave to stand before the judgment throne of God. Further, it is held that Moses and Jesus, would advocate for mercy for their followers, but God will hear the petition for mercy of Prophet Muhammad alone for the Muslims.

Pre-destination (*Taqdir*): Most of the Muslims believe in the absolute decree of God and pre-destination of both good and evil. Surah 3.145 observes, 'No one dies unless Allah permits. The term of every life is fixed'. But the same Surah holds that God is omnipotent to reverse His own decree and that He has endowed man with free will. Hence man can freely choose to obey the commands of God. Thereby he will be accepted for the paradise of Allah.

Many people object to the doctrine of pre-destination. According to them this is the denial of the free will to man. However, the doctrine of pre-destination is an expression of gratitude to God that He saves men out of His mercy and supreme compassion. Hence, as an expression of the mercy of God, Sura 3 observes:

> It is no concern of yours whether He will forgive or punish them. They are wrong doers. His is all that the heavens and the earth contain. He pardons whom He will and punishes whom He pleases. Allah is forgiving and merciful. (3:128-129).

Again,

> Say: O Allah! Owner of Sovereignty! Thou givest sovereignty unto whom Thou wilt, and thou withdrawest sovereignty from whom Thou wilt. Thou exaltest whom Thou wilt, and Thou abasest whom Thou wilt. (*Surah* III. 26).

St. Paul and later on Calvin too support this doctrine of predestination. The Kaṭhopanishad and Muṇḍaka repeat the same doctrine of pre-destination and God's Grace.

> This Soul is not to be obtained by instruction,
> Nor by intellect, nor by much learning,
> He is to be obtained only by the one whom he chooses;
> To such a one that Soul reveals his own person. (*Kaṭh* 2.23; *Muṇḍaka* 3.2, 3).

It will be shown later on that the grant of free will to man is a special gift of God to man. And man is different from the angels, according to the Quoran, for the simple reason that man can freely choose either the good or bad. In contrast, the angels have no free will and they always carry out the will of God. As such the doctrine of pre-destination is an expression of faith, trust and absolute surrender to the will of God. The surrender to the will of God is the meaning of Islam and one has to be faithful to Him when a Muslim is pushed even to the gate of hell.

> "To be the slave of God is the proudest boast of the Muslim."[3]

A Christian too sings,

> Our wills are ours to make them thine

A Ramanuji will also say,

> The absolute surrender to the will of God is the attainment of one's most perfect freedom.

Hence, the doctrine of pre-destination is not a philosophical concept for the religious devotees, but is an expression of piety. No one can miss this note if he goes through the whole Surah 3.

MAN IN ISLAM

Man has been created out of dust, according to the Quoran. There are many references to this view of the creation of man:

> "Allah created you from dust, then from a little fluid, then He made you pairs (the male and female)". (*Surah* XXX. 11).

Again,

> Verily, We created man from a product of wet earth; Then placed him as a drop (of seed) in a safe lodging; Then fashioned We the drop a clot, then fashioned We the clot a little lump, then fashioned We the little lump bones, then clothed the bones with flesh, and then produced it as another creation. (*Surah* XXIII 12-14).

God has created man even above the angels, for he commanded the angels to bow down before Adam.

> And We created you, then fashioned you, then told the angels: Fall ye prostrate before Adam! And they fell prostrate, all save Iblis, who was not of those who make prostration. (*Surah* VII. II).

The same account of the superiority of man over angels has been given in *Surah* 38:73-74; 20.116. Why is this superiority, even when man has been made of dust and angels have been created out of fire? First, because Adam was given knowledge of things, with memory and thinking.

> And He taught Adam all the names, then showed them to the angels, saying: Inform me of the names of these, if ye are truthful.
> They said: Be glorified! We have no knowledge saving that which Thou hast taught us......He (God) said: O Adam! Inform them of their names, and when he had informed them of their names, He said: Did I not tell you that I know the secrets of the heavens and the earth? (*Surah* II. 32-33).

The second thing is that angels have no free will, but man has.

> And when thy Lord said unto the angels: Lo! I am about to place a viceroy in the earth, they said: Wilt Thou place therein one who will do harm therein and will shed blood, while we, hymn Thy praise and sanctify Thee? He said: Surely I know that which ye know not. (*Surah* II. 30).

The thing is that man has been given freedom of will. If he obeys the commandments of the Lord, he will enter Paradise, which is the greatest good for man and His creation. But man is free either to do good or evil.

> "If ye do good, ye do good for your own, and if ye do evil, it is for them (in like manner)". (*Surah* XVII. 7).

Again,

> "Lo! this is an admonishment, that whatsoever will may choose, a way unto his Lord". (*Surah* 76.29).

God has given His commandments to mankind and man is free either to believe or not believe.

> Then whosoever will, let him believe, and whosoever will, let him disbelieve. Lo! We have prepared for disbelievers Fire... ... ...
> Lo! as for those who believe and do good works—Lo! We suffer not the reward of one whose work is goodly to be lost. As for such, their will be Gardens of Eden...... (*Surah* XVIII. 30-32).

Man alone of all the creatures of the Universe has been credited with the task of carrying the trust of God.

> Lo! We offered the trust unto the heavens and the earth and the hills, but they shrank from hearing it and were afraid of it. And man assumed it. (*Surah* XXXIII. 72).

Man has been held in high esteem in the Quoran and three important statements have been made about him. 'Surely We created man of the best stature' (Surah 95.4). First, God has chosen him for Himself and keeps on guiding him.

> "Then his (Adam's) Lord chose him, and relented towards him, and guided him". (*Surah* XX. 122).

And God did this because of His mercy and compassion for Adam who had disobeyed God.

Another great thing has been said about man. God has made man his vice-regent on earth.

> He it is who hath placed you as viceroys of the earth and hath exalted some of you in rank above others, that He may try you by (the test of) that which He hath given you. (*Surah* VI. 166).

Dr. S.M. Iqbal in '*The Reconstruction of Religious Thought in Islam*' has repeatedly mentioned XXXIII. 72 in which it has been mentioned that God has endowed man with the trust of God. Thus, according to Dr. Iqbal, man has been endowed with creative will and as such man is a co-sharer and co-worker with the creation of the world. The most memorable lines of Dr. Iqbal are:

> *Khudi ko kar buland itnā ki har taqdīr se pahle,*
> *Khudā bande se khud puchhe, batā terī razā kyā hai?*

(Develop your individuality so high that before being endowed with God's ordination, God will ask, 'what do you want to be?')

Hence, there is no limit to human spiritual progress. But angels are what they are, and, they have no creative freedom of will to be either more or less than what they are. But is there no doctrine of pre-destination against the freedom of will? Yes, many Surahs support the doctrine of *taqdīr* or pre-destination.

"No soul can ever die except by Allah's leave and at a term appointed". (*Surah* III. 145).

But these lines are not meant to teach so much the doctrine of fatalism, as the doctrine of obedience to the sovereign will of Allah. Under all happenings of the world, the faithful Muslim will have to bow down before the divine decree.

Well, one question may crop up. Has not God limited Himself by creating man free, even to do evil? Dr. Iqbal accepts this self-limitation of God. But why does God permit man to do evil? Free will is necessary in order that at least some men may rise above the angels in goodness by submitting themselves to divine commandments. But by its very nature free will is not possible without the possibility of disobedience leading to hell-fire. Hence God has permitted evil, but has not willed it. Even Iblis has been permitted by God to do his mischief till the day of judgment.

Last thing about man is that God has given His own spirit to man and at the time of death this spirit returns to God. At the time of resurrection man shall rise from his grave and he will be given the same spirit so that he may be judged for his acts. Thus man remains ultimately free, for he remains accountable before His creator on the day of judgment for his acts of commission and omission.

Three things might be noted about man. He did not exist before his creation. Secondly, he was created at some point of time. Third, he is not immortal. We can also say that man will not be sent to this world again before the day of judgment.

The World

The world has been created by God. As such the world has been so created that man may know things for himself for his guidance, and, then again, man may know the glory and power of God. By the orderly movement of the Sun and Moon man will know about the laws planted in the world. Besides, God has created the clouds and rains for nourishing the corn plants and fruit trees for the benefit of man. Certainly this world has not been created for mere sports of God.

> And We created not the heavens and the earth, and all that is between them, in play. (*Surah* 44.38).

The Sun and Moon have been created so that man by knowing their movements may guide his steps.

> He it is who appointed the Sun a splendour and the Moon a light, and measured for her stages, that ye might know the number of the years, and the reckoning............Lo! in the difference of day and night and all that Allah hath created in the heavens and the earth are portents, verily, for folk who ward off (evil). (*Surah* X 6, 7).

The same thought is contained in Surahs II. 22 and XIII. 2, 3. Besides, creations have the purpose of showing God's glory and might, God's commandments for man and lessons for man for his guidance on this earth.

> And of His signs is this: He created for your help—meets from yourself that ye might find rest in them, and He ordained between you love and mercy. Lo, herein indeed are portents for folk who reflect.
> And of His signs in the creation of the heavens and the earth, and the difference of your languages and colours. Lo! herein indeed are portents for men of knowledge. (*Surah* XXX. 21-22).

Again,

> Allah causeth the revolution of the day and the night. Lo! herein is indeed a lesson for those who see. Allah hath created every animal of water. Of them is (a kind) that goeth upon its belly and (a kind) that goeth upon two legs and (a kind) that goeth upon four. Allah createth what He will. (*Surah* 24.44-45).

Thus this world is God-centred and man-centred. God has created this world with all kinds of food for man so that he might eat them and multiply his kind. According to Dr. Iqbal God has created the world without any free will, but He made it so that it may evolve into something better and higher and he quotes the following: "He multiplieth in creation what He will". (*Surah* 35.1).

But everything in the world and much in man are determined by God.

> No female beareth or bringeth forth save with His knowledge. And no one groweth old who groweth old, nor is aught lessened of his life, but it is recorded in a Book. (*Surah* 35.11).

Again,

> He maketh the night to pass into the day and He maketh the day to pass into the night. He hath subdued the sun and moon to service. Each runneth unto an appointed term. Such is Allah, your Lord; His is the Sovereignty;.........(*Surah* XXXV. 13; see also *Surah* 13.2).

Problem of Evil and Suffering

The problem of evil and suffering is brief and sketchy, in the Quoran. At first it appears that God is the doer of all things in His creation. Surah III. 145 says that the human span of life is directly fixed by God. Again, Surah III. 26 says that God gives sovereignty to some and even debases some others. Even births are ordained (Surah 35.11). But does this mean that God is the source of every kind of evil? No.

1. First, many evils are caused by man's disobedience to God by lying and cheating his fellowmen.
2. Then God in His compassion and mercy for Iblis has allowed him (the Devil) to tempt men for doing evil.
3. There are evils to test men so that they may turn to God for getting their sufferings redressed.

Those who disobey God are punished in this world and then again in the next, on the day of judgment.

> Turning away in pride to beguile (men) from the way of Allah. For him in this world is ignominy, and on the day of resurrection We make him taste the doom of burning (*Surah* II. 9).

Amongst the sins of disobedience include 'the filth of Idols' and 'lying' (Surah III. 30). The Quoran teaches to obey Allah, otherwise there is nothing but the garment of fire in Hell.

> Lo! those who disbelieve and hinder (others) from the way of Allah, they verily have wandered far astray. Lo! those who disbelieve and deal in wrong, Allah will never forgive them, neither will He guide them unto a road.
> Except the road of hell, wherein they will abide for ever (*Surah* IV. 167-169).

Many evils are due to the machinations of the Devil (Iblis). Iblis is a disobedient and rebellious angel, but God in His mercy and compassion has allowed him to live till the day of judgment. But this Iblis causes men to deflect from God as in the case of Adam (Surah II. 36) and lurks in ambush for men on God's right path (Surah 7.16) and has beguiled Adam (Surah 7.22-24).

No matter whichever be the evil which befalls men, the faithful are asked and expected to remain firm in their faith. No doubt there are evils which test the loyalty of the faithful.

Job is a clear case in this regard.

> And make mention (O Muhammad) of our bondman Job, when he cried unto his Lord (saying): Lo! the devil doth afflict me with distress and torment.
> ... ...
> And We bestowed on him (again) his household and therewith the like thereof a mercy from us, and a memorial for men of understanding... ...
> ... ...
> We found him steadfast, how excellent a slave! Lo! he was ever turning in repentance (to his Lord). (*Surah* 38. 42-45).

Certainly misfortune and sufferings bring men to God.

> When We show favour unto man, he withdraweth and turneth aside, but when ill toucheth him then he aboundeth in prayer. (*Surah* XLI. 51).

Again,

> And if a wave enshroudeth them like awnings, then they cry unto Allah. (*Surah* XXXI. 32).

Thus, suffering for Islam is a means of repentance and turning towards God.

FINAL DESTINY

Islam starts with the creation of man and this creation culminates on the day of judgment. Those who are judged as the faithful and obedient, will be rewarded by Allah with a life in Heaven with an unending happiness. The unfortunate evil-doers and disbelievers will be hurled into hell-fire where there will be wailing and gnashing of teeth.

> If you do good, ye do good for your own souls, and ye do evil, it is for them (in like manner). (*Surah* 17.7).

For the believers there are the seven heavens which God has created for them, and, for the disbelievers God has appointed hell. (Surah 17.8). Again,

> He is the mighty, the forgiving, who hath created seven heavens in harmony... ... ...
> And verily We have beautified the world's heaven with lamps, and We have made missiles for the devils, and for them We have prepared the doom of flame. And for those who disbelieve in their Lord there is doom of hell, a hapless journey's end!
> When they are flung therein they hear its roaring as it boileth up. (*Surah* 67. 3, 5-7).

Description of Heaven and Hell is scattered throughout the Quoran. The whole Surah 76 is practically given to the description of Heaven. But let us jot down a few points from Surah 37. 40-50.

> Save single-minded slaves of Allah;
> For them there is a known provision,
> Fruits. And they will be honoured
> In the Gardens of delight.
> On couches facing one another;
> A cup from a gushing spring is brought round for them,
> ... .

> And with them are those of modest gaze, with lovely eyes,
> And some of them draw near unto others, mutually questioning.

In the same manner, the description of hell has been given throughout the whole Quoran. A few examples would suffice.

> As for those who will be wretched (on that day) they will be in the Fire; sighing and wailing will be their portion therein. Abiding there so long as the heavens and the earth endure save for that which the Lord willeth. (*Surah* XI. 106-107).

Again,

> Nay, but they deny (the coming of) the Hour, and for those who deny (the coming of) the Hour We have prepared a flame.
> When it seeth them from afar, they hear the crackling and the roar thereof. And when they are flung into a narrow place thereof, chained together, they pray for destruction there. (*Surah* XXV. 11-13).

Finally,

> Hell, where they will burn, an evil resting place. Here is a boiling and an ice-cold draught, so let them taste it. (*Surah* 38. 57-58).

But certainly man was created an excellent being (Surah 95.4) and it was expected that he will remain faithful to his creator to the end.

Dr. S.M. Iqbal has mentioned three very important things about the final destiny of man. First, man was created at a certain point of time and before that he had no existence of his own. Hence, man's soul is not eternal, contrary to what has been taught in the *Gītā*. Secondly, man remains in a state of suspended animation till the time of resurrection. The Quoran also states 'That We may transfigure you and make you what ye know not'. (*Surah* 56.59).

Hence, the state of man after death has not been disclosed to man. Lastly, each man is accountable for his deeds on the day of reckoning. But Dr. Iqbal also hazards his guess: Personal immortality, then, is not ours as of right; it is to be achieved by personal effort.[4]

In like manner, Dr. Iqbal, a great supporter of individuality, regards heaven-and-hell[5] as stages of man's progress and decline.

Ethics of Islam

Islamic faith means inward belief and outward confessions and the way of life as the outward expression of inward conviction Faith is made strong by works and knowledge. The inward experience is most palpable in Sufism. But Islam accepts both the reality of the world and the world to come. Naturally it prescribes certain social laws for the Muslims and these laws have been very carefully laid down in Sharia. These laws cover the whole life from the time of birth to the time of death and burial. When a male child is born *Kalima* has to be said in his ears, and, the burial too has to be attended with recitation from the Quoran. In their lives the Muslims follow the Quoran and Hadith and Sharia. Their aim is to imitate the example of the prophet.

A Muslim has to undergo *wudu* i.e., washing of the hands, feet (up to ankle), face and a part of the head. He has to say his prayers five times a day. Similarly, Muslims have to offer congregational prayer on Friday, Id al-Fitr and Id al-adha and if possible, they have to go on pilgrimage to Mecca, at least once in their life-time.

A Muslim is allowed to marry and is permitted to see his prospective wife. Man and woman, both must give their consent for their marriage. This husband has to provide maintenance for his wife and children. Divorce is permitted, but is not desired. As such several considerations have to be given, before divorce is finalized. The divorced wife cannot be remarried to her former husband as long as she has not been married to another man and that also for the required time. Polygamy is neither forbidden nor required. But under certain circumstances another wife can be had, specially for having a son, if no male issue has been born from the first wife. The wife has a right to inherit property of her husband or parents.

All kinds of drink are allowed, but intoxicating wine from

grapes is strictly prohibited. About food, a Muslim is permitted to eat every kind unless explicitly forbidden. Muslims are forbidden blood, pork, suffocated animals or birds, food offered as a sacrifice before idols. Similarly, frogs, crocodiles, turtles are forbidden for food. But camels, cows, sheep, horses are permitted. Animals and birds with claws are forbidden e.g., tigers, lions, wolves, bears, falcons, hawks, and so on. (Surah V. 3, 4).

When Allah punishes the liars and unbelievers by sending them into hell, then naturally Muslims also are strict in punishing crimes e.g., a thief caught for stealing can be punished by his hands being cut off. Similarly, eve-teasers are given lashings or whippings. Hence, punishment is exemplary and preventive.

Further, Muslims are responsible to society. Hence, they have to offer Zakat and Sadaqa. These are taxes for the maintenance of the poor and needy. Poverty is not a matter of humiliation.

Sufism means a departure from the ordinary Muslim code. Hence, Sufism was not acceptable for the orthodox Muslims for a long time, till al-Ghazati (died 1111). The Sufi emphasizes more the interiority of moral excellence than social ethics. He recommends the renunciation of the world and mortification of his flesh. For him real *jihad* is carried on the passions and the demands of the flesh.

A last question can be raised. Is morality an autonomous body of duties and rights, or, is it so because of the commands of God? Since the time of Kant, in philosophy we accept the doctrine of the autonomy of morals. Even God has to accept the moral duties as binding. But Islam accepts that God reveals all that is moral or immoral. Hence, for a Muslim an action is good or bad, as God wills it. In other words, morality depends on the will of God, and His declaration. A thing is good because God wills it, and bad if He disapproves of it. As a matter of fact the *līlā*-doctrine in Hinduism comes very near this Islamic view.

Sufism

From the Indian standpoint, based on the advaitic way of life, Sufism is the grandest development of Islam. Of course, sufism as a form of mysticism draws upon the contributions of Judaism, Christianity, Buddhism and Advaitism. We must not ignore the contributions of Greek neo-Platonism, for Islam was greatly influenced by Greek thought. But in the end Sufism has remained predominantly Islamic in character, in spite of its protest against the externalism of Islamic practices.

First, we must not forget that the Prophet himself practised contemplation, and, in his absorption in contemplation in the caves of Mt. Hira in 610 A.D. he first received God's commandment of becoming a prophet. Then again, Surah 53 describes the vision of the Prophet in being in the heavens.

> Verily he saw one of the greater revelations of his Lord. (*Surah* 53.18).

Again, the Quoran speaks of God as nearer than the hands and feet of man.

> We verily created man and we know what his soul whispereth to him, and We are nearer to him than his jugular vein. (*Surah* 50.16).

Further,

> Lo! Allah is Seer of what ye do. (*Surah* 2.110).
> Whithersoever ye turn, there is Allah's countenance. (*Surah* II.115).

However, Islamic mysticism remained largely within its prescribed limits of monotheism, because of the two important elements in it. First, Allah is a Person and nobody can coalesce into a person to become one with Allah. Secondly, Islam teaches the overall transcendence of God and no creature can dare to make himself equal to God. Hence, Sufism does not teach the identity of the mystic with God, as is found in *Advaitism* ('I am Brahma'). Of course, in their ecstasy many Sufis came very near declaring this. Al-Hallaj in 922 A.D. and Abu El Futuh in 1191 A.D. were executed for declaring this identity. Mansur al-Hallaj in his ecstasy uttered Anal' Haqq (I am God). He beautifully brings out this feeling of identity in the following oftquoted lines:

> I am he whom I love, and he whom I love is I,

We are two spirits dwelling in one body.
If thou seest me, thou seest Him,
And if thou sees Him, thou seest us both.[6]

This reminds one of the saying of Jesus, 'Father and I are one. He who sees me sees the Father'. But Christ upheld the superiority and the higher position of God. Many Sufis would maintain that the mystic can come very near God and enjoy communion with God. Further, a favoured sufi can participate in many powers and attributes of God (*Sifat*), but cannot participate in His essence (*zat*). This view comes very near the view of Ramanuja who claims that *bhaktas* enjoy many powers of Brahma, but they do not share His powers of creating, maintaining and destroying the world.

'Sufi' has been derived from 'Suf' which means 'wool', standing both for purity and poverty. Sufis regard the life and actions under the so-called five pillars of Islam, comprising five Prayers, Ramadan fast etc., as mere external observances. These are mere words and forms and not the reality behind them, according to the sufis. Their question is; should we worship God, or, love Him? Worship is an outward form, but love alone brings us to the *haqiqa* (reality) behind the veils of outward observances. A whole-hearted act of devotion is higher than the submissive obedience to God's commands. The true teaching of Islam is experienced in the heart. Some of the mystics even disparaged some of the acts of worship. For example, Abu Sa'id (d. A.D. 1049) would not allow his disciples to go on pilgrimage to Mecca and would not allow the interruption in their dancing when the *muezzin* called to prayer. But this is another extreme. For this reason, the Sufis were not respected by a majority of the Muslims. However, Abu Hamid al-Ghazzali (A.D. 1059-1111) tried to reconcile worship and love of God, and thereby reconciled sufism with the *Sharia*, in accordance with the call of Qushayri (d. A.D. 1072). Qushayri held that *haqiqa* does not free one from observing moral obligation under *Sharia*. Al-Ghazzali lived according to strict Muslim law. But he also held that the true meaning of the law is revealed by divine light in the heart through sufi experience of love of God.

The Sufi is so much occupied with his beloved God that there is no place left for the world and its fleeting things. He gets intoxicated with and possessed by the vision of Allah, as was Arjuna who was awe-struck by the *Virāt-rūpa* of Lord Krishna. Love is the sole means of reaching Allah, as was held in India by Alvars and later on by Kabir and Ramkrishna.

> Love means the attributes of the lover (Sufi) are changed into those of the beloved. Now he lives in accordance with the saying of God: 'when I love him, I will be his eye by which he sees and his ear by which he hears and his hands by which he reaches out.[7]

Again,

> Love is the rending of the veil and the revelation of what is hidden from the eyes of men. I looked one day at the light and I did not cease looking at it until I became light.[8]

The well-known couplet is

> *Lali mere lal ki, jit dekhaon tit lal,*
> *Lali dekhan main gayi, main bhi ho gayi lal.*

Indeed, *Brahmavid Brahmaiva bhavati,* (the knower of brahma himself becomes Brahma). The same is also reported of Ramakrishna.

Here the conflict of law and love (devotion) is the same which occurs in Christianity and again, between advaitic *jñāna* and *karma.* As against Shankara's emphasis on *jñāna* against *Karmakanda,* Ramanuja has advanced the doctrine of *Karmajñāna-Samuccayavāda.*

Sufis who observed both worship and love of God, regarded external observances as mere symbols of the real truth. For example, prayers do not constitute a mere set of words and postures, but really mean a spiritual discourse between man and his Creator. The real meaning therefore is a dialogue with God. Similarly, pilgrimage outwardly consisting as moving around Ka'ba, kissing of the Black Stone etc., really stands for movements in the heart for experiencing God within the heart. Sufis use *dhikr* (repetition of the many names of Allah, corresponding to *Rama-Sumirana* in Kabir, Ramakrishna and Sikhism) but really it means contemplation and absorption of the lover in his Beloved.

A sufi no doubt regards God as Creator and Doer and determiner of everything in the world, but He is experienced most in His sufi believer.

A mystic Rabi'a (d. A.D. 801) spurned paradise and the fear of hell, but lived to love God for its own sake.

> O God ! if I worship Thee in fear of Hell, burn me in Hell, and if I worship Thee in hope of Paradise, exclude me from Paradise. But if I worship Thee for thine own sake, withhold not Thine everlasting beauty.[9]

Is this not the same what Alvars and many *bhaktas* clinging to *prapātti* hold? They sought nothing beyond the rapturous gaze of God. However, the utterances of Muhy al-Din Ibn Arabi are most significant for the Indian readers.

Ibn El-Arabi is considered to be the greatest Arabic mystic of Islam. He teaches that Allah is the only reality who is above description and qualifying attributes.[10] El-Arabi states

> that God is only real Being. He is above all qualifying attributes, and the world is a mere illusion.[11]

Further he tells us, 'Glory to God who created all things, being Himself their very essence'. This means,

> God is the object of worship not in the sense that He is exclusively the God of the Muslims, the Christians, or the adherents of any other religion, but in the sense that He is the Essence of everything that is worshipped.[12]

This is the same thing which has been taught in the *Gītā*.

> As men approach me so do I accept them;
> men on all sides follow my path, O Partha (IV:11; *Vide* VII.21).

In other words, Allah is in every form and yet is not limited to any specified form

To confine Him to one particular form to the exclusion of all

> other forms is infidelity, and to acknowledge Him in all forms of worship is the true spirit of religion.[13]

In this not the spirit of Ramakrishna speaking?

> Now I am called the shepherd of the desert gazelles,
> Now a Christian monk,
> Now a Zoroastrian
> The Beloved is Three, yet One;
> Just as the three are in reality one.[14]

Then Ibn Arabi breathes a truly universal spirit of religion which is the precious pearl of the greatest worth of deep religious experience.

> My heart has become a receptacle of every form,
> It is a pasture for gazelles and a convent for Christian monks,
> And the Tables of the Torah and the Book of the Qu'ran.
> I follow the religion of love whichever way its camels take;
> For this is my religion and my faith.[15]

One is reminded of Ramakrishna who practised Islam, Christianity, Shaktiism, Vaiṣṇavism and so on. According to him too there is one God towards whom all are travelling.[16]

Sects of Islam

There are many sub-sects of Islam, but we in India are concerned with two major sects, namely *Sunni* and *Shia*. There is really no difference in the articles of creed or the five pillars of Islam. The real difference lies in the status and position of Ali, the son-in-law of the Prophet.

Ali was wedded to the daughter of Prophet Muhammad. But setting this fact aside he had risked his life for the prophet and was a valiant man and a faithful follower of the Prophet. He was held in high esteem by every one. Even the Prophet not only loved Ali, but respected him for his qualities of head and heart. On three-four occasions the prophet had declared, 'Oh God, who is a friend of Ali, be his friend and the one who is Ali's enemy, be his enemy.[17] Naturally, it was believed that he would be the first Caliph. Unfortunately, after the death of the Prophet, not

Ali, but Abu Bakr became the first Caliph and he nominated Umar as his successor. After Umar, Uthman became the third Caliph. Ali was declared the fourth Caliph, but he was killed when he was praying in the mosque at Kufa. Afterwards, Ali's sons Hasan and Hussain were slain in an unequal battle of forces. Certainly this killing of Hasan and Hussain is a matter of deep lamentations by all the followers of Ali, who are now called Shia.

The real point of difference between the Shias and Sunnis is with regard to the institution of *Imam*. The Shia believes that the Prophet Muhammad has initiated a cycle for the continuing guidance of the community in the person of the *Imam*. This Imam is invested with the qualities of inspired and infallible interpretation of the Quoran. The first Imam was Ali who belonged to the family of the Prophet and inherited the spiritual abilities from the Prophet. As such he was the real leader and infallible interpreter of the Quoran. This spiritual heritage continues in the descendants of Ali till now.

Modern Developments in Islam

Thus, as yet neither the Quoran nor the person of the Prophet Muhammad has undergone the modern test of criticism. In comparison, the textual criticism of the Bible has shown that it is full of mythologies and even the Pentateuch has not been written by Moses. No such textual criticism of the Quoran has been undertaken. Besides, the person of the prophet is regarded too sacred for critical enquiry. Perhaps 'The Satanic Verses' (1988) by Saloman Rushdie has only literary value, if any, but is not a critical study of the prophet. It has been declared irresponsible and offensive work. Yet Islam cannot remain untouched by modern developments.

The Quoran is being translated in the vernaculars of the people, the veiling of women is slowly disappearing in advanced countries, instead of bigamy, monogamy is going to be practised, and more political rights are being allowed to women. Even the system of divorce has become more difficult. Education, industrialisation and secularism are getting their foot-hold, though in Pakistan and Bangladesh there is reversal in favour of 'Islamic State'.

ISLAM AND CHRISTIANITY

There are a number of things in common between Islam and Christianity. More or less, Old Testament is a common heritage of both Islam and Christianity. Besides, they share in common monotheism, the transcendence of God, revelation of God through prophets, the doctrine of heaven and hell, the day of judgment, and so on. But there are some important differences, specially concerning the person of Jesus.

1. Islam accepts Jesus Christ as a prophet. Secondly, Islam also believes in the second coming of Jesus.

2. But Islam does not accept the sonship of Jesus. The reason is that Islam interprets 'Sonship' in physical terms. In physical sense, however God can have no son or daughter. According to Christianity God is spirit and no one has ever seen Him. Jesus is said to be the son of God in a metaphorical or symbolical sense.

3. Islam does not believe that Jesus was really crucified. His substitute was crucified. But Islam believes that Jesus ascended into the Heaven, where he was seen by the prophet in his vision of the Heaven.

4. There is a subtle difference between Islam and Christianity with regard to God. First, Islam rejects the doctrine of trinity. This doctrine, according to Islam, distorts the pure monotheism of the teaching of the prophet Abraham. Secondly, Islam regards God as Judge, but also merciful and compassionate. For Christianity God is essentially love, and out there to receive and redeem the sinners of the sin.

5. Both of them are missionary religions and at times have used violence for propagating their religion.

6. In the last resort, Christians do not regard Prophet Muhammad as a prophet of God, but his religious insight and vision are worthy of any world leader of any religion of the world.

7. According to Christianity the denial of the crucifixion of Jesus, denies the atonement of the sin of the sinners. This is tantamount to the denial of Christian way of salvation.

Islam and Judaism

There is little doubt that the teaching of pure monotheism in Islam was greatly influenced by Parsiism and Judaism. Both Judaism and Islam do not believe in incarnation of God and the sonship of Jesus. Both of them, therefore, would not accept the Christian doctrine of trinity. Both of them accept the doctrines of creation, day of judgment and resurrection of the dead, Heaven and Hell, revelation of God through prophets, and, the transcendence of God. However, there are important differences between Islam and Judaism.

1. The Jews do not regard Jesus as a prophet, but Islam does.
2. The Jews do not believe in the ascension of Jesus, but Islam does.
3. The Jews pay special veneration to Moses and Ezra, but Islam rejects the claim of Ezra, for eminence and traces its monotheism to the teachings of prophet Abraham. Again, the Jews regard Moses as the greatest prophet and calls Ezra the son of God. As against this for Islam, prophet Muhammad is the greatest prophet and the final seal of prophetism.
4. Islam regards that the Jews had corrupted the teaching of pure monotheism by believing in many other gods and idol worship and paid too much reverence to Ezra.

However, these two religions are so close that some Western scholars regard Islam as 'Talmudic Judaism', adapted to Arabia, plus the apostleship of Jesus and prophet Muhammad.

References

1. R.S. Bhatnagar, *Dimensions of Classical Sufi Thought*, Delhi 1984, pp. 137-138.
2. *Glimpses of World Religions*, Jaico, Bombay 1962, p. 213.
3. Picthall, M., '*The Glorious Koran*', London 1948. Translations from Quoran have been taken from this book.
4. S.M. Iqbal, *The Reconstruction of Religious Thought in Islam*, p. 113.
5. S.M. Iqbal, *Ibid.*, pp. 116-117.
6. Afred Quillaume, *Islam*, p. 146.

7. Smith, M., '*Readings from the Mystics of Islam*'. No. 31, p. 35; K. W. Morgan, *Islam*, Delhi 1987 pp. 171-172.
8. Smith, M., *Ibid.*, No. 28, p. 33.
9. Kenneth W. Morgan ed. *Islam*, pp. 175-176.
10. K.W. Morgan, *Ibid.*, p. 177.
11. K.W. Morgan, *Ibid.*, p. 177; Vide A.J. Arberry, *Doctrine of the Sufis*, Camb. 1977, p. 140.
12. K.W. Morgan, *Ibid.*, p. 178.
13. K.W. Morgan, *Ibid.* p. 178.
    Radhakrishnan commenting on Gita IV-11 observes, "The same God is worshipped by all. The differences of conception and approach are determined by local colouring and social adaptations". (*Gītā* p. 159).
14. Idries Shah, *The way of the Sufi*, p. 80.
15. Kenneth W. Morgan, *Ibid.*, p. 178; also see '*My heart can take on any appearance*' in Idries Shah, *Ibid.*, p. 80. It is the same thought of the oneness of every religion.
16. The Gospel of Ramakrishna, p. 128.
17. Kenneth W. Morgan, *Ibid.*, p. 187.

CHAPTER VI

HINDUISM

INTRODUCTION

Initially 'Hinduism' does not mean the name of any religion. It is a Persian word and stands for all the inhabitants who live in and about the Indus Valley and beyond. But now 'Hinduism' stands for the religions of India, other than Islam and Christianity. It is a blanket term which stands for Brahminism, Buddhism, Jainism and even the aboriginal religions of India. Kabirpanthis, Nathas and Sikhs do not accept the nomenclature of 'Hinduism', but they too are regarded as forms of Hinduism. Even the followers of Ramakrishna Ashram do not mistakenly want to call themselves 'Hindus'. Even the Arya Samajists are included in the list of 'minorities'. Is there anything then that characterizes 'Hinduism' that separates it from prophetic religions?

Yes, at present in general it can be said that all those religions that accept the fourfold pillar of *Karma-Saṃsāra-jñāna-Mukti* may be called 'Hindu'. In this sense even Sikhism, Arya Samaj, Kabirism and Nathism may be called 'Hinduism'. In this wide sense of the term Hinduism is really a federation of religions, with their different creeds and practices. We know only this much that the doctrine of *Karma-Saṃsāra-Jñāna-Mukti* is first seen in the clearest form in Ajivikism, Jainism and Buddhism. It is now accepted by even the Orthodox Brahmins. This doctrine is not clearly spelled in Ṛgveda and not even in the oldest parts of the Upanishads called the *Chandogya* and *Bṛhadāraṇyaka*.

In the wide sense of the term 'Hinduism', it has no founder, but certainly there are eminent teachers within this fold. Who can ignore the names of Lord Mahavira, Lord Buddha, Yajñavalkya, Manu, Kabir, Ramakrishna Paramahansa, Chaitanya, Sikh Gurus and many more. Numerous sages and rishis have accepted Hinduism and by their saintly lives and teachings have enriched Hinduism. In this sense, Hinduism is really an encyclopaedic religion which has room for atheism, theism Yogic spiritualism, all forms of devotion, casteism, non-casteism, and so on and so forth. In this wide sense, Hinduism means the entire culture, spiritual values and a general way of life with its roots in Indian origin of about 5000 years. Naturally, Hindus have learnt the task of peaceful living having orthodoxy and non-orthodoxy within their limits. Intolerance in the different forms and sects of Hinduism did not take as violent a form as we find in the case of prophetic religions. In due course, Shankara, the most celebrated orthodox Brahmin and Kabir a Shudra and even an outcaste have forged the most formidable principle of unity amongst religions. In the same manner Ramanuja and Alvars have evolved the most important forms of theism, known to mankind, in the form of *Bhakti* cult.

HINDUISM AND PROPHETIC RELIGIONS

In the wide sense of the term 'Hinduism' and prophetic religions have important points of difference, broadly speaking, which cannot be easily ignored.

Hinduism inclusive of Brahminism and non-Brahminism	*Prophetic Religions (Zoroastrianism, Judaism, Christianity and Islam)*
1. There is one reality, usually Brahman of which this world is either real (Ramanuja) or illusory.	1. The world is real but a creation of God out of nothing, depending on the fiat of His will.
2. The doctrine of emanation is best taught in the Pāñcarātra and Bhagavat Purana. Here the earlier emanations are less contaminated than the later ones. In the same way, the earlier Yugas of Satya and Treta are better than the later ones.	2. The prophetic religions have been presented in the form of a drama. The first scene begins with the creation of man and the last scene includes the day of judgment with Heaven and Hell. There need be no thinking that the first creation was better than the later one. Really the

	teaching of later prophets is considered better than that of the earlier ones. Kirkegaard regarded the disciple at the second hand as better than the earlier disciples of Jesus.
3. Naturally, in general, Hinduism teaches the cycle of creation and dissolution, without any final end. As a matter of fact, Jains and Mimamsakas teach the eternity of the world.	3. As noted earlier in prophetic religions, there is only one creation which is heading, or, progressing towards a final end.
4. With the doctrine of emanation goes the teaching of involution.	4. Here there can be nothing but a final end of the world.
5. God or gods are but manifestation of the one reality called Brahman. Hence, *avatāravāda* is a natural implication of emanation. As everything is a manifestation of Brahman, so even a jiva can seek and attain identity with it. For Shankara's advaitism, the world is illusory and leaves Brahman wholly untouched.	5. God is considered more transcendent than immanent. He might be omnipresent. He can meet His creatures only through prophets. Prophets may enjoy nearness of God, but they dare not think of mergence or identity with God. This is most clear in Judaism and Islam. Some Indian Christians think of Jesus as the Incarnation of God in the form of *avatāravāda*.
6. Naturally Hinduism teaches the doctrine of avidya as the real cause of his coming into the world--cycle of births and deaths, and his miseries.	6. Man in his worldly existence has fallen into sin and requires a deliverer in the form of a Prophet or a saviour.

7. The body is due to *Karma* and is a blemish. It is a product of *avidyā* and can be dissolved only through *jñāna*.	7. This body therefore has to be used in God's service and has to be sanctified, for both the world and man are real.
8. Even insects and trees are the emanation of Brahman. So they too are objects of our reverance, respect and *Ahimsā*.	8. Man is the highest creation of God. Hence, service to fellowmen is the highest duty. Other lower animals and trees have been made for man.

As Hinduism is a federation of religions, so the abovementioned points of difference are valid within limits. The doctrine of emanation is formed clearly only in the *Pāñcarātra* and the theory of four Yugas. Again, for advaitism, the world is illusory, but is not so for Ramanuja.

Again, the term 'salvation' means to be saved from hell-fire, and, for the Hindus, it means to be freed from the endless cycle of births and deaths. Thus, hell-fire and cycle of births-deaths are akin concepts. Why is the cycle of birth-death dreaded? Because life is considered to be essentially painful.

Besides, Mahayanists think that later disclosures of Lord Buddha are far more progressive than the earlier ones. Hence, all forms of Hinduism are not essentially conservative and backward-looking.

Further, *avidyā* is translated as *error*. However, *avidyā* means distortion of intellect and vitiation of human will. And this is also the real meaning of 'fall' or 'sin' in Prophetic religions.

Hence, the difference between the two great traditions are only too general.

A Short History of Hindu Religious Thought

We have already seen that the Iranians and Indo-Aryans formed one tribe. It is also certain that the Aryans came into India from the North-Western region of Asia. There is no evidence that the Aryans of India ever crossed the border of Western India to occupy the land outside of India. Pliny observes

The Indians almost alone among the nations have never emigrated from their own borders. (J.W. McCrindle, *Ancient India*, p. 108).

When the Aryans came to India, they did not find the inhabitants without religion. The natives did have a religion quite different from the Ṛgvedic gods and religious practices of the Indo-Aryans. The natives of India were called dark people with flat nose (*anāsah*), speaking quite a different rough tongue (*mṛdhravak*). These Dasas/Dasyus were called *a-yajña* (without Vedic Sacrifice), *a-devaya* (without the worship of gods), *anya-vrata* (observing quite a different vrata or ceremonies) and *a-Mānuṣa* (inhuman).[1] They were looked down upon as phallus-worshippers (śiśna-devah).[2] These characteristics of the then natives of India, specially of the Indus Valley dwellers are easily borne out by the excavations of Mohenjodaro.

From the excavations it has been maintained that the Harappans, as the people of Indus Valley Civilizations are called, were associated with the worship of Shiva (as *dhyani* with his eyes fixed on the tip of the nose), Liṅgam, Yakṣas, Nagas, Mother Goddess, bull, snakes, trees etc. Most probably these people who lived about 2500 B.C., developed the four pillars of *Karma-Saṁsāra-Jñāna-Mukti*. These views are clearly and most emphatically maintained in the non-Aryan cults of Jainism and Buddhism. In contrast, the Ṛgveda talks of *svarga-prāpti* (desire for heavenly abode). The Harappans had iconic religion too as evidenced by the image of......proto-Shiva and goddesses, bulls, trees etc.

Most of the Harappans have been either absorbed in the larger matrix of Hinduism, or, else were driven in the mountains and in Southern India. The full struggle between the Aryan and non-Aryan cults came to a focus about the 5th or 6th Century B.C. At that time Jainism and Buddhism had fully flourished in Kashi, Videha, Vaishali, Koshala and Magadha. The Ṛgvedic cult could not have won the battle frontally. So the Indo-Aryans slowly and gradually mastered the technique and thought of the non-Aryan people. They assimilated much of the non-Aryan cult of Yoga, Karma-Saṁsāra-Jñāna-Mukti, the *pāñcamahāvrata* of the Jains along with *Ahiṁsā*. Their crowning device was in the acceptance of the doctrine of the Upanishads, which had a good deal of similarities with the Buddhist doctrine of desirelessness and *nirvāṇa*. Could all the non-Aryan people become Aryanized? In this comingling of religious thought, the Ganges and Jamuna lost much of their separateness and became one stream. But not quite Brahminism laid down two conditions for being assimilated into its fold, namely,

1. Vedas are to be accepted as the only religious scripture and,
2. Caste has to be accepted for assigning a place, rank and order in Brahmin society. Of course, Brahmins had to be regarded as the highest caste, and, also as the custodian and interpreters of the Vedas.

The term 'Vedas' in due course included much more than the original 'Veda'. But even then Jainism and Buddhism did not accept caste-distinction and in due course they developed their own scriptural authorities.

Till the rise of Islam in North-West of India, Buddhism was the flourishing religion of that region. But with the spread of Islam, some of the Buddhists came to India. They were not absorbed into the main stream of Hinduism, presumably because they did not accept the two conditions of Brahminism. Hence, they had no option but to accept Shaivism and Vaisnavism which were non-Aryan theistic forms of worship. They had their own scriptures, and, they did not accept caste. Their watch-word was,

> He alone belongs to Hari, who worships Hari.

Shaivism had its long history of Yogic practices, most probably dating from the time of Mohenjodaro. Vaiṣṇavism, either of the Gītā or of the Alvars, developed *bhakti* as the potent means of realization *mukti* (liberation). It is worthy of note that the Gītā admits all worshippers, irrespective of their caste or sex.

> All those who take refuge in Me, attain to the highest end, even though they are of low caste, women, Vaishyas and Shudras. (IX: 32).

In the same way, most of Alvars were shudras, who gave a new and lasting lease of life to the path of devotion.

In due course, these Buddhist shudras have given birth to many Saints, Gorakhpanthis, Kabir-panthis and others. Sikhs may not have been Buddhist Shudras, but they were greatly influenced by the Saints, and, they like the other non-Brahmin Saints repudiated caste and the Brahmin scriptures. It is not a matter of surprise that at the end of his struggle against caste, Dr. B.R. Ambedkar had no other option left to him except the acceptance of Buddhism.

Hence, it is an altogether wrong opinion to hold that Jainism and Buddhism have arisen from Brahminism and that they only protest against the animal-sacrifice of Vedic religion. They are the indigeneous, independent and parallel movement of religious thought. Even now in some form or the other these non-Brahmin and non-Vedic movements are continuing. It is not an accident of history that Tulsidas so successfully combated the heresies of the Saints, mainly Kabir.

Thus every form of Hinduism is neither Aryan nor Vedic. However, it must be admitted that at present by Hinduism is meant largely Brahminism and Vedism. However, if we compare the Ṛgvedic thought with the modern classical Hinduism, then we find that the following elements have been added to the Ṛgvedic religion:

1. The meaning of the Veda now includes the Brahmaṇas and the Vedanta and perhaps also Smṛtis.
2. Hinduism largely accepts the four pillars of *Karma-Samsāra-Jñāna-mukti. Svarga-prāpti* (the heavenly abode) still lingers on in the religious philosophy of Ramanuja and in some forms of Vaisnavism.
3. The doctrine of renunciation is largely accepted, though by far the orthodox view represented by Maṇḍana Mishra is that the *Sannyāsa Āshrama* can be accepted only after the stage of being a house-holder. However, Shankara, like the Buddhists and Jainas, favours *sannyāsa* at any stage, even without undergoing the life of a house-holder.
4. Vedic rituals have become only auxiliary factors in having

jñāna, which is regarded as the most essential means of liberation. Of course, Ramanuja recommended the performance of Vedic Karmas even up to the end of one's life.

The Religious Scripture of the Hindus

The 'Veda' means knowledge. Formerly there were three Vedas only, namely, Ṛgveda, Yajurveda and Sāmaveda. The Ṛgveda contains hymns in praise of the gods; the Yajurveda contains the rituals to be performed, and, Sāmaveda contains the hymns to be sung. Later on, Atharvaveda was added. The Vedas were elaborated into the *Brahmaṇas*, which are more important from the viewpoint of sacrifices than for higher esoteric thought. The last part of the Vedas is known as the *Vedānta* (i.e., the end of the Veda).

The Vedanta comprises about 108 Upanishads of which ten are important. Each Veda has the following Upanishads attached:

Ṛgveda	—	Aitreya and Kaushitaki Upanishad
Yajureveda (White)	—	Bṛhadāraṇyaka and Isha Upanishads
Yajureveda (Black)	—	Taittiriya, Kaṭha, Svetāsvatara, Maitri Upanishads.
Sāmaveda	—	Chhandogya and Kena Upanishads.
Atharvaveda	—	Muṇḍaka, Pras'na, Māṇḍūkya.

The earliest parts of the Vedas were learnt orally and were transmitted from the father to the son, about 3000 B.C. The Aryans are supposed to have come into India between 2500 B.C. and 1500 B.C. Most probably the Ṛgveda, at least its oldest part was written down in the region of Saptasindhu between 1500 B.C. and 1000 B.C. There is every likelihood that a good number of *mantras* might have been lost in their transmission from oral to written form.

The Vedas are known as *Shruti* for here the religious materials were seen or heard by the seers. This was followed by the *Smṛitis* (i.e., remembered). They include almost all the authoritative texts including the *Gītā*, *Dharma Shastras*, the Epics and the Puranas. The most important *Dharma-Shastras* are of Manu and Yajnavalkya. The epics include the *Rāmāyana* and *Mahā-*

bhārata. There are about 18 Purāṇas, representing popular Hinduism. The most important ones are Bhāgavata Purāṇa and Skanda Purāṇa. The Bhāgavata Purāṇa is an amalgamation of Advaitism and *Bhakti* in the cult of Vaiṣṇavism. Skanda Purāṇa is sacred to Shaivism and contains advaitic knowledge, Yogic exercises, tantra etc.

For practical purposes Vedic mantras are even now recited on the occasions of deity worship, marriage and other religious ceremonies. However, the Gītā and the Upanishads are the most important religious books for the learned. Ram Mohan Roy, Rabindranath Tagore and Aurobindo had made the Upanishads as their subject-matter of studies and meditation. However, for the vast majority of the Hindus, the Rāmāyana is the most popular sacred book.

Religious Philosophies (Darshana)

Indian philosophy is largely committed to religious values. But the Brahmins were more interested in the acceptance of the Vedas as the sole authority in the matter of religion than in actual speculation. Hence, they did not recognise Jainism, Buddhism, carvakism. Nay, in the beginning for a long time *Sāmkhya-Yoga, Nyāya-Vaiśeṣika* philosophies too were considered to be non-Vedic. Nay, understandably Vaiṣṇavism was also considered non-Vedic.[3] But at present the position has changed much, for these philosophies have been accepted as orthodox. The criterion of orthodoxy is the acceptance of the Veda as authoritative *darshana.* Those *darshanas* that accept the authority of the Veda are known as *āstika* (orthodox), and those that do not are known as *nāstika* (unorthodox). With these meanings of *āstika* and *nāstika*, we can thus classify the various *darshanas.*

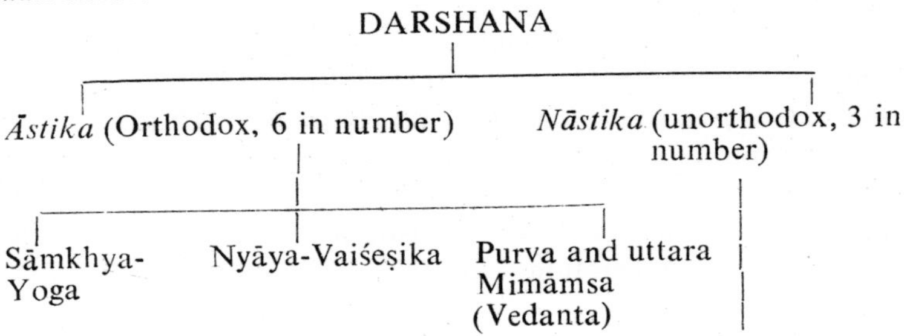

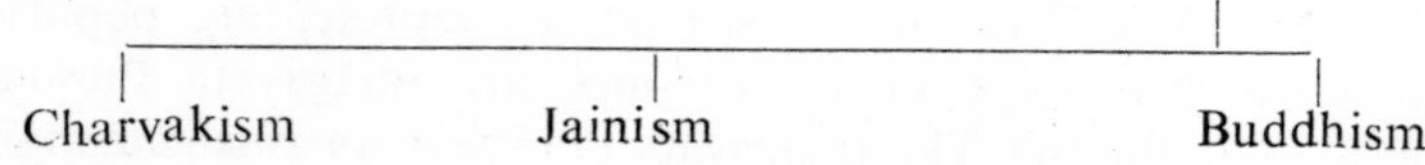

These systems have remained inter-related and have developed after a good deal of give-and-take amongst themselves This inter-relation is so great that even the advaitism of Shankara is considered to be 'Buddhism-in-disguise' (*pracchanna Bauddha*).

Distinctive Features of Hinduism

Hinduism is the oldest religion of the world and it has come in contact with a number of non-Aryan and non-Vedic religions in India. Hence, some of its tenets have been changing their hues. Besides, religion for Hinduism has been taken most seriously and the acute and meditative mind of the Hindus has introduced many shades of opinion even with regard to the current terms of religion. Keeping these considerations in mind, we can mention the following features of Hinduism which distinguish it from prophetic and other Indian religions like Jainism and Buddhism.

The defining characteristics of Hinduism may be called the four-fold pillar of *Karma-Saṁsāra-Jñāna-mukti*. But each term is found in various meanings.

Karma—In general '*Karma*' means activity in a state of infatuation. Usually it means an action under the influence of passions and undesirable emotions. '*Karma*' in this sense binds a creature in the endless cycle of rebirths. Each birth in the cycle is said to be painful.

As distinguished from '*Karma*', the advaitins prefer '*avidyā* or *ajñāna*' as the real starting-point of tumbling into the miserable worldly existence. Ramanuja who criticizes the *māyā*-doctrine of Shankara prefers '*Karma*' to '*avidyā*'. However, this is only a verbal distinction. In Sāmkhya it is pointed out that the pure spirit is essentially inactive. But it falsely identifies itself with the active *prakṛti* and thereby falsely thinks itself to be a doer and enjoyer of its activity. However, actions are due to *prakṛti* and not due to the spirit itself. Thus, action (*karma*) is due to ignorance, infatuation or *avidyā*. Thus *avidyā* and *karma* under the influence of emotions are two inseparable aspects of the same coin. There is not much to choose between karma and avidyā.

The doctrine of *niṣkāma karma* is also a distinctive aspect of *karma*. According to it only *sakāma* (with some desire) *karma* binds a man in the wheel of rebirths. But a disinterested performance of duties in one's station of life (Varṇāshrama *Dharma*) does not bind a man. Of course, this *niṣkāma karma* comes under *Bhakti*. This comes very near Kant's doctrine of duty for the sake of duty, taking duty to be a divine command.

Saṁsāṛa (Painful worldly existence): 'Saṁsāra' means that which is an endless process. Here it means 'an endless chain of rebirths'. Each birth, even a birth into the highest species called 'human being' is full of miseries. It does not mean that life is only suffering. Nobody can deny the fact that an actual life has both moments of pleasure (happiness) and painfulness. But what is contended is that even the worldly pleasure is infected with momentariness and transitoriness. And that which is transitory can never be considered to be 'real or eternal happiness'.

Further, this worldly existence has become worse through the ages because it has been greatly shaped by the twisted wills of the *jivas*. This accumulation of *Karmas* through the ages in countless rebirths of an individual is called *Karma-Samskāra*. One can imagine how difficult it is to get rid of one's *Karma-Samskāra*.

Jñāna: But after diagnosing the cause of human miseries, one can hope to deal effectively with them. Those who take '*ajñāna*' as the real cause of fall into wordly existence, hope to put an end to *ajñāna* by means of true *jñāna*. Others take the performance of Vedic rituals and *niṣkāma karmas*, as a means of terminating the endless cycle of rebirths. Ramanuja advocates the theory of *Karma-jñāna-Samuccaya*. Others advance one of three ways of ending the endless chain of rebirths. These three ways are *jñāna-mārga*, *Karma-mārga* and *bhakti-mārga*. Advaitins recommend *jñāna-mārga*, the Saints and others under their influence advocate *bhakti-mārga* (the path of devotion). B.G. Tilaka has popularized the path of *karma*.

Mukti (*Liberation*): It means deliverance from rebirths. It is both a positive and a negative concept. The most important cause of bondage is said to be the formation of *egoism* (ahaṁkāra). Hence, the loss of one's ego in the differenceless Brahman (as *Sat+Cit+ānanda*) is characterized as *mukti*. This is also known as *layavāda* or mergence. This has been advocated by Shankara.

As against mergence, Ramanuja understands by *mukti* an abode in *Baikuṇṭha* (heavens) in communion with Ishvara. This will also be accepted by all who advocate the path of devotion to a personal God.

The immortality of the Soul: Classical Hinduism accepts the immortality of the soul. Shankara teaches that a jiva is really identical with Brahman (*jivo brahmaiva*). According to Ramanuja, a jiva is only a part of Brahman and remains conserved to the end, whether in bondage or in the state of liberation. This is also maintained by all those who advocate the path of devotion to a personal God.

Here the soul is said to be a spirit and capable of existence, independently of a body. The well-known verses of the *Gītā* (II. 20-25) state that the spirit is unborn, eternal, permanent, and, is not slain when the body is slain. The spirit in its different births, simply changes its body as garments, but itself remains the same, unchanging soul. Hence, this view distinguishes Hinduism from prophetic religions and is in line with the Greek view of the Soul.

Hinduism accepts supernaturalism more firmly than this-worldliness. But by clinging to *āshrama dharmas*, the importance of the duties of a house-holder cannot be under-estimated. But it must be admitted that Hinduism accepts social conservatism much more than progressiveness.[4] This follows from the fact that Hinduism believes in the periodic creation and dissolution of the world.* Further, it also accepts that there are four Yugas which keep on repeating themselves as soon as there is a fresh creation. They are *Satya*, *tretā*, *dvāpara* and *Kali*. An alloyed true dharma prevails in Satya Yuga, in *tretā* truth and falsehood get mixed up in equal proportion. In *dvāpara* there is more of *adharma* than true religious piety. However, *Kalī yuga* is unmixed *adharma*. Hence, the doctrine of four-Yugas teaches that the past has the truth of religious belief and later on this pure

*However, the Mimāmsakas and Jainas accept the eternity of the world.

truth gets gradually lost. Hence, Hinduism teaches religious conservatism.

In contrast Prophetic religion accepts the dramatic beginning in creation and the ending of it in the day of judgment. It also in general holds that God progressively reveals His ways to man.

Caste: At present caste is the most controversial issue among the Hindus. But there is little doubt that even Parsiism has four classes of people. However, there is nothing like 'Shudras' who are like social slaves of the higher castes of Brahmins, Kshatriyas, Vaishyas. The mention of caste has been in Ṛgveda 10:90 and since then it has been repeated in Sat. Brahman 14:4.23 and Taittiriya Brah. 1.2.6.7; 3.2, 3.9. Manu Smṛti has put a final seal on caste, according to which Shudras have to serve all other members of the society.

Gandhiji also had accepted caste. According to him, efficiency of expertise and skill can result from their transmission from the fathers to their sons. Thus, the doctrine of caste by birth was given a social and professional sanction. But later on in April 1945 Gandhiji became dissatisfied with the prevalence of caste and advocated its dissolution.[5]

Of course, non-Sanātani Hindus do not accept caste. (Sants, Nathas, Kabiris, Sikhs). Arya Samaj, Brahma Samaj and Rama-Krishna Ashramite are Hindus coming under orthodox schools, but they repudiate caste.

It is to be noted that some of the most important figures in Hinduism did not belong to higher caste. Vidura was born of a Shudra woman, Vaśiṣṭha was born of a prostitute, Vyāsa was born of a fisher-woman and the sage Parāshara was born of a Chānḍāla woman, and so was Satyakama Jabala.

Varṇāshrama Dharma: The Vedic people were given to ancestor worship. If there be no son in the family, then this ancestor-worship will cease. Therefore, the Vedic religion, even from the time when Indo-Aryan and Iranian lived together had paid special sanctity to the life of a house-holder. Hence, the Vedic Brahmins, even when they accepted the doctrine of *jñāna* and *mukti*, preserved the old sanctity of a house-holder. Thus, compromising with the doctrine of *Sannyāsa* (renunciation), the Brahmins laid down the doctrine of four *āshramas* i.e.. *Brahmacharya Gṛhastha*, *Vānaprastha* and *Sannyāsa*. *Sannyāsa* comes towards the end of life after completing the duties and obligations of a house-holder.

Thus, Hinduism teaches that corresponding to each stage of life there are duties for every caste. Here, the *Gītā* too emphasizes caste-duties (XVIII:40-48).

> Remaining in the imperfect performance of one's own caste-duty is better (more conducive) than the duty belonging to other castes even if performed perfectly (*Gītā* 18:47).

Vaṛnāshrama Dharmas pertain to the conservation of the society.

Karmavāda and Puruṣakāra: 'Karmavāda' is related to '*Karma*' and is a theory about '*Karma*'. In general *karmavāda* simply means 'as you sow, so you will reap'. People get in this life according to what they have done in their past lives. This theory serves to reconcile the needy, oppressed and exploited people to their hard lot. But does it mean fatalism? Yes, some of the *ajivikas* held to *antinomism*. According to this theory this life simply unfolds what has been accumulated in the past lives[6] and no efforts, either good or bad, can change the course of events. However, Lord Mahavira refuted this doctrine of antinomism. If *karmas* have accumulated in the past lives, then even in this life they can be exhausted, and prevented from fructification and fresh accumulation. Hence, there is also the theory of *Puruṣakāra*.

According to *Puruṣakāra*, one can change the course of events in this and future lives by one's efforts either through *bhakti*, fresh *karmas* and *jñāna*.

Karmavāda is also used to explain disparities in life, for which man is held responsible and not his Creator called Ishvara. Hence, this is a way out of the theistic tangle with regard to the evil in the world.

Idolatry: The Aryans themselves were not iconic. But by mingling with the native cult, present Hinduism has become iconic. Is it also idolatrous?

By idolatry is meant that a finite being is taken for the Infinite. Except in few instances, the classical and dominant trend is that an idol is only a means for concentration but the real object is the Absolutely transcendent reality, usually called

Brahman. It can also be said that the unqualified Brahman can be approached through some of its manifestations. For Shankara, even Ishvara in a general sense cannot be called absolutely real. Hence, for Hinduism, an image is only a support (*ālambana*) for the purposes of meditation.

Avatāravāda: Closely connected with image-worship is the doctrine of *Avatāra* (incarnation), specially in the form of 'Rama' and 'Krishna'. This is peculiar to Hinduism, but is also accepted by the Christians who accept 'The Apostle's Creed', mentioned here in this book.

There is also the doctrine of *arcāvatāra*, according to which some shrines are holier than others. This is really the doctrine of the *Pāñcarātra* which was canonized by Ramanuja.

However, the most important religious philosophy of the Hindus is advaitism. According to advaitism, the final conclusion about *avatāravāda* and *arcāvatāra* is thus stated by Appaya Dixit:

> O Lord, I have in my weakness, committed three sins and beg forgiveness of you. To serve as support for meditation I have given a form to the Highest who is really formless; I have tried to define the indefinable by composing *stotras* and litanies and lastly I have confined the omnipotent Lord to particular places of worship and have journeyed to those places.

Thus, a Hindu is fully aware of the fact that man is weak and frail, and, cannot fail to raise his hands in prayer to God, realizing the inadequacies of such an approach.

THE NOTION OF GOD

The Ṛgvedic religion was polytheistic at the start and different hymns were addressed to various gods. Some of these gods are clearly the personification of the powers of nature like the Sun, the Earth, the Winds and so on. Yet among these hymns we find some of them addressed to Varuna who is as nearly the highest righteous God as any conceived in antiquity. However, in due course, God Varuṇa was relegated to an insignificant place.

Later on, Hiraṇyagarbha, Visvakarma and Prajapati are as nearly monotheistic Gods as one could see. However, the trend led the Aryans towards monism, according to which there is one, non-dual reality, without much emphasis on the personality of this reality. At first, gods are praised and worshipped in pairs e.g., Varuṇa-Mitra, Dyāvā-Prithivi, Varuṇa-Aditi, Indra-Varuṇa, and so on. Then came the stage of *Visve Devah*. This worship of the totality of gods paved the way for the adage

> To what is One, sages give many a title;
> they call it Agni, Yama, Matrisvan (*RV*. I.164.46).

In due course, the Vedic priests indifferently chose any one god at the time of worship and at that moment that god was considered to be the highest. This is the stage of what is known as *henotheism*. This is also known as *monolatry* in which case one god is said to be the highest, though other gods are not denied.

Atheistic trend: It seems so surprising that in about 600 B.C. Jainism and Buddhism established atheism. What is more surprising is the fact that early philosophies of India in Sutra form were atheistic. Early Mimāmsā too with its stand on the Vedas was wholly atheistic. For it is correct utterance of the mantras which was all necessary for attaining the spiritual end of man.

Most probably the Vedanta was a little later development. Even the theistic sutras of Nyāya (IV.1.19-21) have been interpreted atheistically.[7] What could be the reason for this atheistic trend?

The reason can only be guessed. It appears that the early development of Yoga made the seeker self-dependent. He hoped that by means of his own efforts it would be possible for him to achieve his highest goal. Tall claims were also made at the beginning, and even much afterwards in the rise of the tantra (c. 900-1200 A.D.). However, it was felt that human powers do not achieve what they want to attain without the help of supernatural power. Hence, the Yoga smuggled in God as *Ishvara-pranidhāna* i.e., one has to surrender oneself to God for one's Yogic attainment (Patañjali's *Yoga-sutra* 1:23; 2.1; 2:32 and 2:45).

Of course, 'God' has been introduced here only abruptly as an object of devotion and one to whom all the fruits of one's action have to be surrendered. He has not been mentioned as the creator or even as *Karma-phala-dātā* (the giver of the fruits of action).[8] But whether as the result of the pressure of theistic cults at that time, or, by the inner need of Yoga itself, God began to assume great emphasis in the later thought of the Hindus. The two elements of *bhakti* and *nīṣkāma karma* came to be fully utilized in the Gītā. But even in the Upanishads, the supreme reality called Brahman, was used both as *nirguṇa* (unqualified or attributeless) and *Saguṇa* (qualified or with attributes). The *nirguṇa* aspect is emphasized in a number of passages viz., Muṇḍ 2:2.11; Chh. U. III.14.1; Kena IV:6; Māṇḍ. VII.12). There are also passages which support theism, or, *saguṇa* aspect of Brahman. Brahman as creator, credited with intellect and desire is also found in a number of passages.

> It bethought itself: 'Would that I were
> Many! Let me procreate myself.' It emitted heat.
> That heat bethought itself: 'Would that I were
> many! Let me procreate myself'.
> (*Chh. U.* VI:2.3-4; *Vide Taitt.* 2:6; *Ait.* I:1.1.

Hence both Shankara and Ramanuja, accept the existence of Ishvara. For Shankara theism is less important than Brahma-realization. Ordinarily for Shankara theistic worship is valuable, both for itself and for its instrumental value in the supreme task of Brahma-realization.

> Nor do we wish to contend against the devotional approach and the unceasing one-pointed meditation on God: for this has been recommended both by *Shruii* and *Smṛti* (*Vedāntasutra Bhāṣya* II:2.42).

Shankara also grants that bhakti of Ishvara leads to *karma-mukti* (liberation by successive steps Vs.III.3.1; Vs.I.1.11; I:1.24: III: 2.21). But it must be conceded that for Shankara, Ishvara-bhakti does not always lead to *Brahma-jñāna* because *bhakti* may be conducted for purposes other than *Brahma-prāpti.* It may lead to Lordship i.e., *svarga-prāpati* (Vs.IV.3.14; to gradual liberation (Vs.III.2.21), to earthly prosperity and power (IV.1.12) and to warding off of calamities (Vs. III.2.21). Besides, bhakti in itself is dualistic, but Brahma is non-dual. Hence, for Shankara, only *Jñāna* will lead to Brahma-realization.

Ramanuja is highly critical of Shankara's doctrine of attributeless, non-dual Brahman. According to Ramanuja Brahman is personal, for he is endowed with 'intellect and will'.

> Brahman bethought itself: 'Would that I were many!
> Let me procreate myself'. (Chh.U.VI.2.3-4).

Besides, the whole world is real and not illusory as Shankara thought. Everything has proceeded from Brahman himself.

> As a spider might come out with his thread, as small sparks come forth from the fire, even so from this Soul (Brahman) come forth all vital energies, all worlds, all gods, all beings (*Bṛhadāraṇyaka* 3:1.20).

For Ramanuja, Brahman is an all-inclusive Ishvara, that comprises both *cit* (conscious beings) and *acit* (non-conscious objects called the whole material world). This Ishvara, therefore, is qualified, with the world and Jiva as the body of Ishvara and He is the indwelling soul of this body.

According to Ramanuja, this personal Brahma may be called *bhagavan*. He is credited with the six qualities of dominion (*aiśvarya*), strength, glory, splendour, wisdom and dispassion (*Śribhāṣya* I:1.1). Besides them five aupanishadic attributes are found in Brahman, namely, Self-luminousness, *ānanda* (bliss), *ananta,* satya and purity (*amalatva*). He is also described as having infinite number of auspicious qualities, specially easy availability (saulabhya) to His devotees and infinite compassion (karuṇā) for them.

The essential attribute of a jiva is to remain dependent on God as his master and the ultimate refuge. Hence, God can be best approached through *bhakti.* Steady remembrance of the Lord is called *bhakti* (devotion), uninterrupted like the flow of oil in a burning lamp (*Śribhāṣya* 1.1.1)*. However, for Ramanuja, this

**Śribhāṣya*, Eng. tr, G. Thibaut, pp. 14,16.

bhakti has knowledge and karma as well (*Vedārtha-Saṁgraha,* padas 127, 129, 136). For Ramanuja steady remembrance means the same thing as *Upāsāna* (meditation).

Again,

> By the term 'Vidya' is meant meditation that has developed into bhakti—In all these and similar cases the term 'Knowledge' (*Vedana*) signifies meditation (*dhyāna*).[10]

However, the most popular form of theism is found in the *avatāras* of Krishna and Rama. Lord Krishna has been raised to the status of the Absolute Brahma, endowed with personality. In the form of religious worship, the Bhāgavata Purāṇa dwells on the playful activities of Lord Krishna. This has formed the centre of many poems and songs of the Alvars and the Saints. In the form of an influential religious philosophy the worship of Lord Krishna is found in the Gītā. Here the doctrines of three pathways of salvation (*jñānamārga, Karma-mārga* and *Bhakti-Mārga*), *niṣkāma karma* (disinterested discharge of one's duty), openness of the Lord to all castes (Gītā 9.32) are very important.

No less important is the worship of Rama. As a matter of fact the Rāmāyana in the form of a drama is very popular in all parts of North India. At the time of Durga Puja, the play of Rama is enacted in Bengal, Bihar and specially Banaras.

Popular theism is found in the Purāṇas, with the doctrine of a triad of Brahma, Viṣṇu and Mahesh. Brahma is the creator, Viṣṇu the sustainer and Śiva is the destroyer of the world. Lord Viṣṇu is the most benign god. He out of his *Sattva*, incarnates himself for upholding righteousness.

> Whenever there is the decline of righteousness and rise of unrighteousness, then I incarnate myself for the protection of the virtuous and for the destruction of the evil-doers, from time to time (*Gītā* IV.7-8).[11]

Krishna and Rama are the most adored *avatāras* and they sustained the most exalted form of Bhakti. Ramanuja was really a Vaisnava and the most important philosopher of *Bhakti*.

Ramakrishna has combined both *nirguṇa* and *saguṇa* forms of Brahman. According to him, Brahma is both with and without forms. Brahma with forms can be approached through *bhakti* and Brahman without form can be realized through *jñāna*.

One point is to be mentioned here, that in the later times, the Nyāya-Vaiseśika has been busy in proving the existence of God. However, in this philosophy, God is taken to be an efficient creator. As contrasted with this conception of an efficient cause, Shankara regards his 'Ishvara' both the efficient and material cause of the world.

With the exception of Mimāmsā, the *āstika* schools of philosophy regard the world to be periodically created and dissolved. This is as much true of advaitism as of Nyāya-Vaiśeṣika school.

Further, Mimāmsā regards the Vedas to be impersonal (*a-pauruṣeya*) and eternal. The Nyāya regards the Veda to be *pauruṣeya* i.e., created by God, but is wholly reliable.

Man in Hinduism

Man is essentially a soul or spirit without any body. This has been stated very clearly in the Gītā II.20-25. Sāmkhya-Yoga, Nyāya-Vaiśeṣika hold on to the plurality of souls. According to Shankara, a *jiva* is essentially Brahmaṇ, just as the ether enclosed in a jar is nothing but ether. Ramanuja also holds that a *jiva* is essentially pure consciousness and is a part of Brahman. This may be, but what about a *jiva* in his earthly existence?

A *jiva* is man with a body. This body is not the essential self. It is an adjunct of the spirit in bondage. How has this bondage in the form of the body come about? Through *avidyā* or *ajñāna* (nescience), according to most of the Indians. However, according to Ramanuja, this bondage has come about according to one's *karman.* But how has this *karmañ* taken place in a pure spirit? Ramanuja does not explain this. But quite clearly this *karman* also could not have taken place without nescience. Ramanuja does not say so, for he is not thinking of the first creation. In the cycle of creation and dissolution, a *jiva* is born in the world because of his past *karman.* A *jiva* gets the body, his caste and his family according to his past *karman.* His social status and many things of this life depend on his past *karman.* Here Ramanuja seems to stand on a sound footing.

But one need not think in terms of creation as a whole. Let us think of an individual jiva. Why is he in bondage? Here karman theory will not be of much use, for it is the result of nescience itself. Hence, for Shankara, Sāmkhya and Nyāya, nescience is the real cause of bondage. Each individual at one time has been the victim of nescience and as such has tumbled in this miserable worldly existence. This account of falling into bondage has been initially explained by Sāmkhya and accepted by the Gītā.

The body essentially consists of *Prakṛti* which has the three constituents of *sattva, rajas* and *tamas*. These three constituents are psycho-physical in nature, for even our mind and intellect are *Prākṛtic* and not spiritual. Sattva is very light as against tamas which is heavy. Again, Sattva is bright. Rajas is dynamic and conative. Tamas is not only heavy but also enveloping things as if in darkness. These three aspects are inseparable. Drawn by the sattvic element of Prakṛti, the pure soul identifies itself with Prakṛti. The spirit, according to Sāmkhya, is essentially inactive (*niṣkriya*)*. In contrast, Prakṛti is always influx (pariṇāmi-nitya). By falsely identifying itself with Prakṛti, the jiva falls in bondage and undergoes pleasure-pain and endless chain of activities.

It is the proximity of the spirits with Prakṛti which makes Prakṛti evolve from subtle states of grosser ones. The gross elements are known as gross *tanmātras*, known as ākāsha (ether), Vāyu (air), Agni (fire), Apah (water) and Pṛthivi (the earth). The gross human body is made of these five elements. However, there is also a subtle body of each jiva, which keeps on transmigrating till this *jñāna* dawns that the jiva is not the doer, nor the enjoyer of the fruits of action. Essentially it is Prakṛti that is the doer. The individual jiva is pure consciousness without any activity.

In general Hinduism accepts this doctrine of nescience as the cause of bondage with the sole exception of Ramanuja. As noted before, Ramanuja regards *karman* and not nescience, the cause of bondage. He prescribes shastric injunctions for *karma* to the end along with *jñāna* and *bhakti*, for release. So he also endows the spirit with activity.

The universal bondage of jivas in the world is *anādi* (beginningless), but this bondage is bound to end (*Sānta*). No Hindu

*Ramanuja grudgingly attributes activity to the jiva.

system undertakes the task of explaining the reason of this cosmic bondage. First, it does not admit of first creation. In this eternal cycle of creation and dissolution of the worlds the question of the *origin* of cosmic bondage is senseless. Secondly, the task for each jiva is to work out his own salvation. One should not therefore remain pre-occupied with the fruitless effort to speculate about the first beginning which never was. This worldly existence is taken to be essentially painful. Three kinds of pain have been mentioned by Sāmkhya, namely, *ādhyātmika* (bodily and mental), *ādhibhautika* (external natural influences) and *ādhidaivika* (supernatural influences). This painful existence is due to *avidyā* (nescience) and is evil. *Avidyā* is that which soils the soul, perverts the will and misdirects men into the path of destruction. The word 'ignorance' is not quite precise. Avidyā really means an erring mind, befogged intellect and soiling of the inmost being of man, called his 'Soul'. Physical pain is also evil, because it weakens the will and prevents the promotion of good. Without a good physique, even Yogic exercises are not possible. Supernatural pain or evil is that which is beyond human control e.g., flood, cyclone, earthquake, and so on. 'Pain' has been explained largely in terms of transitoriness as in Buddhism. Only inactive quietism of the spirit is real. But who can deny that there is pleasure also along with pain? As a matter of fact it is the pursuit of pleasure which is the main reason of births and endless chain of deaths. Hence, it is meaningless whirl of going round and round, as in the story of Sisipus, which means painful existence. Shankara writes about this meaningless chain of endless births and rebirths:

> Once again birth and the death, once again gestation in mother's womb. This worldly existence is difficult to cross, O Lord Shiva, protect me. Again, the same fruitless repetition of night and day, fortnight and month, and the endless flow of years. But even then wish (to be born) is not extinguished (*Charpaṭpañjarika-stotram*).

Hence, pain means the boredom of endless repetitiveness and utter meaninglessness of worldly existence.*

*The thought of repetitiveness and meaninglessness has been expressed in the *Book of Ecclesiastes*:

Generations come and generations go, but the world stays just the same.

However, it is presumed all along that the jiva is essentially free, whether in bondage or release. In this life a jiva no doubt is greatly determined by his past karman. But this life is not only the place where some karmas become exhausted by being played out. Then some karmas are destroyed and weakened and some others are freshly created. This is the doctrine of *Puruṣakāra.* This doctrine of Puruṣakāra maintains that man is free, through his own various efforts either to weaken and destroy past karman, and prevent the formation of new *karman,* and, to live out the *karman* already at work. The doctrine of freedom and determinism assumes importance in the *Viśiṣṭādvaita* of Ramanuja.

According to Ramanuja, an individual soul is the body of God. A body is that which God completely controls and sustains for His own use and purposes (*Śribhāṣya,* II:1.9). When a jiva is wholly dependent and controlled by God, then is he really free?

According to Ramanuja, the chief and only authority in matters of religion are the Vedas. Vedas issue out injunctions in the form of 'ought'. 'Ought' implies that man is either free or not free to carry it out.

> For commands can be addressed to such agents only as are capable of entering on action or refraining from action, according to their thought and will. (*Śribhāṣya* II. 3.40).

Hence, Vedic commands imply that man is free either to obey or disobey. But how to reconcile freedom with the complete and slavish dependence of the jiva on Brahman?

Well, dependence on the finite and imperfect is undesirable, for such a dependence is against the dignity of man. But dependence on God, as the most supreme and the greatest goal of man is his highest freedom and greatest virtue.

> The only one that ought to be served by all who are enlightened about the fundamental nature of the self, is the highest

---

The sun still rises, and it still goes down, going wearily back to where it must start all over again...... .
The water returns to where the rivers began, and starts all over again. Everything leads to weariness......... a weariness too great for words. (Chap. I.4-8).

Puruṣa...'He alone is to be served by all'. (*Vedārtha-Saṁgraha,* pada 250).

Hence in Hinduism man is free either to win his salvation or to remain in the endless cycle of rebirths. He is free to follow either Bhaktiyoga or Karmayoga or Jñānayoga, suited to his temperamental constitution. If a man does not choose to be released, then he will remain in his miserable existence. For this miserable existence, the jiva and not God is responsible. This topic will be taken up again in the context of *mukti.* But now we have to discuss the nature of the world in Hinduism, for it is this world which each jiva has to face.

The World in Hinduism

In some hymns of the Ṛgveda, it appears that sages visualized the mystery of first creation.

> What was that One who is the unborn's image hath established and fixed firm these worlds' six regions. (*RV* I. 164.6).
> In the beginning rose Hiranyagarbha (golden seed), born Only Lord of all created beings. He fixed and holds up this earth and heaven. (*RV*. X. 121.1).

and then, again,

> Prajapati! thou only comprehends all these created things, and none beside thee. (*RV*. X. 121.10).

Further,

> There was not non-existent nor existent:
> there was no realm of air, no sky beyond it. (*RV*. X. 129.1).

It is also stated that there was only darkness, and void (RV. 129.1). If this is so, then who can say with certainty about the origin of this world. Gods were later creatures.

> He, the first origin of this creation, whether he formed it all, or did not form it.......(*RV*. X. 129.7).

Later on, this speculation about the first creation is not found.

It is conjectured that the world is eternal (Mimāṃsakas), or, that there is an endless cycle of creation and destruction. Does not this teaching about non-ending cycle of creation and dissolution mean that the world as a whole is eternal? However, it means that the world of any one time is contingent and is likely to pass away. The four stages of satya-yuga, *dvāpara*, *tretā* and *Kali*, keep on repeating till the world is dissolved.

In one of the cycles of the on-goings of the world, the world is created by God, out of the pre-existing materials (maybe atoms of earth, water, fire etc.) and of *karman*. This may be the view of Nyāya-Vaiśesika, where God is considered to be merely an efficient cause. As against this Shankara regards Ishvara to be both the efficient and material cause of the world. For Shankara, the world is Māyā and Ishvara is the Lord of Māyā. This is also in harmony with the Gītā. Under the guidance of Lord Krishna, the whole world revolves (Gītā IX:10). In either case the world is taken to be orderly and governed by laws.

Has the world emanated from Brahman, or has it been created? In the *Pāñcarātra* the world has emanated from Vāsūdeva in the order of Samkarṣana, Pradyumna and Aniruddha. Ramanuja has taken over the doctrine of *Pāñcarātra.* According to Ramanuja the whole world of Prakṛti is nothing but the body of Brahman. In the evolved form we see the world and in *pralaya* this gets involved in Brahman again, and, remains in its subtle form.

However, the world is said to be periodically created by Ishvara. According to Nyāya-Vaiśeṣika God is only the efficient cause of the world. As against this, Shankara holds that Ishvara is both the efficient and material cause of the world. In either case, the world remains dependent on God. And as such is contingent.

Again, is God transcendent or immanent in the world? The Ṛgveda holds that the absolute reality is both immanent and transcendent.

A thousand heads has Puruṣa,
A thousand eyes, a thousand feet;
He holding earth enclosed about,
Extends beyond, ten fingers length. (*RV.* X. 90.1)

True, the Upanishad Bṛhadāranyaka holds that Brahman holds together all things in the same manner in which all spokes of a wheel are held together in the hub and felly. In other words, Brahman is the immanent being of all things (B.U. II. 5.15). Again, Bṛhadāraṇyaka holds that Brahman is the Inner Controller of all things. This it repeats twenty three times (B.U. 3.7.1-23). According to Ramanuja, then, Brahman is immanent in all things. But he also adds that Brahman consists of *cit* (soul) and *acit* (material things, the world) as his body, and He himself is the indwelling Ātman of this body. In this *Sharīra-Sharīrin* relationship, Brahman as the indwelling Ātman is immanent in the world, and, as an entity much more than the body and beyond it, is also transcendent of the world.

Is the world real or unreal? According to Sāmkhya-Yoga, Nyāya-Vaiśeṣika, the world is real. It is so for Sāmkhya, for Prakṛti is as real as the souls. For Nyāya-Vaiśeṣika the world is constituted of real and eternal atoms. Hence, in that sense it is real. But as a created thing the world is not absolutely real. It is dependent on the creative will of God.

For Shankara the world is not absolutely real. It is *anirvacanīya* or *sadāsada-Velakṣaṇa*. It cannot be as unreal as an *alīka* (e.g. ākāsha, lotus) or as a dream is. For all practical purposes, the world has empirical reality, or, *Vyāvahārika Sattā*. The world remains real till Brahma-Jñāna dawns upon the seeker. The world for all who are not *jivanmukta*, is the real field of working out one's salvation. Swami Vivekananda advises us:

> Arise ye! Awake ye!
> Obtain what is best for and understand it. (*Kath* 3:14).

Then enter into the world and live in it. Let your muscles be of iron and your sinews be of steel. Hence, for the Hindus, the world is the field for working out one's salvation. Can it be called unreal? But one question may be asked, 'What is the purpose of this creation of the world?'

Both Shankara and Ramanuja think that God is spontaneously creating the world. He is full and complete in Himself. Therefore, this world cannot add to His perfection, or, fulfil what is still unfulfilled. Hence, the world is said to be *līlā* or creative sport of Ishvara. For Ramanuja this world makes no difference to Ishvara. He remains untouched by anything happening in the world (*Gītābhāṣya* 7:12; 9:4). But from another point of view this world is a vale of soul-making, for only by pious works and devotion to God a soul in bondage can win release (*Gītābhāṣya* 3:10; 4:7).

Apart from Shankara and Rāmanuja, Alvars and Bhāgavata Purāṇa have mentioned *līlā* in the form of dalliance of Lord Krishna. Whatever the word 'dalliance' may mean, it is interpreted by the *bhaktas* as the condescension of the Lord for His devotees. However, Bhāgavata Purāṇa (X:33:31-32) does not allow the literal meaning of dalliance and its imitation by ordinary men in this literal sense. In the spiritual sense, *līlā* of Gopi-Krishna simply means that God too cannot maintain His being without His devotees (*Gītābhāṣya* of Ramanuja, 7.18 and 8:14).

Hence, even *līlā* has the purpose of helping souls in bondage to win their highest end. This attainment by the jiva also helps the Lord to experience His *ānanda*.

The Problem of Suffering

The Ṛgvedic view of suffering is quite different from the stand of sanatana Hinduism. We must not ignore the fact that the Ṛgvedic and Iranian Aryans of the Gatha times had very similar views of suffering. Suffering is due to transgression of the laws of Varuṇa and Mitra, called *ṛta*.

> Whatever laws of thine, O God, O Varuṇa, as we are men,
> Day after day we violate,
> Give us not as prey to death, to be destroyed by thee in wrath,
> To thy fierce anger when displeased,
> To gain thy mercy, Varuṇa, with hymns we bind thy heart.
> (*Ṛg*. 1:25:1-3).

Again,

> I erred and went astray
> Have mercy, spare me, Mighty Lord.
> When through our want of thought we violate thy laws, punish us not.
> O God, for that inequity. (*Ṛg*. V. VII:89:3, 5).

Hence, by means of hymns of praise and forgiveness, the Ṛgvedic Āryans sought to mitigate their suffering. Later on, Ṛgvedic rituals, sacrifice and utterances of mantras were sufficient for gaining over suffering. But this Ṛgvedic reason of suffering as due to the violation of the laws of *ṛta* was altogether given up. Instead, the law of karman and the doctrine of *Saṁsāra* were accepted.

The worldly existence was taken to be full of suffering. It must not be understood that the Hindus in the past, or at the present time are not aware of pleasant moments of life. But the very word '*saṁsāra*' means that it is a series of fleeting events. Now that which is fleeting cannot yield eternal bliss. Hence, any pleasure is shot through with its evanescence. Hence, worldly pleasures are like the ever-vanishing waves that never are. Besides, this world suffers from sheer repetitiveness, which the view of periodic creation and dissolution of the world generates in us. The world cannot but create boredom and meaninglessness. Therefore, the worldly existence, being fleeting, repetitive and meaningless cannot but be regarded as the scene of suffering.

In contrast, man is looked upon as an essentially eternal, changeless, inactive spirit, characterized by pure consciousness and bliss. How has this pristine glorious existence come into this miserable world? As noted earlier, through *ajñāna*, the pure spirit has been lured into this world which as Prakṛti is known as *parinaminitya* (ever fleeting). Whether *ajñāna* or *karman* under the influence of avidyā be the cause of fall of the spirit, this fall is but unmitigated suffering. No time or plan can be assigned to this fall in this endless creation and dissolution of the world. Hence, suffering is said to be beginningless (*anādi*). But the lives of the *mukta* (liberated) show that this suffering comes to an end, as soon as *jñāna* dawns on the seeker. He, the *mukta* knows that the worldly events, pleasant and unpleasant, do not touch him. As a matter of fact, these worldly events never belonged to him. This Sāmkhyan view appears to prevail both over Shankara and Ramanuja, the two great leaders of Hinduism.

If a jiva himself, by his own choice and *ajñāna* has brought about this suffering upon himself, then no one is responsible for it. He therefore himself has to work out his own salvation by having the knowledge of his own being as quite distinct and independent of the ever-changing, evanescent series of events called the world. Man alone is the architect of his destiny. This was taught by Lord Buddha and Lord Mahavira. And Shankara too has adopted this view by combining his philosophy of *Jñāna* with karmayoga and bhakti. But karma-yoga and Bhakti remain subservient to *Jñāna*. Why did Shankara introduce Karma-Yoga and Bhakti in his philosophy of *Jñāna*?

It appears that the extant practice of Yoga in Jainism and Buddhism did not bring about the desired result. It seemed that some supernatural powers were necessary to put an end to suffering. Hence, Patanjali, a Hindu thinker, introduced *Ishvara-praṇidhāna* for the success of Yoga-practice. Later on, Shankara too regarded the Vedic *Karma-Kāṇḍa* as a necessary preparatory exercise for self-control. He also granted that devotion to Ishvara is an important means for obtaining *Brahma-Jñāna*, which alone puts an end to worldly existence or human suffering. But devotion to Ishvara in present day Hinduism is considered very important and for this the view of Ramanuja has to be given.

According to Ramanuja, Ishvara is essentially a *Karmaphala-dātā*. He creates the bodies of the jiva, in accordance with his Karman. He allows jivas in this world to work out their salvation, due to His *karuṇā* (compassion).

> These immortal atmans are subject to beginningless karman and are, for this reason, created conjointly with bodies that are determined by their various karman.[12]

However, the question may arise, 'If Ishvara is so compassionate, then why does He allow sufferings in this world? Can He not prevent them?

Bringing out of suffering by the jivas themselves, wholly depends on them. For their suffering Ishvara cannot be called cruel.

> For by pity we understand the inability, on somebody's part, to bear the pain of others, coupled with a disregard of his own advantage, when pity has the effect of bringing about the transgression of law on the part of the pitying person, it

is in no way to his credit: it rather implies the charge of weakness. (*Śribhāṣya* II:2.3).

The Lord has to punish the evil-doer both for retributive and preventive ends.

The Lord, however, can grant salvation if the devotee works for it and makes himself a deserving person.

LIBERATION (MUKTI)

The question of *ajñāna* and *mokṣa* does not arise in the Ṛgveda. The people are conscious of their violation of the law of *Ṛta* and the Ṛgvedic Aryans sought for forgiveness of their violation of the ṛta. The ultimate end for them was the attainment of *Svarga*, where their hearts' desires will be fulfilled in company with the gods. However, in extant Hinduism, the seeker pursues the chief end of *mukti* from the endless chain of births and rebirths. Hence, enchained by *saṃsārika* existence is a real bondage. As this bondage to worldly existence is due to *ajñāna*, so this can be removed only by means of *jñāna*. It has to be noted that *ajñāna* does not mean simply ignorance, if by ignorance we mean lack of cognition. *Ajñāna* really means distortion of will and intellect. Naturally, intellect has to be purified, and will has to be put on the right tract. As both will and intellect are guided by ego-feeling (*ahaṁkāra*), so this ahaṁkāra has to be dissolved. Hence, a philosophical knowledge of the ultimate reality is necessary, and, this knowledge can be attained by overcoming the passions for enjoyment or pleasurable feeling. Only by cultivation of will and intellect *Brahma-Jñāna* will dawn. Therefore, attaining *jñāna* really means the culture of the soul. Two things immediately follow.

Loss of ahaṁkāra would mean entrance into an undifferentiated reality. This is tantamount to the acceptance of mergence into differenceless reality, where mother is not a mother, father is not a father, and so on. Shankara accepts this to be the ultimate destiny of the jiva. Secondly, when will and intellect have been purified, then there can be no question of immorality. Hence, a *Brahma-Jñāni* is said to be beyond good and evil. Now the question is, can man, who is responsible for tumbling into this wordly existence, work out his own salvation? Can a fly fallen into a jar of sugar come out of the jar by its own efforts?

Jainism and Buddhism in their classical form do not admit the reality of any supernatural power. According to them, man unaided by any supernatural powers can attain his final liberation. This is not the case either with Shankara or Ramanuja. Let us take the case of Shankara.

According to Shankara, since bondage in worldly existence is due to ignorance (*ajñāna*), so liberation is possible only through *jñāna*. But can *jñāna* be attained independently of *Karmakāṇḍa* and Bhakti? According to Shankara, both *Karmakāṇḍa* and bhakti are necessary for preparing the ground for obtaining *mukti*.

Shankara tells us that there are two paths for the jivas, the *pravṛtti* mārga of action and *nivṛtti* mārga of the renunciation of action (*Karma-Sannyāsa*). *Pravṛtti* mārga has been prescribed for the Kshatriyas in whom there is the predominance of rajas. This path is good for purifying the soul, and, only the purified soul can follow *nivṛtti mārga* called *jñānayoga*.[13] The path of action in general is meant only for unenlightened.[14] Besides, *Karmakāṇḍa* implies the dualism of the doer and deed. But Brahma is one non-dual reality.

Again, all Karmas are born of *avidyā*.[15] Further, nothing produced can be eternal. Hence, *Karmakāṇḍa* cannot produce the external state of mukti.[16] Besides, the spirit is inactive and only *prakṛti* is active, then how can *Karmakāṇḍa* win the release of the inactive spirit?[17] Finally, the Vedic works are performed for having progeny, worldly prosperity and temporary happiness of heaven (Bhagvadgita-bhasya II:42-44; VII: 20; Vedanta Sutra I:1.4; III.4.12). Therefore, Shankara concludes that *Karmakāṇḍa* simply perpetuates the avidyaic existence of *Saṃsāra* (BGB XV.I). If Karma cannot yield mukti, can *bhakti* effect liberation?

By bhakti is meant here *upāsanā* (worship). By worship is meant the concentration of mind on a symbol (*ālambana* or support) as prescribed by the Shastras. By the steady flow of the mental stream in the direction of the symbol, all other disturbing thoughts are warded off. There results then the purification of the mind. This purified mind and intellect ultimately lead to *bodhi* or the enlightenment of the spirit, which is the same thing as release from *Saṃsāra* or liberation. Thus, *bhakti* is a very important auxiliary means of obtaining *Brahma-prāpti* or liberation. But *bhakti* need not lead to *mukti,* for bhakti may be maintained for reasons other than *mukti.* The Gītā VII.16 mentions four kinds of bhaktas, namely, men in distress, seekers after wealth, seeker after wordly knowledge and jñānis. Thus, Shankara holds that the bhaktas worship the Lord for warding off calamities (Vs.III.2.21), for earthly prosperity and even for heavenly bliss; and some for gaining Lordship (IV.3.14). However, those who worship the Lord for *Brahma-jñāna,* then the Lord grants His Grace for this. The *Vivekacudamani,* Verse 3 outlines three gifts of the Grace of God.

1. To be born as a human being.
2. To have the desire for liberation.
3. To come in contact with a jivanmukta. . . . .

Certainly 2 and 3 are important factors that can lead to *Brahma-jñāna.* In addition, Shankara also admits that worship of the Lord may lead to *Krama-mukti* (liberation in successive stages; Vs. IV.3.10; Vs. IV.4.22).

In general Shankara does not emphasize bhakti for release, because it is vitiated by the dualism of the worshipper and the worshipful. In addition he recommends *jñānayoga* as the only reliable means of obtaining *mukti.* Here he mentions four *sādhana-catustaya* for becoming fit (*adhikāri*) for *Brahma-jñāna.*

1. *Nityānitya-Vastu-Viveka* i.e., one has to know and discriminate between the eternal and non-eternal, with a view to withdrawing from what is non-eternal (*anitya*).
2. *Iha-mutrartha-bhoga-virāga* i.e., the seeker has to become indifferent to the enjoyments of ephemeral things of this and other worlds.
3. *Shama-dama-Sadhana-Sampat* i.e., one has to cultivate (quiescence) Shama, dama (self-restraint) etc., and, faith in the teachings of the Vedanta.
4. *Mumuksutva* i.e., longing for release.

After these preparatory steps have been completed, the seeker has to take refuge in a *jivanmukta* guru for final instructions. The competent teacher imparts the final instructions to an *adhikāri* seeker. The seeker has to give his rapt attention to the instructions of the guru. This is known as *Shravana*. Then, he has to ratiocinate on the truth imparted by the guru. This is known as *Manana*. After full deliberations of all *pros* and *cons* of the teaching, the guru initiates the seeker into meditation on the eight *Shanti-Vākyas* of the Upanishads, with a view to the realization of the differenceless Brahman, where a mother ceases to be a mother, a father ceases to be a father, a candala ceases to be a candala. (Brhadāraṇyaka IV:3.22).

Mukti: *Mukti* means for Shankara, the attainment of *Brahma-jñāna*. There is also the Upanishadic aphorism *'Brahmavid Brahmaiva bhavati'* (The knower of Brahma becomes Brahma). Hence, *Brahma-jñāna* means becoming one with Brahma. A number of similes show that 'becoming Brahma' means mergence into Brahma. Just as the rivers merge in the sea, just as the water of a pitcher becomes one with the water once the pitcher breaks, just as the ether of a pot mixes with and becomes one with the ether surrounding it as soon as the pot is destroyed, so the spirit imprisoned in the body becomes one with Brahman once this body ceases to be a part of the jiva. Does becoming Brahma mean mergence and absorption in Brahma, or, does it mean the regaining of the pristine purity and glory of the the soul? Here the beautiful observation of Kabir is worth mentioning.

A tree by the side of a sandal tree, becomes sandalized; an iron-piece coming in contact with Parasa,* becomes gold; water of a drain when merged into the Ganges becomes *ganga-jala* (the "Gangetic water"; *Kabir Granthavali*, pada 274). Do the tree, iron-piece and drain-water lose themselves, or, do they reach their perfection? Yes, *ahaṃkāra* (egoity) is lost, but the jiva becomes one with the creative Brahma. The jiva loses his creature-hood and becomes the creative source of all that is. He has been transformed from being a created being into a creator force itself.** Ramanuja would not accept this doctrine

*A material (Philosopher's.............) touch transforms an iron-piece into gold.

**According to Ramakrishna, mergence means becoming mortal. "What is needed is absorption in God—loving Him intensely. The 'Nectar Lake' is the Lake of Immortality. A man sinking in it does not die but becomes immortal" (The Gospel, p. 108).

of mergence into Brahma. But there is also an important point with regard to Shankara's doctrine of *mukti*.

There are two kinds of mukti, namely, *Jivanmukti* (deliverance in this very life) and *Videhamukti* (liberation after the fall of the body). After attaining *Brahma-jñāna*, the body is not immediately left behind. It continues. But the attachment to the world and bodily movements is lost. The on-goings of the world are left behind, just as the slough of a snake is left behind on a distant hill by the snake. The water of the drain, as if gets purified through the machinery before it falls into the Ganges. Body, intellect, mind, *ahaṃkāra* are all so purified by Vedic performance of *Karmakāṇḍa* and devotion to God that a *jivanmukta* goes beyond good and evil of extant morality of the *ajñāni*. But why and how this mortal body continues even after the attainment of *Brahma-jñāna* ?

Well, knowledge destroys all the past karmas (*sancita karman*) and cancels the fruition of current activities (*kriyamana karman*), but the fructescent (*prarabdha*) karman will continue to work till they are exhausted.

> . . . . since the resultant of the present body must produce definite results, speech, mind and the body are bound to work even after the highest realization, for actions that have begun to bear fruit are stronger than knowledge; as, for instance the arrow that has been let to fly continues the course for some time.[18]

He has a body, but the feeling of embodiment is lost. Just as a burnt rope does not bind, so no karma can bind him. He is in the world, but not of the world, for he has lost the illusory entanglement in it. He is lifted away from the temporal flow, and becomes a thing of eternity.

After the *prarabdha* karman gets exhausted the body falls and the spirit merges into Brahma. However, only a *jivanmukta* can really serve as the teacher of advaitism for an *adhikāri* (fit) seeker. Hence, for advaitism, *jivanmukti* is a necessity.

In this connection four kinds of *jivanmukti* have been mentioned, namely, *Brahmavid, Brahmavidvara, Brahmavidvariyana* and *Brahmavidvaristha*. Brahmavid realizes that Brahma alone is real and this world is illusory. Brahmavidvara rises from his *samādhi*, according to his will. Brahmavidvariyana has to be awakened from his *samādhi*. Brahmavidvaristha cannot be aroused even by others. Ramakrishna had attained the last stage of *Brahma-jñāna*.

Mukti for Shankara is the supreme good of a jiva. The Mukta goes out of the temporal flow and becomes a spectator of all times. He no longer requires this world, for it is God's world, and, God can take care of this world.[19] One should not run away with the idea that *Brahma-prāpti* is a product of any activity. It is an eternal state of *ajiva*. Just as a self-forgetful lady searches for a garland and does not find it anywhere except when she finds it there already around her neck, so a jiva forgetful of his eternal state loses himself in the world. But he can find only when he turns to himself and becomes aware of himself as Brahma. Just as a baby prince lost in a jungle is brought up as a shepherd, thinks of himself only as a shepherd till he discovers his own real identity, so is a jiva who has discovered his identity with Brahma in his state of *mukti*. Of course, for advaitism, jñāna is not an activity.

Though the doctrine of Shankara is acceptable to a large number of Hindu elite and *nirguṇa* poets, yet Ramanuja in his ramifications is no less popular and widespread.

RAMANUJA

Ramanuja does not accept that Brahma is *nirguṇa*, nor that the world and jiva are illusory, nor that through *jñāna* alone one can work out one's salvation, nor the possibility of *jivanmukti*. According to Ramanuja, Brahma is qualified with His body, and, His body comprises the world and jivas and He remains the indwelling spirit of His body. The very nature of the body is that it remains wholly dependent on its spirit which is Brahma Himself.

A jiva falls into *saṃsāra* because of his karma, *Kāma* (passions) and *avidyā*. Further, through countless ages of *Saṃsārika* existence, the jiva gets away from Brahma. The farther away he remains from Brahma, the more entangled he gets in this worldly existence of suffering. However, the jiva is real, both in the state of release and bondage, both in the created world and at the time of pralaya in a subtle form. Ramanuja ridicules the doctrine of mergence. Who does in the state of mergence survive? If he does not survive, then who is there to receive the release? Ramanuja says: 'If mergence or extinction be the nature of *mukti*, then everybody will shrink back from this state of mukti.[20] Hence, Ramanuja, accepts the reality of the *jivas* as distinct from the Lord.

According to Ramanuja, Ishvara is personal and endowed with the infinite number of auspicious attributes. As has already been mentioned, each jiva in this sorrowful worldly existence gets his body according to his Karman. The body keeps on changing with each birth, but the atman within man remains immortal. It is a part of Brahman. The question arises, how can the jiva in bondage attain its salvation? This can be achieved only through *bhakti*.

Bhakti is the continuity of steady remembrance of the Lord, uninterrupted like the flow of oil in a burning lamp. Bhakti is one-pointed devotion, unswerving faith and love. This kind of bhakti is also knowledge, for this is also *Upāsanā* and *dhyāna* (meditation).

> By the term 'Vidya' is meant meditation that has developed into bhakti...... In all these and similar cases the term 'knowledge' (Vedana) signifies meditation (dhyana).[21]

Really this *Bhakti* is much more than *jñānanisthā*. For a bhakta to know God is to worship Him, to lie prostrate before Him, and doing service to Him as his highest beatitude. But is there no place for *Karmakāṇḍa*?

Ramanuja recommends *jñāna-karma-bhakti-samuccaya* for obtaining mukti. He describes the following pathway to Mukti.[22]

1. Accumulation of merits by the performance of Vedic rites, according to one's *Varnāshrama dharma*.
2. Seeking refuge at the foot of the Supreme Person.
3. Then acquiring knowledge of reality through the studies of scripture and instructions of holy teachers.
4. This knowledge enriches the soul. He gets devoted to

the performance of his *nitya* and *naimithika* (obligatory) duties and avoidance of prohibited acts.

5. This kind of knowledge combined with *Karmakāṇḍa* is the worship of the Lord.
6. This worship (upāsanā) turns into bhakti.
7. Finally, there is the state of *prapatti* in which state the *bhakta* completely surrenders himself to Ishvara, and, Ishvara accepts him as such and extends to him His refuge. The devotee cannot live in separation from God's being, qualities, acts and dominion,[23] and, God too cannot maintain Himself without His devotee.[24]

At last by means of Karma-Jñāna-Samuccaya the bhakta gets back his former dependence (Sesatva) which he had lost by his Karman in association with avidya.

Mukti: Ramanuja admits two kinds of mukti:

1. *Kaivalya* in which state the jiva remains totally free, though remaining subservient to the Lord.
2. *Kainkarya-bhava*—Here the freed soul remains in full dependence on and obedience to the Lord for any service required of him by the Lord. In this state *paripurna* Sesa-Virttih (complete dependence) is fully realized.

The freed soul enjoys the life of perfection in *Vaikuṇṭha*. First, the *mukta* attains *salokya* i.e., the same place of abode as of the Lord. Then he enjoys the bliss in the service of the Lord (*Kainkarya*). Further, he reaches the presence of God (*sānnidhya*). Again, he becomes like Him (*Sarupya*) and finally enjoys fellowship with Him (*Sayujya*).

In the state of release, the *mukta* gains the power of beholding the Lord.[25] He gets all his wishes and desires fulfilled.[26] He enjoys all the powers of the Lord except the power of creation and the destruction of the world.[27]

Bhakti and Prapātti

Bhakti requires much effort on the part of the seeker. It is open to the higher castes only, for the performance of Vedic Karman is an essential preparatory requirement for progressing towards *bhakti*. Here the seeker has to be careful in the observances and even then he runs the risk of not being chosen by the Lord. The case is quite different with *prapātti*.

Prapātti means unqualified and absolute self-surrender to God as one's only refuge. Here, the seeker has to put complete trust in God. Commenting on Gītā XVIII:66, Ramanuja writes,

> Renouncing all *dharmas* which consist of Karmayoga, jnana-yoga and bhaktiyoga, which constitute the means for the highest good, and which are being performed with great love as My worship.

By virtue of the complete, and total self-surrender to the Lord, the Lord too out of His *Vātasalya* ignores all omissions and commissions of the devotees and grants him His protection. The main emphasis in prapatti is on *Sharanāgati* (the refuge of the Lord). This means that the devotee throwing himself at the foot of the Lord, trusting in His Grace, surrenders the fruits of his actions to God. The *prapanna* (the bhakta granted the refuge of the Lord) feels that being the dependent body of God, under His total control and guidance, is not the doer but the Lord alone. He lays the entire burden of his salvation to God Himself, and then lives a tranquil life, consecrated to the service of the Lord.[28] Naturally the spiritual progress of a *prapanna* does not depend on his slender resources, but upon the infinite power of God.

Ramanuja did not make this distinction. But he has simply philosophized the bhakti cult of the Alvars, many of whom were Shudras and one of them was Andal, a woman. These Shudras were shut out of the door of bhakti. But they were great seekers after God. Naturally, Ramanuja could not debar them from Salvation through bhakti. In the case of Alvars, the Lord himself chooses them whom He wishes to be saved (Katt. II; 23; Mund. III. 2.3). This is the doctrine of universal bhakti called *prapātti*, open to all persons who seek God's grace, who seek His fellowship and are devoted to Him and worship Him with the utmost love.

> And I (the Lord), dwelling in their hearts am moved by compassion and thereby destroy their darkness of soul born of ignorance by lighting luminous lamp of their knowledge.[29]

Though the doctrine of *prapātti* was practised by Ramanuja, yet he did not make it explicit in his commentary on scriptures. But he does talk of election and implies the doctrine of *prapātti* in his *Gītābhāsya* IX:32. Naturally the later doctrine of *marjara-Kishora-nyaya* (where the Lord Himself takes the initiative e.g., in *prapātti*) and *Markata-Kishora-nyaya* (bhakti) had not arisen for Ramanuja. But it is certain that the Shudras are open to *prapātti* only in whose case marjara-Kishora-nyaya is applicable. Here the cat takes care of her kitten. Similarly, in *prapātti* the Lord Himself takes care of His *prapanna.* However, in *Markata-Kishora-nyaya,* the mother monkey takes care of her young one, only when the young one remains clinging to the body of his mother. This corresponds to *bhakti,* where the seeker has to make efforts in order to deserve the Grace of God. But as the Lord makes no distinction between men, so we can say that bhakti is the earlier stage of devotion and *prapātti* is the final stage.

Human Destiny

The destiny of man in bondage and suffering is quite different from that of the soul in release. The man in bondage keeps on migrating from one birth into another. The gross body dies, but the subtle* body remains constant throughout the sojourn of man in the endless cycle of births and deaths. This doctrine of transmigration is non-Aryan and is now the most distinctive feature of Hinduism. If a man performs good Karmas, then he is likely to be born into a good family and caste. Men doing evil deeds may be born into a lowly birth of a dog and even of an outcast (Chh. U. 5, 10.7).[30]

Though this bondage or suffering is *anādi,* it has an end (Santa). Either through *jñāna* (Samkhya, Shankara) or Karma-jnana-bhakti-Samuccaya (Ramanuja), mukti (liberation) is possible. A reference to this has already been made.

According to Shankara, there is Mukti in this earthly frame and is called *jivan-mukti.* However, when the Karmas

*According to Samkhya-Karika, Verses 39-40, there are eighteen elements which constitute subtle body, namely, Buddhi (Intellect), ahamkara (individuation), the eleven indriyas (five jñānendriyas, manas, five Karmendriyas) and five tanmatras (subtle bodies).

get exhausted, then the *Brahma-jñāna* gets *videha-mukti* after the fall of the body. In this state, the *jñānī* becomes perfect by merging into Brahman.

For Ramanuja, the individual atman is a part of Brahman, forming his body. He remains conserved to the end, both in bondage and release, in the evolved state of creation and in the unevolved state in *pralaya* in a subtle form. After getting release from his saṃsārika sojourn, he enters into Vaikuntha, the abode of Viṣṇu, where he continues to grow in spiritual progress, and passes successively from *Kain-karya* (service of the Lord), to *Sannidhya* (proximity). Then again from *Sarupya* (likeness of the Lord) to Saye......(fellowship) of the Lord. A released soul gets endowed with all the powers of the Lord except the powers of creating the world and dissolving it. He gets all that he wishes, but being a sesi (dependent) he desires most the service of the Lord.

Religious Pathways and Practices

Men are born with different Saṃskāras and *guṇas*. Some have the dominance of Sattva, and some of Rajas and still others of Tamas. As these men are, so are their deities and paths.

> Sattvika men worship the gods, Rajasika persons worship Yaksa and raksasas, and Tamasika people worship nature spirits and ghosts (*B.G.* XVII:4).

In the same manner, Shankara holds that *Karmayoga* is meant for the warrior-class and nivṛtti path of Sannyāsa (renunciation) is recommended for the Sattvikas.*

Again, as the kind and degree of devotion will be in respect to one's deity, so will be its reward.

> Whatever from any devotee with faith wishes to worship, I make that faith of his steady (*B.G.* VII. 21).

Hence, as men are, so are their deities. And just as their deities are, so are the fruits of their action. Hence, the three pathways of *Karmayoga*, *Bhaktiyoga* and *Jñānayoga* have been recom-

*Shankara's Bhāsya of Gītā XVIII. 30.

mended. At present all these pathways are really inter-related. This inter-relation really follows from the nature of *avidyā* which keeps men in their bondage. 'Avidyā' does not mean ignorance in the ordinary sense. It does mean lack of cognition with regard to an object of faith. It means that which distorts the very means of cognition. This distorted intellect not only conceals the real object from being known, but projects quite a different thing in its place e.g., seeing a snake in the snake-rope (*sarpa-rajju-bhrama*) illusion. The infatuated man not only fails to perceive the rope as rope, but in the place of rope sees a snake. This results in a vitiated will. Instead of remaining steady and calm the victim of snake-rope illusion runs away in fright. This is what happens in the cosmic state of *avidyā*, when human beings under the influence of avidyā run after momentary pleasures. In terms of modern psychology we can say that *avidyā* disorients cognition, conation and affection which are the three inseparable aspects of mind. Hence, the three pathways recommended for remedying the whole man cannot but be inseparable. Karmayoga includes *jñāna* of

1. Various ends for which a Karma is prescribed.[31]
2. What is performed by Prakṛti, and not by the agent.
3. The final fact that the Lord alone controls and guides all jivas and *Prakṛti.*

In the same way both *Bhaktiyoga* and *jñānayoga* must be at first preceded by the purifying preparatory stage of *Karmayoga.* Again, Shankara admits that the Vedic Karmas and bhakti are both needed for purifying the intellect, and, only by the purified intellect the seeker can obtain *jñāna* or Brahma-realization. Nay more, Bhakti obtains the Grace of God, and, God's Grace makes the guru available to the appropriate seeker after *Brahma-Jñāna.*[32]

Further, *Karmayoga* does not involve only *Jñāna*, but also bhakti. As is well-known, there are four kinds of Karmas, *Nitya* (like bathing etc.), *naimittika* (for special occasions like warding off an evil), *Kamya* (for obtaining a desire) and *nisiddha* (prohibitions and taboos). But the action has to be *niṣkāma.* This is possible when the fruits of all actions have to be offered to the Lord. And this is not possible without the all-out surrender to God. Hence, devotion and trust in the Lord is necessary.

Again, no *jñāna* is possible without a guru, and, no guru is possible without the Grace of God.

Practices: The real remedy consists in turning will and intellect godward by withdrawing them from the worldly pursuits. Performance of rituals like *sandhyās* and *prātahkriya* is a daily affair. But the muttering of gayatri is considered to be of very great usefulness in warding off evil and obtaining the desired result.*

From the time of the Vedas, the correct pronunciation and utterances of Vedic sutras have been regarded to be very efficacious. Mispronunciation of them was deemed to be very inauspicious. This was specially emphasized by the mimāṃsakas for whom the Veda was eternal. But in due course, short syllables were substituted for constant muttering (*japa*). At the stage of the Upanishads there were mantras (sacred short syllables) like *tajjalana* which were considered to be too secret for the public. They were taught by the guru to the pupil. In due course, the Buddhist developed *mantra-yāna* (the path of mantras, through which the seeker could obtain many desired results. Even now the mantras given by the guru to his pupils have to be recited daily for warding off evils and for obtaining the desired result. But the real meaning of constant repetition is to turn the mind away from wordly desires and their pursuits.

Theoretically even now *Varnāshrama dharmas* (duties in one's station of life and caste) are emphasized in relation to which the following couplets are recited.

---

*Gayatri mantra (R.V. III. 62.10) is as follows:

Om, bhur-bhuvah-svah
Tat Savitur-Varenyam
bhargo-devasya dhimahi
dhiyo yo nah prachodyat (OM)

"Let us adore the supremacy of the divine Sun, the godhead who illuminates all—whom we invoke to direct our understanding right in our progress towards his holy seat". (Wilson)

Or

"We meditate upon the adorable effulgence of the resplendent vivifier, Savitar; may he stimulate our intellects" (V. Raghavan)

"Sve-Sve Karmanyabhiratah Samsiddhim labhte narah" (*Gītā* XVIII. 45).

(Men devoted to their own prescribed karma (duty) attain their ultimate goal). But neither in the past, nor at the present time, this has been observed. In the past Brahmins like Dronacharya were war-Lords, and, Kshatriyas like Bhisma Pitamah have promulgated religious teachings. At the present most of the prominent political leaders have been Brahmins. Even an octogenarian Brahmin like Kamalapati Tripathi is still continuing in political life. Caste really is kept alive by the politicians as their important ballot asset. The *Varnāshrama dharmas* have really lost their religious purposes, notwithstanding the stand of some Shankaracharyas.

The number of *pūjās* are so numerous that if a Hindu begins to observe all of them then he will have no time left for doing any thing else.[33] But some of them are observed by a number of Hindus. New moondays, *Purnimā* (full moon) and one day at least in a week are kept by Hindus, for observing food injunctions and fast. In the same way, lunar and Solar eclipses are observed by taking baths, specially in some sacred rivers. Some ceremonies are important like namakarana (naming), *mundana* (first shaving off the new born child), *Upanayana* (sacred thread ceremony) for the three higher castes, Vivaha (marriage) and *Śrāddha* (funeral ceremony accompanied with feast). Kumbha mela at Prayaga and at Haridwar, specially every twelfth year is observed by a great mass of the Hindus.

There are numerous festivals of the Hindus, of which a few have to be mentioned because of their being observed from antiquity. Holi (colour sprinkling), Chhath which is really sun-worship with a good deal of physical penance and purity, *Dipawali* (the festival of lights) and Durga-Puja, Kali-Puja, Saraswati-Puja and so on. Holi is observed on the first day of the month of Chaitra. The celebrations start with the burning of logs of wood and last for two days at least. This is really a spring festival about March-April.

Then comes Ramanavami which falls on the ninth day of the moony fortnight of the month of Chaitra (March-April).

Raksha bandhana is a festival of sisters who put the protective cover on the wrist of their brothers. This is based on the legend of Viṣṇu as an avatāra in the form of a dwarf, who ultimately succeeded in overcoming the demon Bali, the great foe of the gods. The festival falls on the day of full moon in the month of *Shravana* (July-August).

There is also the festival of Krishnasthami in commemoration of the birthday of Lord Krishna. It falls on the eighth day of the dark fortnight of the month of Bhadra (August-September). On this day, specially at Brindabana, temples of Lord Krishna are illuminated.

Vijaya Dasami falls on the tenth day of the bright fortnight of Asvina (September-October). The festival lasts for ten days and is called *Dasahara*. During this period Rama Lila is staged in Bengal, Bihar, Varanasi and other places. This is also the commemoration of the victory of Rama over Ravana.

Chhatha is really a festival of Sun-worship and is observed with a good deal with austerity, in Bihar and Eastern Uttar Pradesh. It is observed on the sixth day of the dark fortnight of Kartika (October-November).

Do the people really believe in the existence of Saraswati, Kali and other gods and goddesses? At the present time, most of the Hindus regard them as the manifestations of one and the same God. They will quote RV. I. 164.46.

> They call him (one God) Indra, Mitra, Agni, and he is heavenly able winged Garutman. Are Rama, Krishna, Shiva and Vishnu so many names of One? Perhaps it is so for the advaitins.

For the advaitins, the ultimate reality is undifferentiated Brahman, without any name and form. It is non-personal and is usually called *nirguṇa*. However, many Saints, some Kabirpanthis and at times Ramakrishna hold that *nirguṇa* can be attained only through the worship of *Saguṇa* (Brahma with forms or attributes). Hence, even Brahma, Viṣṇu and Mahesha are really *Saguṇa* forms of Brahman. The worship of Saguna is only a means for reaching the highest reality called *nirguṇa* Brahman. Rama and Krishna are most potent *saguṇa* Brahman whose worship ultimately leads to Brahma realization.

The names of Rama and Krishna are important and perhaps they are the most popular deities of the Hindus. They are considered to be the *avatāras* (two important incarnations of Viṣṇu out of ten). Lord Krishna is an object of special veneration of the Alvaras and the Gītā. In the same way Rama is the most popular deity of some of the Saints, but is adorable most in the many versions of the Rāmāyana.

Ethics: There is hardly any pathway to liberation where ethical conduct has not been prescribed. But the ethical culture of the Hindus is remarkably different from the ethical injunctions in the West. This may be termed the inferiority of morals. For the real cause of bondage is avidyā which warps the intellect and will. It has been termed as tṛṣnā (longing, desire). It may be termed as 'drive' or 'urges' in terms of current psychology. The Yogic practice consists in turning the senses from outward things to inward drive. This is the most important feature of *hatayoga* or *Kundalini jāgrana* i.e., the rousing of the latent or dormant power in Spino-cerebral nerve-currents for reaching the Brahma-loka for obtaining ambrosia. This is based on the adage that within man is contained the whole universe, for Brahma is the indwelling spirit in each man. Hence, the ethics of the Hindus emphasize self-culture. The highest reality is not outside, but inside. Hence, sublimation of all the urges within man into one-pointed pursuit of reality is the nerve of Indian ethics. One can easily note here that it is most suitable for purposes of Brahma-realization through *jñāna-mārga*.

Even in Bhaktiyoga steadiness of devotion has to be attained by controlling desire, hatred, anger etc.[34] But Karmayoga in general means outward activities in a society. This Karmayoga is most Vedic. Here Manu recommends the following ten virtues: *Dhṛti* (steadfastness), Kṣama (forgiveness), Dama (application), *Asteya* (non-stealing), *Shauca* (purity), *Indriya-nigraha* (sense-control), Dhī (wisdom), *Vidyā* (learning) and *satya* (truth). Akrodha absence of anger). In general, *pañca-mahāvrata* of the Jains has been incorporated in the social conduct of the people. They are *ahimsā* (non-violence), Satya (truth), asteya (non-stealing), *brahmacarya* (celibacy) and *aparigraha* (non-greed).

Varnashrama Dharmas really aim at social stability, or, what is known as *lokasamgraha*. Hence, Hindu ethics need not be called life-and-world-negation. But the current Hindu ways of morality are more conservative than progressive.

Branches of Hinduism

Hinduism is not the name of any one religion, either Vedic or non-Vedic. At present it is called a way of life, without any fixed creed. However, in due course, Hinduism has evolved into what is called *Sanaṭana Hinduism* which is a synthesis of Vedic and non-Vedic religions comprising several thousand years. This Sanatana Hinduism accepts the Vedas as its holy scripture, caste and the four pillars of *Karma-Saṃsāra-Jñāna-mukti.* Sanatana Hinduism may be said to have different branches. Many branches of Hinduism do not accept the Vedas as their scripture and repudiate caste. Vaisnavism and Shaivism are important branches of Hinduism and they repudiate caste. Still they come under Sanatana Hinduism because many caste Hindus pay respect to Shaivism and Vaisṇavism. Certainly this is true with regard to the devotion of Rama and Krishna who are said to be the *avatāras* of Viṣṇu. Here Sanatana Hinduism has assimilated the worship, specially the bhakti cult of Rama and Krishna exactly as in the past it assimilated the four pillars of *Karma-Jñāna* etc. But this is not the case with other branches of Hinduism.

Jainism and Buddhism are not branches of Sanatana Hinduism. They are really non-vedic and possibly non-Aryan religions. They never had caste and they never owed allegiance to Vedism. In no sense they can be called *sects* of Hinduism that have protested against animal-sacrifice of the Vedas. Certainly they do protest, but as independent religions with their own parallel development. As a matter of fact Vedic religion really came in clash with them and in the long run by assimilating all the important elements of them rendered them empty. *Karma-Saṃsāra-jñāna-mukti* and yoga were certainly non-Vedic and they are quite explicit in both Jainism and Buddhism. But in the long run they all have been fully assimilated in Sanatana Hinduism. As a matter of fact Jainism is much closer now to Sanatana Hinduism than Buddhism. *Pañca-Mahāvrata* of *Satya, Ahiṃsā, asteya, brahmacarya* and *aparigraha* of the Jainas has been adopted by sanatana Hinduism and was fully utilized by

Mahatma Gandhi. There are also intermarriages between the Hindus and Jainas.

In the days of Indian classical Buddhism caste, the Vedas and theistic worship were rejected, and as such Buddhism could not be fully absorbed and assimilated in Sanatana Hinduism, even when Lord Buddha was recognized as an *avatāra* of Viṣṇu. At present Kabir-panth and Sikhism are sought to be assimilated in Sanatana Hinduism, at least in the Constitution of India, article 25. But these two religions seek to preserve their own identity and their followers do not want to be called 'Hindus'.

Leaders of Hinduism

Quite true, Hinduism did not have any one specific founder. It has grown through the years by the seers and sages. But this does not mean that it lacked stalwart leaders. There was hardly an age in which leaders have not sprung up and taught the people.

In the Vedic age Manu, Vaivasvata, Bhṛgu, Atri, Kasyapa and Vaśiṣṭha and their descendants were the great leaders. Similarly, in the age of the Upanishads there were great leaders like Ajatashatru, Pravahana Jaivali, Sanat-Kumara and illustrious Yajñavalkya. In the middle ages there were many outstanding leaders whose contributions are highly relevant even now. Shankara (788-820), Ramanuja (1017-1137) Madhva or Ananda-tirtha (1198-1270), Sayana (1315-1387) were great Hindu thinkers with unparalleled genius. Amongst later thinkers and great leaders and reformers were Ramananda (14th-15th century) with his disciples of Santa poets like Sena (a barber), Ravidas (a chamara), celebrated Kabir (a muslim weaver, about 1398-1495) and Guru Nanak (1469-1538). Some of them would not like to be called 'Hindu', but they belonged to the Hindu tradition. The names of Mira, Suradasa and Tulsidasa cannot be omitted either. But we are more interested to single out a few great leaders of the 19th and 20th Centuries. They might not have contributed anything startling, but they were men of great religious stature and their realizations should not go out from mankind. Rammohan Roy, Keshab Chandra Sen, Ramakrishna and Vivekananda, and, the redoubtable Swami Dayananda Sarasvati. Ramamohan Roy, Devendranath Tagore and

Rabindranath Tagore belonged to those Brahmin families who had made compromises with the Muslim rulers. As such they were not very popular with many Bengali brahmins. For this reason at first their contributions to many fields remained confined to elites only. However, they were greatly mentally alert. They at once transformed their loyalties to British rulers as soon as they perceived the coming political power. Ramamohan Roy (1774-1833) has been justly called 'The father of Modern India'. Though many will not directly owe their allegiance to Ramamohan Roy, yet his influence and reform movements are important even today. He was both a religious and social reformer. He was opposed to idolatry, sati, enforced widowhood, girl infanticide, untouchability and polygamy. As an educationist he saw that only in mastering science and technology, India would be able to make progress. For this reason he pleaded with the British rulers to introduce English teaching for the Indians. He himself was a remarkable scholar and linguist. He had mastered Persian, Arabic, Sanskrit, English, Greek and Hebrew. In his relatively short life he assimilated some of the best thought of the East and West.

Adi Brahmo Samaj

The British Missionaries were preaching and converting a number of Bengalis and Ramamohan Roy had to take note of Christianity. He rejected the doctrines of the incarnation of Jesus and Trinity. He regarded the doctrine of triune Godhead as some sort of polytheism. He himself studied the Upanishads and translated some of them into Bengali. He kept close to the unitarian teaching of the Upanishads. However, his Upanishadic unitarianism was combined with Islamic monotheism and Christian ethical practice and teaching. His religious contributions are said to be eclectic, because these contributions were not logically synthesized. However, he tried to establish universal Hinduism centred round the Upanishadic worship of a formless God.

In 1828, Ramamohan Roy founded Adi Brahmo Samaj which was dedicated to the

> Worship and adoration of the Eternal,
> Unsearchable and Immaculate Being,
> who is the Author and Preserver of the Universe.

Ramamohan Roy never saw that the attributes of being the Author and Preserver of the Universe are the attributes of his God, which do not render Him formless. Later on Ramakrishna justly remarked that this is really a subtle form of idol-worship, for these attributes are merely hard and petrified *forms* of God.[35] However, this Samaj was open to all men, without distinction of colour, caste, creed, nationality and religion. The chief aim of the Samaj was the contemplation and promotion of the worship of the Author and Preserver of the universe, and, of charity, morality, piety, benevolence, virtue with a view to 'strengthening the bonds of union between men of all religious persuasions and creeds'.[36] Against polytheism, he wanted to establish a universal religion on the Hindu base.

We have already referred to the many social reforms that Ramamohan Roy wanted to carry out with the help of the British rulers. He really wanted to have an independent India with a view to enlightening the whole world. This could be achieved if India with the help of science and technology could be turned western socially.

After the death of R.M.Roy in 1833 at Bristol (U.K.), Debendranath Tagore (1817-1905), father of Rabindranath Tagore, organised the Samaj and laid down the four articles of its faith:

1. In the beginning there was nothing. The one Supreme Being alone existed. He created the universe. (Vedic, Upanishadic and Christian traditions are all combined).
2. He alone is the God of Truth, Infinite Wisdom, Goodness and Power. He is Eternal, Omnipotent, the One without a second. (Islamic and Advaitic concepts combined).
3. Our salvation depends on belief in Him and in His worship in this world and the next.
4. Belief consists in loving Him and doing His will.
   (3 and 4 combine Islamic, Christian and the Hindu cult of Devotion, specially of Ramanuja).

In Adi Brahmo Samaj idolatry, polytheism and even the monism of Shankara were rejected. The monotheism of this Samaj was thoroughly dualistic i.e., accepted the dualism of God and His worshippers. But it fully accepted the right of reason to interpret the scripture.

Later on, Brahmo Samaj went into the hands of Keshab Chandra Sen (1834-1884) who changed the whole tenor and texture of Adi Brahmo Samaj. He tried to Christianize Hinduism and Hinduize Christianity with the result that there was a complete break from Adi Brahmo Samaj in 1866. Keshab accepted Christ which is clear from his Easter message of 1879:

> .... My Christ, my sweet Christ, the bightest jewel of my heart, the necklace of my soul—for twenty years have I cherished Him in this my miserable heart.[37]

But he never ignored his Indian spiritual heritage. He refused to be called 'Christian'. He borrowed only the two principles of forgiveness of sins and the spirit of Self-sacrifice. He added to his faith the bhakti-cult of Chaitanya and introduced *kīrtan* into his worship.

Formerly, Keshab rejected idolatry, but under the influence of Ramakrishna he assimilated much of Hindu polytheism. For Ramakrishna Hindu idolatry was nothing but divine attributes materialized. But he avoided the monism of Shankara. Keshab, under the strong influence of Ramakrishna finalised his religious position in New Dispensation (*Nava Vidhan*) on January 25, 1880. According to the publisher of Romain Rolland's 'The life of Ramakrishna', Note II, the New Dispensation emphasized three things:

1. The worship of God as Mother.

No doubt this is as old as the oldest Indian tradition of Indus Valley Civilization, where Mother Goddess was worshipped, but it was a living, realized truth in the life of Ramakrishna. Naturally, Keshab was confined in this native religious tradition under the influence of Ramakrisha.

2. The recognition of all religions and their prophets as true.

This was the central religious insight of Keshab. But this religious truth is also as old as the Ṛgveda (I.164.46). But once again Ramakrishna's influence cannot be discounted, for Ramakrishna too teaches the doctrine of religious harmony and unity. But the words of the New Dispensation are remarkable:

> Every good and great man is the personification of some special element of Truth and Divine Goodness. Sit at the

feet of all heavenly messengers......Let their blood be your blood, their flesh your flesh!.....Live in them and they will live in you for ever.[38]

3. The assimilation of Hindu polytheism into Brahmoism. This was directly based on the insight of Ramakrishna, who held that God is with and also without forms. Any symbol of God is just as valid.

Many followers of Keshab's Brahmo Samaj left him after his New Dispensation because he had softened his stand on idolatry and polytheism. But the Bombay branch of Keshab's Brahmo Samaj continued as Prarthana Samaj without breaking ties with Keshab. This Prarthana Samaj included such eminent men as Mahadeva Govind Ranade, and Sir R.G. Bhandarkar. However, Prarthana Samaj had nothing to do with Christianity. But the greatest religious genius was certainly Ramakrishna (1836-1886).

Ramakrishna

Gadadhar who came to be known 'Ramakrishna' was born at Kamarpukur, a short distance from Calcutta, on February 18, 1836, and, he returned to his eternal Brahman on August 15,1886. He was almost illiterate, but the most learned men of his time came to see him and paid their homage to him. His life was most simple and yet he created a revolution which is still continuing.

Ramakrishna used to fall into Samādhi ever since his childhood. He remained convinced that his Lord is in all forms and this divine polymorphism remained with him throughout his life. His *samādhi* came to be disciplined by one Bhairavi Brahmin who was a devotee of Viṣṇu. She remained with him in a mother-son relationship for six years and taught him the path of *jñāna* through its many steps, including tantras. Throughout his spiritual training under Bhairavi Brahmin, he remained a devotee of his Mother Kali whom he touched, saw and heard Her voice. But even this high spiritual realization had to be perfected.

In 1864, a jivanmukta in the sense and discipline of Shankara's advaitism arrived. His name was Tota Puri. This religious guru prevailed upon him to go beyond the love of Mother Kali in order to lose himself in Nirguṇa Brahma. Ramakrishna sought the permission of Mother Kali, which permission she gave to him. Very shortly Ramakrishna sojourned from Savikalpaka *samādhi* into *nirvikalpaka samādhi*, in which state he remained motionless with almost the stoppage of heart-beat. His state of *nirvikalpa* has been thus described:

> The Universe was extinguished. Space itself was no more. At first the shadows of ideals floated in the obscure depth of the mind. Monotonously a feeble consciousness of the Ego went on ticking. Then that stopped too. Nothing remained but existence. The soul was lost in Self. Dualism was blotted out—Beyond word, beyond thought, he attained Brahman.[39]

As a result of his supreme realization, he taught a great many lessons for the whole mankind.

1. He found that Brahman is both formless and with forms. It is Shiva and Shakti, both in one. Manifest in the many forms of religious deities and at the same time unmanifest in his inactive aspect. Mother Kali is as much formless Brahman.

2. Quite naturally, for Ramakrishna the world is real. According to him it is absurd to think that the world is unreal as long as we form part of it. Even a *siddha* rising from *Samādhi*, returns to this world of *Māyā*. At least his ego remains relatively real to him, and, also the things revealed to him through this ego, on the ordinary plane.

3. Ramakrishna practised Islam, Christianity and other sectarian cults of India. He found the deity of each form of worship in his vision. At first each form appeared external to him, then it vanished into his body and finally he found that he himself had become what he adorned in turn as a Muslim, Christian, Vaiṣṇava, Shaivite etc. As a result of this unique realization, he summed up his position thus:

> I have practised all religions, Hinduism, Islam, Christianity and I have also followed the path of the different Hindu sects . . . . . I have found that it is the same God towards whom all are directing their steps, though along different paths.[40]

4. But he was fully convinced that the life of *Samādhi* is not

all, even though it is the highest spiritual experience. Somehow *samādhi* must lead men to an active life in the service of man. Thus, Ramakrishna revived the notion of Bodhisattvas and jivanmuktas anew in modern setting. He chose his disciples and specially Vivekananda to carry out this task of educating the world in the path of spiritual enlightenment and service to fellowmen for the alleviation of human suffering. In this context, he is reported to have said,

> Jiva is Shiva, who then dare talk of showing mercy to them? No mercy, but service, service for man must be regarded as God.[41]

Again,

> Are you seeking God? Then seek Him in man! The divinity is manifest in man more than in any other object.[42]

Thus, Ramakrishna believed in the unity of all religions and their deities, and, service to whole mankind. He realized the first and bequeathed his heritage of service to all mankind specially to his beloved disciple Vivekananda.

Swami Vivekananda (1863-1902)

Narendra Dutta was a Kayastha by birth. He was roused from his sceptical slumber by the great saint Ramakrishna. By nature Narendra was a Karmayogin. But being converted by Ramakrishna, he became a *jñānin* too. He became Vivekananda as he was awakened to his mission in the world in which contemplation was wedded to human service and enlightenment. After becoming a disciple of Ramakrishna, he was given the following instruction towards the end of his life by his Master:

> You will bring spiritual consciousness to men and, assuage the misery of the humble and poor".

How to fulfil this mission to the poor and miserable masses of India?

Though not invited and without any credential from any official religious body, Vivekananda set out to attend the World Parliament of Religion in 1893. However, Vivekananda was given a chance to speak at the august, memorable Parliament. He spoke extempore and electrified the whole audience. Not only he spoke on September 11, 1893, but he was given the chance again on September 19, 1893. A few lines are worth quoting:

> The Hindu refuses to call you sinners.
> Ye are the children of God, sharers of immortal bliss, perfect beings . . . .

He concluded his speech,

> May he who is *Brahman* of the Hindus, the Buddha of the Buddhists, the Father of the Christians give strength to you.[43]

He established many centres in America, Britain and elsewhere. He returned to India in early 1897. The young crusader of Hinduism was welcome everywhere in India and Ceylon. He now opened centres for helping the miserable masses and the poor. Now he proclaimed his message: "Worship Shiva in the poor, the diseased and the weak".

> What our country now wants are muscles of iron and nerves of steel, gigantic wills . . . and that can only be created by the idea of the *Advaita*, the ideal of oneness of all.

Again,

> "Arise, awake from this hypnotism of weakness. Stand up, proclaim the God *within you*, do not deny him".

On May 1, 1897, Vivekananda founded Ramakrishna Mission with the following detail:

1. The Association will bear the name 'Ramakrishna Mission'.
2. Its aim is to preach the doctrine of Ramakrishna for the good of humanity.
3. Its duty is to direct the activities of the movement initiated by Ramakrishna 'for the establishment of fellowship

among the followers of different religions knowing them all to be only so many forms of one undying eternal religion'.

4. Its methods of action are: (a) to train men as competent teachers; (b) to promote and encourage arts and industries; (c) to propagate the Vedantic and other religious doctrines elucidated in the life of Ramakrishna.
5. It was to have two branches: The first branch is to be Indian consisting of 'Maths' (monasteries) and 'Ashramas' (retreat houses) in various parts of India. And the second branch is to be foreign consisting of 'Spiritual Centres' in Western countries.
6. The aims and ideals of the Mission being purely spiritual and humanitarian, it would have no connection with politics.

Vivekananda accepted advaita Vedanta, and yet immersed himself in social activities like famine relief, maintenance of orphanages, opening of training centres, educational institutions, dispensaries and the like. Following the instructions of his Master 'jiva is Shiva', he gave a call for social service.

> Where should you go to seek for God? Are not all the poor, the miserable, the weak, good? Why not worship them first? . . . Let these people be your God . . . .

He was also against the exploitation of the low caste in the guise of caste system. He advised people to go in for inter-marriages between different castes.

For practising religions tolerance, Vivekananda proclaimed:

> I accept all religions that were in the past and worship with them all: I worship God with every one of them . . . . . The *Bible*, the *Vedas*, *Koran*, and all other sacred books are but so many pages, and an infinite number of pages remain yet to be unfolded.[44]

Both the Master (Ramakrishna) and his disciple (Vivekananda) were not simply intellectually convinced of the unity of all religions, but they experienced and lived it through.

Now we come to another religious reformer who created more ripples in Hindu society than the reformist movement in Bengal. This man of iron character was Dayananda Sarasvati.

DAYANANDA SARASVATI (1824-1883)

The real name of Dayananda Sarasvati was Mulashankara. He hailed from Gujarat, the State from where Mahatma Gandhi also came afterwards. Dayananda was born of orthodox Brahmin parents who were quite rich. Whilst still a boy Dayananda saw a rat running over the body of the Deity Shiva and nibbling the offerings made to Him. The faith of the boy in the idol-worship was greatly shaken. Afterwards not wanting to get married, he left home and came to Mathura where he studied *Ashtādhyāyi*, Mahābhārata and *Vedanta*, under the blind Swami Virijanandji. After three years of study he left his Guru with the avowed aim of preaching the pure Vedic cult without its admixture of Purāṇas, Shastras, Tantra and Vedanta. Even Veda meant for him, without Brahmanas and the Upanishads. His religious cry was 'Get back to the original Veda'.

Dayananda Sarasvati was not only a real Hindu reformer, but he was a great social reformer and an equally great nationalist. In the beginning he lectured only in Sanskrit, but after coming in contact with Keshab Chandra Sen and Ramakrishna, he was advised to preach in the native language of Hindi. As a nationalist Hindu Dayananda Sarasvati was violently opposed to Christianity and Islam. He was opposed to any foreign cultural invasion. This could be expected of him, because he had not learnt English, without which it was difficult for him to understand and assimilate Western things. He was also opposed to Jainism and Buddhism. Though opposed to the West, Swamiji borrowed the rationalism of the 19th Century and its then prevailing emphasis on science and technology.

In his cry 'Back to the Veda', Dayananda spoke against polytheism, idolatry and caste. According to Swamiji, the Veda spoke of four classes of Brahmins, Kshatriyas, Vaisyas and Shudras, and not the hereditary caste. Classes depend on social functions and not on hereditary. Could the worship of pure monotheism and anti-caste proclamation go without violent protest and agitation? But Swamiji with his indomitable courage continued his preaching. He went to Banaras, the citadel of Sanatana Dharma and engaged three hundred Brahmin pandits in a monumental contest in 1869, and came out victorious. In 1875 Dayananda Sarasvati founded *Arya Samaj* in Bombay and later on made Lahore his headquarters. Afterwards many branches of Arya Samaj were established all over India. In Lahore however he wrote his great gospel *Satyartha Prakasha* (The torchlight of truth), in which the Bible was put to severe criticism.

The sweeping reformation preached by Dayananda Sarasvati created a mass movement, which can be contrasted with Brahmo Samaj. The latter was confined to a few intellectuals only. His religion of the Veda was a nationalist religion. The Veda itself was venerated as eternal and *a-pauruṣeya* (non-personal), and as such infallible. For Swamiji it contained all truths, even scientific ones. Its propagation was considered to be highly desirable. Therefore, Dayananda Sarasvati translated the Veda in Hindi, and made it available for the masses. However, Swamiji retained the doctrine of Karma, Saṃsāra and Mokṣa. This doctrine is considered non-Vedic. However, Dayananda's rejection of caste was not merely theoretical. It soon came to have practical effect. He came to be regarded as the saviour of the untouchables. For him any untouchable can enter into any holy temple of the Hindus. The present fight of Swami Agnivesha, against the Shankaracharya of Puri, for the right of the untouchables relating to temple-entry hearkens back to Dayananda Sarasvati. The following is the creed of Arya Samaj:

1. God is the primary cause of all true knowledge and of everything known through knowledge.
2. God is *sat-cit-ānanda*: existent, intelligent and blissful. He is formless, omnipotent, omniscient, omnipresent, unborn, endless, unchangeable, without beginning, unequalled, the support of all, the master of all, unaging, immortal, fearless, eternal and the cause of the universe. To Him alone is worship due.
3. The Vedas are the books of true knowledge. It is the first duty of every Arya to read them, teach them and recite them, or to hear them being read by others.

4. One should always be ready to accept truth and give up untruth. (This was accepted both by Jainism and Buddhism, which Arya Samaj rejects).
5. Everything should be done according to the dictates of Dharma, i.e., after reflection over right and wrong.
6. The primary object of Arya Samaj is to do good to the world by improving the physical, spiritual and social conditions of mankind.
7. One's dealings with others should be regulated by love and justice, and in accordance with the dictates of Dharma.
8. One should promote knowledge and dispel ignorance or *avidyā*.
9. No one should be content with his own good alone, but should look for one's welfare in the welfare of all.
10. In all matters which affect the social well-being of the whole society one ought to discard all differences and not allow one's individuality to interfere; but in strictly personal matters everyone may act with freedom.

Arya Samaj maintains the equal right of all to serve as priest, and it is not confined to Brahmin caste alone. Besides, the Samaj maintains the equality of sexes and the right of everyone to study the Veda. The Samaj allows widow remarriage and is against child-marriage. For advancing the cause of the country, the Samaj has always laboured to found educational institutions with the teaching of science. Very early Dayananda Anglo-Vedic College was opened at Lahore, and Kanya Mahavidyalaya at Jullundur. The famous Gurukul was opened at Kangri and Haridwar. The Samaj is a great protagonist of Hindi.

Not only the Samaj fights against Islam and Christianity, but is willing to re-convert (*Shuddhī*) Muslims and Christians into Hindu fold.

In spite of the fact that Arya Samaj started as a mass movement and encouraged national movement for the freedom of the country against British rulers, it has not made much progress at the present time.

Conclusion: Many other religious reformers of very great stature have appeared in the 19th and 20th Centuries. We can name the following stalwarts: Rabindranath Tagore, Aurobindo Ghose, Mahatma Gandhi, Radhakrishnan, Ramana Maharshi and others. On the whole their insistence is on anti-idolatry and anti-casteism. The Bengal movement emphasized Brahma-realization far more palpably than others. The harmony and unity of all religions is another theme. The reader alone can judge the effect of their lives and teaching in the current modern life of the Hindus. The following excerpts from the statements of 'All India Nationalist Forum' condemn the action of the Shankaracharya against the temple-entry of Harijans. The forum adds:

> We aim at creating casteless and egalitarian Hindu Society free from discrimination, exploitation and superstition" (*The Times of India*, July 16, 1988).

References

1. R.V. I. 51.8,9; VII. 59.11; X. 22.8.
2. R.V. X.99.3; VII. 21.5.
3. M.M. Gopinath Kaviraj, *Bharatiya Samskrti Aur Sadhna*' Vol. I. pp. 89, 120, 126.
4. "Ramakrishna once asked ironically: 'If you happen to meet God face to face, will you plead O God, please grant that I may dig a canal, build a school and found a hospital", *The Gospel of Ramakrishna*, p. 143. But Ramakrishna entrusted social work to his disciple Vivekananda.
5. M. Gupta, '*Varnashramadharma aur achutodharana se jujhate hue Mahatma Gandhi*, RAVIDAS, February 24, 1986.
6. Antinomianism simply means that there is nothing intrinsically good or bad. This doctrine was held by a number of unorthodox 62 or 63 schools, mentioned in *Brahmajāla-Sutta* of the Buddhists and *Sutrakṛtanga Sutra* of the Jains. See also A.L. Basham, *History and Doctrines of the Ajivikas*, 1951. Purana Kassapa, Pakuda Kaccayana and Makkhali Gosala were famous *akoriyavadi* (antinomian).
7. The reader is referred to D.P. Chattopadhyaya, '*Indian Atheism*', and Sarvananda Pathak, *Carvaka Darshan Ki Shastriya Samiksha* for a fuller account of atheism.
8. *Vide* author's *Nirishvaravada*, pp. 50-52; *Classical Religious Philosophy of the Hindus*, pp. 42-45.
9. *Sarva Khalvidam Brahma* (All this is Brahma), Chh. U. III.14.1; also *vide* Maitri 4:6.
10. *Vedārtha-Saṁgraha*, pada 127.
   Gita IV.5 mentions the many *avatāras* of Viṣṇu.

11. The ten incarnations of Viṣṇu are in the forms of fish, tortoise, boar, man-lion (*nṛsimha*), Dwarf Brahmin, Parashurama, Rama, Krishna, Buddha and Kalki (yet to be).
12. *Gītābhāsya* II.13; also vide IV.14; IX.10; XIV.4,5.
13. Shankara's comments on B.G. IV.IV:33; V:10-11; XVIII:5.
14. Shankara's bhāṣya of the Gītā II:17, 19, 21.
15. Shankara bhāṣya of Gītā XVIII:48.
16. *Ibid.*, Introduction of Chap. III and IV.
17. *Vedānta-Sutra* II.4.30.
18. Bṛhadāraṇyaka Shankara Bhāṣya I.4.7,10.
19. A.G. Warrier, *The Concept of Mukti in Advaita Vedanta*, p. 496.
20. Shribhāṣya I. 1. i; I. 4.21; II.1.15.
21. *Vedārtha-Samgraha*, pada 127; *Vide pada* 129, 136; *Shribhāsya* I 2.23.
22. *Vedārtha-Samgraha*, pada 126.
23. *Gītābhāṣya* VI.1.
24. *Gītāhhāṣya* VII.18; VIII.14.
25. *Shribhāṣya* IV. 4.17.
26. *Shribhāṣya* IV. 4.13.
27. *Shribhāṣya* IV. 4.13; IV. 4.17; IV. 4.20.
28. *Shribhāṣya* I.2.23; *Vedartha-Samgraha*, pada 126.
29. *Vedārtha-Samgraha*, pada 125 ; also vide *Shribhāṣya* II.2.3.
30. Also *vide* Kaṭh. 5.7; Kaushitaki 1.2; Shvet. 5.11-12.
31. Ramanuja, *Gītābhāṣya* 16-17.
32. *Viveka-Cūḍamaṇi*, Verse 3.
33. K.M. Sen, *Hindūism*, p. 34.
34. Ramanuja, *Gītābhāṣya*, III.34-37; VI. 26-27.
35. Romain Rolland, *The Life of Ramakrishna*, p. 182.
36. Ibid, p. 109.
37. Romain Rolland, *Ibid.*, p. 121n.
38. Romain Rolland, *Ibid.*, p. 186; Here one is reminded of St. John 15.4.
39. Romain Rolland, *Ibid.*, p. 63.
40. Romain Rolland, *Ibid.*, p. 90; The Gospel of Sri Ramakrishna by M. p. 129.
41. Romain Rolland, *Ibid.*, p. 96.
42. Romain Rolland, *Ibid.*, p. 231.
43. Swami Vivekananda, *The Complete Works*, pp. 19.20.
44. Romain Rolland, *Vivekananda*, p. 266.

CHAPTER VII

BUDDHISM

INTRODUCTION

Buddhism is a truly Indian religion for it belongs to the tradition of Indus Valley Civilization. It is essentially non-Vedic and possibly pre-Aryaṇ world-view of India. In it the doctrine of *Karma-Saṃsāra-jñāna-mukti* was clearly defined and adopted. It appears to have been influenced by 62-63 heretical views which have been mentioned in *Brahmajāla-Sutta*. However, non-Aryan Yoga along with the *tapas* (austerities) of *Sannyāsa* (renunciation) has been fully assimilated. These heretical views of Brahmajāla Sutta do not have any kinship with the then prevailing Brahminism. Besides, Sāṃkhya is considered non-Vedic and Lord Buddha at first was instructed by Alara Kalama, and this Alara is identified with Arada who was an exponent of early Sāṃkhya. Even the word 'Buddha' is said to have been derived from the Sāṃkhyan 'Buddhi'. Further, 'Kapil' of 'Kapil-vastu' is said to have hailed from this place, who is said to be the founder of Sāṃkhya philosophy.

Lord Buddha and Lord Mahavira were both kshatriyas, like the many teachers of the Upanishads. These kshatriyas were regarded as inferior kshatriyas (Manu X. 22). They were related to tribes that have not been mentioned amongst the Aryan tribes. Hence, Buddhism and Jainism cannot be called 'offshoots' of Vedic religion. They are independent and parallel development of thought. Of course, in due course, they came in clash with Vedic religion. For this reason a good deal of struggle arose between Buddhism and Brahminism, which led to sharpness in the tool of thinking and deepening of philosophical speculation. Even when Buddhism disappeared from India, its many contributions have been used and fully assimilated in Hinduism of today.

Even when Buddhism has been assimilated by Hinduism, its distinctiveness cannot be denied. It has developed its own scripture. Instead of appealing to the scripture as an authority (as in advaitism and Ramanuja), the Buddha encouraged independent thinking without appealing to any authority. It never held the doctrine of caste and theoretically it held fast to atheism (*nirishvaravāda*) and salvation through one's efforts alone without taking recourse to any supernatural agency. Buddhism, unlike Hinduism, has centred round the life and teaching of its founder, Gotama, the Buddha. Further, it has international ramification and is a missionary religion. It adopted the vernacular of the people for the propagation of its faith. This also shows that it is quite different from Vedism which is based on Sanskṛta.

Lord Buddha (c. 560 b.c.—c. 480 b.c.)

Lord Buddha was born of Shuddhodana and Maya. Shuddhodana was a chiefpin and ruler of Shakya clan, which in turn was related to Iksvaku of Kosala. Lord Buddha was known as Gotama or Siddhartha before he was called the enlightened one (*Buddha*). He was married to Yashodhara and to them a son named Rahula was born.

Meantime Gotama going out of his palace on three different occasions saw a sick man, an old man and a dead man. These sights convinced him that life is misery and a way out of this life of suffering should be found out. At that moment he saw a serene recluse and then he thought of himself becoming one. One day Gotama after having the last look at Yashodhara and the baby Rahula sleeping, left them, and became a wandering monk, put on the garment of a renunciate. In his search for a way out of suffering, he placed himself under the two teachers of Alara Kalama and Uddaka Ramaputta. Alara Kalama gave him the doctrine and necessity for enlightenment, according to Sāṃkhyan philosophy. However, mere intellectual doctrine of enlightenment did not make him enlightened. So he went to another teacher Uddaka Ramaputta who taught him the necessity of *tapas* and bodily mortification. Lord Buddha practised the path of bodily mortification, till he became too weak even to walk. At last when he was meditating under the banyan tree at Bodh Gaya, he gradually found the riddle of suffering opening before him. He remained dazed by what he had found out. He became enlightened. A struggle remained within him: should he or should he not proclaim this gospel of enlightenment? At last he decided to transmit this gospel to the whole world. This gospel is now known as Buddhism, whose distinctive features can be thus outlined:

The Distinctive Features of Buddhism

1. The four pillars of *Karma-Saṃsāra-jñāna-mukti* are most clearly defined and accepted by Buddhism. The doctrine of Yoga was not only adopted, but was perfected by Buddhism. The practice of *tantra* is largely Buddhist.

2. In the oldest Hinayāna school, silence is maintained about the existence of God. The whole subject-matter was treated as a metaphysical heresy (*avyakṛta*). Towards the end, it was felt in Mahāyāna Buddhism, that some sort of theistic worship is desirable for the masses. Hence, the doctrine of *trikāya* Buddha was introduced, namely, Rupakāya (historical), Sambhoga kāya (heavenly God) and Dharmakāya (an embodiment of dharma). The worship of Bodhisattvas also became prevalent. However, theoretically Buddhism remains atheistic. The last words of the Master were *appo dipo bhava* (Be a light unto yourself: and seek your salvation with diligence). A follower of Buddha, himself becomes a Buddha and does not worship Buddha or any supernatural power.

3. The distinctive feature of Buddhism is that everything is momentary, life is painful (*sarvam dukham dukham*) and there is soullessness (*anātmavāda*).

4. It has three vows to be taken for being initiated into Buddhism.*

(i) I seek refuge in the Buddha (*Buddham Sharanam gacchāmi*).
(ii) I seek refuge in dharma (*Dharmam Sharanam gacchāmi*).
(iii) I seek refuge in Samgha (*Sangham Sharanam gacchāmi*).

---

*Here Lord Buddha has been compared to a physician who diagnoses and prescribes the cure of human suffering:

1. Dharma is the medicine prescribed, and
2. Samgha is the nurse who administers the medicine.

5. Reason is accepted as the sole guide in matters of religion, and not any authority of any scripture.

Buddha is reported to have said that his teaching has to be carefully weighed and reasoned out, and then and then alone has to be accepted,

> "not because it is a report, not because it is a tradition, not because it is said in the past — nor because it is suitable, nor because your preceptor is a recluse, but if you yourself understand that this is so meritorious and blameless, and when accepted, it is for benefit and happiness, then you may accept it".*

6. Buddhism never had any caste distinction. Lord Buddha was totally opposed to caste and has given very sound reason for its rejection.

7. The four noble truths (*catvari arya satyani*) most systematically sum up the whole teaching of Buddhism.

8. The highest end of life is the attainment of Nirvāṇa, which has been interpreted both affirmatively and negatively.

9. Buddhism is termed middle path, for it avoids the extremes of both ascetism and worldliness.

10. Without becoming a *bhikshu* (a renunciate in a monastery), one cannot attain one's *nirvāṇa*. There is no mokṣa possible for a house-holder.

11. The three steps of *Shīla*, *Samādhi* and *Prajñā* epitomize the religious striving of a Buddhist.

12. Lord Buddha taught in the language of Pali, which was the language of his country. This distinguishes Buddhism from Brahminism. Later on when many important Brahmins were converted into Buddhism, Sanskrit was adopted as the language of Buddhism.

13. Buddhism is the most successful missionary religion of India. It is now an international religion.

Buddhist Sacred Books

Buddhism in due course established Universities at Nalanda, Vikramashila and Taxila. Many monks and chieftains studied in

**Anguttara Nikāya*, Pt. I., III.65.

them. As a result of these Universities a large number of Buddhist literature has cropped up. Many of these Buddhist writings are found in Tibetan texts, Chinese translations, and even in distant North West countries. However only a few can be mentioned here.

Shortly after the death of Lord Buddha a Council was set up about 477 B.C. at Rajagriha. A second Council was held at Vaishali about 377 B.C. to canonise the Buddhist sacred books. In the third Council about 241 B.C. held at Pataliputra the books were canonised. The early canonised books are known as Tripiṭakas i.e., three baskets. They form the canonised books of Hinayāna or Theravādi schools.

1. The *Vinayapiṭaka* contains the teaching of the Buddha regarding the rules of conduct of monks.

2. *Suttapiṭaka* contains the doctrine of Buddha and a number of his dialogues. It is divided into *nikāyas* or collection.

(i) Dīrghanikāya (Long Discourses)
(ii) Majjhimanikāya (Medium sized discourses)
(iii) Samyutta-nikāya (Mixed Discourses)
(iv) Anguttara-nikāya (Graduated Discourses)
(v) Khuddaka-nikāya (Miscellaneous Discourses).

3. *Abhidharma-nikāya* which contains philosophical matter and creed. For the Mahāyānist *Vaipulya* Sutras and *Prajñāpārmita* Sutras are most important. *Visuddha-Magga* of Buddhaghosa and *Milindapāñha* are also important works.

The Buddhist Teaching

Buddhism evolved its doctrine and practice for about 1500 years in India. It was also the most significant movement from the time of the Buddha up to 1200 A.D. Naturally it has become a vast and complex religious system. One can study it for himself to convince oneself about its vastness. Two out of many books can be recommended.

1. A.K. Warder, *Indian Buddhism.*
2. Acharya Narendradeva, *Buddha-Dharma-Darshana.*

Buddhism is based on three philosophical tenets:

1. Momentariness, 2. Universal suffering and 3. Soullessness.

Perhaps the doctrine of momentariness is most fundamental doctrine, which also means that nothing in the world and jiva can be regarded as substantial. Nothing has any permanent nature of its own (*nis-svabhāva*). As such everything is in flux. From this it follows that every pleasant moment is bound to die out. No reliance can be made on things in constant change.* Hence, pain is inevitable in relation to evanescent things if we set our heart on things. Soul too has no permanent self, but is a stream of ever-flowing mental events.

From the viewpoint of practice, leading to *nirvāṇa* (cessation of suffering), there are the three jewels (*triratna*) of *Shīla*, *Samādhi* and *Prajñā*. Through *Shīla* or moral discipline one has to prepare oneself for attaining *nirvāṇa*. Then there is the next step where *Shilā* is carried further into *Samādhi*. However, *Samādhi* can yield only temporary relief. The seeker, even when *Samādhi* is complete, has to return to this miserable world. As such Shīla and Samādhi are perfected into Prajñā, in which there is sorrow but not of the *jivan-mukta*, but of the world.

The whole teaching of Buddhism is included in the doctrine of four noble Truths.

The Four Noble Truths (*chatvari arya satyāni*) are:

1. There is suffering.
2. There is the cause of suffering.
3. There is the cessation of suffering.
4. There is the path leading to suffering.

I. *There is suffering*: Indian religious systems are soteriological. Naturally they are interested in the practical result of the riddance of suffering. No Indian religious thought has denied the existence of suffering, and, the consequent need for release from this suffering. Buddhism gives reason for this suffering in terms of its doctrine of momentariness and non-substantiality of things. But Buddhism is concerned with the task of getting

*According to Sāṃkhya Prakṛti is *nitya-parināmi*, but the soul is eternal.

away from it. Hence, it does not encourage people to think about the first origin of evil or suffering. Any attempt at knowing the first cause of suffering, is a metaphysical heresy for Buddhism. This advice has been tacitly followed by other Indian religious systems. This doctrine of suffering has been epitomized as '*jara-maraṇa*' (old age and death).

II. *Twelve links of Dependent Origination* (*Dvādaśa-Nidāna*): There is suffering because there is the cause of suffering, for nothing can take place without a cause. This doctrine is known as *pratītya-Samutpāda*, which means this exists, therefore that exists. The miserable life of earthly existence has been explained in terms of a chain of twelve links.

From past lives	1. Ignorance (*avidyā*) 2. The Gestalt (*Saṃghata*) of body, speech and thought, transmitted to us through our former lives. This is known as *Saṃskāra*.
Relating to present existence	3. Consciousness (*Vijñāna*) 4. Name and Form (*Nāma-rūpa*) 5. Six doors of sense-organs (*saḍāyatana*) (Five traditional sense organs and mind) 6. Contact (*Indriya-Vastu-Sampark*). 7. Sensations as a result of this contact. It also includes feeling (Vedanā). 8. Cravings for pleasures of senses (*Tṛṣṇā*). 9. Grasping or clinging to *tṛṣṇā*. 10. Desire to be born (*bhava*) on account of (*Tṛṣṇā*).
Pertaining to future birth	11. Birth (jāti). 12. *Jara-maraṇa* (old age and death).

It is said that bhava i.e., the desire to be born is the father and *tṛṣṇā* is the mother of our present existence. If there were no *tṛṣṇā*, then there will be no *bhava*. Hence, both the Upanishads and Buddhism aimed at realizing a state of desirelessness. That life is suffering is also the theme of the Biblical book of Ecclesiastes:

I envy those who are dead and gone; they are better off

> than those who are still alive. But better off than either are those who have never been born. . . . (4:2-3)

This is also in the Greek Myth of King Midas who wanted to know what is best for man. God Mercury unwillingly had to blurt out:

> O Children of misfortune and chance! Why should I tell you what is best for you, that is, not to be, not to exist and not to be born.

Goethe has also remarked,

> "Why live a life so twisted; Better if it had not existed".

Fortunately, Lord Buddha emphatically holds that this life of suffering can be overcome, for there is a state of the cessation of suffering.

III. *There is Nirvāṇa*: *Nirvāṇa* literally means 'blown out' as a flame is blown out. This is the final aim of human striving. It can be said to be a state without pain, without desire and without any prospect of rebirth. Perhaps it can be described as a permanent state which is wholly indescribable, because it is completely transcendental. The nature of *nirvāṇa* is the most controversial issue in Buddhism, and we shall discuss it again under the heading 'Final destiny or *mokṣa*'.

IV. Path to the cessation of suffering (*Dukha Nirodha Mārga*): As there is *nirvāṇa* which was attained by Lord Buddha himself, so there must be a path which leads one to one's final destiny of *nirvāṇa*. Before embarking on the path, the seeker must fully understand the doctrine of momentariness, dependent chain of causation, (*pratītya-Samutpāda*) and *anātmavāda* (Soullessness). After being fully intellectually convinced of these principles, the seeker has to undergo the eightfold path:

1. Right Views, 2. Right resolve, 3. Right speech,
4. Right conduct, 5. Right livelihood, 6. Right effort,
7. Right mindfulness, 8. Right concentration.

These steps when analysed fall into three inter-related stages of path:

Morality (Shīla)	1. Right speech (Samyagvâk) 2. Right conduct (Samyak-Karmânta) 3. Right living (Samyagajīva)
Samādhi	4. Right effort (Samyagvyāyāma) 5. Right mindfulness (Samyak-smṛti) 6. Right concentration (Samyak-Samādhi).
Prajñā (Wisdom)	7. Right resolve (Samyak-Saṁkalpa) 8. Right View (Samyagdṛṣṭi).

We have already described *avidyā* (nescience) as the state in which the mind is distorted, intellect is befogged and the inmost being of man is soiled. Hence the will of man has to be purified, and, man has to be oriented in the right direction (*Samādhi*) and finally *ahaṁkāra* (egoity) has to be destroyed by reaching the state of *Prajñā*.

Samādhi means training the whole mind and developing deep insight into the essentials of Buddhist teaching, concerning *pratītya-Samutpāda, Shīla* and *Prajñā*. It is said to have been analysed into *Sam-ā-dhi* which means synthesis of body-mind-will. The very aim of *Samādhi* is to have egoity dissolved. This is possible in stages.

1. In the first stage of *Samādhi*, the mind is withdrawn from impurities of passion, emotion, attachment and there is withdrawal from all tempting objects of the world. Here there is a good deal of thinking and reasoning concerning the teaching of Buddhism.
2. In the second stage reasoning ends and a deep conviction into Buddhist teachings arises. Here gross bodily sensations tend to become subtle.
3. In the third trance there is happiness and tranquillity of mind.
4. Lastly, there is neither pleasure nor pain. There is the *Upekshā-bhāva* i.e., complete indifference and serenity.

In the later development of Buddhism eight stages have been mentioned. In Tantra, the eightfold *ṛddhīs-siddhīs* (attainments) have been described.

PRAJÑĀ

One finds that in the state of Samādhi, towards the final stage, egoity is lost. The centre of pleasure-pain is lost in *upekshā-bhāva*. But this complete indifference lasts as long as *samādhi*. On returning to the ordinary world, the seeker finds himself in the world again, even when his attitude to the world gets detached. But to reach the state of feelinglessness, the seeker has to practise *prajñā*. In this state, pain in the toe or in any part of the body is felt, but is not owned.

GOD IN BUDDHISM

In the early phase of Buddhism, still represented in the Hinayāna school of Ceylon, Burma and Thailand, there is no place for God. God does not come in any of the Four Noble Truths, neither in the causation of suffering nor in the path of winning *nirvāṇa*. Nay, Lord Buddha remained silent about God. For him it was useless to speculate about God. Any venture in this direction was called a metaphysical heresy. From this silence of Lord Buddha, it has been inferred that the Buddha did not deny the existence of God. But in the long history of Buddhism, the Buddhist have tried to refuṭe every proof in favour of the existence of God. Hence, Buddhism may be regarded as an atheistic system of religious thought.

If there is any entity which may be called supernatural, then it is *nirvāṇa*. Many thinkers regard *nirvāṇa* as a positive entity, corresponding to the *nirguṇa* Brahma or even Brahma of the Upanishads. In the *Milinda Pañha*, Sage Nagasena thus describes *Nirvāṇa* to King Milinda,

> O King, Nirvana is not born, neither does it grow old, it dies not, it passes not away, it has no rebirth.[1]

Again,

> Nirvana is not past, nor future, nor present, nor produced nor not produced, nor producible.[2]

One can easily compare the passages quoted here with the one passage in Kaṭhopanishad:

> The wise one (Brahman) is not born nor dies.
> This one has not come from anywhere, has not become anyone.
> Unborn, constant, eternal, primeval, this one is not slain when the body is slain". (*Kaṭh.* II.18)*

But this is too slender a thread to support theism.

True, at one time Lord Buddha was credited with omniscience. But Lord Buddha has so defined it that from this omniscience one cannot conclude his Divinity. Lord Buddha claimed Omniscience in a very limited sense i.e.,

1. He remembered his past lives,
2. He could see beings born into new births, according to their Karmas i.e., the law of trasmigration.
3. He got release and had knowledge of this i.e., the path leading to the cessation of suffering.

But certainly in Mahāyāna School, the doctrine of Bodhisattvas arose. Is bodhisattva a God?

By 'bodhisattva' is meant one who has *bodhi* (enlightenment) as one's *Sattva* or essence. Bodhisattvas have to be distinguished from Arhats or *pratyekabuddha* of Hinayānism. A bodhisattva, having attained *bodhi* refrains from entering into *nirvāṇa*, for working out the nirvāṇa for the whole world and working also for his *parinirvāṇa*. After living a great many lives of compassion, friendliness, helpfulness and equanimity, he attains omniscience. In the long run Manjushri (personification of wisdom, *Prajñā*), Avalokitesvara (personifying *Karuṇā*, mercy) and Maitreya (personification of friendliness) became objects of *bhakti*. But they are at best helpers of men. They are not the creator or sustainer of the world. Hence, they cannot be called 'God'. Besides, in Buddhism, *nirvāṇa* has to be attained by oneself and it cannot be a gift which can be given by the grace of any supernatural power. Therefore, we once again repeat that Buddhism does not admit the existence of God.

However, towards the final phase of Buddhism, the doctrine of *Trikāya* Buddha came into being. The truth is that man can-

*Substantially this is repeated in Bhagavadgītā II.20.

not live without God. Hence, even atheistic Yoga in the beginning had to introduce the doctrine of *Ishvara-pariṇidhāna.* Similarly Buddhists, finding it difficult to work out their salvation developed the doctrine of trikāya Buddha.

The Buddha is pictured in three forms, namely, *rūpa-kāya* or *nirmāṇa-kāya* or historical Buddha who lived from c. 580 B.C. to c. 460 B.C.; *Sambhoga-kāya* Buddha corresponding to the Hindu conception of Ishvara in His heavenly abode; and, Dharmakāya Buddha. It is the notion of Dharma and Dharmakāya which is important for philosophical theology.

'Dharma' is a loaded word in Indian philosophy. It means:

1. The ultimate truth.
2. Scripture, doctrine and religion.
3. Righteousness or virtue i.e., ethically toned thought and conduct.
4. Moral law (e.g., dharmashastras).
5. Attributes of substances.

But in Buddhist sense, *Dharmakāya* means the ultimate reality which is the support or substratum of the world. As an abstract entity *dharmakāya* means the indescribable, immanent and cosmic entity of the world. As a concrete and personalized being *dharmakāya* means the ultimate Being full of Compassion. Thus *dharmakāya* stands both for the Vedantic *nirguṇa* and *saguṇa Brahma.* Thus the first vow '*Buddham Sharanam gacchāmi*' took the form of *bhakti* i.e., refuge in the Buddha.

If there is any place of Ishvara, then it is in the doctrine of *Dharmakāya* Buddha. However, philosophically Buddhism remained atheistic* but practice belies the theory.

The World According to Buddhism

We have already seen that Buddhism does not accept the existence of a creator God. Consequently, the world cannot be treated as 'creation'. Is it then eternal, as the Mimāṃsakas and Jainas think? No. Nothing is permanent. Everything is in constant Heraclitean flux. Then why do we talk of the same moun-

*Readers are advised to consult A.K. Warder, *Indian Buddhism*, pp. 152-158.

tain or river or other things of everyday life? It is due to the continuity of change without abruptness, as David Hume said. It is like one candle that lights another and unthinking people seem to think that it is the same light. A little reflection will show that one volume of water flows down the river and another volume immediately takes its place. Similarly, the cells of the body keep on dying and taking birth. But we say it is the same river 'Ganges', and, the same person Rama. Why? Because of *Saṅghāta* or *skandha* (Gestalt) of the momentary events. Each moment dies the moment it is born as A.N. Whitehead had described 'events'. But the momentary events are synthesized, according to the doctrine of dependent causation. But even here the events are momentary, and, no event continues for more than a moment (*Sarvam Kshanikam Kshanikam*). But the momentary events form more or less recognizable aggregate, characterized by name and form (*nāma-rūpa*). We call that it is the same table, because the aggregate of passing events continues to have the same recognizable shape which we can conveniently call 'table'. When the shape undergoes a good deal of change, then perhaps it would cease to be called 'table'. It might be called 'fuel or wood'.[3]

Though the Buddhist take the help of causation, they do not subscribe to the *satkāryavāda* of sāmkhya. Their theory of causation is called *asatkāryavāda* i.e., the effect is not implicitly contained in its cause. Hence, the Buddhist totally deny the existence of eternal atoms. Is the world then totally unreal?

In this context we are reminded of George Berkeley who has advised us to talk in the language of the vulgar and think with the learned. Here Lord Buddha advises us that there is the conventional language of everyday life and the world disclosed by it is practically true (*Sdmvṛti*). But as against this there is the higher language of Buddha's teaching which discloses the real nature of things. This *Samvṛt* world is illusory and is based on *avidyā*. However, this world is based on the principle of *pratītya-samutpāda*. Is the principle of causation itself then eternal?

Perhaps, Buddhism would not admit that. Here Buddhism faces the same predicament in which the advaitin and later on Wittgenstein find themselves. The four noble Truths and the detailed teaching and discourses of Buddha are tools and convenient devices for generating insight in the seeker. Once *bodhi* is attained, the ladder is left behind and the convenient scriptural language is seen to be illusory.

Hence, the world, as long as no *nirvāṇa* has been attained has to be taken real in the *Vyāvahārika* sense.

The Buddhist were divided into monks-nuns and laity. Monks-nuns had to renounce the world, but they had to resort to a monastery and its Order. Here also the monks had to undergo strict discipline of the monastery. The laity had to support the monastery. Thus, here too the tenuous existence of the monastic life and its world had to be accepted. By living in the world one cannot live out of the world.

Man and Soul-less-ness (Anattāvāda)

Everything is momentary. Therefore, there is no substantial man or his soul. When Buddha was asked, 'Is there any permanent soul', he kept silent. Is there no soul? Again, the Buddha kept silent. Why did he keep silent? For he did not accept the doctrine of the annihilation of man after death, as the materialist in his day maintained. He believed that man does transmigrate from one birth to another. Therefore, he did not accept the doctrine of annihilation (*ucchdavāda*). Nor did he believe in *Shāśvata-Veda*, according to which soul is eternal. The Buddha believed that man as the mind-body complex is not eternal. One day this complex is bound to be dissolved by following the theory and practice involved in the Four Noble Truths.

Hence, man for the Buddha was *nāmarūpa* complex or psycho-physical complex of *rūpa* (matter), *Vedanā* (sensation, emotion), *Samjñā* (perception), *Saṃskāra* (predisposition due to past accumulation of karmas) and *vijñāna* (consciousness). Each of the five skandhas, is itself complex.[4] However, man has an illusion about himself.

1. He thinks that he (man) is his body, calling it as 'me' or 'mine'.
2. He also thinks that he owns his own sensation.
3. Man may think of this mind-body complex as 'me' or 'mine'.

How to explain this illusion of 'me' or 'mine'? What is this 'I' or *ahaṁ* (ego)? When it is analysed then it (i.e. I or ego) disappears. Man is found to be a stream of passing events, as Hume has shown in the west much after or G. Ryle even much later (1950, *The Concept of Mind*). Explaining the non-existence of a permanent man, Nagasena asks King Milinda

> Is it in the outward form (*rūpa*) that is Nagasena, or the sensations (*vedanā*), or perception (*Samjñā*) or predisposition (*Saṃskāra*), or the consciousness (*Vijñāna*), that is Nagasena?[5]

Hence, an individual man is only an aggregate with a pattern of psycho-physical stream. If there is no permanent self, then what passes from birth to birth in transmigration?

The changes in man are insensible and continuous from moment to moment. For example, we say that it is the same candle which is burning, even though changes keep on going in it every moment. What counts is the pattern. The stocking is said to be the same even when in due course during its repair all the threads in it are replaced. The same is true of the jiva in transmigration. The continuity of the pattern remains.

> One comes into being, another passes away; and the rebirth is, as it were, simultaneous.[6]

Hence, any permanent Soul for Buddhism can be called in the language of David Hume 'an idle figment of imagination'. Or, 'a category-mistake due to the bewitchment of language.[7]

Thus, the doctrine of man as an aggregate of *rūpa* (corporeal passing events) and *nāma* (psychical events), follows from the doctrine of momentariness. And, that which is transitory is painful. Naturally, Buddhism does not accept that this illusory notion of man as a permanent self can be maintained. This illusion will land him into a state of painfulness, for analysis reveals that man is but a stream of psycho-physical events.

> What is transitory, is painful, what is painful, is *anaṭṭā*, what is *anattā*, is not mine, this am I not, this is not myself.[8]

Naturally for Buddhism this ego-consciousness has to be destroyed, or, what is the same thing, this aggregate has to be dissolved. Then is it only a negative way? Is there nothing that remains after this aggregate has been dissolved?

Whether Lord Buddha denied the existence of a permanent individual Self, or, he denied only the empirical Self? These are tall questions. The term '*nirvāṇa*' simply means a flame blown out. Does not remain in any other shape or form. Perhaps it is an idle metaphysical question for Lord Buddha. His negative way is perhaps final

> You teach the Atta, but I teach what Atta is *not*.
> You know the Atta, but I only know what the Atta is *not*.
> Therefore, you are always talking about the Atta, but I only speak of *anatta*.[9]

It is still a more difficult question to decide whether Lord Buddha meant to retain the notion of an absolute Self.[10]

Evil and Suffering or Bondage

The whole human life is an unmixed evil and suffering according to Buddhism.

> This, O Monks, is the sacred truth of suffering: Birth is suffering, old age is suffering, sickness is suffering, death is suffering, to be united with the unloved is suffering, to be separated from the loved is suffering, not to obtain what one desires is suffering . . . .[11]

The whole train of human suffering is due to his *avidyā*, caused by the jivas themselves in their past lives. They alone are responsible for the evil and are advised to remove suffering by their own efforts. Buddhism is essentially atheistic and does not recommend to seek divine power for removing either *avidyā* or suffering.

A little glance at the enumeration of human suffering will show that it will be called natural evil for us. In *jarāmaraṇa*, man will not be said to be responsible for his birth or sickness and death. Suffering, therefore, is not due to social exploitation so much or natural calamities. Of course, Lord Buddha was fully conversant with the social evil of wars, greed, exploitation of man by his rulers. But Lord Buddha did not think of improving society or conquering nature. The serious thinker can work out his salvation by withdrawing from society, and, by means of self-conquest. Though *avidyā* is the main cause, because it completely orients man in the wrong direction, yet *tṛṣṇā* (the desire for pleasure) is the cause which keeps the chain of suffering (twelve links of dependent causation) alive. It also keeps man rooted in the world and sows the seed of future birth by producing the tendency to take fresh births.

No matter how many births a man may take, his *tṛṣṇā* cannot be satisfied. On the contrary, his desire for many more lives will be greatly strengthened. Naturally, this *tṛṣṇā* should be overcome by minimizing the opportunities for pleasure. This is possible if one withdraws from the world and gets initiated into the life of a monk or nun. It is useless to call Buddhism or any Indian system as pessimistic. Self-conquest which lies in each individual life's own self-effort was regarded as the panacea of all evil. Here Buddhism and other Indian systems of Advaita, Bhakti and Yoga were eminently successful. Will anybody call Buddha, Shankara, Ramanuja, Chaitanya, Kabir, Ramakrishna, Vivekananda, Aurobindo and so on, to be unsuccessful? It is only when we think now, due to science, technology, banking, commercial and industrial enterprises, and so on, that we consider self-conquest or the culture of the soul by withdrawing from the world as pessimism. Life-and-World-negation was as much the accepted creed and world-view of the ancient Indian thinkers, as world-and-life-affirmation is the accepted postulate of the Western and West-Oriented Indian politicians today. These two stands should not be mixed up when we turn to the ancient Indian philosophy like Buddhism. Why did Buddhism, and, as a matter of fact Indian religious philosophy accept life-and-world-negation and the culture of the Soul so important?

Buddhism accepted the doctrine of *Karma-Saṃsāra-Jñāna-Mukti* as its *Weltanschauung*. The wheel of transmigration will continue as long as one does not attain *nirvāṇa*. Besides, this world and the jiva as psycho-physical complex are infected through and through with momentariness. How can anything transitory be taken as real or pleasant? The whole world appears continuous with the wheel of dependent causation, without anything which has a permanent nature of its own (*nis-svabhāva*). Hence, the worldly life is painful. Not even suicide will release a man from his chain of suffering. For death is always followed by another birth. One candle before being extinguished lights another. Nothing and not even Gods are exempt from impermanence and consequent suffering.

> The three and thirty gods, and the Yama-gods, the happy deities, the gods who joy in creation, and the ruling gods, bound by the chains of desire, return within the power of Mara. The whole universe is consumed with flames, the whole universe is enveloped in smoke, the whole universe is on fire, the whole universe trembles.[12]

Is suffering totally useless?

Suffering has its own use. It shocks man into his pitiful existence. Man is kicked into his awareness for realizing his own authentic existence. Once awakened, and he not only works out his own salvation, but out of compassion for others, who are unmindful of their pitiful lives, he lights the lamp for them. The working out of the usefulness of suffering has been thus outlined by Mrs. Rhys Davids:

1. The realization of the fact of suffering gives rise to a quest and faith.
2. Faith gives rise to joy.
3. Joy ripens into rapture.
4. Rapture in due course gives way to serenity.
5. Serenity paves the way for happiness.
6. Happiness gives way to concentration.
7. Concentration yields knowledge and insight leading to *Nirvāṇa*.

Final Human Destiny or Nirvāṇa or Release or Liberation

What is the cause of human suffering or human bondage? Of course, the cause has been explained through the twelve chains of dependent causation. But there are three main elements in this *dvādasha nidāna* i.e., *avidyā*, *tṛṣṇā* and *ahaṁkāra* (egoity).

First, ignorance means nescience concerning the four noble truths.

> And what, monks, is ignorance?
> Whatever is not knowing concerning ill, its arising, its stopping, the course leading to its stopping—this, monks, is called ignorance.[13]

This *avidyā* is very akin to the later doctrine of Māyā. Lord Buddha asks his disciple Subhuti.

> What thinkest thou now, Subhuti, is illusion one thing and material form another? Is illusion one thing and sensation another? Perception another? Conformations (*saṃskāras*) another?
>
> . . . . . . Subhuti answered: Nay, Master, nay; illusion is not one thing and material form another. Material form itself is illusion and the illusion itself is material form, sensations, perception.

And Lord Buddha continues:

> It is in the nature of illusion that lies which beings what they are. It is, O Subhuti, as if a clever magician, or the pupil of a clever magician, caused a vast concourse of men to appear at a cross road, where four great thoroughfares meet, and, having caused them to appear, caused them again to vanish.[14]

This *avidyā* allows man to remain in *tṛṣṇā* and this is the real cause of human suffering.

> This, O monks, is the sacred truth of the origin of suffering: it is the thirst (for being), which leads from birth to birth, together with lust and desire, which finds gratification here and there: the thirst for pleasures, the thirst for being, the thirst for power.[15]

This thirst keeps the flame of desire burning and this desire has its focus in the ego. On account of tnirst, desire located in the ego, keeps on from birth to birth. The individual suffers not only in this life, but through countless rebirths. In this chain there is some continuity of the individual which is not the same (as the eternalist maintain) nor quite different (avoiding the thesis of the annihilist). There is the *criss-crossing* of skandhas throughout the cycle of endless rebirths. The lamp neither remains the same nor different from hour to hour. Suppose a first hut is burnt by some one in the row, then other huts too are burnt by succeeding fires. Is not the man who caused the first fire responsible for the rest?

> Just so . . . . . . it is one name-and-form which has its death and another-name-and-form which is reborn. But the second is the result of the first, and is therefore not set free from its evil deeds.[16]

And again,

> Just so great King, this (one) name-and-form commits deeds, either pure and impure, and by that Karma another name-and-form is reborn. And therefore is it not set free from its evil deeds.[17]

The cessation of suffering is known as *nirvāṇa*. It is the cessation of all those states in the *skandha* which constitutes individuality. Hence, any talk of individuality after attaining *nirvāṇa* is not possible. This *nirvāṇa* is attainable even in this life and is called *jivanmukti*. This *jivanmukti* means peace, equipoise, wisdom and virtue unruffled by outward happenings. Any further metaphysical speculation cannot but disturb this peace. Hence, Lord Buddha regarded metaphysical speculation about the self a heresy. Then what is *nirvāṇa*?

> As a flame, blown out by the wind, disappears and cannot be named, even so the recluse when released from name and body disappears and cannot be named.[18]

Again,

> A monk whose mind is thus released cannot be followed and tracked out even by the gods.[19]

Nirvāṇa is really a state of mind in this life in which state a *jivanmukta* enjoys perfect equipoise. But it is also spoken of as an entity and this description fits as much into what is called Brahman.

> O King, *Nirvāṇa* is not born, neither does it grow old, it dies not, it passes not away, it has no rebirth.[20]
> Nirvāṇa is not past, nor future, nor present, nor produced, nor not produced, nor producible.[21]

Hence, it is maintained by Mrs. Rhys Davids, A.K. Coomaraswamy, I.B. Horner, George Grimm and others that *Nirvāṇa* is the denial of the persistence of the empirical self, but not of the immanent Man in men.

> Nothing in the world any longer applies.
> The Perfected One in his purity, rid of the dross of his personality, thus beyond death, is something unrecognizable; but he exists, he still is, namely, something inscrutable.[22]

The denial of nihilism gives some support of the view that in some sense there is a non-empirical Self which remains, of course without egoity. Again, the life of a *jivanmukta* supports the view that *nirvāṇa* need not mean annihilation of the Self. But the truth is that Lord Buddha was genuinely not interested in any metaphysical enquiry. The important thing for Lord Buddha was purely therapeutic. He only wanted an end to the chain of endless rebirths, by reaching *nirvāṇa* which is a state of painlessness. This *nirvāṇa*, for Lord Buddha, was real to him. Beyond this for him was a no-man-land of useless disputation and profitless controversy. Any metaphysical pre-occupation for Lord Buddha, meant restlessness, doubt and uncertainty. And this would mean the denial of peace and equipoise. Why should we not maintain that Lord Buddha maintained silence about metaphysical question as a genuine conquest over idle curiosity. Hence, *nirvāṇa* means extinction of any and every vestige of name-and-form (*nāma-rūpa*) even of the idle curiosity for metaphysical knowledge.

LIFE AFTER DEATH

Those who overcome all desires and get their ego dissolved by withdrawing from the world and by obtaining knowledge through Samādhi may enter *nirvāṇa*, but a vast majority of people remain outside the pale of *nirvāṇa*. What happens to them after their death?

Lord Buddha followed a middle path between the nihilist and eternalist. The nihilist, largely materialists, believe there is total extinction (*ucchedvāda*) of the man after his death. The eternalist believe that there is a permanent soul which survives death. But Lord Buddha rejected both the views. There is no proof of the immortality of the soul. Further, this view unsupported by any sound piece of knowledge is likely to lead to laxity in morals, possibly antinomianism of Buddha's days. The nihilist view is equally devoid of sound knowledge, and, most certainly it is likewise fraught with moral depravity. But Lord Buddha was fully convinced of transmigration. The question naturally would arise, what is that which transmigrates when there is no permanent Self?

Of course, there is an individuality, a psycho-physical complex (*nāma-rūpa*) which continues from birth to birth. Is it the same individuality? No. The individuality keeps on changing. However, this changing individuality is not the same as the previous one at the time of death. But it is not quite different from the earlier one before death. The pattern involved in the psycho-physical complex continues. So there is the endless chain of continuity in the interminable chain of rebirths. This transmigration of the continuous chain has been called by Wittgenstein as criss-crossing of changing events constitutive of the empirical self or psycho-physical complex. Some elements of the previous moments may resemble the later ones and yet other events may change considerably from the previous moments. But as long as it is the same continuous chain, the responsibility of any individuality at any moment remains. For example, one candle lights another. Here the light of one is responsible for the next succeeding light of the next candle. Again, an individual may set one hut on fire, and, this fire of the first hut lights up the next and in this way the fire continues from huts to huts. Will not the man or the individual who put the first hut on fire, responsible for all fires? Again, are not the gains and doings of the father visited on the succeeding generations? Hence, in spite of the momentary events constitutive of psycho-physical complex* (rūpa and nāma consisting of vedanā, samjñā, saṃskāra and vijñāna) there is the continuity of the *series*, and this *series* keeps on transmigrating in the endless chain of countless rebirths.

But no matter whatever be the different individuality in this series, there cannot be any unalloyed happiness. Even gods are infected with momentariness, for the adage is, 'whatever is transitory is painful'.

In the whole account of transmigrating individuality, no permanent self is maintained, and yet every kind of persisting individuality is endowed with moral responsibility. As man in this life of his individuality is nothing but a bundle of material and psychical events, so he continues likewise in all succeeding series of rebirths. If a man suffers because of his deeds in this life, so he is said to suffer throughout the whole cycle of endless rebirths. The difference between the eternalist and Buddhist middle path lies in the difference in the accounting of individuality. There might be differences indeed with regard to the concept of individuality, but no Indian system regards the psycho-physical complex as eternal and real. The Vedantist may call this psycho-physical complex as *Upādhis* (mere name-and-form), and Buddhist also call this individuality as only empirically real. However, in many systems (Sāṃkhya, Vedanta, Jainism) over and above the empirical Self, there is an eternal, unborn soul. Buddhism maintains complete silence about the eternity of the soul, whether individual or Brahman. This silence is a matter of very great discipline and later or after the dawning of *nirvāṇa*, this idle curiosity also falls away like all other events of the empirical Self. Keeping of silence is a part and parcel of peace and equipoise of a *jivanmukta*. The lesson is hard, but has to be learnt.

Sects in Buddhism

At the second council at Vaishali in B.C. 377, the Vajjians differed from other Buddhist elders (*theras*). The Vajjians called

* *Rūpa* material events and *nāma* psychical events.

themselves Mahāsanghika and the rest were known as theravādins. The aim of the Theravādins was to attain *arhatahood* with the help of *Shila, Samādhi* and *Prajñā*. Later on, the Mahāsangika called themselves Mahāyāna and called the rest through the nickname of Hinayāna (smaller vehicle).

On the whole the Hinayāna represents the conservative group and interprets the Buddhist scripture literally. In contrast, the Mahāyānist were progressive, liberal and in due course spread all over North India, North-West regions of Asia and China. In due course, they developed esoteric circle and tantra. In certain essentials Hinayāna and Mahāyāna did not differ. They both accepted the following:

1. Nirvāṇa is inexpressible, has no origin and is unchangeable.
2. *Nirvāṇa* has to be realized by oneself alone, without making reference to any supernatural agency.
3. Personal self is lost in *nirvāṇa*.
4. *Nirvāṇa* means tranquillity.
5. It means the barring out of any more *Saṃsārika* birth.

However, they differ in the following points:

Hinayāna	*Mahāyāna*
1. Nirvāṇa is a state of bliss, and, is a matter of acquisition.	1. Nirvāṇa is *ajāti* (unborn) and cannot be acquired. It is a state as a result of attaining bodhi. It cannot be described at all, not even as bliss. It is *Shunyatā*.
2. *Arhatva* or one's own salvation has to be won. Hence, it is also known as the theory of *pratyeka-buddha*.	2. Here one has to attain not arhatva of the individual selves, but of all beings. Hence, *bodhisattva* is the ideal and not *nirvāṇa* but *parinirvāṇa* has to be won. Not Buddhatva, but Sambuddhatva has to be acquired after many more efforts as Bodhisattva.

3. Hinayāna emphasizes the dissolution of ego-consciousness by the removal of Kleśāvaraṇa i.e., the veil of passions, tṛṣṇā. It is firmly based on Samādhi.	3. Mahāyāna in addition to Kleśāvaraṇa emphasizes the removal of *jñānāvaraṇa* i.e., the veil over true knowledge. Hence, it takes the help of Dialectic (*Prasangikavāda*). Hence, even *pratitya-Samutvāda* has to be shown as only an initial stand, for the dialectic shows that ultimately it is also self-contradictory, leading finally to the acceptance of *Shunyatā*.

Has Buddhism Ceased to Exist in India?

From the viewpoint of direct followers and their number, Buddhism has not much vitality in India in spite of neo-Buddhism of Dr. B.R. Ambedkar. But from the standpoint of its teaching and thought, it is still very much alive on the Indian scene. Without Buddhism, it is doubtful whether Gauḍapāda and Shankara could have developed Advaitism. This is admitted even by Brahmin thinkers who call Shankara crypto-Buddhist or a Buddhist-in-disguise. But apart from this very close influence, the whole Saint movement in India was initiated by Buddha Tantrikas, and, Gorakhnath and his Guru Matsyendranath have been said to be Buddhist before they become Shaivite. Further, there is a direct influence of Nathas on Kabir, Dadu, Ravidas and through them on Guru Nanak. Even Bauls of Bengal and Sahajiyas were greatly indebted to Buddhist Tantra. Hence, really Buddhism has been absorbed both within and without the rank of Hinduism. In this sense Buddhism is still alive in India.

References

1. *The Questions of King Milinda, Sacred Books of the East*, Vol. 35, p. 193.
2. *Ibid.*, p. 195.
3. F. Waismann, '*How I See Philosophy*', reprinted in Logical Positivism, ed. A.J. Ayer.

4. A.K. Warder, *Indian Buddhism*, p. 303.
5. Harvard Oriental Series, Vol. III. p. 154.
6. *The Questions of King Milinda*, SBE Vol. 35, p. 64.
7. G. Ryle, *The Concept of Mind*, Chap. I.
8. George Grimn, '*The Doctrine of the Buddha*', 161n; see also pp. 167, 171, 187.
9. *Buddhist Sutta*, Sacred Books of the East, Vol. XI, Delhi 1965, p. 369.
10. Some opinions with their reason have been given in the author's *The Hindu Religious Philosophy*, pp. 381-394.
11. Hermann Oldenberg, *Ibid.*, p. 216.
12. H. Oldenberg. *Ibid.*, p. 216.
13. Samyutta Nikāya II. 2-4, 43.
14. H. Oldenberg, *Buddha*, p. 219.
15. H. Oldenberg, *Ibid.*, p. 223.
16. *The Questions of King Milinda*, p. 74.
17. *Ibid.*, p. 112.
18. Sutta Nipata, SBE Vol. X. VV 1073, 1075, pp. 198-199.
19. E.J. Thomas, Early Buddhist Scriptures, p. 107.
20. *The Questions of King Milinda*, p. 193.
21. *Ibid.*, p. 195. This description of *Nirvāṇa* is the same as of Brahman, Kaṭha, II. 18.
22. G. Grimm, *Buddha*, p. 183.

CHAPTER VIII

JAINISM

INTRODUCTION

Jainism is a very old non-Vedic religion and some of its features go back to the times of Indus Valley Civilization. Like the Upanishads and Buddhism, Jainism was a kshatriya movement. It had its locus in a religion which was not yet touched by Brahmin cult. These regions East of *Sadanira* (modern Gandaka) were inhabited by non-Aryan tribes. Jainism was formerly allied to Ajivikism. It is said to have been held by a number of 24 Tirthankaras and Lord Mahavira (B.C. 599-527) the last and the most important Tirthankara belonged to the clan of Licchavis of Vaishali. This Vaishali was a janapada or oligarchy and was later on destroyed by Ajatashatru.

Jainism is not an offshoot of Vedic Brahminism. It belonged to the people who were essentially agriculturist, who valued bulls and cows. They therefore had simple living and could practice *ahiṁsā* and austerities. In contrast, the Vedic Aryans were essentially pastoral people and they were used to animal-sacrifice. Naturally the Aryan and non-Aryan people of India were always in conflict, and, so in their religious beliefs too they held opposite views. In the long run, the Vedic Aryans accepted all that was of importance in Jainism and Buddhism. The present Hinduism is a commingled stream of Aryan and non-Aryan cults. Keeping in mind the independent and parallel development of Jainism, we can proceed further.

Jainism is essentially a religion of Tirthankaras. Jainism has come from the word 'Jin' which means one who has conquered his passion. It essentially means the conquest of one's own self in bondage. Again, a Tirthankara is one who has built a ford which takes one across the ocean of bondage and suffering. A Tirthankara has not only conquered himself, but has taught people, the way out of this ocean of suffering. These 24 Tirthankaras have been mentioned, namely, 1. Rishabha, 2. Ajita,

3. Sambhava, 4. Abhinandana, 5. Sumati, 6. Padmaprabha, 7. Syparshva, 8. Chandraprabha, 9. Pushpadanta or Suvidhi, 10. Shitala, 11. Shreyamsa, 12. Vasupujya, 13. Vimala, 14. Ananta, 15. Dharma, 16. Shanti, 17. Kunthu, 18. Ara, 19. Mali, 20. Munisuvrata, 21. Nami, 22. Nemi or Arishtanemi, 23. Parshanath, 24. Vardhamana or Mahavira.

Rishabha muni has been identified with the image of an ascetic God on a seal amulet of Indus Valley Civilization. However, this cannot be Rishabha Muni as this God is linked with *liṅga-worship*. Excepting Parshanath and Lord Mahavira, other tirthankaras are more legendary figures than historical persons.

Basic or Special Features of Jainism

1. Jainism having its close association with Ajivikism is the oldest non-Aryan religion of India.

2. It is non-Vedic in the sense that it does not recognize the Veda as its religious scripture,—does not admit caste distinction, and, is opposed to the Ṛgvedic religion. It accepts *mokṣa* and not heavenly abode as the highest human end. It also accepts non-Vedic Yoga and austerities as important means for securing liberation.

3. Unlike the Ṛgvedic principle, it accepts the four pillars of *karma-saṃsāra-jñāna-mukti* as its creed.

4. It is wholly atheistic, but intensely spiritual form of religion.

5. As there is no place for God in its system, so Jainism regards the world as eternal in its on-goings.

6 Though Buddhism too accepts *ahiṁsā* as an important moral creed, yet *ahiṁsā* is the central teaching of Jainism (*ahimsa parmo dharmah*) and, accounts for the moral conduct of Jaina seekers and Sadhus.

7. From the viewpoint of essence, Jainism is dualistic, for it admits the distinction between the two entities of *Jiva* and *Ajiva*. But from the viewpoint of number it accepts the plurality of spirits and of atoms.

8. In order to give a system to its plural ontology it takes resort to *anekāntavāda* and *syādvāda*.

9. Jaina doctrine of soul is very distinctive, for it admits spatial dimension to it. Again, Jainism also admits that karmas

are like subtle material objects that cling to the soul. This shows that Jainism has very primitive concept of soul.

10. Jainism, however, has a great deal of modern tone in the form of its rationalism. A Jaina thinker Ratna Shekhara in his book *Sambadha Sattari* states that each man can realize his own self-sameness of the soul by his own efforts without reference to any supernatural agency.

11. Unlike Hinduism and very much like Buddhism, Jainism is associated with the historical figure (of Lord Mahavira), who might not have originated Jainism, but has given an authoritative seal to its principal tenets.

12. Not only Jainism has no place for caste, it has no place for either Buddhist Scripture or the Ṛgveda as its religious scripture. It has its own religious books.

Jaina Religious Scripture

Originally there were 14 Purvas and 11 Angas. Purvas were transmitted orally and in due course have been lost. Hence, 11 Angas form the main Jaina religious literature. Besides, there are 22 Upangas, 10 Pakinnakas, 6 Chedas, 4 Mula-sutras and 2 other Sutras. Out of 11 Angas the *Acharāṅga* formulates the rules of conduct for the monks, and, *Sutrakṛtāṅga* describes the Jaina rites and points out its distinctive features.

Uvasagadasao is the 7th Anga and was translated into English by A.F.R. Hoernle in 1888. English translation of Jaina Sutras in Sacred Books of the East, Vol. 22 and 45 is also important.

Formerly the Jaina scripture was written in Ardha Maghadhi. Later it was written rather more systematically in Prakrit and Sanskrit.

Jainas are essentially traders from the time of Makkhali Gosala, for they desist from agriculture. They fear that in digging the soil, they are likely to kill insects and this killing would mean *hiṁsā*. They own a good deal of wealth of India. The Jainas have survived all these years, but Buddhism has almost disappeared from the land of its origin. The main reason is that Jainas have nothing to oppose Brahminism. They do not admit caste, but accept Brahmin priesthood at many of their functions. Secondly, they have adopted a great many popular gods from popular Hinduism. Besides, their own four pillars of *Karma-Saṃsāra-*

jñāna-Mukti have been assimilated into Hinduism. The *pañca-mahāvrata* of Jainism (*Satya, asteya, brahmacharya, ahiṁsā and a-parigraha*), has been fully adopted by Hinduism though not with the same rigour. Yoga and austerities now are as much Jaina as Hindu for the last many years. Jainas have become so much Hinduistic that they also adopt Vaiṣṇavism. As a matter of fact even inter-marriage is permitted between some vegetarian Hindus and Jainas.

Jaina Philosophy and Religion

Jaina philosophy and religion are intimately inter-mixed. Hence, in a very brief outline its philosophy too has to be presented.

According to Jainism, ontologically there are two kinds of substances, namely, *Jiva* and *Ajiva*. A jiva is either *nitya-Siddha, siddha* or Baddha. A jiva in his pristine nature has infinite jñāna (knowledge), ananta darshana (infinite perception), *ananta caritra* (pure conduct) and *ananta virya* (infinite power). Through karmas of beginningless rebirths, the soul it soiled, for these karmas stick to the soul, make its vision and action limited, obscured and obstructed in every way. Of course, the original soul in its pristine nature is pure spirit and karmas are like material particles. Ordinarily no material particles can stick to the pure spirit. Alongwith this materialized view of the spirit in its embodied body remains either small or big. For example, in an ant, the jiva is small in size, but in an elephant it is big in size. Hence, a jiva has also spatial features. For this reason, critics tend to think that Jainism is more primitive than Buddhism. Of course, Jainism has a much older history.

Again, the karmic matter may hinder the perception of a jiva by restricting its sense-organs. According to the development of *baddha* jivas there is an ascending order of one-sensed, two-sensed, three sensed, four sensed and five sensed jivas. One sensed jiva remains immobile like plants and man is said to be five sensed jiva because he has the traditionally five sense-organs of eye, nose, ear, tongue and skin. But a jiva might win his own salvation by shedding off all the karmic matter. He becomes a *siddha* (perfected). And a perfected siddha who has laid down scriptural teaching and preaching is called a Tirthankara, and, they are 24 in number, and, Lord Mahavira is the last and most illustrious of all of them. But a *nitya-siddha* is one who is eternally free and has not been a *baddha* at all.

Apart from an infinite number of jivas there are five *a-jivas* of *dharma*, *adharma*, *akasha*, *kala* (time) and *pudgala* (matter). Dharma and Adharma are used in peculiar meanings. Dharma is an all-pervasive subtle material substance in which motion is made possible e.g., water for fish and air for birds. It is only a medium for motion. As against dharma, *adharma* is that subtle material substance which accounts for rest. Pudgala is that matter which consists of atoms and molecules. We can put the jivas and a-jivas in a tabular form for easy comprehension.

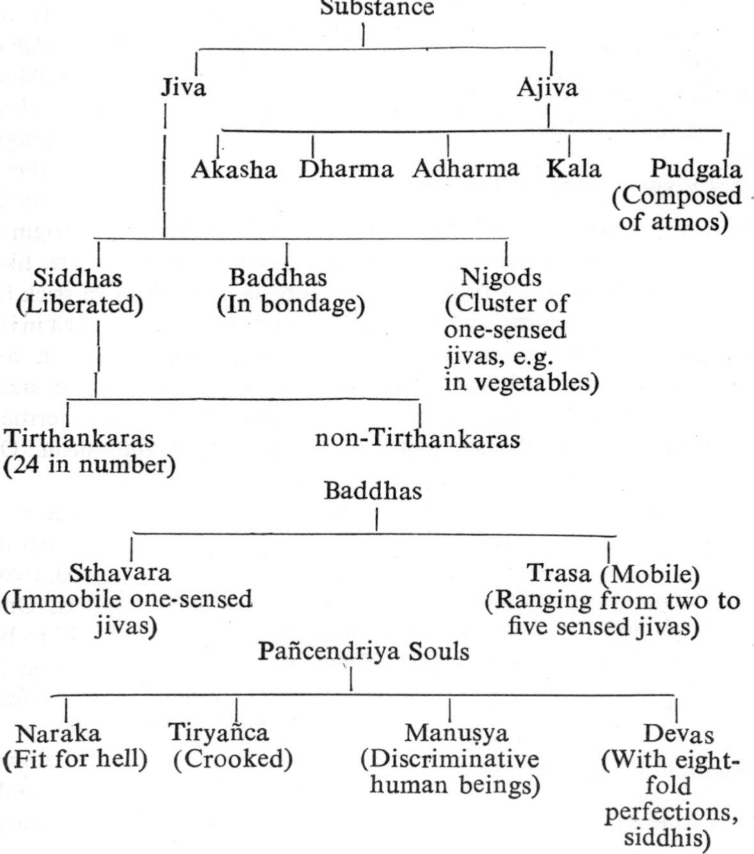

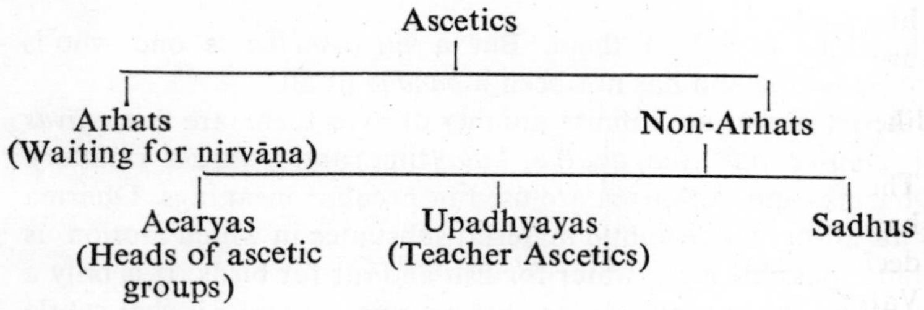

Siddhas, Arhats, Acaryas, Upadhyayas and Sadhus form as pancaparamesthin i.e., the supreme judge and advisory council.

For all practical purposes Jainism is concerned with the soul in bondage, and, this bondage is due to karmic matter which envelopes the soul and keeps the bondage throughout its countless rebirths. Hence some account of the karman will be given under the heading of 'Bondage'. First of all we have to consider the views of Jainism with regard to God.

The View of God in Jainism

Jainism regards the world eternal. Naturally there is no room for any supernatural entity who can be the creator, sustainer and destroyer of the world. Hence, there is no God in Jainism. Further, for Jainism each soul in his pristine nature is alone and solitary. He does not need any help from other souls, and does not give any help to others. As a matter of fact all souls, freed and *nityasiddhas* have the same status. Thus, there is no room for worship. Consequently each soul in bondage is said to be an architect of his own soul. Either he can work out his own destiny for liberation or sink further into deeper bondage. Hence, J.L. Jain observes[1]:

> Alone he accumulates merit; alone he enjoys the various happiness of heaven; alone he destroys *Karma*; alone also he attains to mokṣa" (*Anupreksha* 76).
> 'He alone is doer and experiencer of his status'
> (*Amritchandi Suri*, 10)

Again C.R. Jain writes,

> None can help the jiva in his troubles; he alone has to bear

his pain and suffering; friends, relatives, wife and children are powerless to combat suffering.[2]

In like manner Mrs. S. Stevenson writes:

> The soul is the maker and non-maker, and itself makes hapiness and misery, is its own friends and its own foe, decides its own condition good or evil, is its own river Vaitarani.[3]

Not only Jainism has no place for God in its system, but has advanced very powerful arguments against the existence of God. But in spite of its atheistic thinking Jaina temples are full of idols, specially of Lord Mahavira. How to account for this, specially when any Tirthankara is not there to grant any grace for the release of his devotee?

Yet the Jainas do great deal of *bhakti* towards the idol of Lord Mahavira, for according to them the mere sight of the Tirthankara serves as a reminder for them to lead a life in such a way as to win one's own release. Of course, the desire for release lies in dormant form in each man and the sight of the idol makes this desire for release awakened in the believers. Hence, an idol is a support in meditation and its sustaining aid. H. Zimner states this with a great insight in the following way:

> If one holds a red flower before a glass, the glass will be red; if one holds up a dark blue flower the glass will be dark blue. Just so, the mind is changed by the presence of the image. Contemplating the form of the passionless Lord in a Jain temple, the mind becomes filled automatically with a sentiment of renunciation. The mind straightway becomes purified. But given purity of mind, one is already on the way to final bliss.[4]

For this purpose a statue of Lord Bahubali at Shravanabelagola in Karnataka has been erected. It is 70 feet high and the *Mahabhiseka* (coronation) of this occurs every 12 years. This ceremony is attended by lakhs of Jaina devotees.

Thus, the Jaina view about God is most consistent with its beliefs and tenets. Guru and religious scripture are only guides towards winning its *nirvāṇa*. But this is not pure humanism, for the goal to be achieved is wholly spiritual. Further, this goal is not to be attained by improving human society and by undertaking ameliorative measures for secular benefits. Hence, Jainism may be called spiritual humanism, as different from the naturalism of John Dewey and the materialistic humanism of communism.

Man in Jainism

That which is eternal in man is his spirit or soul. Keeping to the philosophical principle of *identity-cum-difference* according to Jainism, the soul is both eternal and non-eternal. It is eternal with regard to its substance, but non-eternal with regard to its modes. Again, the soul is without any pain or sorrow in its eternal state of pristine glory, but suffers on account of its identification with body of its karmic matter. Hence, man is essentially a pure spirit, but is now in bondage due to his karman in countless past lives. As pure spirit, he is infinite knowledge, has unhindered intuition of all things, infinite power and faultless ethical conduct. But karman is a sticker and has covered his knowledge, perception, and ethical conduct. The worst thing is that the karmic matter and soul get so much mixed up that the embodied soul behaves like a material thing. This soul gets big or small according to the size of the body in which the spirit indwells. As such the jiva gets restricted on all sides. Hence by 'man' is understood an embodied spirit, an amalgam of karmic matter and soul. This man is caught up in the endless cycle of births and deaths, which really means that he is condemned to a life of suffering, evil and bondage.

This bondage is beginningless and karma is said to be the cause of this bondage. It is karma alone which darkens the soul, distorts his intellect and will and hurtles him down towards his destruction.

Thus, in the doctrine of man i.e., the embodied spirit two things have to be noted. Jainism, the most ancient non-Vedic religion, accepts the doctrine of karman and transmigration. *Karmavāda* is so deeply accepted by Jainism that its doctrine of liberation and enslavement is rooted in it. Karmas enslave a man and by working them out from the embodied spirit, man can become his former pure spirit of infinite knowledge and unfettered pure consciousness. Besides, man by his own effort by listening to the still small voice of his own imprisoned spirit, can remove every vestige of karmas. Thus bondage is through karma, and, liberation from bondage is through *nirjara* and other special spiritual exercises like *dhyānas*.

The important thing to realise is that even a good karma called *punya* (virtuous act) is also a binding force. All karmas forming *saṃskāras* have to be eradicated for winning one's *nirvāṇa* from bondage. Naturally *nirvāṇa* can be attained only by the monks. Laity (Shrāvakas) by following the *anuvrata* (milder way of observing pañca-Mahāvrata) can hope to get the opportunity of becoming monks in succeeding births. Shrāvakas, however, can follow trade or any skilful work without committing *hiṁsā* as far as possible. Utilizing plants for food is less harmful than animal-slaughter. The greater and lesser *hiṁsā* depends on the kind of organisms. A goat is five-sensed organism but a plant is one-sensed organism. Hence, taking away a plant's life is a lesser crime than killing a goat.

Karmas which conceal and distort the nature of soul may be classified into two, and, each of them can be further subscribed. This may be made clear through a table of Karman.

Karman

Ghatiya	*Aghatiya*
(Karmas that obscure the soul so much that they are difficult to be eradicated.)	(Karmas that do not soil the soul in an essential way).

GHATIYA KARMAS AND THEIR KINDS

I. *Jñānāvaraṇiya* which obscures five kinds of knowledge.
   (a) *Mati* which is sense knowledge of things present.
   (b) *Shruti* or scriptural knowledge.
   (c) *Avadhi* knowledge concerning distant things, ordinarily known as clairvoyance.
   (d) *Manah-prayāya* i.e., knowledge of the thought and feeling in other minds.

(e) *Kevala-jñāna* which is omniscience inherent in each individual.

II. *Darśanavaraṇiya* which distorts right attitude, conviction and faith.

III. *Mohanīya* which befogs right belief.

IV. *Antarāya* which obstructs charity, enjoyment and effective power.

Ghatiya Karmas are also of four kinds.

1. *Nāmāvarnīya* which is related to having bodies and their organs.
2. *Āyuh* which determines one's life-span.
3. *Gotra* which determines the family of one's birth.
4. *Vedanīya* which determines one's pleasure and pain.

Hence man under the influence of karma is in bondage and suffers from all kinds of disabilities. As long as karmas are not eradicated men will continue to suffer. Hence, karmas have to be totally and completely destroyed.

The Ultimate Destiny or Liberation

The inflow of karmas soils the soul. Naturally these karmas have to be eradicated. In general it means that fresh inflow of karmas (*āshravas*) has to be stopped, known as *Saṁvara.* Lastly, the past karmas have to be burnt out or eradicated through the process known as *nirjarā.* For achieving the stoppage of fresh karmas and eradication of past karmas psycho-physical discipline has to be adopted. Again, moral austerities have to be enforced. For stopping the inflow of fresh karmas, tapas has to be adopted and it also is supposed to consume the accumulation of past karmas. In like manner, *pañca-mahāvrata* known as *Satya, asteya, brahmacarya, aparigraha* and *ahiṁsā* has to be enforced strictly for the monks and with less rigour for the laity. For achieving mental control three *ratnas* (jewels) of right conduct and right (firm) faith and right (proper) knowledge have to be assiduously cultivated. But above all eight *dhyānas* and fourteen steps of *gaṇasthāna* have to be resorted for final deliverance, or, what may be called the attainment of the pristine state of a *Kevali,* characterized by Omniscience. In other words, present inflow of karmas can be stopped, and, past karmas can be eradicated by a rigid discipline of mind, body and speech.

Ratna-Traya: Right faith means trust in the Tirthankaras, one's Guru and the knowledge imparted by the Guru. It also means conviction of and a proper attitude to Jainism in general.

Right knowledge at the preparatory stage means the understanding of six dravyas, five astikayas, seven tattvas and nine padarthas (categories). Right conduct (*samyak caritra*) is the natural outcome of right faith and right knowledge. This also means strict observance of five vows (*pañca-mahāvrata*). Let us elaborate a little on *tapas* and pañca-mahāvrata for reaching one's ultimate destiny, according to Jainism.

The inflow of fresh karmas can be stopped and past karmas can be eradicated by *tapas*. This tapas (austerities) is wholly non-Vedic. This largely means 'the mortification of the body'. It may be external or internal. By *bāhya* (external) tapas is meant observing of fast, restricted begging of food and eating tasteless food. It also means standing in summer under mid-day sun, residing by the river side in winter and under a tree during rains. By internal tapas is meant doing penances for all acts of commission and omission. It also includes faith in elders, saints and scripture. But tapas has to be followed up in observing the five vows involved in *pañca-mahāvrata*.

Ahiṁsā (non-injury) is the most distinctive moral view in Jainism. Even in Buddhism it is not as strictly carried out as in Jainism. Killing (*hiṁsā*) means separating the body from the subtle body. It means also the inflicting of pain to any organism whatsoever. As the Jainas believe that all particles of matter are inhabited by souls, so they take great precautionary measures against destroying life in water, air and earth. They do not take food after sun-set for abstaining the killing of insects attracted by the lamp light. It is not only a negative precept, for it also means 'respect for life, whether in your person or in any living beings'.

However, kings and rulers do no wrong if they have to fight their battles in defending their countries and their welfare. Gandhiji maintained that *ahiṁsā* is a weapon which can be wielded only by the strong and not by the coward.

Satya does not require much elaboration. Here it means moral excellence. It has to be observed in thought, word and deed. One should speak out the truth, should speak to create pleasantness, but should refrain from talking unpleasant truth, as far as possible.

Asteya (non-stealing) means not appropriating a thing which does not belong to one e.g. a monk is not permitted to use an umbrella or a begging bowl of Sangha without the permission of the appropriate authority of the monastery. In others words, it means respecting the ownership of things not belonging to oneself.

Aparigraha (non-possession). A monk or nun renounces the world and possesses nothing which one can call as one's own. It also means non-attachment of worldly objects and things. Of course, a laity has to acquire means for his existence. Here it simply means honest living and avoidance of avarice. Gandhiji and before him Kabir have developed the idea of trusteeship. In other words, the people have to regard their wealth as Trust, and they have to be mere custodians of wealth in this life.

Brahmacarya (celibacy). It means abstinence from sexual pleasure. Hence, a monk or nun has not to marry and has not to commit adultery. It also means avoidance of fornication i.e., sexual life without marriage and without adultery i.e., prohibited [sex life with a married person. For example, Makkhali Gosala lived with a rich potter woman without marriage. Lord Mahavira considered this life of fornication as the violation of the vow of *brahmacarya*.

Guṇasthāna and Dhyānas

Through the fourteen steps of *guṇasthānas* and eight stages of Dhyānas a monk or a nun makes progress from this worldly life towards liberation and in the direction of right knowledge, faith and conduct. Ultimately the seeker ends in the realization of his pristine glory and omniscience.

The fourteen steps of guṇasthānas are:

1. Mithyādṛṣṭi; 2. Śasvādana Samyagdṛṣṭi (slight foretaste of right belief); 3. Samyag-Mithyādṛṣṭi (mixed right and false beliefs); 4. Avirata-Samyagdṛṣṭi (Sufficient insight into spiritual truth dawns). 5. *Deśavirata Samyagdṛṣṭi. 6. Pramatta-Samyata* much abstinence is achieved, but negligence has to be avoided.

7. *Āpramatta Saṁyata* (Here one gets into the foretaste of mokṣa). 8. *Apūrvakaraṇa* (Here sufficient discipline and right vision dawns. 9. *Anivṛtti-bādara-Samparāya* (gross passions are subdued, but subtle ones remain to be further controlled. 10. *Sukṣma—Samparāya*. Here unconscious attachment for rebirth continues to be operative. 11. *Upaśānta-Kaṣāya*. Here all passions are subdued. 12. *Kṣiṇa-Kaṣāya*. Here even subtle passions are annihilated, but omniscience not attained. 13. *Sayoga-Kevali-Guṇasthāna* (Omniscience achieved and the stage corresponds to that of *jivanmukta*. 14. *Ayoga-Kevali-Guṇasthāna*. Here all vibrations cease and the monk passes into omniscience, immediately on attaining this stage. Eight steps of dhyanas are complementary of Guṇasthānas. Dhyānas are really the form of Yogic practices of the Jainas. Here the orderly development of knowledge leading to omniscience has six stages:

1. *Mati* i.e., the acquisition of empirical knowledge.
2. *Shruti* i.e., Scriptural knowledge.
3. *Avadhi* i.e., knowledge of things beyond the range of sense-perception.
4. *Manahparyāya* is the knowledge of what is in the mind of others i.e., telepathy.
5. *Kevalijñāna* is the knowledge of things past, present and future.
6. *Nirvāṇa* i.e., the stage of complete omniscience.

These dhyānas have to start after some progress has already been made in guṇasthānas. Naturally without faith in a guru and his guidance, the *guṇasthānas* and *dhyānas* cannot be undertaken. These dhyānas have been subdivided into four Dharma Dhyānas and four Shukla Dhyānas. As a result of guṇasthānas and Dhyānas, the Jaina monk attains *nirvāṇa*. It is a positive state of painless perfection. It is an eternal state, but difficult to approach. Those who reach this stage are free from sorrows and who have put an end to the endless cycle of rebirths.

THE WORLD

According to Jainism, the world is eternal and real. Following the Jain principle of *identity-cum-difference*, the world is finite in its spatial dimension, but infinite in time and its modes. The world consists of *Ākāśa, Dharma, Adharma, Kāla* and *Pudgala.* Ākāśa, Dharma, Adharma have no parts. Thus *pudgala* is real matter which consists of atoms and molecules. Thus it is found both in atomic form and aggregate.

Even an atom is a substance and a substance is always found with attributes. Hence, atomic substances are those that persist through their changes. A substance has the three changes of *utpāda* (origination), *Vyaya* (going out of existence) and, *dhrauvya* (continuing in being). *Utpāda* and *Vyaya* in a thing refer to the difference (or changes), but *dhrauvya* refers to the aspect of identity by virtue of which a thing persists its changes.

Jainism is not interested in the improvement of this world order. It is surprising that Lord Mahavira's uncle was the head of the Republic of Vaishali, and, yet Lord Mahavira does not think of improving either the public or social life of the people. The point is that he himself had renounced the world and naturally he could not be anymore occupied with it. It was the period of self-conquest and not of the world-conquest. One lives in one's intellectual climate and weather, and, one can no more shake off one's intellectual atmosphere than one can live without one's shadow. After all it is neither a small achievement nor an unworthy end to have conquered one's passion and emotion. A *jin* is as much valuable as a scientist or a social reformer, or, many other valuable lives whom mankind adores.

However, as far as the world was thought of, according to Jainism, it was fully scientific. It maintained atomism which was the earliest theory of its kind in the world. *Dharma* has been used in the peculiar sense, i.e., that which makes motion possible, and, *Adharma* is that which accounts for rest. Time is that in which changes take place, and, Ākāṣa is that which serves as the receptacle of things.

Jainism, keeping to its doctrine of self-conquest and self-culture, does not advise its adherents to get involved in worldly pleasures. It taught respect for life, and, the greatest respect for man, the highest of organisms.

From the viewpoint of biology, the order of organisms in terms of the number of senses is thoroughly scientific. Most probably from the viewpoint of the evolution of senses in the organic world, the Jaina view is scientific. Before J.C. Bose showed to the world that plants have life, Jainism held this belief some twenty five hundred years ago.

Not only the view of Jainism, with regard to the world is scientific, it also keeps to the doctrine of compromise and in one sense goes even beyond Buddhism. According to Buddhism, everything is momentary and nothing is substantial. But the Jainas, in their doctrines of *anekāntavāda* and *syādvāda* maintain that things are both momentary and substantial. With regard to man, Jainism holds that the soul of man is eternal and substantial, but its body of karmic matter is non-eternal. Similarly, atoms constituting a thing are eternal, but their groupings are non-eternal.

But in spite of the fact that Jainism regards the world eternal and real, its advice is that one should not lose oneself in it.

The Problem of Evil or Suffering

The soul apart from the body in which it is encased is characterized by *ananta jñāna* (infinite knowledge), *ananta darshana* (infinite faith or intuition) and *ananta caritra* (pure conduct) and *ananta vīrya* (infinite energy). But man is an embodied spirit. Hence, it is fettered and restricted in its knowledge, perception, action and power. What more can be the evil for the infinite, omniscient and self-existent spirit? What could be the cause of this evil? Jainism offers no answer. Its purpose as that of Buddhism is purely therapeutic. It lays down ways and means for winning release from this state of unmixed evil. One thing is certain for Jainism. Karmas have befogged the intellect and darkened the soul. Karmas are sticking substance and they have completely covered the soul. These karmas keep on accumulating throughout the endless cycle of rebirths. If one ponders over the problem of evil posed by Jainism, then the release of the soul appears to be almost insoluble. However, the practical solution is possible.

From a realistic stand karmas are the real cause of one's bondage, suffering and evil. Man is restricted in his knowledge. Therefore, he makes mistakes. Because he lacks faith in the Tirthankaras, Scripture and his guru, so he does not undertake the task of winning his own release. He does not see that even a life of pleasure is simply his snare and a trap. Even a life of a deva in heaven is no way out of the tangle. The most important thing is that Karmic matter has to be eradicated. In explaining bondage or evil, Jainism refers to karmas as the real cause. Karmas dwarf the intellect and produce *avidyā*. Hence, it will be a mistake to suppose that *avidyā* is the fundamental reason of one's evil or suffering. Only Ramanuja, apart from Jainism, regards karmas as the cause of evil for man. But he also adds that karmas in association with *avidyā* lead to bondage of the jiva.

Jivas are many. So it means that there is a continuous influx of pure spirits into this world, leading to their bondage or suffering or evil. No pure spirit as *nitya-siddhas* can be the cause, nor of the siddhas or perfected soul can cause karmas. And there is no God. Hence, the jivas alone are the creators of the evil of bondage which they have brought about upon themselves. In like manner, there is no God to help the jivas out of their misfortune. Hence, man alone is the architect of his final destiny. He can either work up for his deliverance, or, remain in his sorry state of affairs. Man is his greatest friend and at the same time his greatest enemy. Thus man alone is responsible for his evil.

Hence, the existence of man in the world, in any walk of life is evil for Jainism, Buddhism and even for Shankarite advaitism. Perhaps Buddhism and Advaitism, specially in neo-Vedantism, there is some room for amelioration. Jainism is wholly negative with regard to the world. But by encouraging the Jaina laity for undertaking trade and industry, Jains are the richest people of India. Here actual life lived belies the theory.

Though the doctrine of evil in Jainism is most devastating, yet the path to put an end to evil is quite clear. The influx of Karmas has to be stopped and the accumulated Karmas of the past lives have to be totally eradicated. The stoppage of Karmas is known as *samvara* and its eradication is known as *nirjara*. These two go together. First step is to adopt the three jewels of right faith, right knowledge and right conduct (*Samyag-darshana-jñāna-cartiani mokṣamargah*). For the cultivation of right conduct *pañca-mahāvrata* has to be strictly followed. Lastly, for the removal of *jñānavaraniya* and *mohaniya* (i.e., covering of jñāna and passions) one has to take to *guṇasthāna* and *dhyānas*.

The removal of all karmas is a difficult thing. But the greatest achievement requires our utmost effort.

Life After Death

Two things may happen to a man after death. If a person has practised *tapas* (austerities), *pañca-mahāvrata* (five vows), *dhyānas* and *guṇasthānas* under a guru, then he may attain the pristine glory of Omniscience. He becomes immortal and no more enters into the cycle of rebirths. But a vast majority of jivas have to transmigrate from one birth into another, in an endless chain. The Jainas were the first to have maintained the doctrine of *karma-saṃsāra-jñāna-mukti*. They have made a detailed classification of karmas, leading to the rebirths of a jiva either in a higher or lower rebirths. There are karmas that determine specific body and their organs, age, family and pleasure pain in next lives. There is no way out of the rigour of *Karmavāda,* except by the path of liberation. We have already made reference to this path. The important thing to repeat and emphasize is that man alone can work out his liberation through his own efforts. There is no possibility of making prayers to any supernatural agency for one's release.

Anekāntavāda and Saptabhaṅgi Naya

Buddhism might have adopted a middle path in its theory and practice. But Jainism has worked out a world-view of compromise in relation to the conflicting views. At least there were at least 62 views regarding the world, soul and God at the time of Lord Mahavira and he resorted to *anekāntavāda* and *syādvāda* with a view to striking out a compromise between them.

According to Jainism, reality is multifaceted (anekāntavāda, many ends or adages, *aneka antas*) and *naya* means many views from many perspectives. What is true from one perspective need not be true from another. *Syāt* simply means 'from a certain point of view and in a certain sense'. Keeping this meaning of 'syāt', seven-fold predication is said to be exhaustively possible.

1. In a certain sense and view, the jar *is* (syadasti ghatah).
2. In a certain sense, the jar *is not* (*Syannasti ghatah*).
3. In a certain sense, the jar *is* and *is not*.
4. In a certain sense, the jar is indescribable.
5. In a certain sense, the jar *is* and is indescribable.
6. In a certain sense, the jar *is* and is not indescribable.
7. In a certain sense the jar is and is not and is indescribable.

For example, a jar is in the room on a table at 9.30 A.M., and yet may not be there at 10 A.M. Again it is and is not between 9-10 A.M. If a man is forced to say whether it was between 9-10 A.M., then he would keep silent. In this way the Jainas maintain seven-fold predication going beyond the *catuṣ-koṭi* of the *ajivikas*.

By combining the *Anekāntavāda* with the principle of identity-cum-difference, Lord Mahavira could wriggle out of the perplexing views of the 62 heterodox schools of his time. For example,

1. The Soul aspect of a jiva is eternal.
2. Its modes in terms of its karmic material are non-eternal.
3. A jiva is both eternal and non-eternal, if we take an embodied jiva.
4. If it is asked to declare it either eternal or non-eternal, then like Lord Buddha one has to say it indescribable or call it is *avyākṛta*.
5. Thus the soul *is* and is indescribable.
6. The Soul is and is not indescribable, if a *Mukṭa* is in view.
7. The Soul is and is not and is indescribable by combining (4), (5) and (6).

The Monk and the Laity

Buddhism did not take care of instructing the laity, with the result that a large number of Buddhists till now have remained at a very low level of religious beliefs. However, unlike Buddhism, Jainism has kept close to the laity and laid certain religious vows for them to observe. Both the monk and the laity have to maintain the three jewels of right faith, right beliefs and right conduct. Both of them have to observe *pañca*-mahāvrata of satya, asteya (non-stealing), *ahiṁsā* (non-violence), *brahmacarya* and *aparigraha* (non-attachment). The difference between the monk and the laity is that a monk has to observe these vows with far greater rigour than a laity. For example, a monk has to abstain from sex in word, deed and speech. A laity can become a house-holder by marrying. He has only to desist from adultery and fornication. The observance of a vow in a lesser degree is also known as *anuvrata* in relation to *mahāvrata* of a monk.

But certain other restrictions have to be maintained even by the laity. For example, a laity is discouraged from farming his land for fear of destroying many lives in the soil. In modern times he can hardly help in destroying the pests if he has to introduce green revolution in his farm. Similarly, a householder has to observe certain vows for his self-discipline e.g., setting certain periods per day for meditation on the teachings of Jainism, Guru and Tirthankaras. He may induce himself to maintain silence for himself on certain days in the week or month. Everyday, a laity has to meditate every morning.

A monk is a renunciate and he has to practise tapas, accept three jewels of his faith, observe mahāvratas with rigour and at last has to enter dhyānas and progress along the fourteen steps of *Guṇasthānas*.

Sects

There are two sects called Digambaras and Svetambaras. Digambaras live naked as Lord Mahavira was. They appear to be older of the two. Svetambaras put on clothes and cover their mouth with a piece of cloth for fear of injuring insects. Both of them do not differ essentially in their beliefs and practices. For practical reasons, the Digambaras do not admit women as nuns. But Svetambaras have no objection against women in accepting them as nuns.

The two sects differ with regard to their beliefs relating to their religious Scripture. The Svetambaras accept the extant Aṅgas, Upaṅgas and other canonical works as genuine whilst the Digambaras hold that original works have been lost. The Digambaras have a number of collections in their custody, but they are reluctant to make them public. On the whole, the Jainas have preserved a good deal of literary works of India.

It seems almost unbelievable that Jainism without holding beliefs in supernatural agencies should have indulged in having idols. In about the sixteenth century, Lonkashaha protested against image worship. According to him image-worship is against Jaina religion. He established a sect called Sthanakavasi in Western India. In about 1817 Acharya Bhikanji Maharaja organised *Terapantha* which is really a sub-sect of Sthanakavasi sampradaya.

References

1. J.L. Jaini, *Outlines of Jainism*, pp. 80-81.
2. C.R. Jain, *The Practical Path*, p. 53.
3. Mrs. S. Stevenson, *The Heart of Jainism*, p. 192.
4. H. Zimmer, *Philosophies of India*, p. 216.

Chapter IX

SIKHISM

Introduction

Sikhism took its rise in the Punjab in the 15th Century and at present it has assumed great importance on the Indian scene. Sikhism is Hinduistic in the sense that it accepts the four-fold principles of *Karma-Saṃsāra-Jñāna-Mukti*. It also adopts a general Hindu view of life, poetry and music.

Sikhism was born at a time when India was in a state of political upheaval, social instability and religious ritualism, externalism without much inner illumination and spiritual experience in depth. Sikhism at the hands of the first Guru, named, Nanak was not primarily a political movement. From the social point of view it was founded on the rejection of caste and it promoted egalitarianism. Naturally it did not support untouchability. Sikhism of Guru Nanak was essentially a religious reformist movement in the direction of Saint poets of India. Guru Granth Sahib the sacred book of the Sikhs contains four poems of Trilochan, 62 of Namadeva and 240 Sakhis and 227 padas of Kabir. Most of the characteristic teachings of Sikhism like monotheism, crusade against idolatry and caste, externalism (bāhyāchāra), ritualism could be easily traced to these saint poets, specially Kabir. Kabir appears to be a contemporary of Guru Nanak.

Again, in the beginning, terms like Sikh, Saint, Sadhu, Bhakta and Sevak were used in the same sense. However, now, the term 'Guru' is to be used for the first ten Gurus and for Adi Granth Sahib. All poets whose lines have been included in Adi Granth Sahib are called 'Saint'. But 'Guru' is not to be called 'Saint'. However, one can note that Guru Nanak was greatly influenced by Saint Kabir.

'Sikh' is really derived from the word '*Śiṣya*'. Hence, Sikhism is the religion of ten Gurus and their followers Śiṣyas.

A Sikh is one who is willing to lay down his life for the sake of his Guru.

Ten Gurus[1]

Guru Nanak was the real founder of Sikhism. He was born in 1469 in a village called Talwandi, some fifty miles south-west of Lahore. It is now in Pakistan and has been named Nankana Sahib. True, Sikhism of Guru Nanak was largely a religious and spiritual movement, but even Guru Nanak advised his followers to resist evil 'even to the point of sacrifice and martyrdom'. Later on Guru Hargobind Singh girded on two swords '*miri*' (to defend and pursue political end) and '*piri*' (for safeguarding spiritual pursuit). But it was the last Guru Gobind Singh who infused martial spirit into his Sikh followers called 'Khalsa' and who were to be called 'Singh' (lion). The new order of Khalsa had to fight in defence of their faith, home and hearth and their honour.

1. Guru Nanak (1469-1539).
2. Guru Angad (1504-1552). He introduced Gurumukhi script.
3. Guru Amar Das (1479-1574).
4. Guru Ram Das (1534-1581).
5. Guru Arjan Dev (1563-1606).
   Guru Arjan Dev built a temple 'Hari Mandir' which developed into Golden Temple in the 19th Century through the munificence of Maharaja Ranjit Singh. He also prepared what ultimately took the form of Adi Granth Sahib in 1604.
6. Guru Hargobind (1595-1644). He assumed two swords *Piri* and *Miri* and sat on a seat and called it Akal-Takht. 'Miri' stands for earthly power, and, 'Piri' stands for spiritual power. Thus a Guru is a soldier and a saint.
7. Guru Hari Rai (1630-1661).
8. Guru Hari Krishan (1656-1664).
9. Guru Teg Bahadur (1621-1674).
10. Guru Gobind Singh (1666-1708).

A short reference to Guru Gobind Singh is necessary, for, he changed the whole tenor of life of the Sikhs. He was born at Patna, and, was only nine years old when he was called to assume the sacred trust of being a Guru. Sikhs always had to struggle against the Muslim rulers and there is little doubt that Sikhs were turned into incomparable soldiers as a result of that struggle. However, it was the cruel assasination of the bold but highly virtuous Guru Teg Bahadur that created a sense of revolt against the Muslim rulers in the mind of the Sikhs. After all Guru Teg Bahadur died to safeguard the honour of Sikhism.

Guru Gobind Singh thought and meditated over the matter deeply. His sons too were all killed by Wazir Khan. Naturally the question was 'Do or Die'. On Baisakhi day in 1699 Sikhs had assembled, as usual in a large number. He announced in the assembly that he needed five heads as offerings to the Guru. Sword in hand, with unflinching courage he waited for the response. First one and then other four also offered themselves for the supreme sacrifice. Kabir writes,

Sir rākhe sir jāt hai, Sir Kāte Sir hoe
(He who would cling to his life would lose it, and he who would sacrifice it would gain.)

A new code was announced with emphasis on moral excellence, heroism and strict discipline. In a bowl sweet drink was prepared and from that one bowl all of them were made to drink symbolising brotherhood within the rank and casteless-ness and absolute equality. They all were to bear the name of 'Singh' (lion) and they were given five vows to observe. These five vows known as pañca-Kakara i.e., *Kesh* (keeping of long hair), *Kaṛā* (iron bracelet), *Kachh* (under drawers), *Kaṅghā* (comb) and *Kirpāṇ* (Sword). The five heads offered to the Guru were known as *pañj pyāre*. They are remembered even now in the daily prayers of the Sikhs. These Sikhs with five K's are now known as Khalsa (the pure).

These vows of strict discipline and *pañca-Kakara* have infused new militancy and a close-knit brotherhood. In addition to this, Guru Gobind Singh abolished the succession of personal Guruship. Adi Granth Sahib was to serve as Guru. Its *Bāni* would serve as the guide of the holy assembly. Further, he gave this injunction that wherever five Sikhs with pure heart would gather together, he would be present in their midst for their guidance in spirit. Thus, Guru Gobind Singh invested Guru Granth Sahib with spiritual power, and, Panth with temporal sovereignty.

Guru Granth Sahib

What the Bible is to the Christians, the Quoran to the Muslims, the Veda to the Brahmins, Guru Granth Sahib is for the Sikhs. It contains *Bāni* which stands on the level of 'the Word' of the Christian and of the followers of Shabda Brahma and of the Śaivites. Guru Nank himself had composed a number of songs, the best of them may be named *Japji*, *Asā-di-vār*, *Rahi-rāsa Patti*, *Dakani Oṃkāra*, *Siddha Goṣthi* and *Bārā Māh.* Other Gurus after Guru Nanak have also added their compositions. Guru Granth Sahib was composed in 1604 by Guru Arjan Dev who was assisted by the great devotee Bhai Gurdas. It was written in Gurmukhi Script so that the Sikhs may remain Guru-centred. Guru Granth Sahib includes not only the compositions of Gurus but also of many Saint poets. It includes verses of Ramanand, Jaideva, Namadeva, Trilochan, Veni, Dhanna, Pipa, Sain, Kabir, Rai Das, Shaikh Bhikhaji, Sadhna, Surdas, Poona Nane and of Muslim Sufis. However, the compositions of Kabir are far more numerous than of any other non-Sikh composers. 243-245 *Sakhis* and 227 padas of Kabir have been included in Guru Granth Sahib.[2] This shows the great esteem in which Kabir was held by Sikh Gurus. Kabir was a non-Vedic Hindu influenced by Gorakhnath and some Buddhist poets. Hence, much of Sikhism has to be understood and interpreted in terms of Saints' religious philosophy. However, Sikhism in course of its historical development has to be understood as an independent religion like Jainism and Buddhism. But it is an Indian religion and wholly embedded in the culture and tradition of India, more non-Vedic than Vedic.

Basic Features of Sikhism

Sikhism is wholly an Indian religion in the sense that its founders were all of Indian origin. Secondly, its religious scripture and teachings are wholly Hindu and hardly Muslim. With these standpoints we can submit the following points as the outstanding features of Sikhism which distinguish it from any prophetic religion.

1. Sikhism fully subscribes to the fourfold principles of Karma-Saṁsāra-jñāna-Mukti (*Japuji* XX, XXV). These principles are the differentiating features of any form of Hinduism, at the present time.

2. Sikhism is marked out as a Guru-centred religion much more than any other Indian tradition. True, Guru is given a place of great importance in Nyāya, Advaitism, Nathism and Kabir panth, but the Guru is held in the highest esteem in Sikhism. Even God is called *Wahe guru.* The script of Guru Granth Sahib is called Gurmukhi because it is calculated to make the Sikhs God-ward instead of becoming self or ego-centred (manmukh). In the last resort Adi Granth Sahib is now known as 'Guru' i.e., a spiritual guide of the whole community (*saṅgat*).

3. There is the vow of five K's i.e., keeping of long hair (of head and face), iron-bracelets (Kaṛā), *Kachh* (under drawers), comb (*Kaṅghā*) and *Kripāṇ* (Sword). In one sense, they are merely external observances, but in another respect they are the vows of self-discipline, martial spirit, brotherhood and submission to the Guru. These five K's not only mark out the Sikhs from the Hindus but from all other people of the earth.

4. Unlike any other form of Hinduism, it enjoins upon the Sikhs to fight against social injustice and in defence of one's faith. Though it appears to have some resemblance with the Muslim doctrine of *Jehād,* yet it appears to have arisen among the Sikhs as a result of religious persecution and social injustice in the form of *jizya.* Even the first guru, Guru Nanak had advised his followers to fight against social evils. Guru Hargobind wielded the two swords of *mīrī* and *pīrī.* But it was Guru Gobind Singh who infused the martial spirit into the Sikhs in defence of one's faith. Hence, one of the salient features of Sikhism is that there is a fusion of *bhakti* and *Śakti,* and Khālsā is a symbol of a saint soldier.

5. Sikhism teaches strict monotheism. The highest entity is both non-personal and attributeless and personal. In the non-attributed form it is called One-Oṃkara of *nirākshara,* and, in the attributed form He is the creator, sustainer and destroyer

of the world. For His devotees He is *dayālu* (kind) and Kripālu (compassionate).

God as both manifest and unmanifest is in accordance with Indian tradition, but is most marked in Dadu and Rai Das, the Saint poets of medieval India. To some extent even Namadeva admits the worship of Paurānic deities, though his deity is essentially without attributes.

6. In consonance with strict monotheism, Sikhism does not admit *avatāravāda* (the doctrine of incarnation) and does not believe that there can be any first and last or special prophet of God. But an earnest seeker can obtain the light divine and can be said to be a realized soul. Such a person can be a Guru, but he is not an object of worship, but only of veneration.

The refutation of *avatāravāda* is found most pronounced in Kabir by whom Guru Nanak was certainly influenced. By the way this rejection of *avatāravāda* shows that it could have no relationship with Christianity, and, the rejection of any special emissary of God differentiates Sikhism from Islam.

7. But Sikhism admits that there is only One God *ek-Oṃkāra* (unmanifest) and also *Oṁkāra* (in manifest form) with an infinite number of attributes. He can be variously named as *Wāhe guru*, *Kartar* (creator), *Akal* (eternal), *Satt-nāma* (the holy name). He is also known as *Allah*, *Khudā*, *Karim* (benevolent), *rahim* (merciful), Sahib (Lord). The same Lord may be variously named and worshipped in different languages.

This is also a strongly marked feature of Kabir's teachings. On the basis of this Kabir has tried to unify the Muslim and Hindu differences.

8. Sikhism is against caste, idolatry, ritualism and external observances.

These features are found in most Saint poets, but specially in Kabir.

9. Sikhism teaches that *Māyā* is the creative manifestation of God, but is also the source of five traditional evils in man, namely, *Kāma* (passion), *Krodh* (anger), *lobha* (greed), *moha* (infatuation) and *ahaṁkāra* (egoity). These can be removed through prayer, meditation and social service.

Kabir also teaches that *Māyā* is the power of God, called

Raghunath, and, that it is a great enchanting power which leads to man's spiritual fall.

10. *Nāma-sumirana* (constant muttering) of God's name with complete surrender to him has been emphasized by Guru Nanak. This is a powerful means of winning the Grace of God.

Kabir too takes recourse to *nāma-sumirana*, but it was Namadeva who dwelt upon this method of meditation. We must not ignore the fact that Sikhism is also known as *sant-mat*. Hence, it is but natural that it should have been influenced by Saint poets.

11. Sikhism prescribes *bhakti* for gaining release and this is also a strong feature of Saint poets like Dadu, Rai Das and Kabir.

12. Guru Nanak does not recommend *sannyāsa* as a means of *mukti*. He himself was a house-holder and considers the life of a house-holder as very important in society.

13. Like Kabir (Sakhi 31.7-9; Pada 103 of Kabira Granthavali), Sikhism is beyond both Hinduism (Vedic) and Islam. Sikhism is no doubt an Indian religion and embedded in Hindu culture and world-view but is an independent religion.

14. But Sikhism does not teach that either Hinduism or Islam is wrong. It teaches both Hindus and Muslims to practise their own faiths with a view to strict moral life and social service, without caring much for rituals and external observances. In this sense it was a reformist religion.

15. Sikhism favours local language and its script is gurmukhi, which is also its distinctive feature.

God in Sikhism

Sikhism has arisen from the devout hearts of Ten Gurus. They were not philosophers. They have set down what they could experience about the Supreme Reality. Their language has been shaped by the Saint poets and mystics of the medieval times.

Sikhism teaches strict monotheism. There is only One God. But he can be conceived both as unattributed and attributed. In the unattributed form He is called *Ek-Oṁkāra*, and, in the attributed form, He is called *Oṁkāra*. It is useless to seek any philosophical concept to explain the two aspects of God.

Nirguna our saguna ek
Saguna nirguna thapai nao,
Duha mili ekai tino thao—(Guru Granth Sahib).

In reality nirguṇa and saguṇa (attributed) Brahma are one and the same. In order to escape from idolatry, Guru Nanak talks of God as *nirañjana, nirakshara*, beyond human understanding.* The famous lines from the mūla mantra with which the Granth Sahib begins:

There is one God, Eternal Truth in his Name;
Maker of all things, Fearing nothing and enmity with none.
Timeless is His Image; Not begotten, Being of His own Being,
By the grace of the Guru made to me.
This nirguṇa Brahma can be attained only through.

Samādhi. In the famous three jewels of advaitism *Shravaṇa, manana* and *nididhyāsana*, Guru Nanak enjoins upon his followers *suniyai* (listening to the holy words), *mannai* (pondering over the truths heard) and *dhyāna* (meditation over the truth).

But the Supreme Reality has also been called the maker or creator. Hence, He is endowed with will and intellect. Therefore, *Pārabrahma* is also *Oṁkāra*, Saguṇa Brahma or Ishvara. Thus, the same supreme reality is both formless and with form. As Ishvara, He becomes an object of worship and devotion. In this aspect He is known as kind, benevolent (*dayālu* and *kripālu*), and as formless He is called *Saṭt-nāma, nirākshara, akāla* (eternal).

Lord as an object of devotion is invested with *māyā* which is the manifesting and creative power of God. This is exactly what Kabir takes *māyā* to be. But this māyā for Guru Nanak conceals the real nature of God, and, man under the influence of māyā becomes a victim of the five evils known in Indian thought as *Kāma* (lust), *Krodha* (anger, violence), *lobha* (greed),

* At the very beginning of Japuji, Guru Nanak describes the One God as immortal, unborn, self-existent. He is also stated to be formless in Japuji XVI-XXI. Again, He is said to be primal, the pure, without beginning, the indescribable and the same from age to age (XXVII-XXXI).

moha (infatuation or attachment to worldly objects) and *ahaṁkāra* (egoity, pride and self-seeking). This is really the enslavement of man and his bondage from which he is to be freed. Otherwise he will be in the endless chain of miserable rebirths. As will be detailed later, man can free himself only with the grace of God and for this he has to engage himself in prayer, meditation and selfless service to mankind.

Along with this doctrine of God there is also a negative side. Though God is creator, kind and benevolent, yet He does not incarnate Himself in what is known as *avatāra*. This is a doctrine which was held by Kabir in a very special way (*Bijak, Shabda* 8, 45).* In the same way, Sikhism does not maintain that there are special or exclusive prophets of God. Hence, Sikhism maintains strict monotheism by indirectly criticizing Islam and almost directly Christianity and Paurānic Hinduism.

Guru Nanak calls Saguṇa Brahma, the object of worship and devotion by various names of *Kartār* (creator), *Akāl* (eternal) *Satt-nāma* (holy name). *Wahe guru* also was used in post-Nanak literature. Guru Nanak has also used the name of Allah, Khuda, *paravardigār* (the cherisher) and Sahib (Lord). He has also used the various names of God, used in Paurānic bhakti like Rama, Gopala, Murari, Narayana, Madhava. Why has Guru Nanak used so many appellations concerning God.

The meaning is obvious. Sikhism seeks to spread its message to all adherents of different faiths, with a view to reconciling them and also with a view to deepening their faiths in the interest of strict moral rectitude and service to all mankind. Keshava-Karim, Allah-Ishvara, Rama-Rahim are but different names of the same entity which is both formless and with form.

> The Guru of Gurus is but one, though He has various forms. Hence, 'The Guru is Shiv; the Guru is Viṣṇu and Brahma; the Guru is Parbati, Lakshami, and Saraswati.

Thus difference is superficial and underlying reality in all reli-

---

* *Kabir Granthavali*, pada 6, 335; Sakhi 33.11; Bijak Kabirdas Mula, Shabda 8; Ramaini 54, 75. Guru Nanak was influenced by Kabir not only in the denunciation of *avatāravāda*, but also in his tirade against religious formalism and externalism, casteism and idolatry.

gions is deeper and far more fundamental. Why quarrel and fight amongst ourselves over names?

By pointing out the underlying reality which undergirds all names and forms of religions, Guru Nanak makes a point against ritualism and external observances that divide one man from another. Guru Nanak appeals to the inner depth in the real seeker after God, and, here Rama and Rahim are one and the same reality.

Again, Guru Nanak does not favour *sannyāsa*. He commends himself to the life of a house-holder who works hard for his honest living and makes sacrifices for the needy.

Thus, a Sikh house-holder is expected to observe *Kirt Karnā, wand chaknā, nām japnā*' (hard honest work, sharing the wealth with others and reciting the name of God). Prof. Gurucharan Singh Talib quotes the following lines from Guru Nanak:

He whose livelihood is earned through work,
And part given away in Charity—
Such one, Nanak, truly knows the way to God.[3]

The charitable distribution of food called *laṅgar* was introduced by Guru Nanak, and, every Sikh is expected now to contribute towards it. Is it any wonder now that Sikhs are not only excellent soldiers, but are also excellent farmers, successful businessmen and industrialists-entrepreneur?

Lastly, as personal God, He is the Saviour of His seekers. If we sincerely seek Him, then by bestowing His Grace the Lord frees his devotees from the shackles of *Māyā*. The highest end of man is God-realization, whether through Samādhi or through *bhakti*.

The Concept of Man in Sikhism

Man no doubt is an embodied soul. Not the body, but the soul is immortal.

This conscious soul dieth not,
The precious jewel, for which men go on pilgrimages.
Dwelleth within the heart.[4]

This soul, apart from the body is said to be a spark from the burning light of God. At times the embodied soul, called man has been compared to the water of the ocean in a glass. This glass is only the container, but the water is of the same nature as the ocean. This will remind one of the Vedantic metaphor of *ghaṭākāsha* (i.e., ether enclosed in a jar). Unless this enclosure of the body is destroyed, the water cannot mix with the water of the ocean. Unfortunately man does everything for the continuance of this body, and, keeps on transmigrating in endless rebirths of countless sufferings. Here Sikhism shares the Indian thought that life is suffering, and, unless liberation is won, man will keep on transmigrating in endless rebirths, attended with suffering. But the question is, why does man fall into this countless rebirths?

In one sense, it is the *līlā* of God. Because of His spontaneous creative power called *Māyā*, the world has come into being. This māyā, however, conceals the real nature of God. Through this concealment man falls into five evils of *kāma* (lust), *krodha* (anger, violence), *lobha* (avarice, greed), *Moha* (infatuation, attachment to worldly pleasures) and *ahaṁkāra* (pride, selfishness). As long as these five evils are not removed, man will continue to suffer in the endless circle of countless rebirths.*

Man thus has twofold nature. Because of the pure spirit of God within him, there is a tendency within him to move Godward (Gurumukh). But there is also the tendency to continue in worldly pleasure. This would remind one of the Buddhist teaching about *tṛṣṇā* and *bhāva* (the desire, to be born for the worldly enjoyment). This desire for the worldly pleasure has been called in Sikhism *manamukh* i.e., turning one's mind towards his selfish interest and pleasure. What is the remedy? Remedy lies in the surrender of one's will to the will of God. But who is responsible for human *Haumai* i.e., the state of bondage of the soul by the five evils of lust, greed, attachment, anger and egoity.

True, there is the enthralling māyā that conceals the true nature of God and the real duty of man towards God. But man has been endowed with reason, and, also a tendency within him to move Godward. If man does not use his reason for knowing

* Macauliffe, I, LXVIII-LXIX.

his ultimate end of realizing God, then he is responsible for his further continuance of misery in endless rebirths. Thus *Haumai* is the state of rebellion against God, and, separation from His being. This means turning away from divine presence for the greater allowance of beastly pleasure. But human existence is a very precious opportunity of turning towards God and winning one's release from endless sufferings in countless rebirths. Only in this life can one win his mukti.* This human birth is a rare good fortune in the wheel of transmigration and is not likely to happen again in this ceaseless turnings of the wheel.

True, this body is the source of enchantment, but then it has not to be neglected or looked upon with contempt. The body has to be used in the service of man and God. This body is a temple of God and only by having a sanctified life can one have a knowledge of God and his duty to mankind.

In the body God is present,
The body is His temple,
In the body is the place of pilgrimage,
Of which I am the pilgrim.[5]

This will remind one of the Biblical teaching which requires man to offer himself to God as 'His holy temple'. This insistence of Sikhism to treat one's body as the temple of God is a new departure in Indian religious thought, as also his insistence to serve humanity will also be regarded as a very healthy religious tradition. It is in keeping with the doctrine of *Sarvamukti* of Vedantins and of the Bodhisattvas. This has been taken up further by Ramakrishna Ashrama. To keep one's body as the temple of God, a Sikh has to resort to prayer, meditation and concentration on God in both aspects as attributed and ultimately as unattributed.

Sikhism further maintains the equality of all men, brotherhood of the Sikhs and the rejection of caste.

The World

M.A. Macauliffe** has presented the views of Guru Nanak which

* Macauliffe, Vol. 6, p. 311.

** Max Arthur Macauliffe, *The Sikh Religion*, Vol. I pp. 164-167. That He has no caste is repeated several times.

strongly has the flavour of the Ṛgvedic (X. 90, 121, 129) hymns. The story of creation given by Guru Nanak has also a touch of the Quoranic doctrine of creation of the world.

> He fixed the heavens without pillars by the utterance of a word,
> Having created the sun and moon, He infused His light into them.
> Thou has no father or mother; who begot Thee?
> Thou art devoid of all form, outline, or caste.

According to this account at the beginning there was utter darkness. There was neither the earth nor the sky, neither the day nor night. God remained in His own being. Then He created the world and entered into it,[6] as is also given in the Upanishads.[7] God sustains the world. Mere command of God has brought the world into being.

If we emphasize 'God said and there was the world', then the mere word of God may be understood to have created the world out of *nothing*. But at another place Guru Nanak has mentioned that God has created the world, not out of four, but five elements. The whole world is a wonderful creation of God and shows His power and glory. This will strongly remind one of Psalm 19 singing the glory of creation.

> How clearly the sky reveals God's glory!
> How plainly it shows what he has done
> ... ...
> No speech or words are used,
> No sound is heard,
> Yet their voice goes out to all the world.

Now Guru Nanak says that the ignorant or foolish people do not heed the voice of God, revealed in His creation. But Sat-Guru teaches that God is omnipresent and He indwells in everybody and in everything.[8] Those who turn to God, find the world to be the wonderful creation of the Lord and His *līlā* (sports). This knowledge of the dependence of the world on God and His *līla* fills the devotee with admiration and praise for the Lord and helps his devotion to Him.

True, the world has no reality of its own. But knowing this world as dependent on and the creation of God, the world has to be taken seriously. This is the field of his duties and by performing them a devotee can please God and win his release by His Grace from endless transmigration.[9] Hence, every Sikh has to fulfil his duty, largely as a house-holder. Out of 10 Gurus 9 were house-holders. Thus the world is real and is the creation of God so that man in bondage may win his release.[10] One should notice that according to Sikhism only in this human existence on earth can one win his release. Hence the world is real and the human existence is also very precious.

This view in Sikhism distinguishes it from advaitism where the world is said to be illusory. The world is real because God has created the world and He indwells in it. How can it be unreal or in any way slighted? If one is Godward, then he takes the world as real and takes his opportunity to work out his release by doing his duties in this real world very seriously.

> True, service to God and devotion to Him are means of release, but knowing the world and society as real, Guru Gobind Singh has emphasized *puruṣakāra* (self-effort) and social service, known as (*Muktināma*).
>
> O Sikhs, borrow not, but if you are compelled to borrow, faithfully restore the debt. Speak not falsely and associate not with the untruthful. Associating with holy men practise truth, love truth, and clasp it to your hearts. Live by honest labour and deceive no one . . . . Covet not money offered for religious purposes . . . . He who distributeth sacred food should do so in equal quantities, whether the recipients be high or low, old or young . . . . Abandon at once the company of Brahmanas and Mullas who cheat men out of their wealth,...

Again, 'Let him contribute a tenth part of his earnings for religious purposes'.[11]

The Problem of Suffering

Sikhism admits that the world is a creation and God is *Kartār* (creator). He has created the world because of the creative power of māyā. This māyā conceals the real nature of God, and, as a result of this ignorance man becomes *manamukhi* and falls into the five evils of lust, anger, infatuation, greed and egoity. Is God, then responsible for the evil or suffering of man in endless transmigration. No doubt a creator God is beset with this difficulty. Whether God creates out of nothing, or with the five elements, because of His līlā in the form of His māyā He becomes responsible at least in part for the evil and suffering of man. In Zoroastrianism, it has been pointed out that God can create only finite things because it is the very meaning of things created. And, finitude cannot but be invested with imperfection which in the domain of creatures with powers of discrimination can be interpreted as māyā, ignorance, limitations (as in Jainism) and suffering (moral and philosophical). But God has also given reason to man and his capacity for knowing his ultimate end or divine purpose. That purpose is that man should surrender his will to the will of God.

> Our wills are ours, but they are to make them thine.

God has made man finite—infinite, *manamukh* (wordly) and Gurumukh (Godward). Man is also endowed with free will and reason, either to move in the direction of God-realization or to lose himself in endless transmigration fraught with endless sufferings. Thus, man is now responsible for his moral fall and sufferings. But there is also a way out of sufferings.

If one remains immersed in the enjoyment of the world, then the bondage of ignorance continues. However, if one gains knowledge about the world and moves Godward then there is the prospect of release. This has been illustrated by the metaphor of two birds.

> Of these two, the one eats sweet fruit;
> The other looks on without eating (*Muṇḍka* 3.1; *Śveṭ*: 4.6).

Hence, man in a sense now is his own architect of the soul, as Jainism would say.

True, *haumai* i.e., living in and enjoying the world cannot be forever allowed. God sends sufferings so that man may turn Godward. Thus suffering can be also good in disguise.

This worldly existence of man is the result of his past karmas and God is not responsible for his worldly existence. But quite naturally good karmas give rise to better status and opportunity to man. But there are pathways to God-realization to which we may turn now.

Pathways to God-Realization

There is one eternal God, both attributed and unattributed. Unattributed God is the same as *Nirguṇa Brahma.* He can be realized by means of constant concentration and *Samādhi.* Like Shaṅkara, Guru Nanak recommends *Suniyai* (*Shravana*, listening to the lesson given by a Guru), *Mannai* (*Manana*, pondering over the truth given by the Guru), and *dhyāna* (*nididhyāsana* i.e., realization through deep meditation). But this is a difficult path attended with many risks. Guru Nanak also refers to Haṭhayoga where there is the discipline of the body and the control of breath. But this path is bogged down in the marsh of *ṛiddhi-siddhi* (attainments of powers) and is likely to lead to distorted path of *pañcamakāra* of the perverts.* Against this Guru Nanak recommended the path called *Sahaj* (easy and in accordance with the nature of man). This is a path of prayer, meditation or bhakti leading to the Grace of God.

> Make continence thy furnace, resignation thy goldsmith
> Understanding thy anvil, divine knowledge thy tools,
> ... ...
> Divine love thy crucible, and melt God's name therein,
> In such a true mint the Word shall be coined,
> This is the practice of those on whom God looketh with an eye of favour.**

Thus, the practical approach for God-realization means devotion to Ishvara or Brahman with attributes. Whether one wants to realize *nirguṇa* or Saguṇa Brahma, the guidance and instruction of a Guru is absolutely necessary. Of the Guru himself

* Guru Nanak was a widely travelled man and his experiences about the Kapālikas of Assam had filled him with repugnance for the path of haṭha-yoga.

**Japuji (XXXVIII).

is a man who has realized God, and is called a sat-Guru. This is also in keeping with advaitism where a Guru is said to be indispensable and this guru himself should be a *jivanmukta* (liberated in this life) and *Brahmajñāni*. According to Guru Nanak, in a true guru God has installed His own spirit, and through him the ways of God are revealed to the pupil. Without a Guru man will remain in the state of misery.

> The heart is an elephant, the body is a forest,
> The Guru the good; when the mark of the true World is made on the elephant.[12]

In *Japuji* Guru has been thus described:

> The word of the Guru is the inner music,
> The word of the Guru is the highest scripture;
> The word of the Guru is all pervading.
> The Guru is Shiva, the Guru is Vishnu as well as Brahma.
> The Guru is Parabati, the mother goddess.

There is the teaching of Guru-trinity in the sense that the highest Guru is God Himself (Wahe guru).* Then there are ten Gurus, from Guru Nanak to the last tenth Guru Gobind Singh. Lastly, Guru Granth Sahib is the last Guru for the future spiritual guidance of the Sikhs. But apart from these three, there are realized souls who also are to be counted as gurus. But no guru is likely to come across a seeker without the Grace of God. How to obtain this Grace?

First thing is the constant utterance of the name *nāma-sumirana*), with complete surrender to God.

> If I repeat the Name, I live; if I forget it, I die;
> It is difficult to repeat the true Name.
> If a man hungers after the true Name,
> His pain shall depart when he satisfieth himself with it.

*This is in harmony with Indian tradition. According to advaitism *Brahmavid* (knower of Brahma) becomes Brahma himself. Kabir too writes,

Gur Govind tau ek hai, duja yahu ākāra (Isakh 1.26).

Guru and Govinda 'God' are one, only difference is of form. Ramakrishna repeatedly holds that God is the only Guru.

It is immaterial by which name the devotee is most concerned. It is the magic of mantra which has been recommended in Indian tradition from time immemorial.[13] The technique of *nāma-sumirana* leads to concentration on God, purifies the mind, makes the seeker *Gurmukhi* (Godward). Each and every name of God is efficacious in reaching Him. The point is that name is a word and the primal word, which has led to the creation of the world, is likely to be touched, and, the power of being saved may be thus invoked. Naturally *nāma-sumirana* has its relation with the doctrine of *Shabad*.

According to the Vedantic doctrine of *Shabad-Brahma*, the whole world is the creation of *Shabad*. Both in Islam and Christianity, the world was created by the Word of God. God said, 'Let there be light and there was light'. In Shaivism there is the Vibration in Shiva-Shakti and this vibration takes the form of sound, and the world is the manifestation of this sound. Hence, *Shabad* of Sikhism is the creative and indwelling power of this Universe. Again, the teaching of Guru and of Guru Granth Sahib is through word.

Now through the repetition of name (*nāma-sumirana*) of the Lord, the devotee gets connected with the creative Shabad. Once this connection is established, the seeker gains higher inner illumination. Thus, Guru Nanak observes:

> In the Name of the Lord's spirit abides,
> May the name in me be indwelling.
> Without the Guru we walk in darkness,
> Without the Word we understand not life.
> The word of the Guru is Light,
> His word's Light leads to Truth.
> From the Word has emanated the Name,
> Through the Word is union attained.[14]

This point has also been made by Kabir,

> *Sabad ju bāhya ek,*
> *Lāgat hi bhain mili gaya, paṛya Kaleje chhed.* (1 *Sakhi* 1.7)

(The Guru shot at me his word-arrow, which immediately vanquished me by piercing through my heart).

But God-realization ultimately depends on the Grace of God.

Grace of God is a free gift of God to His devotee to one with whom He is pleased.[15] But this requires that the seeker must be a worthy recipient. In order to be a worthy recipient, the seeker must be devoted to God. Devotion to God is most necessary for God-realization. It is the Grace of God which induces the seeker and his Guru to come together. It is the Grace which enables a seeker to have a right name for repetition. It is the Grace of God which ultimately prepares the soul to have real devotion to Him.* Hence, Guru Nanak recommends unswerving devotion to God.

> On the unending, immeasurable path of death,
> Devotion to God is man's sure provision;
> On that frightening path, obscured by smoke and dust,
> Devotion to God is the source of light,
> On the path where friend thou has none,
> Devotion to God is thy true helper
> On that way where terrible heat will oppress thee,
> Devotion to God will give thee cooling shade,
> There where unbearable thirst will suffocate thee,
> Saith Nanak, God's Name showers joyful amrita.
> (Prof. Gurucharan Singh Talib, *Religions of India*, p. 175)

Finally, according to Sikhism, no matter whichever path be followed, one thing is always there, without which no pathway can lead to God-realization. This is proper ethical conduct and purity of heart. Hence, Sikhism does not teach the doctrine of going beyond 'good and evil'.

Final Destiny

In Guru Granth Sahib, a few lines of Kabir have been included according to which there are four states of the liberated soul,**

* According to Shaṅkara three indispensible things for release are due to the Grace of God.

1. To be born as a human being.
2. To have the desire for liberation.
3. To come in contact with a *jivanmukta* Guru.
(Viveka-cūḍamani, Verse 3 (Gita Press).

**M.A. Macauliffe, Vol. 6, p. 250*n*.

namely, gaining of heavenly abode, nearness with God, similarity with God and fellowship with God. These four kinds of final destiny have really been maintained by Ramanuja. Again, in these very lines it is said that one reality appears to be many, but finally manyness is absorbed in the non-dual reality. This metaphor of reflection* is really advaitic which supports the theory of mergence into nirguṇa Brahma, as the final destiny of the liberated soul. Hence, the Sikh writing supports both the doctrine of the conservation of individual souls, and, also at times the doctrine of absorption into *nirguṇa* Brahma.

Like the Buddhist theory of *nirvāṇa* what matters most is the view that in the final stage, there is an end of suffering. Hence for the Sikh the final destiny of God-realization is freedom from suffering due to the endless transmigration of the soul.

As water blends with water, when
Two streams their waves unite,
The light of human life doth blend
With God's celestial light.
No transmigration then awaits
The weary human soul;
It hath attained the resting place,
Its peaceful crowning goal.[16]

In this state there is no misery or pain. The theory of mergence really is indicative of mystic trance. We have already seen that the ultimate reality for a Sikh is both *Oṁkara* and *One-Oṁkara* (*nirguṇa Brahma*). This unattributed Brahma is realized through *Samādhi* (meditation). Hence, mergence is the real outcome of *Samādhi*, for in this state the outer world ceases to be felt, and, again, in the last stage even the ego appears to be lost. Again, even when attributed Brahma becomes an object of devotion, then here too the individual gets so much absorbed in the object of his contemplation, that he no longer is aware of his own existence. Hence, mergence is really a reflected state of *Samādhi* or of even intense devotion.

* The reflection metaphor states that One moon reflected in the waves of the river appears to be many. Similarly, all Jīvas are really one non-dual Brahma in which manyness of reflected moon is absorbed.

In the last resort Guru Nanak dwells upon the presence of God in one's own heart and conscience. This was also emphasized by Kabir who talked of *Ātmārāma*. Nanak also says:

Ap pachane Har mile (Guru Granth Sahib 1410-11)
(The Lord is within man).

Again,

Gurumukh bujhaya ek livalāya, nij ghar basaya sāch Samāya
(G.G.S. 222).

But is the seeker really lost? This is more of a feeling of unattached living, rather than the state of final destiny of an individual.

Brahma jñāni sadā nirlepa, jaise jal mahi Kamala alepa
(G.G.S. 272).

One has to remain as detached, as a lotus remains unwetted by water. If service to humanity be stressed then disinterestedness of the devotee has been emphasized as it is in the Gītā (II. 47). Though both the theories of mergence and conservation have been stated, really the theory of conservation in heavenly abode (*Sach Khanḍ*) is more in keeping with the energetic life of a hard working, honest, social worker Sikh. Here in *Sach khanḍ*, friends and relatives recognise one another and enjoy everlasting beatitude. But Sikh tradition gives weightage to mergence as the supreme end of Sikh devotion and aspiration.

Life after Death

Sikhism accepts the theory of karma and transmigration. Even if a man does good work in this life, but without devotion, then he has to take birth in the next life. He will not get *Sach khanḍ*, but must undergo purgation after death.* Such a person has to work again for either mergence or *Sach khanḍ*. But as long as he does not have God-realization he will have to undergo countless rebirths.

If a man does evil, his punishment will be severe. After the punishment, he will take birth into lower animals. Then again

* Here the Sikh view is neither Muslim nor Hindu.

going through the windmill of countless transmigrations, he will be reborn as a man. After having the priceless birth as a man, he has to work out his salvation by prayers, meditation and self-surrender to God.

> Comfort pervadeth the hearts of those whose minds are attached to God's feet.
> They whose minds are so attached are saved,
> O Lord, and obtain happiness by Thy Favour.

One thing is clear that man is responsible for his transmigration. 'The recording angels' take with them a record of man's acts.

> It is he himself soweth, and he himself eateth.[17]

This karmavāda has been ordained by God.

> Rebirth and deliverance depend on Thy Will:
> Nobody can interfere with it.[18]

Sikhism and Hinduism

At present all kinds of sects are called Hindus, irrespective of their beliefs and practices. Negatively Hinduism means non-Christian, non-Muslim and non-Parsi faiths and practices. This cannot but produce confusion. We have divided Hinduism into Vedic and non-Vedic. Vedic Hinduism, excepting Arya Samaj, simply means the acceptance of the Vedas as the only religious scripture and the acceptance of caste. Non-Vedic Hinduism is largely of Jain and Buddhist tradition in which atheism, anti-avatāravāda, anti-casteism etc., are maintained. Kabirpanth, Gorakhnath panth and Sikhism are really non-Vedic Hinduism. But like all other forms of Hinduism, Sikhism has family resemblance with even the prevalent form of Sanatana Hindu Dharma.

1. All form of Hinduism at present accept the four pillars of *Karma-saṁsāra-jñāna-mukti.* Sikhism too accepts them. Therefore, Sikhism comes under the family name of 'Hinduism'.

2. Besides, at the time of the origin of Sikhism, it did not differentiate itself from caste-Hinduism. Almost on all religious occasions, Brahmin priests presided over the functions. M.A. Macauliffe in 1909 writes:

> Notwithstanding the Sikh Gurus' powerful denunciation of Brahmans, secular Sikhs now rarely do anything without their assistance. Brahmans help them to be born, help them to wed, help them to die, and help their souls after death to obtain a state of bliss.[19]

Again, Khushwant Singh observes that contrary to the instructions of the Gurus, Sikhs maintain caste, go to Hindu and Sikh places of pilgrimage.[20]

Under the circumstances, how can one say that Sikhism is not Hinduism?

3. Many verses of Kabir, Tukaram, Rai Das, Trilochan and other saints have been included in Guru Granth Sahib. On the whole these saints will come under-non-Vedic Hinduism. As a matter of fact Sikhism is much nearer to Kabir panth than other forms of Hinduism.

Sikhs and Hindus have remained in a close-knit relationship. Sikhs are as much Indian as any Sanatani Hindu will claim for himself. They all are soaked in Indian culture and ways of living.* But one should not ignore same differences between Sanatani Hinduism and Sikhism.

Sikhism does not accept idolatry, *avatāravāda* (incarnation) and caste. Guru Amar Das states his anti-caste views in the following:

> Let none be proud of his caste.
> He who knoweth God is a Brahman.
> O stupid fool, be not proud of thy caste;
> ... ...
> Everybody saith there are four castes,
> But they all proceeded from God's seed.
> The world is all made out of one clay,
> But the Potter fashioned it into vessels of many sorts.[21]

4. Keeping to the rejection of many external forms of devotion, pilgrimage, idolatry, caste, one Inderjit Singh, a Sikh has given the following statement of Guru Granth Sahib to show that Sikhs are not Hindus.[22]

* Under the Constitution of India article 25, 2B, Explanation 11, Sikhs have been called 'Hindus'.

I do not keep the Hindu fast nor those observed by Muslims during Ramzan......"
I have broken away irrevocably from the Hindu and the Turk and it is a great relief.
I will not go on haj or pay obeisance to a Hindu Temple...
I shall not worship idols or say namaz
We (the Sikhs) are neither Hindus nor Mussalmans.

As a matter of fact Guru Nanak is said to have declared to the high priest of Baghdad about his sect in the following way:

> I have appeared in this age to indicate the way unto men. I reject all sects, and only know one God, whom I recognize in the earth, the heavens, and in all directions.[23]

5. But there is little doubt that the following features differentiate a Sikh from a Hindu.

(a) The adoption of five vows of long hair, iron bracelet, *Kachh* (under drawers), comb and Kirpan.
(b) Intense loyalty to the Guru '*Sir rākhe sir jāt hai*'.
(c) Belonging to Sikh Khalsa or militancy.
(d) The adoption of Gurmukhi Script as distinguished from Devanāgari Script, differentiates Sikhism from Hinduism which recognizes Sanskrit in Devanagāri script.

References

1. *Religions of India,* Indian Library, p. 153, 167, 169.
2. M.A. Macauliffe, *The Sikh Religion,* Vol. VI. In the Appendix of Kabir-Granthavali 192 Sakhis and 222 padas from Guru Granth Sahib have been mentioned.
3. *Religions of India,* Clarion Book, p. 175.
4. M.A. Macauliffe, *Ibid*., Vol. I. p. 291.
5. J.P. Suda, *Religions of India,* p. 253, quoted from Guru Granth Sahib.
6. *Taittirīya Up*. 2.6. (Having created the world, Brahma entered into it).
7. M.A. Macauliffe, *Ibid.*, p. 178.
8. M.A. Macauliffe, *Ibid.*, p. 210.
   There dwell congregations or Saints. They rejoice; the True One is in their hearts, God dwelleth in the true realm. Japuji, XXXVII.

9. M.A. Macauliffe, *Ibid.*, p. 214.
10. M.A. Macauliffe, *Ibid.*, p. 212.
11. M.A. Macauliffe, *Ibid.*, Vol. V, p. 5, p. 5, pp. 116-118.
12. M.A. Macauliffe, *Ibid.*, Vol. I, p. 276.
13. Interested reader in *nāma-Sumirana* can consult the author's *Kabīr Kā Dharma Darśhan*. An exhaustive reference to *nāma-mahimā* is given in *Kalyaṇa*, 1965, number 1.
14. Quoted by J.P. Suda, *Ibid.*, p. 251.
15. M.A. Macauliffe, *Ibid.*, Vol. I. 198, 208-209; Japuji IV, XXIV.
    'Rebirth and deliverance depend on Thy will;
    He to whom God hath given the *boon* of praising and lauding Him', *Japuji* XXV.
16. M.A. Macauliffe, *Ibid.*, Vol. I, Introduction LXIV-LXV.
17. M.A. Macauliffe, *Ibid.*, Vol. I, *Life of Guru Nanak*, p. 5; p. 209.
    Angels keep a record of one's work, Vol. I XXVII, 206, 210.
    This is essentially Muslim view.
18. M.A. Macauliffe, *Ibid.*, p. 206, Japuji XX.
19. M.A. Macauliffe, *Introduction to Sikh Religion*, p. LVII.
20. Khushwant Singh, *The Sikh To-day*, p. 23.
21. M.A. Macauliffe, *Ibid.*, Vol. II, p. 238.
22. *The Times of India*, July 3, 1983.
23. M.A. Macauliffe, *Ibid.*, Vol. I. p. 179.

CHAPTER X

A CRITICAL AND COMPARATIVE STUDY OF THE KEY-CONCEPTS OF RELIGIONS

THERE ARE SOME fundamental differences between prophetic religions and Indian religions. The prophetic religions accept creationism, but Indian religions on the whole do not accept that the world and jivas have been created at any time. Creationism accepts that the world and man have been created at one time and this creation will culminate in the day of judgment.

INDIAN VIEWS

Indian tradition holds different views about the world.

1. (a) Jainism and Mīmāṁsā accept the eternity of the world. So they do not accept the doctrine of creation.
   (b) Nyāya-Vaiśeṣika Schools and the Vedānta accept the periodic creation of the world.
      (i) According to N.V. School, God the creator is only the efficient cause of the world, who creates periodically after each dissolution of the world with the help of atoms and Karmas of the Jivas.
      (ii) The atheistic Sāṁkhya believes that the world consisting of Sattva, Rajas, and Tamas keeps on eternally changing. So its views resemble those of Jainism and Mīmāṁsā.
      (iii) The Vedānta accepts the doctrine of periodic creation and dissolution, but holds that Ishvara is both the efficient and material cause of the world.

In general Indian tradition holds that the world is composed of five constituents of earth, water, fire, wind and ākāsha (ether).

2. An attitude to the past is an important differentiating factor amongst religions. Brahminism (strict *sanatani* Hinduism) holds that the past ancient time alone has the most excellent 'truth' of any religion. As Hinduism is the most ancient religion of the Satya Yuga, so it alone contains the whole of religious excellence. Other religions were born in other Yugas of *dvapara* (where truth is mixed with falsity) and *Kaliyuga* (largely mixed with falsehood). So they cannot be credited with full excellence of religion. Hence, Hinduism cannot but be conservative, for it has to conserve the full excellence of Vedic religion.

According to Islam (excepting Dr. S.M. Iqbal), the Prophet Muhammad is the final seal of revelation. Hence, according to this view, God progressively realizes Himself through the prophets, but after the Prophet Muhammad, no further revelation is possible. At best the Shias can accept the right of better interpretation of the Quoran and Hadith. Naturally, Islam is committed to *fundamentalism* of final revelation by Prophet Muhammad.

Christianity and Buddhism are committed to the theory of progressive revelation. Christianity believes that God has been revealing Himself progressively through the prophets and in the fullness of time Christ finally revealed the nature of God most fully. In due course, Soren Kierkegaard propounded the view that the disciple at the second hand is superior to the earlier disciples of Jesus, because the modern disciple of Jesus is better intellectually equipped than the earlier disciple. In this century R. Bultmann by presenting the case of de-mythologising the writings of the New Testament, tacitly accepts the theory of the superiority of the disciple at the second hand.

In the same manner, the Mahāyāna School of Buddhism kept on harping on the superiority of Buddha's revelation at later times, because in the earlier age the disciple was not fully prepared to understand the hidden depth of Buddhist teaching.

Jainism accepts the final authority of reason in determining the excellence of religious truth, but it has been more conservative than progressive in its views with regard to the earlier teaching of Jainism.

MAKING OF SOULS IS THE FUNCTION OF RELIGION

3. There is another point which has to be kept in mind. According to Christianity all that we can say that there is God, but we cannot say *what He is* (Exodus 3.14). This is how St. Thomas Aquinas and Paul Tillich teach us.* Again, the well-known Vedāntic teaching (B.U. 2.4.14; 3.4.2; 3.7.2) is that the absolute reality *Brahman* is essentially unknowable. Kabir and Guru Nanak too accept this. Then, why should we talk about God or Brahman?

The aim of religion is not so much to know God or Brahman, but to know reality in order to *become* that entity. Here knowing is pressed into the service of becoming. After all ideal man and God are one and the same thing, for example, Rama is considered to be God and yet an ideal man. In the same manner Jesus Christ is taken to be a perfect man and yet God. Hence, the function of religious language is to evoke a vision of an ideal self into which the worshipper seeks to transform himself. According to advaitism a knower of Brahman himself becomes Brahman (*Brahmavid Brahmaiva Bhavati*). A Christian seeks to imitate Christ, so that finally not he, but Christ may live in him. In the same strain, a Muslim seeks to imitate the prophet Muhammad so that he may become Muhammad-like. This is also the meaning of the last utterance of Lord Buddha '*appo dīpo bhava*'. Each Buddhist has to use his own light to become a Buddha, for a follower of Buddhism does not *worship*, but himself becomes the Buddha (the awakened one).

This is also true of Kabir. He meditated on *nirguṇa* Rama in order to become Rama himself. Ramakrishna taught this very eloquently. He practised Christianity and he became Christ; he practised Islam and finally the ideal Muslim figure entered into him and he became one with it.

Radhakrishnan has powerfully advocated this view.

> Religion is not a movement stretching out to grasp something, external, tangible and good and to possess it......It is a new birth into enlightenment.[1]

* The doctrine of *analogiaentis* of St. Thomas Aquinas, and, its modern vision of Tillich's doctrine of Symbolism interpret (Exodus 3.14) in the sense that we know that there is God, but not *what He is*.

Again,

> The mandate of religion is that man must make a change in his own nature in order to let the divine in him manifest itself.[2]

God or Brahman is not a Being so much external to the worshipper as He is the indwelling spirit in the worshipper himself. The Upanishads (Brahdāraṇyaka) 3.7.1-23, Ramanuja and Kabir have emphasized the importance of indwelling Rama (Kabir) and indwelling Brahman (Ramanuja). Hence, life, teaching and death of a votary of a religion alone pertain to the excellence of a religion.

In comparing religious concepts, one has to keep in mind that they do not connote or denote the same thing. There is a good deal of subtle differences in such a common concept as 'God'. Gandhiji thought that 'Ishvara' and 'Allah' mean the same thing for they refer to the same entity whom we may call as the ground of all being, or, simply the Supreme Reality. This will be clear when we take up the concept of 'God'.

God

First, we do not think that there cannot be any religion without the concept of God. Jainism, Buddhism and early Mīmāṁsā are taken to be atheistic systems. Even in one phase of Sāṁkhya, there is no room for God, for the world goes on changing without any mover, and the individual soul falls into bondage and also some of them win their own liberation without any reference to God. Hence, God is not needed either to explain the world or the bondage or liberation of individual souls. Even in Yoga, God is neither a creator nor the sustainer-destroyer of the world. He is only an aid for helping the success of Yoga-practices. But all these atheistic systems have very great interest in promoting the supernatural or transcendental being of man. So much of pre-occupation with the transcendental entity and the destiny of man cannot but be called religious. Thus, we submit that there can be religion without God.

Personality of God

Even when we accept God as an article of faith, this concept differs with different religions. The Hindu God is essentially a Being who creates this world out of *Līlā* (Shaṅkara, Ramanuja, Kabir and Ramakrishna). The Muslim believes in a God of justice tempered with mercy and compassion, but demands utmost obedience. The Christian God is essentially a redeeming, forgiving and suffering God who looks out for the return of the sinner to Him. Besides, the attached stories and histories make a good deal of difference to the concept of God. Lord Krishna cannot be understood without His *līlā* with the gopies or the part he played in the Mahābhārata. In the same manner, Judaic God has meaning in reference to the exodus of the Jews from Egypt, the covenant with Abraham, Isaac and Jacob, and, exile into Babylonia and return of the Jews from Babylonia to their own country under Ezra. Similarly, Christian God cannot be understood without the life, teaching and death of Jesus on the cross, the Pentecostal events and the persecution of the early Christian converts. Hence, the concept of God is not intelligible in itself, without reference to contexts and use in the daily life of His various types of adherents.

Christianity, Judaism and to some extent even Islam would hold God not to be fully knowable. But these religions do believe in the personality of God in the sense that He is supreme Will and Intellect, and, is able to respond to the prayers of His devotees. For example, Sikhism regards God to be *nirākāra* (formless), but still it teaches devotion to God. How can there be any kind of devotion without crediting God with personality. Islam too takes God to be a Person who has not only created man but is benevolent and most merciful. Hence, any theistic system has to accept the personality of God.

However, some thinkers, specially advaitic ones seem to hold that advaitism does not accept either personal or impersonal God, but *super*-personal God. Even Shaṅkara does not wholly deny the reality of a personal God, called 'Ishvara' in his system. But he considers the worship of a personal God as only a means for having *Brahma-jñāna.* In several places Shaṅkara grants that theistic worship may lead to *Krama-mukti* (liberation by successive stages). But he thinks that Ishvara is invested with *Māyā*, though this Māyā is within His control. For him, the supreme reality who alone can be realized through *jñāna*, transcends 'Ishvara'. So it is regarded that the supreme reality is super-personal, in the sense that Ishvara is superseded in the reality of Brahman. Does this supersession of personality mean its loss or its enrichment?

Kabir holds that God's personality is infinitely much richer than man's personality. In this sense, Super-personality simply means the infinitely enriched personality of God and human devotees gaining *Krama-Mukti* are enriched in God. He illustrates by saying that the dirty water of a drain loses its dirtiness and becomes Gaṅgā-jala (the Gaṅgetic water) when it falls into the river Ganges. Similarly, human personality is perfected by being superseded in the infinite personality (super-personality) of God. Hence, the denial of human personality means enrichment in the super-personal God. Therefore, Super-personal God is infinitely enriched personality, and, does not mean the denial of personality.

One more point has to be emphasized. We also credit God with infinite love, justice, mercy and so on. What does 'infinite' mean? According to Spinoza, God has an infinite number of attributes, each of which expresses His nature infinitely. Hence, it means that infinite love, mercy etc., do not limit God. If love, mercy etc., do not limit God, then they are not attributes at all. Hence, St. Thomas Aquinas used the term infinite degree of love, mercy and other attributes found at the human level. He meant that God is transcendent and His attributes transcend human attributes so much so that they can hardly describe God's attributes. Our best exemplification of love, mercy, kindness are at most 'floor concepts' and not ceiling concepts. Hence in speaking about God we reach the utmost limit of human knowledge and language. In the Upanishadic language *turīyā* is the real state in which consciousness remains, but the duality of subject-object is lost.

> For where there is a duality, as it were, there one sees another; there one smells another . . . . Where, verily, everything has become just one's own self, then whereby and whom one smells, then whereby and whom would one see?
>
> (*B.U.* 2.4.14)

One should not ignore this analogical or symbolical nature of language when one talks about God. Strictly speaking one should keep silence, but language when used tends to be metaphorical, analogical and symbolical. The utmost function of religious language is to deepen and widen the apprehension of man of what is the source and ground of his being . . . a being which indwells within the heart and beckons man towards it. Religious language by means of its picture, metaphor etc., evokes in a vision of that Being by becoming which we reach our final destiny and goal. This is clearly demonstrated in the mystics of all ages, eastern and western, Muslim-Christian-Hindu.

Oneness of God

Strictly speaking Judaism and Islam alone have pure monotheism. The eloquent language of Judaism is,

> 'God is one and thou shalt have no other God besides me'

Islam also proclaims,

> 'God is great, there is no God but Allah'.

Christianity tends to be monotheistic, but the doctrine of Trinity seems to hold tritheism instead of monotheism. The humanity and divinity have never been satisfactorily reconciled in the person of Jesus Christ. But *trinity* should not be reduced to the triad of *Brahma, Viṣṇu* and *Mahesha.* If these are three deities with their specific function, then the oneness of God is lost and, if they are three functions of one God relating to creation, sustenance and destruction of the world, then the separate divinities of Brahma, Viṣṇu and Mahesha are lost. Hinduism tends more towards Monism than Monotheism. The prevailing Hindu view is that there is one common referent of different kinds of worship.

> As men approach me so do I accept them; men on all sides follow my path (*BhG.* IV. II).

Radhakrishnan comments:

> Name and form are used to reach the Formless.
> Meditation on any favourite form may be adopted.

However, Sikhism may be said to have pure monotheism. Really in Zoroastrianism, monotheism is primary and dualism is secondary and not final.

Creator God

The Christian believes that God has created the world out of nothing (*ex nihilo*). The same point is made by saying that by the mere utterance of God, things have come into being. God said, 'Let there be light, and there was light'. We need not emphasize 'nothing' or *asat* as in Indian philosophy. Creation by God simply means that God's will and thinking are creative, productive and presentative. In contrast, human thinking is only representative and reproductive, as Berkeley has pointed out. God creates the material and fashions it by the mere fiat of His will. This is also found in Indian tradition where the curse or blessing by ṛṣis bears fruit by mere wish or the words of the sages. But He created man in a very special way, for a very special purpose. According to Judaism, Christianity and Islam God is said to be both the material and efficient cause of the world, in the Aristotelian sense of 'Cause'.

In the Indian tradition, *Shaṅkara* holds that Ishvara is the material and efficient cause of the world. But he does not tell us about the material. Does Ishvara bring about the matter by the mere fiat of His will? At least this is so in the *Chhandogya Upanishad*:

> It (Brahman) bethought itself: 'Would that I were many! Let me procreate myself' (6.3.3).

This Brahman emitted heat. How? We do not know, but 6.3.1 says that this creation proceeds from nothing or non-Being. 6.3.2 corrects this by saying that creation proceeded from Being. Hence, it comes very near the Biblical account that creation resulted from Being alone.

However, this Upanishadic account is not maintained later on. First, Shaṅkara and Ramanuja do not hold that the world had any First beginning. There is a cycle of creation-dissolution. Secondly, Shaṅkara's Ishvara at the end of each dissolution is sublated or reabsorbed in qualityless Brahman. The views of Ramanuja are a bit different from those of Shaṅkara.

According to Ramanuja Brahman is personal and He is both the material and efficient cause of the world, in the cycle of creations. But for him, the world and the jīva form His body. So the material world (*acit*) simply means the passing of matter from the subtle into its gross form. Here the doctrine of creation turns into the doctrine of emanation. God also turns out to be more of an efficient than the material cause, in the sense that God creates jīvas with the help of their past Karmas.

The Nyāya-Vaiśeṣika philosophy clearly opts for God as the efficient cause of the world, who fashions the world out of atoms and past karmas of the jīvas.

Thus, we find that the Upanishadic account of creation and that of the prophetic religions are very much alike. Otherwise Indian theistic religions differ widely from the prophetic religions in relation to the doctrine of creation.

TRANSCENDENCE AND IMMANENCE OF GOD

The meaning of 'transcendence' has to be clarified. First, transcendence means a state in which the entity is in the thing and in continuation with it goes beyond it. For example, ether not only is in the room but also extends beyond it. This is the meaning of transcendence in the Puruṣa Sūkta hymn.

A thousand heads has Puruṣa,
A thousand eyes, a thousand feet,
He holding earth enclosed about,
Extends beyond, then fingers length (*RV* X 90.1).

But we also know from Bṛahadāraṇyaka Upanishad (3.7.1-23) that Brahman is the inner controller of everything and indwells the human heart. Hence, for Shaṅkara, Brahman transcends the phenomenal existence, having no relation with it. In other words, Brahman remains untouched by the illusory empirical world. But the inner core of a jīva is identical with Brahman (*Brahmaiva jivah*). Hence, a jīva is in Brahman, but Brahman goes much beyond him, according to Ramanuja.

There is another sense of 'transcendence' in the Upanishads and Kant. Brahman is the very basis of hearing, thinking and knowing, but it cannot itself be an object of knowing.

> He is the unseen Seer, the unheard,
> Hearer, the unthought thinker, the ununderstood Understander. (*B.U*. 3.7.23).

Again,

> You could not see the seer of seeing.
> You could not hear the hearer of hearing.
> You could not think the thinker of thinking. (*B.U*. III. 4.2).

Kant calls this as the synthetic unity of apperception His statement is:

> Now it is, indeed, very evident that I cannot know as an object that which I must presuppose in order to know any object......[3]

There is a third meaning of 'transcendence' in Judaeo-Islamic concept of God, according to which God is absolutely 'Other'. In St. Thomas and Paul Tillich, God is so much the other, that no words or speech can ever describe Him. No segment of the phenomenal word can ever reach Him. He can only be analogically (St. Thomas) or symbolically (Paul Tillich) approached. Then how can He be known at all, at least for mutual dialogue, communicability and teachability about God? God can be approached only through His revelation. Revelation of God takes place through dreams, vision, angels, but above all through the prophets. In this context, Christians also believe that in the last days God became incarnate in His son Jesus Christ. If this sonship is used symbolically in Tillichian sense, then there is no harm. But if this sonship is used in literal meaning, then God's transcendence is lost, and, the concept of God ultimately becomes a form of anthropomorphism, albeit refined and highly sublimated. But if God simply means 'wholly other', then Christ can only be a symbol, though unique and almost final as a revelatory event.

This by the way has raised the question of incarnation.

According to the theory of incarnation God assumes the form of man to redeem mankind. Though in the Gītā, Lord Krishna is said to incarnate himself for the protection of the good, for the destruction of the wicked and for the establishment of righteousness (Gītā IV.8), this also means the redemption for all mankind. Thus, God assumes human form for redeeming man. Hence, the doctrine of incarnation (*avatāravāda*) as the special revelation of God is found in the Gītā, Paurānic Hinduism and Ramanuja. This is also accepted in popular form of Christianity.

However, Kabir, Guru Nanak and Gorakh Nathapanthis do not accept the theory of *avatāravāda.* In the same way Islam and Judaism do not accept the doctrine of incarnation. Incarnation means that God Himself descends in human form to teach and redeem mankind.

As against transcendence, 'immanence' means that which pervades, embraces and completely indwells the universe. For example, the tendency in the egg to transform it into a chick. Hence, by immanence is meant a controlling spirit and agency in the world. This was the sense of Aristotle according to which God is the form of forms that shapes, controls, guides and draws the whole universe towards itself. Essentially this is the same meaning of 'The Idea of the Good', according to Plato. Most probably the emergentists like Samuel Alexander regarded God as the whole universe with its *nisus* towards the deity, in this sense of Aristotle or Plato. However, the Upanishads and later on Kabir looked upon God, as both transcending and indwelling within man (RV. X. 90.1). Christians also speak of God as both 'transcendent and immanent'. Christian theologians have not clarified this notion of 'immanence'. But in Islam 'immanence' simply means omnipresence. This is only one sense of Judaeo-Christian and even Islamic tradition, according to which God created man in His resemblance, and further He breathed life-giving breath into the nostrils of man formed from soil. This 'breath' is God's breath *in* man, and, may be termed His image or even indwelling spirit of God in man. According to Islam, this breath on the death of a man returns to God. One can see that if the divine image or His controlling breath remains external to God, then God cannot be said to be immanent in man or the earth. The important Christian theologians like St. Thomas Aquinas, Karl Barth and Paul Tillich have fully maintained the transcendence of God.

'Immanence' should be distinguished from emanation. According to the doctrine of emanation the Supreme Reality manifests itself in different degrees. This doctrine is found most prominently in pantheism as in neo-Platonism. In general, as emanation proceeds in stages from the beginning towards its end, the perfection gets diminished. This doctrine of emanation is also found in the *Pañcarātra* known as the theory of *Vyūhas*.

To summarise in prophetic religions God's transcendence is emphasized and His immanence has not been fully worked out. In Hinduism God is both transcendent and immanent, but even here His transcendence is less important than His immanence. Only in a metaphysic where it is held that the whole universe is a living organism as in Bruno, Samuel Alexander and to some extent in Plato and Aristotle, that it can be said that God is immanent in the whole universe and yet transcends each finite thing and man. For example, according to Samuel Alexander, the deity is yet to be and looms ahead of the highest emergent at the rung of the ladder. In this sense, the futuristic deity is transcendent of man; yet, it remains within the evolutionary drive of the whole universe, spinning it towards ever higher emerging beings. Most probably this might have been the sense of Plato and the Upanishads. Akin to the concept of transcendence and immanence, there is the concept of *nirākāra* and *sākāra* in Indian philosophy.

Nirākāra (without Attributes) and Sākāra (with Attributes)

When we say that the highest object of reverence is without attributes, we mean that nothing can be predicated or said about it except that it has Being or existence. Advaitism is said to support the doctrine of attributeless Brahman. But even Shaṅkara accepts the validity of theistic worship with a view to attaining *Brahma-jñāna*. Then the question is, how is *nirguṇa Brahma* related to *Saguṇa* or theistic worship of Ishvara credited with all auspicious qualities? Shaṅkara says only this much that Ishvara is "in proximity to the higher one, there is nothing unreasonable in the word 'Brahman' being applied to the former" and, that the scripture enjoins upon theistic worshipper that he can also obtain (by mere worship) liberation (Brahma-Sūtra Bhāṣya IV. 3.9). But apart from this relationship of close proximity between *saguṇa* and *nirguṇa Brahma*, Shaṅkara does not further detail their inter-relationship. However, much later Ramakrishna holds that *saguṇa* and *nirguṇa* Brahma are one and the same, and, like the inseparable relation of Shiva-Shakti in Shaivism. Ramakrishna also holds that they are inseparable.

> My Divine Mother is none other than the Absolute. She is at the same time the One and the Many, and beyond the One and the Many.[4]

But some of the commentators of Bijak and also Ramakrishna hold that *saguṇa* is the indispensable means for realizing *nirguṇa* Brahma. This is not only supported by Kabir-Granthavali, *pada* 180 and Bijak's *Ramaini* 77, but is in line with Kabir's meaning of *Pūrṇa* (perfect) Brahma. According to Kabir, Brahma has an infinite number of attributes, and each of these attributes is far fuller than any finite attributes even of an incarnate being.* In modern language we can say that *saguṇa* is a symbol of *nirguṇa* which points to the *nirguṇa* without taking its place.

The important thing is that *nirguṇa* Brahma can be directly realized only through *dhyānas* or *samādhi* (meditation) and only indirectly through worship. According to Jainism, meditation alone is the most potent means of attaining *apavarga* (liberation). But even meditation to be sustained at least in the initial stages, requires an object for fixing one's meditation. Here Lord Mahavira can become an object of meditation, knowing fully well that Lord Mahavira does not respond to the prayers of his worshipper, nor is he the creator of the world. He is made an object of meditation with a view to purifying the intellect and the soul of a *dhyānī*.

We have already seen that even in Judaeo-Christian tradition (Exodus 3.14) God is essentially unknowable and whatever

* For defining 'purṇa Brahman', see *Bṛhadāraṇyaka* 5.1; Atharva Veda 10.8.29; MBH 5.4.10.

attributes we ascribe to God really do not literally describe Him. This view of God held by St. Thomas Aquinas, Paul Tillich and Brunner brings Judaeo-Christian concept of a transcendent God very near to that of *nirguṇa* Brahma.

The Concept of Man

The whole of Indian tradition prevailing today accepts the four pillars of *Karma-Saṁsāra-Jñāna-Mukti.* Each individual jīva is born in the world in bondage. This bondage is due to ignorance (*ajñāna**) of his own reality and of other things. But why has he fallen into this worldly existence of bondage and miseries? According to Sāṁkhya this is due to infatuation of the jīva, lured by the *Sattva* element of Prakṛti. This infatuation is akin to the doctrine of Universal ignorance of all individuals in bondage. Ramanuja would say that this bondage is due to *Karma* associated with ignorance. But Ramanuja does not elucidate the exact way this Karma associated with *ajñāna* caused the miserable worldly existence. However, Jainism alone holds that *Karma* alone is the cause of bondage and in due course, this Karma has transformed the omniscience (*sarvajñatā*) of a jīva into his ignorance. But Jainism too does not explain as to how the initial *Karma* came into being which ultimately paved the way for the worldly existence of bondage for any individual. Quite naturally this difference concerning the cause of bondage of an individual would mean also difference in finding out the way of salvation.

However, this doctrine of bondage is very much akin to the Christian teaching of original sin of man. Both in Indian tradition and in Christianity man is born with a heavy load of the past. In the case of Christianity, this doctrine of original sin means that the sin of the primeval father of man is visited ever since on his descendants. But in Indian tradition each individual is responsible for his past *Karma*, and, the individual is responsible for this. However, the world in which each individual is born, is in general sustained by the same kind of ignor-

*The word '*ajñāna*' is usually translated as ignorance. Better word is *nescience*. Further, this nescience is cosmic which envelopes the whole mankind.

ance. In this sense, in spite of differences with regard to the cause of worldly existence, fraught with original sin of man, a Christian and a Hindu do not differ much in their disabilities of life. But one important difference has to be noted. Christianity holds that sin or moral evil came into the world due to disobedience of the commandment of God. Hence, the real cause of the burden of sin is moral. Naturally the way of Christian salvation will differ from that of Indian tradition. There is a further difference between the prophetic and Indian religions with regard to the real nature of man. According to Indian religions man is essentially spirit, whose real nature is pure Consciousness. Barring Buddhism which teaches the doctrine of no-Soul (*anattāvāda*), it is spiritual darkness (ignorance, ajñāna) that sustains the worldly existence of each jīva. However, Sāṁkhya, Advaita Vedanta, Nyāya in general would hold this view. The Vaiśeṣika philosophy holds that consciousness is not the essential nature of a jīva. According to it, consciousness is an extrinsic attribute of Jīva, for consciousness arises only when the spirit comes to acquire a body with senses. Again, the spirit of a jīva is held to be inactive. Ramanuja protests against this view and holds that a jīva in its pristine glory is both conscious and active. Shaṅkara too regards N.V. of jīvas as akin to materialism.

As contrasted with Indian and Greek view about the essential nature of an individual as pure spirit, Hebraic and Christian view holds that spirit is essentially embodied. Hence, Enoch, Elijah and Jesus Christ are said to have ascended into heaven with their bodies. St. Paul holds that even after resurrection of the dead, each individual self will be provided with indestructible body (1 Cor. 15. 42-45). Islamic view on the whole means that on death, the breath or spirit of the dead man will return to God. But on the day of resurrection, each individual will get back his body.* In contrast, the Indian tradition holds that man is essentially spirit and his body is constituted of his *Karmas*. Hence, his body is extraneous to his *ātman*. Just as men throw away the garment and put on another, so is their

* The distinction of spirit, soul and body appear to be quite clear in Christianity. Soul is spirit conditioned by the body. The spirit belongs to God who imparts it to man, and, is essentially 'holy'.

bodies in different births (Gītā 2.22). However, we must not forget that even the Lord assumes Sattvic body to help His devotees. And, according to Ramanuja, the redeemed souls too, at the behest of their Lord and Master may assume Sattvic Body.

There is a further point to note that in prophetic religions including Zorastrianism the soul or spirit is a created entity, but remains eternal, whether in heaven or hell*. But in Indian tradition, the soul is eternal and does not undergo any destruction (Gītā 2.20).

It is true that religion is man-centred. Naturally man has been given a very high place in the scheme of things. According to Judaeo-Christianity man was created in God's image and was given dominion over all the creatures of the earth (Genesis 1. 26-28). Christian theologians also hold that man was created so that he may have a holy will, deserving the fellowship of God. According to Islam too man was created to become higher than the angels, because they alone have freedom of will and intellect (Surah 33.72) and was deemed to be a co-worker with God in relation to the world. This view of co-working with God in the struggle of good against the evil is much more marked in Zoroastrianism.

This view of man reaches its extreme in Advaitism where man is considered to be essentially Brahma (*jīvo Brahmaiva nṛpah*). In Ramanuja, jīva is the body of Brahman whose essential nature is to depend on the Lord. Here the highest destiny of man is to surrender his own will to God, so that man may come nearest to God. In Sāṁkhya, Nyāya and Jainism after liberation, each individual jīva regains .his pristine glory without any finitude and miseries.

Naturally, whether in prophetic tradition or Indian tradition, man is credited with freedom of will. In Indian tradition man is born with the load of past *Karmas* in the form of *apūrva*, but the past *Karma-Saṁskāras* can be overcome and destroyed by the means prescribed in different sects of Hinduism. Yoga, *jñāna*, Vedic

*However, the Bible says that only the worthy person will be conserved to the end (Luke 20.35) and that God can destroy the Soul in hell (Matthew 10.28).

sacrifice and *bhakti* are some of the ways in which the past Karmas can be destroyed and fresh accumulation of Karmas can be stopped. Working out of one's salvation by one's own efforts (*puruṣakāra*) largely depends on the free exercise of one's will. Even in *bhakti*, according to Ramanuja, one must prove his worth and show his fitness for the Grace of God. One has to surrender one's will to God in order that the Grace of God may save the devotee. But this surrender of one's will is as much the work of free will, as withholding it from God's Grace is.

So far there is no difficulty in refuting the charge of fatalism concerning Indian tradition, but there is special difficulty in accepting the doctrine of free will in Ramanuja. However, we need not dwell on this. In other atheistic systems of Jainism and Buddhism, man himself is said to be responsible for his bondage due to the abuse of his free will. However, it is accepted that man can use his free will for working out his own salvation. Man is his own architect either for his further fall or rise.

In prophetic religions, man was created free because he was made in God's image. God himself breathed into his nostrils His breath and Spirit. Man was created free either to obey or disobey the commandments of God in Judaeo-Christian concept of man. Adam in his fall is said to have abused his freedom of will by eating the forbidden fruit of the tree of knowledge. However, according to Christianity, Jesus remained obedient to God even in his death on the Cross. In Islam also man is free either to obey or disobey the commandments of God. However, there is one point of misunderstanding about Islam. It has been already pointed out that for a Muslim it is the proudest thing to be the slave of Allah. Hence, it is contended that Islam teaches that the highest virtue of man is to surrender his free will.

One thing to be noted here is that to be the slave of Allah is not a small achievement. In this context one has to remember that one has to become the slave of Allah by constant remembrance of God, fasting, meditation etc. These acts of obedience purify the man and bring him closer to God. He is divinized and becomes a holy will for which man was created. The moral practice in the spirit and letter of religion alone allows one to become the slave of Allah. This point has been further pursued by Ramanuja.

According to Ramanuja, a jīva is nothing but a part of the body of Brahman. And a body is that which wholly remains subservient to God as its spirit. Does this dependence mean a blemish? According to Ramanuja, dependence on anything or anyone other than the supreme person is painful and a defect in one's spiritual growth and development. However,

> the only one that ought to be served by all who are enlightened about the fundamental nature of the self, is the higest Puruṣa. . . . He alone is to be served by all.
>
> (*Vedārthaangraha*, *pada* 250)

Nay, for Ramanuja, *mokṣa* is nothing but the privilege of service to God.[5]

Hence, to be the slave of Allah is the perfection of man and his highest destiny. A Christian hymn is,

> Our wills are Ours to make them thine,
> So that in thy ocean flow they may richer and fuller be.

The Concept of the World

According to prophetic religions, including Zoroastrianism, the world has been created by God. This is also accepted by Sikhism, according to which in the beginning there was only darkness and God has created this world by his mere command.[6] However, Sikhism appears to be influenced by Islam in this account of creation of the world. But Chhandogya Upanishad does hold that Brahman wished to be many (6.3.3.) and that he became so in due course in an orderly manner. It appears however, that Indian thought does not hold the *First* beginning of the world at any time. Nor does it hold that there will be any final end of the world. It supports the view that the world is periodically created and in due course is also periodically destroyed. In this cycle of periodic creation and dissolution, the world undergoes four orderly stages of *Satya*, *Tretā*, *Dvāpara* and *Kaliyuga*. In the last stage of Kaliyuga, the world becomes too much vitiated and has to be destroyed in order that the world may be re-created afresh. Only Jainism and Mīmāṁsā take the world to be eternal. Buddhism does not say anything either about its periodic creation and dissolution. For Buddhism the world is simply a stream of momentary events. Hence, it is essentially painful. But even Buddhism cannot deny the importance of the world for gaining *Nirvāṇa.*

The world has a meaning and an end for human beings. According to Zoroastrianism creation by God means an end in bringing about finite creatures and things. This finitude necessarily entails evil. This world therefore is an arena for man to side with God for the conquest of good over evil.

According to Judaeo-Christian and Islamic teaching the world has been created by God by His mere wish and command, with man as the centre of the world. In this tradition man has been created in the world to conquer the world by knowing the laws implanted in Nature by God. These laws are meant for the guidance and well-being of man. Hence, the world is God's world by knowing which man can know the omnipotence and infinitude of God.

> Ever since God created the world, his invisible qualities, both his eternal power and his divine nature, have been clearly seen; they are perceived in the things that God has made.
>
> (*Romans* 1.20).

Hence, the world is sacred and manifests His nature and will. Man therefore has to come to grips with it for his own guidance.

This view of the world is clearly taught in the Quoran. The world has been created not as His sport (Surah 44.38). The world with its laws has been created for man for his guidance. (Surah X.6,7; XIII,2,3; XXX. 21.22).

In Zoroastrianism the purpose of creation is that man should be a co-partner with God in defeating the evil which has been introduced by Ahriman. Hence, in general, in prophetic religions this world is a vale of soul-maiming. This world too has a soteriological purpose to serve. Man has to become god fit for the heaven. In prophetic religions man can fulfil this divine purpose of creation by his obedience to God's commands and by surrendering his will to God. This soteriological purpose is also found in Indian tradition.

True, according to Brahmasūtra II.1.33, this world is only a sport of Ishvara. Both Shaṅkara and Ramanuja believe in this theory of *līlā*. However, this *līlā* is not a playful activity for a *bhakta*. In this sportive activity Ishvara descends into human flesh as His condescension to His devotees. Sāṁkhya too advances the theory of unconscious teleology on the part of Prakṛti, with a view to helping man to win his liberation (Sāṁkhya-Kārikā 17, 21, 31, 56, 57-59, 60).

In most Indian systems man comes into the world with his mission to win his salvation. The world is real which man has to know. It is real in the sense that it is not a dream or as unreal as a sky-flower. In the *Nyāya-Vaiśeṣika* school the world consists of eternal atoms which can be combined by an omnipotent God alone. For Sāṁkhya the world is *prakṛti* which is constituted of *sattva, rajas* and *tamas* that are there eternally. However, in *Vijñānavāda* of Buddhism, the world is taken to be a dream. In general for Buddhism the world is just a stream of passing events. Does Advaitism regard the world as illusory?

The *Mithyatva* of *Advaitism* has been translated as 'Illusion'. And this word 'illusion' does not convey the correct meaning of *mithyatva*. First, Ishvara creates this world out of his *māyā*, and, this māyā is within the full knowledge of Him. Hence, this māyā is real for Ishvara. However, for the seeker, from the phenomenal viewpoint it is both *Sat* and *Asat* (*Sadāsat*). It is Sat, real from the empirical or phenomenal stand for all men. Thus, for practical purposes, the world is real, and, for the daily practical concern of life man has to know it and its laws. But this is contended that this world is not absolutely real. It is negated or transcended when *Brahmajñāna* dawns upon the seeker. This transcendental existence of a *Brahmajñāni* is inexpressible in words. If, however, we have to speak about both the characteristics of *Sat-asat*, then according to *catuṣkoṭi* of Nagarjuna and *Saptabhañginaya* we have to say that the world is inexpressible. In the last resort, however, the world is real for man in his practical course of life.

For Jainism too the world is real with its *padārthas* and *guṇas*. In the same way the Mīmāṁasakas regard the world to be eternally real. Ramanuja too regards the world to be wholly real, and, along with Nyāya offers a realistic explanation of psychological illusions like that of snake-rope or conchshell-silver illusion. However, there is one more point about Ramanuja.

Ramanuja holds that the world and jīva (*acit and cit*) both form the body of Brahman who remains the soul of His body. This body of Ishvara remains real for all times. Even at the time of *pralaya* (dissolution of the world), this body which includes the world remains in *subtle* (*sukṣma*) form. For Ramanuja however, the body and Soul of Ishvara are inseparable, so he tries to maintain some sort of organic unity in his system.

Finally, the Kaṭhopanishad exhorts the seeker for winning his liberation.

> Arise ye! Awake ye!
> Obtain your boons and understand them! (III.14)

And Swami Vivekananda interprets this clarion call as a call to service and sacrifice in this world which is the field of working out one's liberation. Hence, Hinduism at present regards the world to be real.

The dependence of the world on God in some sense is accepted both in the prophetic and some important Indian systems of thought. In prophetic religions, the world has been created by God, and, it'll come to an end at the end of the age, determined by God. Hence, the world remains dependent on God.

In Jainism and Mīmāṁsā, the world is eternal and as such the question of its dependence does not arise at all. Similarly, for Buddhism in principle, there is no substance and no God, at least in principle. Hence, the question of dependence on God cannot be asked in this system. According to Advaitism, Ishvara is the efficient and material cause of the world, and, He creates the world for His sport. Naturally, the world remains dependent on Ishvara. But in another sense, the world remains depended on *nīrguṇa* Brahma too, since it provides the white canvas on which the whole world is projected. In Ramanuja, Brahman includes the world (*acit*) as its body along with *cit* (the jīvas). And, the nature of the body is that it remains wholly dependent on its indwelling spirit, which in the case is Brahman.

In *Seshvara* Sāṁkhya, the world remains dependent on its Creator and, this is also the case in Nyāya-Vaiśeṣika system of thought, even when here God is only an efficient cause of the world.

Thus, in theistic systems, the world remains dependent on God, and, even when created it is real with its soteriological purpose to fulfil in the interest of man.

The Problem of Evil and Suffering

Suffering need not be evil, for suffering has a corrective, preventive purpose, and may even manifest the glory of God. In Christianity suffering may turn out to be redemptive too, transforming men into their higher nature e.g., the expiatory and redemptive death of Jesus on the Cross. Besides, suffering serves the purpose of shocking him to realise his fallen nature and to help him to rise in spiritual excellence. It is not only illustrated in the parable of Prodigal Son, but is so in Hinduism too. Then, what is evil?

Evil is that which pertains to deeper fall in man. For example, fall into the nature of beasts and animals, as is taught in the Hindu tradition of transmigration. But more, Ramanuja holds that those who persist in sins are made to sink in still lower nature.

> If . . . . an individual is pursuing what is most contrary to the divine will, the Lord gives him evil intellect and will and actuates him to proceed along evil lines".—*Vedārthasaṁgraha*, pada 124)

According to Christianity, sin is evil, and, this sin is evil in the sense that it leads the sinner towards damnation into hell. Besides, it may mean the destruction of the soul in hell—(*Matthew* 10.28).

Thus, evil is more moral and spiritual rather than physical. One can easily see that physical evil, specially in nature has an educative purpose to fulfil. Flood, famine, pestilence etc., are natural calamities that serve as challenge for man to overcome them. In Indian tradition, there is *dukha* of three kinds, namely, *ādhyātmika* (psycho-physical suffering), *ādhibhautika* (natural) and *ādhidaivika* (transcendental). In Buddhism, suffering is more of existential nature of anguish and nameless anxiety. Main reason for existential suffering is due to the momentariness of changing events which constitute a stream called the world. It has been termed as *jarā-maraṇa* (old age and death). Really, it is the moral evil which constitutes the problem of suffering.

In prophetic religions, as well as in Indian tradition, the supreme object of religious experience is untouched by any evil. In prophetic religion, moral evil with its attendant psycho-physical sufferings came into the world because of the disobedience of man in keeping God's commandments and maintaining strict monotheism. But God Himself is Holy and untouched by any moral imperfection. God is also transcendent of human failures. For example, the book of Job states: Can the mortal man be more just than his creator? (*Job.* 4.17).

> Are you trying to prove that I am unjust—to put me in the wrong and yourself in the right? (*Job.* 40.2)

Job is silenced by the overwhelming might of God. In Islam and Judaism there is the doctrine of resignation to the inevitable decree of God, for what God does is just. This stoical resignation to all things that happen to a man is thus reflected:

> After all this, there is only one thing to say: Fear God, and obey His commands, because this is all that man was created for? (*Ecclesiastes* 12.13).

However, there is one problem that has baffled the prophetic theists. Why did God make man with freedom of will when He fully knew that he would misuse it? This is the question which the angels asked God.

> Wilt Thou place therein one (man) who will do harm therein and will shed blood, while we hymn thy praise and sanctify Thee? (*Surah* II.30).

God silenced the inopportune question by His Omnipotence and Omniscience. But this poses the dilemma.

> Is deity willing to prevent evil, but not able?
> Then he is impotent. Is he able but not willing?
> Then he is malevolent. Is he both able and willing?
> Whence then is evil?

According to the theist, the purpose of God's creation is the emergence of holy wills. A holy will cannot be created or made in the fashion as the angels of heaven who always do the right. A holy will has to create itself, through many falls and, as Kant has suggested, through many lives. A holy will has to conquer its own evil nature, and, finally only through the Grace of God. This becoming of the holy will by surrendering itself to the richer and fuller flow of divine ocean cannot be achieved in a day or even in one life. But this end of the emergence of holy wills far outweighs the abuse of free will. Hence, God does not will evil (i.e., the abuse of free will), but permits it for the purpose of evolving holy wills. Hence, Bergson puts it that this universe is a machine for the making of gods.[7]

Suffering in Christianity occupies an important place and the points may be thus repeated.

(a) Suffering is for the sake of awakening a man to realise his own essential nature. This is well illustrated in the case of the parable of Prodigal Son (Luke 15. 11-31). This is also true in Hinduism.

(b) Suffering is corrective.
"The Lord corrects those he loves, as a father corrects a son of whom he is proud" (*Proverb* 3.12; also *Job* 5.17; *Hebrew* 12.9).

(c) Suffering of the saintly persons and prophets is intercessory, vicarious and redemptive (e.g. in the cases of Moses, Jeremiah and Jesus Christ).

(d) At times suffering is for the manifestation of the Glory of God, (*St. John* 9.3) e.g., in healing a man born blind.

(e) Suffering is purificatory (*Hebrew* 5:8). This is illustrated in the examples of Abraham, Joseph, Job and Jesus. This is also true for the expiatory and penitentiary sufferings in Hinduism.

(f) As the follower of the Cross, it is a privilege for a Christian to suffer for the sake of Jesus. (Phillipians 1.29; 1 Peter 4.13-15).

(g) The doctrine of atonement, according to which Christ

died for the sins of the whole world, is unique in all the major religions of the world.

JUDAIC SUFFERING

Suffering is corrective and retributive. But there is one very grim aspect of Jewish suffering. The Jews have been often persecuted and even massacred. They still hold fast to God. Hence, according to them the Jews alone are the chosen people of God. Hence, they alone are fit to be sacrificed for the redemption of the whole mankind. Thus, Jewish persecution and massacre are in the plan of God for redeeming mankind. Hence, the Jews resigned themselves to their inevitable fate. So did Spinoza and Freud.

SUFFERING IN INDIAN TRADITION

In Indian tradition there is no concept of First creation. Creation and dissolution continue endlessly. In this creation, suffering is a hard fact of life. This has to be faced and every effort has to be made for its eradication. Hence, Indian tradition resorts to therapeutic measure for its removal. In this context, Sāṁkhya mentions three kinds of suffering; Viz., *ādhyatmika* (psycho-physical), *ādhibhautika* (natural) and *ādhidaivika* (supernatural). But the analysis of suffering in Buddhism is remarkable. It dissuades people from entering into the metaphysical origin of suffering. It is a metaphysical heresy. But it accepts suffering as a hard fact of life. Therefore the nature, the cause, the way and cessation of suffering are detailed and discussed. Buddhism, Jainism and early Mīmāṁsā are essentially atheistic. Hence, in these systems God cannot be held responsible for human suffering. Hence, in the atheistic systems of Jainism, Buddhism, and in early atheistic Sāṁkhya, man alone is the architect of his own destiny. In Jainism man is responsible for his many kinds of limitation and suffering due to his *Karman*. In Buddhism and in atheistic Sāṁkhya, the cause of human suffering is *ajñāna* (*avidyā* in Buddhism and infatuation in Sāṁkhya). Further, Buddhism also holds that desire (*tṛṣṇā*) in this worldly existence is a powerful cause of endless births and deaths and these constitute suffering (*jarā-maraṇa*). The whole Buddhist doctrine of wordly suffering is based on its metaphysical theory of momentariness.

However, even in theistic systems of India, God is said to be untouched by inauspicious attributes. He is essentially good, pure light without any shadow in it. Then, whence suffering? Theistic Indian systems do not undertake the task of metaphysical explanation of *first* suffering or the *First metaphysical cause* of suffering. Largely, *ajñāna* or *avidyā* is the immediate cause of suffering and attachment to the world which leads to the endless cycle of births and deaths. For Indian systems, worldly existence is essentially miserable. As *ajñāna* is the real cause of endless rebirths, so the removal of this *ajñāna* by means of *jñāna* is the only remedy.

In the *Viśiṣṭādvaita* of Ramanuja, the doctrine of *ajñāna* is sought to be replaced by *karma*. But he too ultimately holds that *karma along with ajñāna* is the real cause of the miserable worldly existence.[8]

Further, Ramanuja holds that the real nature of a jīva is to remain in subservience to God. Hence, revolt against this dependence on the Lord and the violations of injunctions and prohibitions mentioned in the scriptures, due to *ajñāna* may be mentioned as the specific cause of human bondage and suffering. Hence, this is very much akin to Christian doctrine, according to which sin (moral suffering) came in the world as a result of the disobedience to the command of God by Adam. However, there is some difficulty in Ramanuja's philosophy of qualified monism.

According to Ramanuja, *cit* and *acit* (*jīva* and *prakṛti*) form the body of God, who is the indwelling spirit of this body. Again, according to *Sharīra-Sharīrī* relationship of his system, Ramanuja defines body as that which the Lord *completely controls* (Śribhāṣya 1.2.2; II. 9). If it is so, then the jīvas, forming the body of the Lord, have no freedom of will. Hence, not they but God is responsible for the evil and suffering of the jīvas. However, Ramanuja proves the freedom of the jīvas on the basis of Shāstric injunctions and prohibitions.

For commandments can be addressed to such agents only

> as are capable of entering on action or refraining from action, according to their thought and will.[9]

Like Kant, Ramanuja maintains that commands mean 'thou oughtest'. 'Ought' implies the capacity of free choice of either obedience or disobedience. In another place too, Ramanuja maintains that each individual jīva has the complete power of initiative in taking action or abstinence from it.[10]

But is not God benevolent, merciful and omnipotent? Why then does He not liberate the jīva from the burden of miserable existence, seeing that He is the Lord of Karma? No doubt God is merciful and through His Grace He grants salvation to His devotees. Yes, God does grant salvation to all those jīvas who seek their refuge in Him.

> And I, dwelling in their hearts am moved by compassion and therefore destroy their darkness of soul born of ignorance by lighting the luminous lamp of their knowledge.[11]

Why does the Lord not show any pity for the disobedient evil-doer?

> For by pity we understand the inability, on somebody's part, to bear the pains of others, coupled with a disregard of his own advantage, when pity has the effect of bringing about the transgression of law on the part of the pitying person, it is in no way to his credit; it rather implies the charge of weakness.[12]

The Lord has to punish the evil-doer both for retributive and preventive ends.

Thus, for Ramanuja, man alone is responsible for his karman, suffering, and not God, who remains untouched by human weakness and evil.

Human Destiny

As noted earlier, according to Indian tradition this worldly existence is essentially miserable. This is the starting-point of the soteriological consideration and the way out is taken up as a therapeutic measure. The real cause is *avidyā* or *ajñāna*. Jainism accepts *karma* as the real cause of bondage and Ramanuja too regards karma in association with avidyā as the cause of human bondage and miseries.[13] But some other peculiarities have also been mentioned already in the Viśiṣṭādvaita of Ramanuja.

Naturally for Jainism by eradicating karma, a jīva can win his final destiny of infinite power, knowledge and bliss. According to Ramanuja, the ultimate destiny can be won only by *bhakti.* In the state of release, the jīva regains his ultimate destiny of dependence on and servitude to the Lord. He is also endowed with agency, which the released soul carries out according to the behest of the Lord.

In other systems of Indian thought, the ultimate destiny is really liberation from the endless cycle of miserable births and deaths. This state of liberation is called *nirvāṇa* in Buddhism. This *nirvāṇa* is really indescribable and can only be described as the state without any sorrow, without egotism and desire, and, without the prospect of any further fall into the cycle of births and deaths.

According to Sāṁkhya, Jainism, Nyāya and advaitism, the ultimate destiny of an individual is to regain its pristine glory of pure consciousness. Only Vaiśeṣika system does not admit consciousness as the ultimate nature of consciousness. According to it, consciousness is only an accidental attribute of a jīva, for it arises only when a jīva comes to have a body, sense-organs and their contact with an object.

According to Shaṅkara, liberation is really regaining the pristine state of consciousness, existence and bliss. In its ultimate state it is without any body. Very often it is mentioned that a jīva merges into Brahman, just as the rivers merge into the sea. However, mergence really means perfection and freedom from the limitation (or *upādhis*) which egotism entails. In the language of Kabir, the dirty water of a drain by losing itself in the river Ganges, gets rid of its dirtiness and becomes perfect by becoming Ganges-water (*Gaṅgā-jala*); a piece of iron by coming in contact with *pāras* (philosopher's stone) becomes gold by shedding off its nature as the piece of iron. Here ironness is lost, but iron gets perfected as gold.

In prophetic religions, God has created man so that he may become as holy as God is. In Christianity God has created man so that he may be a child of God. He can become a child of God by being united with God through his faith in the redemptive death of Jesus Christ on the Cross. By remaining in union with God through Christ, man will inherit the Kingdom of God or Heaven. Heavenly abode is said to be full of bliss, without any life of sensuousness. His life will be as holy as of angels who do not have any marriage-relation. He lives in heavenly glory of holiness and the praise of God (Luke 20.35). Though God has been progressively revealing His laws and commandments through prophets and through history, yet there are men who disobey the commandments of God. They are said to be the children of Devil. On the day of judgment they will be cast out into hell, where there will be weeping and gnashing of teeth because of their being burnt there in never-quenching fire. Hence, heaven for the righteous and hell for the sinners or unrighteous are two fates which await men as their final destiny.

For Judaism also heaven and hell are two things that await for the faithful and the unfaithful respectively. Of course, they do not believe in Jesus Christ as the Messiah. Hence, there can be no talk of union with God through Jesus Christ.

In Islam, after death, the spirit of man returns to God. On the day of resurrection he will rise from his grave. If he is proved faithful to God and His prophet Mohammed on the day of judgment, then he will be led into the Paradise, where he will have a life of never-ending enjoyment. In like manner, the evil-doer will be consigned to never-quenching hell–fire. In other words, on the day of judgment all persons will have to cross the bridge of *al-Sīrat*. Those who fall will go to hell, and, those who get across will go to heavens. Hence, the inheritance of heaven and hell is the ultimate destiny, according to Islam.

In the same manner, in Zoroastrianism, on the day of reckoning, every person will have to cross the bridge of *Chinvat*. The pious soul will easily pass the bridge and will go to heaven. However, the impious, the worshipper of Ahriman will fall from the bridge to pass into hell. However, the Parsi believes that hell-life is not eternal, for on the day of restoration, people suffering in hell will be purified and ultimately they will remain in heaven afterwards.

But what happens to souls from the time of death to the time of resurrection and the day of judgment? For the Jews, souls live in Sheol in a weak state of animation. Christians also have developed the notion of a region of purgatory (under the influence of Plato and Parsiism) where they will be purged of their sins and evil nature. Dr. Iqbal also suggests that heaven and hell are not permanent resting places, but they are stages of the progress of the soul.

Of course, in Ṛgvedic Aryan Hinduism certainly there is the concept of heaven. Heaven is pictured where all desires are fulfilled (RV IX. 113.7-11). This is reserved for those who risk their lives in battle, arrange sacrifices and give offerings and pious gifts (RV X. 14.8). In heaven the pious will have the fellowship with their Father (I. 109.7). The heavenly abode of Viṣṇu has also been mentioned in RV. I. 154.5-6. In like manner, there is something like hell for the wicked, mentioned as of 'deep place' (RV IV. 5.5) or 'pit' (RV VII. 104.3), reminding one of Jewish Sheol. This concept of heaven and hell was greatly elaborated in later Paurāṇic Hinduism, no doubt under the influence of Islam.

Salvation and Liberation

The concept of salvation is found in prophetic religions and of liberation in Indian systems of thought. 'Salvation' means escape from the anger of God which leads to the eternal damnation of the sinner into hell. Hell has been pictured as a place of very great physio-psychical torture. On the other hand, 'liberation' means escape from the endless cycle of births and deaths. As any form of worldly existence in Indian tradition is said to be miserable, so liberation ultimately means escape from miseries. Hence, there is hardly much difference from salvation and liberation, for in both cases it means escape from miseries. Positively both mean a life of unending bliss (in heaven for the prophetic religions, and, restoration of the pristine existence of the jīvas before their fall). This is also true for Buddhist *nirvāṇa.* But the respective means of attaining salvation and liberation markedly differ.

For the Jews salvation can be attained by means of obedience to the laws of Moses and by the culture of moral life of compassion, mercy and by having a contrite heart for the many sins of omissions and commissions. One has to remain true to one's Judaic tradition even at the cost of one's martyrdom.

The Christian seeks union with God by having faith in the sacrificial death of Jesus on the Cross. It is said to have full faith in the redemptive and vicarious death of Jesus on the cross. By 'redemptive' is meant that sins are so many cases of debt one owes to God. Hence, debt has to be paid for. Now faith in Jesus means that Jesus by his crucifixion has paid this debt to God. Secondly, it is vicarious death in the sense that in the place of the sinner, Jesus himself has carried away the sins of the believer. This sacrificial death of Jesus is an arrangement made by God for redeeming man of his sins. Hence, it is the free gift of God for all those persons who believe in the sacrificial death of Jesus.

> For God loved the world so much that he gave his only son, so that everyone who believes in him may not die but have eternal life. (*St. John* 3.16).

This forgiveness of sins is not only found in the peace of mind of a true Christian, but also reflected in his transformed life in the spirit of God. He is a new creature. (Galatians 6.15).

For Muslims one can win salvation by strict obedience to the commandments of Allah, and, by observing the five pillars of faith. One has to accept Allah as one God, Mohammed as His last and final prophet. On the day of judgment, the prophet will intercede on behalf of his true followers for the forgiveness of sins of omission and commission. A true believer has to resign himself to the sovereign will of Allah.

A Parsi is a co-worker and co-sharer with God in the struggle of Goodness over evil. He has to triumph over the evil by means of *Humta* (good thought), *Hukhta* (good word) and *Hvarshta* (good deeds).

The doctrine of liberation has been taken up in Hinduism with a good deal of detail.

'Liberation' in Indian tradition has been named '*mokṣa*', '*mukti*', 'tṛṣṇā' etc., (and literally means 'escape'). Hence, liberation means escape from the cycle of endless births and deaths, entailing miseries. As in general, the cause of bondage or miseries of rebirths is said to be *ajñāna*, so escape from bondage means regaining of the true *jñāna* of the nature of jīva himself. This *jñāna* means the realization of the pristine glory of the jīva as pure consciousness (Sāṁkhya, Nyāya, Jainism). However, in this connection the views of Shaṅkara and Ramanuja are important, and, a summary of their views can be given here, since they have already been mentioned earlier under 'Hinduism'.

SHAṄKARA

For Shaṅkara escape from the miserable existence of endless rebirths and deaths can be obtained from *Brahma-jñāna* only. *Brahma-prāpti* really means *becoming Brahma itself*. This is a state where all differences of father-mother, low-high, caste and so on, are utterly lost. *Brahma-jñāna* is re-finding one's real nature which a jīva is (*jivo Brahmaiva nṛpah*).

There are two kinds of *mukti*, namely *jivanmukti* (liberation in this very life) and *videhamukti* (liberation after the fall of the body.

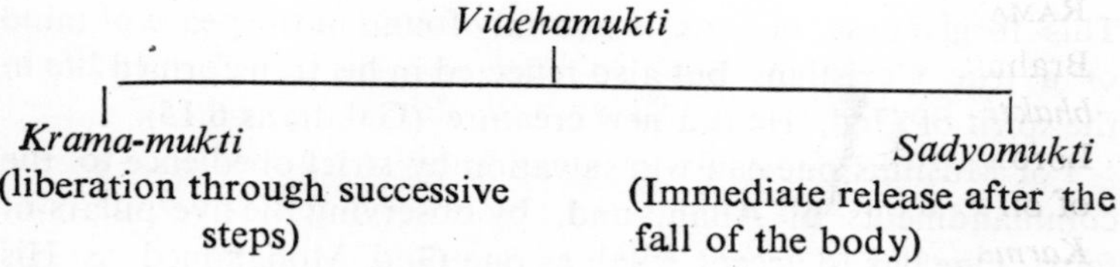

The problem of *jīvanmukti* is important for Shaṅkara for a *jīvanmukta* alone can be the upholder of *Brahma-jñāna*, exemplified in his life, and, can be the competent guide for seekers after *Brahma-jñāna*.

Maṇḍanamishra and Ramanuja do not regard the state of *jīvanmukti* as true liberation. The very existence of the body is the mark of the persistence of *ajñāna* according to Maṇḍana and Ramanuja. Shaṅkara would not accept this objection, since for Shaṅkara, *Brahma-jñāna* destroys accumulated and current Karmas, but fructescent Karmas (*prārabdha*) continue till the fall of the body. For Shaṅkara *Brahma-jñāna* destroys *ahaṁkāra* (egotism), desire and the reality of the world. The feeling of embodiment is lost, but not the body which continues as the momentum even when the push of the karmas is lost. Even here there are stages:

1. *Brahmavid* who knows and realizes Brahma and the illusoriness of the world.
2. *Brahmavidvara* who rises from his *samādhi* (trance) according to his will.
3. *Brahmavidvariyāna* whose *samādhi* can be terminated by external agency.
4. *Brahmavidvariṣṭha* whose samādhi cannot be terminated even by external agency.

The example of Brahmavidvariṣṭha (i.e. the most realized soul of *Brahma-jñāna*) was found in Ramakrishna.

After the fall of the body, a seeker devoted to Īshvara with a view to obtaining Brahma-realization, gets liberation in successive stages, due to the Grace of God. His final liberation comes only after the dissolution of the world (Brahmasūtra-Shaṅkarabhāṣya IV. 3.10; IV. 4.22). *Sadyomukti* is obtained by a *jīvanmukta* who obtains his *Brahma-jñāna* by means of *jñānayoga*.

RAMANUJA

Brahma of Ramanuja is personal and can be obtained through *bhakti*. Bhakti is a constant and steady remembrance of the Lord. This remembrance remains as uninterrupted as the flow of oil in a burning lamp. This *bhakti* is not pure feeling, but is *Karma-jñāna-Samuccaya* (i.e., an intermixture of *Karma and jñāna*, action and knowledge). Liberation is obtained through the Grace of God by seekers who seek it by deserving it by virtue of their love and devotion to God. God grants liberation to man by restoring the dependence (or refuge) of the seeker on God.

Liberation is of two kinds:

1. *Kaivalya* in which stage the jīva remains totally free, though subservient to the Lord.
2. *Kaiñkarya-bhāva* in which the jīva fully enjoys the dependence of the Lord. Here are also stages of development that continue indefinitely.
   (a) The liberated attains *salokya* i.e., the abode of the Lord.
   (b) Further, reaches *Sānnidhya* i.e., the presence of God.
   (c) Further still the *mukta* (liberated) becomes like the

Lord (Sārūpya). In this state he enjoys all the powers of the Lord except the creation and dissolution of the world.

(d) Finally, the mukta enjoys followship with the Lord.

One can note that the doctrine of Grace and the attainment of fellowship with God in Ramanuja and Christianity are very similar ideas.

Sin

The concept of sin has relevance in theism only, where God is taken to be a person. 'Sin' means disobedience of the law and commandments of God. It should be distinguished from crime which means violation of the legal code of a country e.g., theft, murder, fraud etc. Again, sin is to be distinguished from moral lapses e.g., cruelty, greed, ingratitude etc. Crime is related to laws external to man, and moral lapses are related to the internal laws written in one's heart or conscience. Sin, however, has its relation with God as Person, who asks man to obey, observe and carry out his commandments and laws. The concept of sin is most pronounced in Zoroastrianism, Judaism, Christianity, Islam, Ṛgvedic worship of Varuṇa and Ramanuja. As distinguished from sin is the concept of *ajñāna* or *avidyā*. *Ajñāna* not only makes man ignorant of his real nature, but makes him commit many immoral acts. Hence, *ajñāna* is deeply related with morality. Sin requires penitence leading to forgiveness and finally reconciliation with God whose commandments and laws have been violated by the sinner. As against penitence, forgiveness and reconciliation, moral lapses under the influence of *ajñāna* require penances and in general internalization of morality. For example, in Indian system in order to overcome the endless cycle of rebirths, the seeker has to renounce his desires (*tṛṣṇā*) for women, wealth, name and fame etc. In other words, it is a matter of self-culture and self-conquest, if one wants to gain liberation (*mokṣa*).

With this introduction, we can take up the problem of sin in different theistic systems.

Parsiism: There is only one God called Ahura Mazda. He is also the law-giver for the guidance of man. As Ahura Mazda has created man with free will, so man can either obey or disobey the law of God. This law in the form of *asha* (corresponding to *ṛta* of Varuṇa of the Ṛgveda) is moral, natural and spiritual. Disobedience of the law given by Ahura Mazda is sin. Why disobedience, specially when man was created pure? Because there is Ahriman who not only creates natural calamities but distorts the mind of man for evil things and disobedience.

Judaism: The first sin came into the world by the first Adam. This sin consisted in the disobedience of man in eating the forbidden fruit of knowledge. As the further story of Judaism continues, God gave His commandments in the form of law, injunctions and prohibitions. Disobedience of God's commandments was deemed as sin. The two great sins of the Jews were defiling the Sabbath (i.e., working on that day) and Idol-worship. The history of the Jews when they were ruled by others, were defeated and even taken into exile, is the story of worshipping of idols of Baal, Asherah and many others. Jesus was accused of defiling the Sabbath, for he performed many miracles of healing on Sabbath. Again, Jesus was accused of blasphemy when he claimed that he and God are one (St. John 10.30) and that he claimed that he was before Abraham was born (St. John 8.58). Hence, idol worship, defilement of Sabbath and blasphemy were great sins.

Christianity: In Christianity too sin means rebellion against God, and, this disobedience is widespread. Adam sinned by his disobedience and this spirit of disobedience has enveloped the whole human race (Romans 5.12). This is known as the doctrine of *original sin* of man. This means that man's evil nature has deep root in him. St. Paul writes that man is torn into conflict between his human (animal) nature and God's spirit within him. This human nature is so strong that man falls a prey to his passions and animal desires, and, becomes a creature of sin. In other words, by following his animal nature, he substitutes his animal image for the image of God planted in him at the time of creation. True, God has given us the Law to guide us. But we are compelled by our human nature to violate the law.

——I am a mortal man, sold as a slave to sin. I do not understand what I do; for I don't do what I would like to do, but instead I do what I hate. (Romans 7.14-15).

The conclusion is that knowing the Law is not enough, for the animal passion is so strong in man that knowing the law he becomes helpless and he keeps on violating the Law. The more he knows about the law, the more miserable he becomes, for he becomes conscious of his not keeping the law. The more he becomes aware of his rebellion against God, the more he suffers from his sense of guilt. Hence, there is need for a way out of sin in man. Here we are led to faith in the redemptive death of Jesus on the Cross. But we find that there is a good deal of similarity between the load of karma in Hinduism and the doctrine of original sin. A Hindu is born a prisoner of his past karma which determines his conduct to a great extent. How can a Hindu get rid of the load of karma? As in Christianity the Grace of God saves a man from his burden of sin, so in Hinduism too in the *bhakti* school of Ramanuja and others, the Grace of God overcomes the burden of karma and helps a *bhakta* to get his salvation.

Islam: No doubt for Islam too, sin means rebellion against God. This was the besetting sin of Iblis, who disobeyed God by not bowing down before Adam. Ever since the Devil is at work and he beguiles human beings into sin. A Muslim is advised that he should have a great deal of faith in God in order to escape from Sin. No doubt he should get repentant for any act of violating the law. But it is hoped that by observing the five pillars of five prayers, Ramadān fast, zakat etc., it would be possible for him to overcome the sin the Muslim commits.

It appears that insistence on faith in God and His apostle and daily prayers are forms of devotion standing on *par* with *bhakti*. Of course, the vivid picture of hell is also calculated to instil fear in the heart of the possible violation of the Law. The dependence of a Muslim on the mercy and compassion of God and the efficacious advocacy of the prophet Mohammed on the day of judgment would suffice to have the forgiveness of his sins.

Ṛgvedic conception of sin: We have already held that Indo-Aryans and Iranians lived together before their parting. Naturally some sort of Parsiism concerning monotheistic worship might have been the common faith of all Aryans. This monotheistic worship lingers in the worship of Ṛgvedic god Varuṇa.

The Ṛgvedic Aryans in the presence of Varuṇa were quite conscious of the moral laws of *ṛta* promulgated by God Varuṇa. They were also conscious of their violation and seek forgiveness of their sins of commission and omission.

1. Whatever law of thine, O God, O Varuṇa, as we are men,
   Day by day we violate.
2. Give us not as prey to death, to be destroyed by thee in wrath,
   To thy fierce anger when displeased. (RV. I 25).

In the same vein RV. VII. 89 the Ṛgvedic Aryans plead for God's mercy.

> O Varuṇa, whatever the offence may be which we as men commit against the heavenly host,
> When through our want of thought, we violate thy laws, punish us not,
> O God, for that inequity. (RV. VII. 89.5)

It is to be noted that both in the New Testament (Romans 5.12) (7.24) and RV. 1.25.2 and 1 Cor. 15.56 the wages of sin are said to be death.

Ramanuja: For Ramanuja, sin is rebellion against God. God has given man his freedom of will and in Shāstras has given him instructions for his guidance. These instructions are in the form of many injunctions and prohibitions. By his violation of God's commandments in the Shāstras man is condemned to the endless cycle of rebirths and deaths. This doctrine of endless rebirths means endless suffering and compares favourably with the doctrine of hell-fire in prophetic religions. Nay more. For the vile offender God,

> gives him evil intellect and will and actuates him to proceed along evil lines. (*Vedārthasangraha*, *padas* 124, 125)

This evil disposition is really a punishment and saintly nature is a reward of the righteous. This again means the same thing that holy lives fit for the fellowship of God are the supreme end of creation. Here Ramanuja and Christianity join hands. According to Ramakrishna, sin follows from the acceptance of free will. But man is not free. Everything depends on the will of God. Hence, there is neither free will in man nor is he a sinner (M. 274, M. 677, M. 820) from the viewpoint of a man who has realized God, everything good and bad is the play of God's māyā. Man is a machine and the Lord alone is the operator (M. 211). But Ramakrishna also admits that for the neophyte there is a feeling of sin in the beginning (M. 403).

Expiation and Atonement

'Expiation' means reparation of wrong acts, and 'atonement' means wiping out one's sin, or, freeing oneself from the stain of sin. *Parsi* religion holds that it is better not to sin than to expiate oneself for it. Usually prayers were made for atoning sin. Sincere penance was necessary, along with the recital of sacred gāthā. It was supposed that the recital of one gātha routs at least one demon. Only in this life expiation through prayers is possible. True repentance means a change of will. Confession of one's sin has to be made before a Parsi priest known as *Dastur*. Loud confession and bathing one's face with tears were deemed efficacious for expiating one's sin. However, non-repetition of the same sin is the only mark of purification.

Judaism has very many prescribed rites for cleansing one's sins. Commonly animal sacrifice along with repentance was deemed efficacious for wiping out one's sin (Leviticus 6.24-27). Later on feeling of repentance was emphasized in the place of animal sacrifice.

The sacrificial animal had to be without blemish. It used to be a pet domestic animal. At the time of sacrifice, the man seeking expiation, had to put his hands on the head of the animal to be sacrificed, effecting identification with the animal to be slain (Leviticus 1.3-5). Secondly, the sacrificer himself had to slay the animal he once loved as his pet. The slain animal is killed as the substitute of the sacrificer. Hence, the sacrificer confesses his sin of his omission and commission, seeking the Grace of God for wiping out his sin. A portion of the sacrificed animal was burnt in fire as the sweet savour pleasing to the Lord. Here one can easily see the similarity between Vedic and early Jewish rites of sacrificing the animal and burning in the fire. For the Vedic people Agni was the mouth of Gods through which the slain animal was consumed.

But animal sacrifice without repentance for the sin was unavailing. Later on repentance was emphasized.

> The Lord says, "I hate your religious festivals———when you bring me burnt offerings and grain offerings, I will not accept them————Instead let justice flow like astream——" (*Amos* 5.21-24).

Again,

> 'I want your constant love, not your animal sacrifice'. (*Hosea* 6.6).

Repentance was so much emphasized that a Jew took to fasting, alms giving, the study of Torah, and even submission to stripes as means of atonement. But living Grace was the final and only way out of one's sin. Confession of one's sin in public and before God was also another expedient for atonement.

On the day of atonement, even the sin of the people as a whole had to be expiated by animal sacrifice and repentance on the part of the people concerned (Leviticus, Chapters 16, 17).

Christian doctrine of Atonement cannot be understood without Jewish doctrine of expiation and atonement just mentioned above. It was the doctrine of 'original sin', which distorted the will of man. This original sin simply means that by virtue of this deep-rooted inclination in man makes him more of an animal than a spiritual being. Man is torn into conflict on account of his human nature which works against his spiritual nature given to him by God at the time of the creation of man. No doubt there are the laws for the guidance of man. But man knows these laws, but the animal nature within him is so strong that he becomes powerless.

> When I want to do good, I don't; and when I try not to do wrong, I do it anyway. (*Romans* 7.15,19).

The result? Man remains a helpless victim of his own human

nature and sin. But God has created man in His own image and He wants man to remain holy by turning to him and being obedient to Him. How is this possible?

In Christianity the concept of God as Judge and Law-giver is changed into loving, forgiving and redeeming God. God sent Jesus as His only Son, who remained obedient to Him in every way. Nay, he remained sinless to the end of his life. Therefore, he alone was fit to be sacrificed, as in the past animals without blemish were sacrificed for the atonement of the sins of His people. Hence, the New Testament records,

> Behold the lamb of God that taketh away the sin of the world.[14]

How is it possible for the believers to overcome their human nature and consequent sin?

Well, the death of Jesus has shown two things very clearly. First, God loves man and is ready to forgive his sins and to take him back to His fellowship. He has shown that Christ on the Cross was praying for forgiving the people who conspired to kill him. So God too is willing to take back a sinner to His fold. Further, this shows that without coming to God through Jesus, man will remain sinning and conspiring to kill saintly men. Hence, the death of Jesus shows the depth and degradation of man under the influence of sin. What should a man do to get the forgiveness of his sin and a life of virtue over one's sinfulness?

By faith in the sacrificial death of Jesus, as the people in the past got their peace of mind by yearly sacrifice of animals, God has accepted the voluntary sacrifice of Jesus for remitting the sins of every one who puts his trust in Jesus. This faith in Jesus strengthens the life of spirit within man and this strengthened spirit means the restoration of the image of God which God had planted in him at the time of the creation of man. One can easily see the resemblance of Indian tradition, according to which man in his liberation regains his pristine glory that was lost to him by *ajñāna*. In Christian doctrine of atonement (i.e., the remission of one's sins) too, man regains his lost image of God.

Again, this doctrine of faith in the sacrificial death of Jesus is taken to be the Grace of God. Man, by his own merits of good works can earn this forgiveness of sin and reconciliation with God. It is a free gift of God for all those who believe. *Kathopanishad* holds that the Grace (*prasāda*) of the creator enables a man to behold His greatness (2.20).

> This soul (Atman) is not to be obtained by instruction, nor by intellect, nor by much learning. It is to be obtained only by the one whom he chooses.[15]

And Ramanuja has accepted this doctrine of Grace, as before him the Alvars also did the same. But apart from this doctrine of *bhakti* which has already been explained earlier, the *dharma-kanda* of Manu, Yajñavalkya has also mentioned a detailed account of expiation (*prāyaścita*). A very brief account can be mentioned here to illustrate the various means of expiation.

Drinking of intoxicating liquor was strictly prohibited. Those who violated this prohibition could expiate this violation by drinking the same liquor when boiling hot. A killer of a Brahmin had to be killed by archers appointed for this purpose. A theif of gold was considered pure by being killed. Wrongful appropriation of a field, a well etc., could be expiated by taking *pañcagavaya* (five things belonging to a cow, namely, milk, ghee, curd, cow-dung and urine). This is known as *go-vrata*. At times generous gifts to Brahmins, pilgrimage to sacred places could be the means of expiating heinous crimes.

Worship and Prayer

Worship: Both worship and prayer involve dualism, for worship is of a deity, and prayer is also made to a personal deity who can respond to the entreaties of his devotees. We are not said to worship attributeless Brahman. Brahman can be realized only by trance (*Samādhi*) or *nididhyāsana* as Shaṅkara tells us.

'Prayer' comes under 'worship'.

Worship includes not only prayer but much more. The object of worship, as Rudolph Otto tells us, is tremendous mystery (*Mysterium tremendum et fascinosum*). 'Mystery' does not mean an unsolved problem, for a problem is one which is in due course soluble. But God is mystery for He is essentially indescribable and unknowable in the sense that no factual cognition of God is possible. God is said to be most mysterious to the person who has the most favoured vision of Him. He can be described only as *neti, neti* (not this, not this). In prophetic tradition, God is recognized as one's Creator, and, the worshipper realizes his state of creatureliness and absolute dependence, as even Ramanuja would concede. Hence, God requires utmost obedience and complete surrender of His worshippers. Can this God, as the object of one's worship be finite?

William James, John Stuart Mill think that God with so much evil in the world cannot be infinitely powerful and good. But theists do not think so. A worshipper has to surrender himself to God without any reserve. This total, all out surrender is possible only when the object of worship is infinite, as J. N. Findlay has pointed out.

Not only the object of worship is Infinite on whom the worshipper depends for his being, but he also feels that God is holy and no man with unclean lips and moral lapse can even approach Him. Hence, the worshipper is filled with holy dread and regards himself nothing but dust and ashes. He is also afraid at times that he is really not worshipping an infinite God, but a finite caricature of Him. This is what Appaya Dikshit felt that he had confined the Omnipresent Lord to particular places of worship.

Worship matures into *bhakti*, which, according to *Bhagavata Purāṇa,* consists in listening to His deeds, praising Him, remembering Him, washing His feet, paying obeisance, prostrating before Him, doing service to Him humbly overwhelming love for and full dedication to God. With some modification it applies to the worship of every kind of God.

In *bhakti*, the worshipper has to be constantly vigilant, lest he may slip away from his devotion to God. It has been likened to the effort of a baby monkey who has to cling to his mother, lest he falls. This is known as *markata-kishora-nyāya*. But the final stage of *bhakti* is called *prāpatti* in which stage the Lord Himself comes down to the help of His devotee, and the devotee completely surrenders himself to God as his only and last refuge. *Prāpatti* has the following features:

1. Favourable goodwill to all human beings and creatures.
2. Absence of ill-will towards any being.
3. Full faith in God that He will protect him and would provide him his daily needs.
4. Taking refuge in God as his redeemer and saviour.
5. Feeling one's helplessness in saving himself without the help from God, as St. Paul too holds.
6. Surrender of one's whole being to God, known as *Sharaṇāgati.*

According to Gītā 7.16 there are four kinds of devotees:

1. There are devotees who seek the Lord for granting them earthly prosperity (*arthārthi*).
2. Devotees in distress for its removal (*arthārthi*).
3. For obtaining *Brahma-jñāna,* by sharpening the intellect and purifying the heart of the devotee (*jijñāsu*).
4. Devotees who desire communion with God (*sāyujyārthi*).

Sāyujyārthi is the best and *jijñāsu* is the second best. For worship the following features are necessary:

(i) God has to be regarded as Infinite, having the characteristics of mystery, Omnipotence, personality and so on.
(ii) God has to be regarded as having surpassing excellence and beyond the grasp of human intellect.
(iii) Feeling of absolute dependence.
(iv) Surrender of one's total being to God.
(v) Throwing one's burden on God with full commitment and self-involvement.
(vi) In the last resort a *bhakta* cannot help praising and chanting His goodness to Him and to all men.

Prayer: Prayer is worship in which outpouring of heart can be verbalized either explicitly or implicitly (intenrally). It is the experience of the worshippers that prayers are most certainly answered. Even when the prayer is not immediately replied as the worshipper wants, still it helps him in the most unexpected ways. According to the Gītā just as the worshipper is temperamentally and in accordance with his *saṁskāras,* so is his deity

(17.4); just as his devotion to his deity is, so is the reward of his worship (7.21). A contrite heart, full of faith in God, brings even God to his worshipper. Ramanuja holds that God, unable to endure separation from His worshippers, cannot maintain His own atman.[16]

It is also held by theistic devotees that God provides all the needs of His devotee. Jesus said that men should first seek the kingdom of God and then God will provide all their needs (Matthew 6.33). Similarly, Kabir holds that God cannot allow His devotees to remain in want. Again, Jesus has said, 'Ask, seek and knock at the door'. If man can give good things to his children when they ask, then how can God deny his worshipper what he wants (Matthew 7.7-12)?

We have already given Christians' Lord's Prayer and the Gāyatrī of the Hindus. A Muslim has to pray five times every day and he begins the invocation with 'Allah is Great'. Prayers are obligatory and optional. It is obligatory to pray five times daily, attending congregational Friday prayer in a mosque. Optional prayers are of many kinds e.g., after the death of a Muslim, after the successful haj pilgrimage and so on. The purpose of prayers is to keep the Muslim believer in communion with God, and, to keep him free from evil thought and works.

Prayer and Magic

Prayer has to be said with full awareness of its subject-matter and full faith. God may or may not grant what the worshipper wishes. A worshipper gets what is best for him, but one cannot force God to grant what the worshipper wants, no matter with what earnestness he makes his supplication. This need not be the case of magic, where the desired result must follow from the magical incantation. Here magic is most like the natural law where the result must follow if the correct formula has been adopted. Again, in a prayer there is always a benign deity to whom the appeal is made. In contrast, in magic there may or may not be any deity who can be bent to the wishes of the magic-users.

1. Both magic-spell and prayers are verbalized responses to the supernatural agencies, but there are significant differences.

(a) Prayers are used for the well being of all and a worshipper remains without any ill-will towards anybody.
In contrast, magic spell might be used for doing harm.

(b) In prayer, the wish of the worshipper may or may not be granted. However, magic is believed to bring forth the result by the mere force of the spell, for the spell itself is said to be efficacious.

(c) Prayers are made in ordinary language, which is intelligible and meaningful. But magic spell consists of meaningless words.

(d) The order of words in a prayer can be altered almost at will or otherwise, but the order of meaningless words in magic incantations is fixed, and, words have to be pronounced most correctly. Alteration in the order of words, or, its incorrect pronunciation is supposed to be followed by calamities for the user of the spell.

(e) In prayer, there is always a personal deity to whom supplication is made. In magic there might or might not be a deity, but the important thing is that the spell be corrcetly pronounced, word-order be kept intact and the spell be repeated for a required number of times.

In early Mīmāṁsā it was held that there are no gods. The so-called deities, namely, Indra, Varuṇa, Mitra etc., are mere names and occasions for repeating the Vedic mantras. What is necessary is that the mantras be correctly pronounced with the proper order of words. But this view did not last long.

PRAYER AND CONCENTRATION (SAMĀDHI)

In Indian tradition especially in Jainism and Buddhism, the existence of God is denied, at least in principle. Here, *dhyāna* (Jainism) and *Samādhi* (meditation in Buddhism) take the place of prayer:

In the advaitism of Shaṅkara, at times, prayer and worship are regarded as mere means for obtaining *jñāna*. Here God takes kindly to His worshippers. He purifies the head and heart of his devotees. After this purification, the seeker can resort to the *jñānamārga* consisting of *Shravaṇa, manana* and *nididhyāsana*.

However, the system of Ramanuja is fully theistic and here

there is room for prayer and *bhakti*. We have already made a reference to it.

Comparison between Indian Religions

Karma-saṁsāra-jñāna-mukti are the four-fold pillars of Indian religions, even though they may differ in many other features. Further, whatever might have been the original languages of these religions, in the end they all adopted *Sanskrit* as the medium of their thought. For example, Buddhism was propagated at the beginning in the language of Pali, and, Jainism was written in Prākṛta. But towards their final form they have presented their systems in Sanskrit. Again, Jainism and Buddhism are not offshoots of Hinduism. They are parallel and independent religious movements. But on the whole they have the same cultural background of music, literature, script and iconology. However, each of these religions mentioned here has different religious history. For example, Jainism is considered pre-Vedic with Ṛsabha Muni as its founder, and, certainly Lord Buddha was the founder of Buddhism and Buddhism has its own separate and independent history of different councils, schools and missionary enterprise. Again, Sikhism hearkens back to non-Vedic cults and cannot be traced to Vedism at all. Its religious concepts, practices and martial discipline are its distinctive features, though Sikhism is Hinduistic in a wide sense. It shares in common with Indian religions, the four-fold pillars of *Karma-saṁsāra-jñāna-mukti*.

With the points mentioned above, we can make very brief comparison with one another.

Jainism and Hinduism

1. Jainism is nearer Hinduism than Buddhism. Its doctrine of *Ahiṁsā* is accepted by all the systems of India, at least in principle. Both Hinduism and Jainism accept the four-fold principles of *Karma-Saṁsāra-jñāna-mukti*.

2. In the same manner, the Jain doctrine of *pañca-mahāvrata* is the most accepted moral principle of all the religious systems of India.

3. Jainism and Hinduism, both accept the substantial concept

of Soul. However, Jainism has its own distinctive features that differentiate it from Hinduism.

1. *Ahiṁsā* (non-violence) is the most distinctive feature of Jainism. Even when it is accepted in principle by other Indian system, yet animal-sacrifice is even now in vogue in Hinduism in certain quarters e.g., buffalo-sacrifice in Nepal and Kalighat in West Bengal.

2. As noted earlier, Jainism has its own Scripture and it does not accept the authority of the Vedas. For this reason Jainism is considered as unorthodox (*nāstika*) school of thought.

3. Jainism in principle does not support theism, for according to it the liberated souls or eternal spirits do not respond to any supplication and have no part to play in any mundane affairs. But Hinduism is largely theistic.

4. No doubt Jains instal the image of Lord Mahavira, but it is done as a support (*ālambana*) of concentration (*dhyānas*). But Hinduism indulges in idol-worship in the form of *arcā*.

5. Jainism does not accept idol-worship or God. On the other hand, it accepts the role of reason as authority in matters of religious choice. In contrast, Hinduism accepts the existence of God and regards the Vedas as authoritative religious scripture, for the spiritual guidance of man.

6. Jainism has no place for caste, but caste is the most distinctive feature of Sanatana Hinduism.

Jainism and Buddhism

1. Both Jainism and Buddhism accept the four-fold pillars of *Karma-saṁsāra-jñāna-mukti.*

2. Both of them in principle are wholly atheistic, even when Lord Buddha in the end came to be worshipped in the form of *trikāya* Buddha, and, Lord Mahavira is accepted as a support for sustaining *dhyāna* (meditation).

3. Both of them accept *Yoga*, *dhyāna* and *Samādhi* (concentration) as the means of winning liberation.

4. Both of them accept reason for reaching right belief, and, do not advise to accept scripture as an infallible guide for spiritual attainment.

5. Both of them do not accept caste, and, Buddhism is opposed to casteism.

6. Comparatively Jainism is much older than Buddhism, though both of them are equally non-Vedic, and, are independent and parallel religious movements. They cannot be considered as off-shoots of Brahminism. They have a separate history of their own, independently of Brahminism. However, Jainism is nearer Hinduism than is Buddhism.

7. Both of them are Kṣhatriya movements and are not due to any Brahminical teaching.

8. *Tri-ratna* (three jewels) of right-faith, right knowledge and right conduct in Jainism really correspond to *Shīla, Samādhi* and *prajña* (wisdom) in Buddhism.

9. Finally, both of them are instances of spiritual humanism. But they have their differentiating features too:

1. Jainism and Buddhism differ with regard to their metaphysical postulates. Jains believe in substances, specially spirits. Buddhism has its basis in momentariness and regards everything without any essential character of its own (*nis-swabhāva*). For Buddhism so-called soul or spirit is only an aggregate or *gestalt* of passing events.

2. Naturally, they differ with regard to the final destiny of each jīva. For Jainism in the state of release a jīva attains omniscience, unhindered intuition of all things and omnipotence (*ananta jñāna, ananta darshan, ananta cāritra*, and *ananta vīrya*). For Buddhism the state of release is indescribable *nirvāṇa*.

3. In logic too they differ; Jainism believes that reality is multi-faceted. So it advances the logic of *anekāntavāda* and *saptabhanginaya*. As opposed to this Buddhism advanced the doctrine of *anattavāda* (soul-lessness) and momentariness.

4. The original language of Jaina Scripture is *Prakṛt* and of Buddhism is *Pāli*.

5. But Buddhism became a great missionary religion and even now is found all over the globe. But Jainism remained a conservative religion, and, is not found anywhere except in India.

6. In relation to Hinduism, Jainism has become almost a part of Hinduism. But Buddhism has consistently remained opposed to Hinduism.

7. Buddhism has avoided the extreme of *tapas* (austerities) and *ahiṁsā* of Jainism and calls itself as middle-roader (*madhya-mārgi*).

HINDUISM AND BUDDHISM

Whatever might have been the differences between Vedic Aryans and Buddhism, at present all forms of religion of Indian origin accept the four-fold principle of *Karma-saṁsāra-jñāna-mukti.* But apart from this fundamental similarity, there are deep-seated differences between Brahminical Hinduism and Buddhism. These differences clearly show that Buddhism and Hinduism are parallel and independent religious movements, and, Buddhism cannot be said to be an offshoot of Hinduism.

1. Hinduism, specially of Shaṅkara and Ramanuja, accepts the authority of the Vedas as the ultimate court of appeal for all religious issues. In contrast, Buddhism advises us not to take any authority for granted. Every religious truth has to be rationally evaluated.

2. As noted earlier, Hinduism accepts the reality of God in general, and, more so in modern times. However, Buddhism accepts the postulates of momentariness. According to it there is nothing with its substantial character and essence. Naturally there are no eternal and immortal souls, and, there is no creator God. Hence, Buddhism in principle is atheistic, and, Hinduism is on the whole theistic.

Of course, much later in the history of Buddhism, Lord Buddha came to be worshipped in the form of *Trikāya* Buddha, and, even some Bodhisattvas came to acquire the status of deities. Again, in Shaṅkara's religious philosophy, the place of God may be of secondary importance, but then His existence is not denied.

3. Buddhism has no place for caste, and, Lord Buddha has presented very convincing arguments against caste. In contrast, Hinduism is based on caste with the superiority of Brahmins in that caste-system.

4. Lord Buddha was also very much opposed to animal-sacrifice. However, though on the whole animal-sacrifice in Hinduism is not very popular now, yet in Nepal and at Kalighat, Calcutta,

animal-sacrifice is performed. But Buddhism is not opposed to non-vegetarian food.

5. Buddhism was formed by a Kshatriya, and, not by Brahmins. So with the rise of Brahminism, Buddhism has almost disappeared from India. This shows that Brahminism and Buddhism were opposed in their religious outlook, social order, metaphysics and logic.

6. Even the language of Buddhist teaching was the language of people, which was Pali. But Hinduism has maintained Sanskrit as its language.

7. Buddhism was a missionary religion and it spread throughout the whole of Asia. Even now it is a living religion of Asia. However, Hinduism never believed in missionary enterprise and, in this century Radhakrishnan was opposed to missionary enterprise. Only now Arya Samaj has taken up the work of missionary enterprise.

8. Buddhism favours *Sannyāsa* for obtaining *nirvāṇa*. Hinduism does not favour *Sannyāsa* without undergoing the earlier three stages of studentship, house-holdership and forest-dwelling. Maṇḍana was opposed to Shaṅkara, when the latter advanced the acceptanee of *Sannyāsa* without observing the first three stages of life.

But apart from conceptual comparison, religions have interrelations in general, and, we can now take up the problem of 'Encounter of Religions'.

References

1. *Fragments of a Confession*, p. 69 in '*The Philosophy of Sarvepalli Radhakrishnan*', 1952.
2. *Ibid.*, p. 80.
3. The Critique of Pure Reason, tr. N.K. Smith, abridged edition, p. 201.
4. Romain Rolland, 'The Life of Ramakrishna', 1930, p. 76.
5. M. Yamunacharya, *Ramanuja's Teachings in his own Words*, p. 53.
6. M.A. Macauliffe, *The Sikh Religion*, Vol. I, pp. 165-166.
7. H. Bergson, *The Sources of Morality and Religion*, p. 275.
8. Y. Masih, *The Classical Religious Philosophy of the Hindus*, Patna 1988, pp. 466-475.
9. Shribhāṣya, II. 3.40.

10. Vedarthasamgrah, pada 124.
11. Vedarthasamgrah, pada 125; also Shribhāṣya II. 2.3.
12. Shribhāṣya, II. 2.3.
13. Gītābhāṣya IV.14; IX 10; XIV. 4, 5; Shribhāṣya II.1.34; Vedarthasamgrah pada 209.
14. St. John 1.29. This view has been repeated throughout the New Testament, Romans 3.25; The Hebrews 10.9; 1 Peter 1.19; 2.22; 2.24; 3.18; 1 John 3.5.
15. Muṇḍaka III.2.3; Kaṭha II.23.
16. Ramanuja's Comment on Gītā VII. 18; VIII.14; IX.2.

CHAPTER XI

ENCOUNTER OF RELIGIONS

INTRODUCTION

Very often some religions clash and this produces political problem and the failures of human beings to live together in peace. Different views and problems are advanced in this context.

1. First, it is pointed out, 'why raise problems of inter-relation of religions, seeing that with the advance of science, technology, industrialization, religions are bound to disappear in the near future.

2. Even if it be replied that there is a deep-seated tendency in man for religion and religion must persist, then it might be further held that religions in that case are all relative and are bound to clash with one another. Why try to find a solution of bringing religions together on a common platform?

3. However, it might be replied that there is an absolute standard in relation to which all religions point. Here it may be further objected that this standard may not be accepted by all. And further, it might be difficult to realize this absolute standard.

4. Even if the point be conceded that for years the relativity of religions will continue, then the problem of their co-existence will continue to plague mankind.

5. Religion is really implicit in every political party, and political institution has also an implicit religious overtones. For example, Hinduism, Sikhism and Islam have political purposes and ambitions. Again, a political party like Communism assumes a religious commitment on the part of the adherents.

Most probably the questions posed here are much weightier than their solution. But reason is our only weapon with which we can attempt at solving our problems. In the history of human civilization, religions have caused wars and yet they have also promoted peace. For example, Jews, Christians and Parsis violently clashed among themselves, and, with the rise of Islam a good deal of peace was established by the progress of Islam amongst the Arabs and Persians. Why not try to promote this unity? Hence, an intellectual attempt is needed for the mutual understanding of different adherents of various religions.

Case for Religion a Priori

It is a fact that with the advance of science, technology, banking, industrialization, inter-relational trade etc., the hold of Christianity in the west has greatly loosened. The pre-occupation with other worldliness has given rise to this-worldly pursuits. Secularization in this sense is bound to increase all the world over. Even modern India is not untouched by the doctrine of this worldliness. However, we note that natural and super-natural are the two attitudes which keep on oscillating from one end of the extreme to the other end. In ancient India and in medieval periods in the West, supernaturalism loomed large. We are at present going to the other extreme of this-worldliness. But we have to remember the Upanishadic and Biblical teachings in relation to worldly pursuits. Maitreyi said to Yajñavalkya:

> Why should I do with that through which I may not be immortal? (*Bṛhadāraṇyaka* 2.4.3).

Similarly, Jesus replied to Satan,

> Man cannot live on bread alone, but needs every word that God speaks. (*Matthew* 4.4).

Even when all men have their bodily need satisfied, they will still crave for that which is immortal and eternal. What shall a man gain, if he gains the whole world and loses his own soul? Religion has to deal with man's own depth and stirring of one's whole personality. This is what is known as religion *a priori*, which means that there is a deep-seated proclivity in the psychical constitution of man by virtue of which he cannot find rest till he finds a religion that will give him peace and *pistis* under all circumstances in his life. This doctrine of religion *a priori* has been variously stated by the thinkers. The Bible says that the spirit of God is within us which makes us cry out, 'Father, my

Father' (Galatians 4.6). In the same strain St. Augustine has said,

> Thou hast created us for thyself and our heart knows no rest until it may repose in thee.

Anselm of Canterbury (1033-1109) was so convinced of religion *a priori* that he felt that even if a fool could understand the meaning of God, then he would not say that there is no God. But the most convincing case for religion *a priori* comes from an organismic theory of man and his psyche.

In our own day, it was Paul Tillich (1886-1966) who has most powerfully advanced the doctrine of religion *a priori*. In the concluding lines of '*Dynamics of Faith*', Paul Tillich writes:

> . . . . faith is not a phenomenon besides others, but the central phenomenon in man's personal life, manifest and hidden at the same time. It is religious and transcends religion, it is universal and concrete, it is infinitely variable and always the same. Faith is an essential possibility of man, and therefore its existence is necessary and universal.

Faith depends on the presence of an ultimate concern of man for the ultimate.[1]

> The ultimate concern is unconditional, independent of any conditions of character, desire or circumstance. The unconditional concern is total: no part of ourselves or of our world is excluded from it; there is no 'place' to flee from it.[2]

Then again Paul Tillich writes,

> The fundamental symbol of our ultimate concern is God. It is always present in any act of faith, even if the act of faith includes the denial of God, where there is ultimate concern. God can be denied only in the name of God. One God can deny the other one. Ultimate concern cannot deny its own character as ultimate.[3]

Of course, Tillich grants the possibility of remaining unconcerned about one's own ultimate concern,[4] even though it is questionable for Tillich for one to be without one's concern. The reason for saying this is that, according to Tillich, man is always placed in his paradoxical and existential situation of anxieties, insecurities, estrangements and other ambiguous conditions of life. On the whole, 'A God disappears; divinity remains'.[5] Again, a symbol and myth are the expressions of one's faith.

> One can replace one myth by another, but one cannot remove the myth from man's spiritual life.[6]

Even humanism which ostensibly denies religion is a form of faith, according to Tillich

> .... if faith is understood as the state of being ultimately concerned about the ultimate, humanism implies faith. Humanism is the attitude which makes man the measure of his own spiritual life . . . . For ultimate concern of man is man.[7]

The ontological reason for Tillich is that man is infinitely concerned about Being-itself to which he belongs, from which he has been estranged. Here one finds the echo of Augustine and St. Paul, according to whom one cannot find rest unless one finds rest in God. Thus Tillich writes,

> Man is totally concerned about the totality which is his true being and which is disrupted in time and space. Man is unconditionally concerned in time and space. Man is unconditionally concerned about that which conditions his being beyond all the conditions in him and around him.[8]

Thus, Tillich subscribes to the doctrine of religion *a priori*.

Organismic Theory of Man and His Psyche

It was Aristotle who first advanced the theory of *horme* by virtue of which every organism tends to become a whole and complete. Later on, Spinoza declared that there is a central drive or *conatus* in each organism which preserves it in its own being. Without elaborating the concept of 'holism' it can be said that Samuel Alexander, Field Marshall J.C. Smuts, A.N.

Whitehead, Paul Tillich have all maintained an organismic theory in their philosophy. Now keeping to the level of science, we can say that it was Hans Adolf Eduard Driesch (1867-1940) who emphasized the working of a holistic drive in each organism. This drive is specially noticeable in an embryo which takes the form of its species and because of this drive tries to repair any injury done to the embryo in the process of its development. Later on Lashley working on the injury of the brain in the study of learning process emphasized the holistic process of the brain, that is, the remaining part of the brain after the lesion of some of its parts, takes over the function of the parts removed from the brain.

But the doctrine of holism becomes interesting when it is applied to the study of the total personality. It was indirectly hinted at by S. Freud when he stated that each organism trends to maintain an equilibrium of certain potentials.[9] Again, C.G. Jung has always maintained that there is a holistic tendency in each individual by virtue of which after making successful adaptation to the outer world, each individual tries to realise the full potentialities of his inner psyche in the second half of his life. He mentions the four stages of Shadow, anima-animus, mana personalities and maṇḍala experience. The whole process of individuation described by Jung, in general outline is an echo of the advaitic and Buddhistic teaching of reaching the ultimate goal of Brahman and nirvāṇa, respectively.

Very interestingly the organismic theory has been advanced in the building of human personality according to Kurt Goldstein, Andras Angyal, Abraham Maslow, Prescott Lecky, Carl Rogers and others. Like Jung, Goldstein emphasizes the adjustive processes within the organism itself in the task of self-actualization. This process is known as *autonomy*. Apart from autonomy, there is the process of *homonomy* by virtue of which an individual expands and enriches his personality by appropriating and incorporating things and values from the environment. At the psychological level the individual forms an image of his whole personality which, according to Andras Angyal may be termed as his 'Symbolic Self'. It is this symbolic self which gives rise to the formation of one's deity or the notion of one's highest self either as Brahman of Nirvāṇa.

As a psychological organism, an individual gets conscious of his drive to become his symbolic self, which embodies the whole meaning of life, in relation to his total lived sphere of his environment, as Lewin has termed it. Thus the centring or central driving force within the individual to become his own symbolic self makes an individual transcend his own narrow individuality to become his spiritual self. It is this drive which is at the basis of religion *a priori*. A theist would say that God Himself has left His Seal on each individual by virtue of which he would not find rest, except when he finds his rest in God. Others tend to realise their spiritual 'whole' in other than theistic ways. But no man can live without some religion.

Objectors and scoffers would say that it is a worthless attempt to make people religious by defining it. But our attempt has been made as a result of a consensus on this point by appealing to the views, ancient and modern, empirical, historical and psychological. After all philosophy is concerned with the vision of the whole reality, specially with regard to the ultimate human destiny. No views can be final. First, because we are all finite. Secondly, we are still in the midst of evolution, the beginning and end of which are shrouded in the cloud of unknowing. But decision has to be made with all the resources at our disposal. In the 'Yeh' and 'nay' of religious thought and its many and varied promptings, a philosopher discovers his own depth, and, in this discovery of self-disclosure one finds his own authentic self which is the prize of human living.

Relativity in religion follows from the psychological account of the ideal self. Of course, accepting the adage of Feuerbach, a talk about God is really a talk about the ideal man. Hence, the ideal self, projected into the form of God will vary with individuals. This follows from the fact that the ideal self in relation to which an individual feels himself perfect, complete and whole, must vary with the various individuals in response to their needs and aspirations. The same conclusion about the relativity of deity follows from Jung's theory about the differences of individuals who vary according to their types, functions and mental structure. But this relativity of deity also follows from another account about the religious situation.

Christianity, Islam and various forms of Hinduism maintain

that the supreme reality is essentially unknowable. According to Christianity (also Judaism) we know that God *is*, but we do not know *what He is*. Caliph Abu Baker is quoted to have said:

> Praise to God who hath given His creature no way of attaining to the knowledge of Him except through their inability to know Him.[10]

As a matter of fact God is transcendent to His world, according to Islam and He, therefore, can be known only through His Prophets. Similarly, there are too many *neti, neti* texts about Brahman in the Upanishads.[11]

Again, for L. Wittgenstein, God is the meaning of the Universe. Hence, it cannot be described through any segment of the universe.

> It is logically impossible for the sense of the world to be itself a part of the world, since the meaning of anything cannot be a part of that of which it is the meaning.[12]

Further,

> The solution of the riddle of life in space and time lies outside space and time.[13]

Hence, man remains in a predicamental situation. He cannot literally or meaningfully talk about God, and yet by virtue of his psychical constitution he is condemned to know the unknowable, because of religion *a priori*. How is this possible?

Relativity of Religions

True, Brahman transcends everything, but it is also in everything, specially in man.[14] He who controls this world and everything is the inner controller of man. 'He is your Soul, the Inner Controller, the Immortal.'

> That which is the finest essence......the whole world has that as its soul.
> That is Reality. That is Ātman.
> That art thou, S'vetaketu.[15]

Hence, Brahman pervading and controlling the whole universe transcends it in the language of Ṛgveda X. 90.1,3.

> (Puruṣa) He holding earth enclosed about,
> Expands beyond, ten fingers length
> ... ...
> All creatures are one fourth of him,
> three-fourths eternal life in heaven.

Because Brahman indwells in everything, so it can be described though very imperfectly through any finite segments and by the ideal drawn up by man. But whatever description we give of Reality, it is very imperfect since Reality transcends everything. Yet man and his self hold the key to the unknowable reality. How?

According to the evolutionary scheme of Samuel Alexander there are two principles of *conatus* and *nisus* in men. By virtue of *conatus* man is maintained in his being, and, by virtue of his *nisus* he is made to rise above his finite self in the direction of the deity. But God is the whole universe tending towards deity.[16] In other words, the Supreme Reality contains all the possible deities and yet goes beyond all of them.

Thus, following the advaitic philosophy of Radhakrishnan it can be said that some contemplate one name and some another. These names are to be contemplated, lauded and at last denied when they ultimately lead to the Absolute Brahman.[17] Hence, the names and forms in the form of religious deities are all relative, and, are bound to be transcended, though they are pointers and eminent clues to the absolute. In other words, we can apprehend the unconditioned, transcendent reality only through relative symbols called deity, but each deity is only relative. As such there can be no quarrel about the ultimacy of any deity. Krishna and Christ are but necessary, though relative deities for taking us to the absolute Brahman which alone is ultimately real. Paul Tillich states the relative character of Christianity thus:

> The Christ is God-for-us. But God is not only for us, he is for everything created.[18]

Again,

> Christianity as Christianity is neither final nor universal. But that to which it witnesses is final and universal.[19]

Thus, faith in any one's deity should have tolerance on account of the relativity of any object of worship. Hence, the relative character of the object of our worship should pave the way for tolerance amongst all religious believers. However, we can state the view of Wittgenstein too who also maintains the transcendent nature of God and also the difficulty of God-talk.

Linguistic Analysis of Religious Statements

Later Wittgenstein has concentrated more on the meaning than the truth of the statements. He found three kinds of statements, namely, factual statements whose meaning can be determined by appealing to the actual states of affairs to which they apply. He was also much concerned to elucidate statements which ordinarily deal with 'private' experiences like pain, hope, expectation and so on. Here his contributions are considered very important inasmuch as he has laid down the conditions under which pain-statements and the like are used. When Wittgenstein comes to religious language, then he hardly makes any positive contributions towards its understanding. All that he had to say is that religious language cannot be assimilated to scientific, factual or even painlike-statements. He is equally emphatic that God-talk is not non-sensical.[20] He most probably meant that religious language is part of an activity, or a form of life. 'Form of Life' in Wittgenstein is quite a difficult concept to explain. But before taking it up, we must state two more things in this context.

In the *Tractatus*, Wittgenstein held that God is the meaning of the world. He does not manifest Himself in the world (Tract. 6.432). Naturally it lies beyond our language which for him at that time meant that it deals ultimately about some facts of the world. Hence, he consigns God-talk to silence.

> What we cannot talk about, we must pass over in silence. (Tractatus, 7).

Again, God is transcendent, and no finite segment of this world can describe Him. Thus Wittgenstein, Nagarjuna, Nagasen would maintain silence in relation to what we consider our highest Being. But then one must speak and communicate with other fellow beings about God. Silence is the logical outcome of considering God as outside the universe of human language. But man is condemned to talk about that which is beyond talk. He knows that any talk about God will trivialize Him. But compelled by his psychological proclivities about finding God, man must talk. Then what happens?

Of course, God-talk is also a kind of language-game. The intelligibility and justifiability of God-talk depends on this kind of language-game in a religious community. On what does this language-game depend? This depends on the picture which the believing community has of its God. Here one should not think that this picture is of anything existing. The picture simply may point out to what is *Shunyata.* God is illusive and mystical and our picture of Him is a mere pointer. What we want to emphasize is that our picture is not of something. It is used in a variety of ways. It is used as a moral-booster, as Kant and Braithwaite would say. It may be used in support of religious rituals for maintaining our existence in a believing community, or in maintaining our existential decisions. But we also keep on purifying this picture to meet the exigencies of life. For example, the creation-theory was modified in the light of the theory of evolution. Might be, again, the picture gets modified in clash with other religious pictures. For example, the tribal God of the Jews was greatly transformed in relation to the Zoroastrian monotheism. Similarly, Brahman-talk was modified into monotheistic mysticism of the Sufis.

Religious pictures well up from the depth of our being, as Freud's theory about God in the form of Father-image of one's infancy holds, or, it might come up from the Unconscious by way of supplementing the conscious demands of life, as C.G. Jung would maintain. Whatever psychological or ontological explanation of God-picture may be, the picture powerfully moves the believers, explains his involvement and commitments. But this picture must differ with one's bringing-up in one's community, one's personality-type and so on. The result?

Every form of religion is relative and in one way or other keeps on slowly changing. This is quite clear from the existence of many sects in any large religious community. How can any religion claim absolute monopoly of religious Truth and finality? Unfortunately, religionists do not accept their respective religion to be relative. They maintain that their respective religion alone is true and all other religions to the extent they differ from their *true* religion are utterly false. For example, it is claimed by Christianity that it alone is true and all other religions are either partially true or false. The same claim is made by Judaism, Islam and other religions. As their practices collide, so they conflict and cause tension and religious wars. Hence, we have to analyse 'knowing' and 'truth' in order to ascertain the claims of the Absolutists.

'Knowing' has many meanings. For example, Adam knew his wife and begat Cain. Obviously 'knowing' here means sex-intercourse. When you say to an unfriendly man 'I know you' it means that I know your character and I can very well guess what your next move will be. But in this context of religion to know God is to have numinous experience of God. However, 'numinous experience' is more affective than cognitive, even for Otto who has tried to analyse it. Hence, to know God simply means understanding the scriptural information about God and the performance of rituals in relation to Him. At times this kind of scriptural information is said to be God's revelation. Unfortunately an unbeliever can easily set aside the claim of revelation as a form of reliable knowledge. One thing is certain that knowing God or Brahman cannot be assimilated to empirical knowledge of facts of science or everyday life. We have been maintaining that religious knowing is creative with a view to changing, transforming the believers in the direction of morality and friendliness to the world and other fellowmen. Here the paradigm statement is *Brahmavid Brahmaiva Bhavati.* Hence, very often religion has been assimilated to morality. For example, religion has been called 'Morality touched with emotion'. In our day R.B. Braithwaite holds that religious assertions entail a certain behaviour policy, coming under a general moral principle, backed by a story. Here by 'religious assertions' we mean typical religious statements, the paradigm case of which are God-statements, or even Brahman-statements. Besides such statements, any religion contains historical, eschatological, mythological statements, commands, rituals, prayers, exhortations and so on. In any case, typically religious knowing cannot be assimilated to factual statements, as has been done by the positivists. This is very clear from our analysis of the meaning of 'truth'.

In modern parlance in philosophy a statement is said to be empirical if and only if it can be either verified or falsified in principle. J.N. Findlay and A.G.N. Flew have shown in '*New Essays in Philosophical Theology*' that religious assertions can neither be falsifiable nor verifiable. So they can be deemed to be non-factual, and not that they are meaningless, vacuous or nonsensical. Only an empirical statement when verified can be said to be true, and, if falsified is said to be false. Quite clearly then a non-factual statement which religious assertions are, cannot be termed either true or false. Hence, it is inadmissible to say that religious statements, belonging to any one religion are true, and belonging to other religions are false. According to Partick Sherry 'truth' does have two important senses.[21]

1. Actual States of affairs, reality.
2. True beliefs, judgments, propositions, etc.

Hence, let us briefly take up these two senses of 'truth' in relation to religious claims.

In recent philosophy, there is much insistence on language and propositions. Hence, a proposition alone is called either true or false. But when a religion is said to be true and other religion to be false, then we are really saying something about the ontology of religious entities, namely the reality of professed God or angels or heaven-hell etc. In other words, 'truth' is used as synonymous with reality, and, reality is a value-loaded term. In contrast with religious truth, the things of the world are said to be merely passing shows. Hence. Lord Buddha presented the metaphysical theory of *momentariness*. Again, Mahatma Gandhi declared that 'Truth' is God. Mahatma used the term 'truth' ambiguously, for according to him, 'truth' cannot be denied. This is the sense in which propositional value of truth is used, but not in the sense of ontological use of it. For example, the Carvakas denied the existence of any supra-natural world, and, made no distinction between appearance and reality. Hence, 'Truth' in the ontological sense can be denied. 'Truth' in the ontological sense in Platonic and Upanishadic, namely, the supreme reality is timeless, immutable and indestructible. In contrast, the worldly things are transitory, phenomenal and momentary. What is the upshot of this kind of analysis?

Well, God or any such religious entitles are not propositional values, for a propositional 'true-false' depends on repeatable, shareable, public sensible facts, and, God is not a sensible event in time. Hence, God or any religious entity can be said to be true only in ontological sense. But a metaphysical being which in the final analysis religious entities are, is neither verifiable nor falsefiable. Hence, a religious entity is not an empirical fact. It might be an object of scriptural authority, or, untestable religious experience, or, even a matter of mythology depending on one's unscientific world-view. All these means of obtaining religious information differ from religion to religion, and, even in the same religion. Everybody can see that different religions have their own respective scriptures. Even mystics only repeat what they are expected to find in terms of their religious upbringing. Again, in the same religion there are religious fundamentalists, and, there are also liberals. Under these circumstances, it is too much to claim the sole monopoly of spiritual truth in favour of one's own religion, and, declaring other religions to be either false or partially true. Should we then declare that all religions are absolutely relative, and, that each form of religion

> appeals in precisely the same way to the inner certitude and devotion of its followers? It is the deepest apprehension of God and God's fullest revelation to them.[22]

It comes to this, that each religion is true to the person who believes in it. And, yet in spite of the relativity of religions, it cannot be held that each religion is equal and in the same precise way relative.

Radhakrishnan may be presumed to have based his statements on the Gītā:

> Whatever form any devotee with faith wishes to worship, I make that faith of his steady. (VII. 21).

Again,

> The faith of every individual, O Bharata, is in accordance with his nature. (XVII. 3).

In general it means that men differ in their Sattvic, rajasic and tamasic nature. And as they are, so are their gods.

> Sattvic men worship gods......and the dull worship the spirits and ghosts. (XVII. 4).

And in accordance with their faith, they get their rewards (VII. 22). But does this mean that every faith is equally true? Certainly not. The worship of rakshasas, the spirit and ghosts is lower than the worship of gods. Further, the worship of the manifested is inferior to that of the unmanifested.

> Men think of Me as the manifested, not knowing
> My higher nature, changeless and supreme. (VII. 24).

Thus, even relative objects of faith are higher and lower, pointing to what is the Absolute.

The Absolute Principle of Unity of Religions

In the same way, Gauḍapāda analyses the worship of OM (AUM, *amātra*) into the four stages of *Viśva*, *Taijasa*, *Prājña* and *Turīya*. Such is also the view of Shaṅkara as contained in his comment on Gītā VIII. II. Hence, *relative* has no meaning without reference to the Absolute.

The gods refer to God, and, God finally leads to that which is 'God beyond God'. It is a stage beyond description and verbalisation (*vāco nirvartante aprāpya manasā saha*).

> It is not a place where one can live, it is without the safety of words and concepts, it is without name, a church, a cult, a theology. But it is moving in the depth of all of them.[23]

It is a stage which one reaches in practising one's own religion. This is the stage as the climax and end of one's religious endeavour. This is the stage where all desires are extinguished and all sorrow ceases.

> There a father, becomes not a father; a mother, not a mother; the worlds, not the worlds; the gods, not the gods ......a thief, not a thief. (*Bṛhadāraṇyaka* 4.3.22).

The state is *anirvacaniya* (indescribable). By speaking about it, it is trivialized. Kabir would say that speech will distort our meaning of Brahman or whatever name a person chooses to give it.

> *Bolat bolat tat nasai* (Kabir).

By reaching this state all differences, certainly religious differences altogether disappear. The stages of ultimately reaching it are fairly obvious in what has been stated above. From the worship of spirits and ghosts we reach the stage of gods where ghosts disappear. The worship of gods leads to the worship of One God. This too must lead to the state of 'God above God'. The same point has been made by C.G. Jung in describing the processes of Individuation. Here he mentions the four stages of *Shadows* (spirits and ghosts), *anima-animus* (male and female deities), archetypes (an ideogram of God) and *Maṇḍala experience* (a stage without any deity).

The processes of individuation have been mentioned here by showing that one can pass from the worship of God to the realization of 'God beyond God'. For example, a Muslim, a Jew and a Christian have the great advantage of worshipping One God, without having any other God besides Him. But remaining at this stage, without passing into the realization of 'God beyond God' can only lead to conflict. And this conflict denies whatever good a religion can have. Hence, any theist passes to a state where differences are swallowed up,—where a Muslim, is not a Muslim; a Christian is not a Christian; a Hindu is not a Hindu. How can we do that?

First, a Muslim will do well in practising the brotherhood of all Muslims, without making a distinction of rich and poor, and, without the differences of nationalities. After reaching this state, he has to reach a still higher state in which the differences of a

Hindu or a Christian or a Sikh disappear. Finally comes a stage when religious names and forms drop away and men are but men as children of God, without heeding their frailties and weaknesses. At last dawns the feeling that all is God, and, God is in all. After reaching this state can a Muslim practise *jehad*? Some Sufis have certainly reached this final end.

A Christian does not ordinarily have the flesh and blood of Christian brotherhood. He has many differences to overcome. He has to overcome the differences of caste (as is the case in Kerala), nationality, colour, language and regional loyalties. The life of a Christian has been sundered into many fragments and few Indians have reached the stage of Brahma-realization, which one can see in the life of a few Sufis or a Ramakrishnaite. But in the interest, both from the viewpoint of religious achievements and national or international integration, a Christian too has to pass to a stage where all differences are swallowed up. Jesus said,

> Be as perfect as your Father in heaven is.
> For he makes his sun to shine on bad and good people alike, and gives rain to those who do good and to those who do evil. (*Mat*. 5.46).

The highest stage for a Christian is to reach a state of differencelessness. The Christian love is divine which cannot be rejected, rebuffed or insulted.

The same principle of differencelessness is certainly open to a Hindu, for a Hindu believes in the Upanishads. Whether he follows the *jñāna-mārga* of Shaṅkara, or, the bhakti-mārga of saints, he has to outgrow the differences of caste, colour and creed. A *Brahma-jñāni* if he offers something to an outcaste, then he does so not to an outcaste, but to the universal *Ātman* or Brahman in him (Chh. U.V.24.4). Again, a *Brahma-jñāni* makes no difference between a Brahman and an outcaste (Gītā V.18). Brahman itself has no caste (Muṇḍ. U.I. 1.66) and those who want to realize Brahman, ultimately have to rise above all castes and all other differences. For a *Brahma-jñāni* a Muslim is not a Muslim; a Christian is not a Christian; a Hindu is not a Hindu.

Even from the viewpoint of Bhakti, the Lord accepts even

the Shudras, lowly born and even women given to sinful ways (Gītā IX. 30, 32). Hence, the bhakti-cult holds, 'Rama belongs to him, who worships Him'.

The absolute principle of differenceless Brahman has not only been based on the intuition of the Upanishadic sages, but has been philosophically defended by the Upanishads, Shaṅkara, and even by Kant in his doctrine of the transcendental unity of apperception. This also follows from the view of Wittgenstein who maintained silence in relation to God, for any description of God would trivialize Him. Further, Kabir has laid down that any description of Brahman or *nirguṇa* Rama would be tantamount to His distortion. Thus, the principle of differenceless Brahman alone can serve as the unity of religions.

In the last analysis the state of Brahma-realization means to be divested of everything distinctive of the seeker, even his egoity. This is known as the doctrine of mergence, and, this doctrine of mergence has been interpreted by Ramanuja as the annihilation of one's own Self. According to Ramanuja nobody would cherish the idea of one's annihilation. So Ramanuja rejects the doctrine of mergence.[24] But Kabir has beautifully supported the doctrine of mergence which here means to become the differenceless Brahman. For Kabir it means 'becoming nirguṇa Rama'. In Kabir *Granthavali*, pada 274, Kabir holds that the doctrine of becoming *nirguṇa Rama* or Brahman means perfection.

> True, a thistle tree by remaining in close proximity of a sandal tree, becomes itself a sandal tree (losing all its distinctiveness); an iron piece remaining in close proximity of *paras* (philosopher's stone) becomes gold losing its distinctive nature; any drain-water merging into the Ganges becomes *Gaṅgā-jala* (holy water of the Ganges). Hence, anybody living in nearness of attributeless Rama, becomes Rama Himself.

Hence, becoming differenceless Brahman is to lose one's base nature and to gain the perfection of Brahman.

For over two thousand years at least thinkers have been proclaiming that there is only one Supreme reality whom people worship in different ways. For example,

> The bird that is one, priests and poets with words make into many. (*Ṛgveda* X. 114.5).

Again,

> To what is One, sages give many a *title*;
> they call it Agni, Yama, Mataris'van (*RV.* I. 164.46).

Again, the desire for the unity of religions is contained in Ṛgveda X. 191.2.

> Assemble, speak together, let your minds be all of one accord.

Further, the Śvetasvatara Upanishad foreshadows the advaitic principle of unity thus:

> The One who, himself without colour, by the manifold application of his power,
> Distributes many colours in his hidden purpose,
> And into whom, its end and its beginning, the whole world dissolves—He is God.
> May He endow us with clear intellect. (IV.I)

But it is not enough to say that One reality is worshipped in various ways. The nature of this One reality has to be stated so that in relation to this one the unity of religions can be established. For example, at the beginning of *Mahanāṭaka* (or *Hanumānnāṭaka*, about 850 A.D.) it is stated:

> May Hari, Lord of the three worlds, whom the Shaivas worship as Shiva, the Vedantins as Brahman, the Buddhists as Buddha, the Logicians, clever in the means of knowledge, as the Creator, devotees of the Jaina doctrine as Arhat, and the Mimamsakas as Karma.

Again, Udayanācārya about 924 A.D. in *Nyāya Kusumañjali*, Chap. I, Karika 2 states:

> Now with regard to that Being whom all worship no matter what end they strive to attain; the followers of the Upanishads as the One by Nature pure and enlightened; the dis-

ciple of Kapila as the perfect First knower, the disciple of Patañjali as the One untouched by hindrance, karma, fruition and impressions of karma.........

Quite clearly the One adored by different religions is not one and the same. Hari and *Karma-phala-dātā,* the efficient cause of Udayana are not one and the same. In the same way the Christian sages also speak of one God.

St. John even in the first chapter, verse 9 says that there is one light which lightens every man.

Again, God has not left Himself without a witness to all nations (Acts 14.17). Further, God has written his own laws in the hearts of men. Finally,

> Is God the God of the Jews only? Is he not the God of the Gentiles also? Of course, he is. (*Roman* 3.29).

Even Church Fathers have expressed the same sublime thought. Heiler quoting Nicholas of Cusa (1453) writes,

> God is sought in various ways and called by various names in the various religions, that he has sent various prophets and teachers in various ages to the various peoples.[25]

Again, Heiler reminds us of the eloquent witness of Joseph Gorres:

> *One* Godhead alone is at work in the Universe,
> *One* religion alone prevails in it, *one* worship, *one* fundamental natural order, *one* law and *one* bible in all.
> All prophets are *one*; they have spoken on *one* common ground in *one* language, though in different dialects.[26]

Unless one clarifies the meaning of 'one bible' and 'one common ground', the statement is pious, but factually it cannot be acceptable.

In the same vein, the Quoran says,

> Teachers are sent to each race that they may teach it in its own tongue, so there may be no doubt as to the meaning in its mind.[27]

Again,

> Unto each nation have we given sacred rites which they are to perform; so let them not dispute with thee of the matter, but summon thou unto thy Lord. (Surah 22.67).

THE VIEWS OF RADHAKRISHNAN

Radhakrishnan has raised the following problems for himself:

> What is wrong with Hindu religion? How can we make it somewhat more relevant to the intellectual climate and social environment? Such were the questions which roused my interest.[28]

Again, Radhakrishnan was against missionary enterprise, which favoured conversion of the people from one religion into another. Thus, as a Hindu apologist he makes several statements which are not altogether true.

His first claim is that all religions are equally true, since subjective elements in all religions are of the same degree of intensity.

> Each form of faith appeals in precisely the same way to the inner certitude and devotion of its followers.[29]

Again,

> The greatest requirement of human life is to be loyal to truth as *one* sees it.[30]

Is religion then purely a matter of subjective certitude? Radhakrishnan himself does not subscribe to this view.

> It (religion) is not a subjective phenomenon, not mere cultivation of the inner life but the apprehension of something that stands over against the individual.[31]

Further, Radhakrishnan holds that a true spiritual life must express itself in social service and detached performance of duties for collective perfection.[32]

Quite obviously any emphasis on subjective certitude would contribute more to fanaticism and fundamentalism than unity of religions. Again, does the social service of Mother Teresa prove the truth of Christianity, or, the inner certitude of her religion?

Again, Radhakrishnan holds that there is one religion of the Supreme Spirit and all other religions are mere names and forms in relation to it. As an advaitin he makes the following statements:

> Some contemplate one name and some another. Which of them is best? All are eminent clues to the transcendent, immortal, unembodied Brahman;......*

Are all equally eminent clues to the transcendent? Are tamasic and rajasic religions of the same order as Sattvic religions.

The Gītā holds that distorted minds resort to gods (VII. 20) and again, 'men of no understanding think of Me' as manifest. (Gītā VII. 24).

Hence, all relative religions are not equally acceptable nor are they equally eminent clues to the transcendent Brahman.

Then, Radhakrishnan thinks that unity of religions can be brought about by some sort of syncretism.

> The different religious traditions clothe the one Reality in various images and their visions could embrace and fertilise each other so as to give mankind a many-sided perfection, the spiritual radiance of Hinduism, the faithful obedience of Judaism, the life of beauty of Greek Paganism, the noble compassion of Buddhism, the vision of divine love of Christianity, and the spirit of resignation to the sovereign lord of Islam.**

Can the polytheistic paganism of the Greek be reconciled with the strict monotheism of Judaism and Islam? Only Radhakrishnan can think that every religion is equally nearer Brahman or equally excellent for social service. The divine love of Christianity is out to change a sinner into a saint. But Judaic resignation to the inevitable does not spell any change for the better. It is just the acceptance of what is inevitable, as we find in

* *Fragments of a Confession*, p. 78.

** *Ibid.*, p. 76.

Freud's teaching of humanism. It is useless to bundle together atheistic Buddhism, polytheistic paganism and monotheistic Islam and Judaism.

Only on the basis of acceptance of differenceless Brahman as the absolute standard of one's spiritual progress, unity of religions is possible. Only on the basis of gradual overcoming differences can one rise higher and higher till he reaches a stage of Brahma-realization where all differences are altogether lost. Most probably this principle of unity of religions will be better appreciated in the light of Ramakrishna's view about the harmony of religions.

Ramakrishna's Unity of Religions

Ramakrishna saw things which human beings are not permitted to see, and, described and spoke about things which is not lawful for any mortals to utter. For him the purpose of life is to realize God.[33] But he also knew very well that apart from various sects of Hinduism, there are other religions too like Islam and Christianity. So he attempted to establish unity of religions.[34] Ramakrishna desired something infinitely greater than the reconciliation of warring creeds. He wanted that man as a whole should understand, sympathise with and love the rest of mankind. In one word, each religious man should identify himself with the life of humanity.[35] Nay, more. At the point of deep spiritual realization,

> You realise that all things live, like your own Self, in God. You become the willpower and the Conscience of all that is. Your will becomes that of the whole Universe.[36]

Ramakrishna was a sadhaka who put faith above reasons (M 130). Nonetheless his points can be jotted down which unmistakably show the basis of his solution to the Vedāntic. One is not quite sure whether he was advaitic or Viśiṣṭādvaitic.

1. Ramakrishna's first important point is that God or the absolute religious entity is both with and without forms (M 32, 104, 128, 175, 191, 217, 218 and so on).

> The Primordial Power is ever at play. He is creating, preserving, and destroying in play, as it were. The Power is

called Kali. Kali is verily Brahman, and Brahman is verily Kali. It is one and the same reality. When we think of it as inactive, that is to say, not engaged in the act of creation, preservation, and destruction, then we call it Brahman. But when it engages in these activities, then we call it Kali or Shakti. The Reality is one and the same, the difference is in the name and form.[37]

Again,

......the true religious teachers of all times and ages are like so many lamps through which is emitted the life of the spirit, flowing constantly from one source......the Lord Almighty.[38]

The Avatara is always one and the same,
Plunging into the ocean of life, He rises up in one place and is known as Krishna; diving again and rising elsewhere, He is known as Christ.
On the tree of Satchidananda grow innumerable fruits such as Rama, Krishna, Christ and others......[39]

The difference between one deity and another is one of name and form. For example, gold is one, but it can assume various forms in different kinds of ornaments.[40] The same chameleon can assume different colours.[41] In this context the following statement cannot be taken otherwise than what has been mentioned above.

It is like water, called in different languages by different names, such as 'jala', 'pani', and so forth...All three denote one and the same thing, the difference being in the name only. In the same way, some address the Reality as 'Allah', some as 'God', and some as 'Brahman', some as 'Kali', and others by such names as 'Rama', 'Jesus', Durga, Hari.[42]

Again, Ramakrishna holds that God is all-pervading spirit. He exists in all beings, even in an ant.[43]

O Mother, Thou art verily Brahman, and Thou art verily Shakti. Thou art Purusha and Thou art Prakriti. Thou art

> Virat. Thou art the Absolute, and Thou dost manifest Thyself as Relative. Thou art verily the twenty four cosmic principles.[44]

In the light of the above-mentioned statement Riencourt thinks that Ramakrishna's theology is pantheistic.[45] Rolland states that according to Ramakrishna, the Lord moves under a diversity of forms......pious, hypocrite and even the criminal.

> I say: Narayana in the pious man,
> Narayana in the hypocrite, Narayana in the criminal and the libertine.[46]

Again,

> I believe in my God the wicked, my God the miserable, my God the poor of all races.[47]
> ...it is God who manifests Himself as the atheist and the believer, the good and the bad, the real and the unreal; that it is He who is present in waking and in sleep; and that He is beyond all these.[48]

Though God is manifested in all, but not in the same degree. Spinoza too held that God is in all things but not in the same degree. There is more of God in an angel than in the mouse. Ramakrishna also holds that the manifestations of God are different with different things. God is more manifest in some than in others,[49] more in man than in the stone[50] and certainly more in the heart of His devotees than elsewhere,[51] the more in the holy than in the wicked.[52]

As God is manifest in everything, so He is present in idols as much as in His attributes. So even idol-worship is valid and helpful for the beginners.[53]

> God is with form and without form. Images and other symbols are just as valid as your attributes. And these attributes are not different from idolatry, but are merely hard and petrified forms of it.[54]

As all deities are valid, so sincerity and earnestness of faith are necessary for reaching God.

> To be sure, God exists in all beings,
> God can be realized through all paths. All religions are true. The important thing is to reach the roof.
> You can reach it by stone stairs or by wooden stairs or by bamboo steps or by a rope. You can also climb up by a bamboo pole.[55]
> The Christians, the Brahmos, the Hindus, the Mussalmans, all say, 'My religion alone is true'. But, Mother, the fact is that nobody's watch is right. Who can truly understand Thee? But if a man prays to Thee with a yearning heart, he can reach Thee, through Thy grace, by any path.[56]

Thus Ramakrishna renouncing the narrow path of the monopolist and fanatic held that through earnestness and yearning all lovers of God will reach the same goal.[57] If a man has faith, then Ramakrishna states that it does not matter whom he worships.[58] Hence, Ramakrishna concludes,

> All religions and all paths call upon their followers to pray, to one and the same God. Therefore, one should not show disrespect to any religion or religious opinion. It is God alone who is called Satchidananda Brahman in the Vedas, Satchidananda Krishna in the Puranas, and Satchidananda Shiva in the Tantras. It is one and the same Satchidananda.[59]
> Different creeds are but different paths to reach the Almighty. Diverse are the means by which this Kali temple may be reached......some come here in boats, some in carriages, some on foot. Similarly, different people attain God by following different creeds.[60]

If all gods and all paths are true, then which one deity should one follow? Also one should realize that men differ in their taste and temperament,[61] and trees in the garden are of different kinds.[62] Under the following conditions Ramakrishna advises us thus:

> I should say, 'Fix your attention on that form which appeals to you most; but know for certain that all forms are the forms of one God alone'.[63]

Knowing that all paths lead to the same Truth, we should not despise other Deities, but maintain an attitude of respect towards other religions.[64] The Lord has provided different forms of worship to suit different men with different capacities and with different stages of spiritual development.[65] As God has many aspects, so God is described according to the particular aspect in which He appears to his particular worshipper.[66]

> ......the Lord of the universe, though one manifests Himself differently according to the different likings of His worshippers and each one of these has his own view of God which he values most. To some—He is a kind master or a devoted friendly.[67]

Hence, one should know that only through 'ignorance one harbours sectarian views and quarrels.[68] One should know that men differ in their types, temperament and spiritual development, so their objects of worship have to differ and God reveals Himself to different men differently to suit their requirements. Two things have been emphasized by Ramakrishna. First, sincerity, earnestness and faith in worship of any deity whatsoever; secondly, belief in one God.

> Whoever performs devotional exercises, with the belief that there is but one God, is bound to attain Him, no matter in what aspect, name, or manner He is worshipped.[69]

In order that earnestness and seriousness for one's own religion may not degenerate into fanaticism, Ramakrishna enjoins the believer to have belief in one God, as ultimate referent underlying all religious faiths. He states:

> Remain always strong and steadfast in thy own faith, but eschew all bigotry and intolerance.[70]

Again,

> .....One may have that single-minded devotion to one's own religion, but one should not on that account hate other faiths. On the contrary, one should have a friendly attitude toward them.[71]

Ramakrishna did not stop there, but advised that one should practise other faiths for a time.[72]

> I had to practise each religion for a time........Hinduism, Islam, Christianity. Furthermore, I followed the paths of Shaktas, Vaisṇavas, Vedāntists. I realized that there is only one God toward whom all are travelling; but the paths are different.[73]

For this purpose Ramakrishna took to Islam and uttered the name of Allah in 1866. Similarly in November 1874 Ramakrishna took to Christianity. In a vision Christ whispered to him thus:

> Behold the Christ, who shed his heart's blood for the redemption of the world, who suffered a sea of anguish for love of men. It is He, the master Yogin, who is in eternal union with God. It is Jesus, Love incarnate.[74]

An Appraisal

It is a matter of wonder that a man so intoxicated by God could ever walk on this earth. Hence, his followers regard him as an Incarnation. Whatever he said was experienced by him most palpably. His doctrine of 'unity of religions' is not to be criticized, but is to be humbly followed and duly acknowledged. But it is the verdict of a mystic who never left behind his intoxication. We humble men can only show our difficulties in relation to his verdict.

1. There is little doubt that Ramakrishna was a Hindu of Hindus,[75] but not narrow and local. It is Hinduism at its best which also means the highest point reached of an uninterrupted tradition which was nourished by Indian seers at least throughout three thousand years. He worshipped Shiva, Kali, Rama and Krishna and, yet meditated on and realized formless Brahman. He thought and has epitomized the paradoxical aspects of idol-worship and the worship of one God. He was wholly soaked in Rama, Krishna, Chaitanya, Kali without deviating from Brahma-realization. He was a Hindu without any nomenclature and a sect. His spirit hovers over India and mingles with the spirit of the world.

2. In Indian thought different religions are taken to be so many paths that lead to the same mountain top, or, the many rivers that lose themselves in the sea. But God-realization is not a place, but is a matter of becoming. The Master himself noted that Bhakti leads to the service of the Lord, and, Jñāna-marga leads to the mergence into Brahman. This mergence does not mean extinction but perfection. Hence, all paths do not lead to God-realization, certainly not the five-fold Makāra-principle. He himself noted that some paths may be devious.[76]

We also know that some deities like ghosts, devils and Satan (Gītā 17.4-6) are not to be worshipped. The God-intoxicated mystic was too saintly a man to overlook these difficulties.

3. True, the Master recommended worshipping any deity with the awareness that this will lead to God-realization. But the Gītā itself observes that the worshippers may be mistaken in this regard (1.24). No doubt, the Master very often took to pantheism to include all kinds of deity, standing for even wickedness and criminality. But he has also emphasized the higher and lower manifestation of God. Lower deities will pull down the worshipper e.g., towards worldliness. Mammon and sex are also deities. Matter bereft of spiritualism is also an object of adoration. In one's enthusiasm for establishing harmony of religions one should not overlook the demerits of lower forms of worship.

4. The most important concept is of a reality which is both with and without forms.

Apparently this is self-contradictory. The Master himself states the following in this context:

> He who is attributeless also has attributes. He who is Brahman is also Shakti. When thought of as inactive, He is called Brahman, and when thought of as the Creator, Preserver and Destroyer He is called the Primordial Energy, Kali.

Brahman and Shakti are identical, like the fire and its power to burn.[77]
Again,

> ......Brahman and Shakti are identical.

> ......You cannot think of the milk without the whiteness, and again, you cannot think of the (milk) whiteness without the milk.[78]

Conceptual framework cannot be stretched to include Kali (representing forms) and Brahman (formless) in any consistent manner. The illustration refers to a concept of substance-attribute relationship. But Kali and Brahman are both substances and the two substances cannot be identical.

Besides, Ramakrishna thinks that Kali and Brahman are two modes or aspects for *thought*, but are they also apart from our (human) thinking? The two aspects of the Supreme Reality cannot be entertained in the same thought, but in two separate thoughts taken up successively.

Again, Ramanuja has tried to reconcile multiplicity with unity in his own way. For him, Brahman is qualified with *cit* and *acit* as his body, but Brahman is one body-spirit complex. In the state of *pralaya*, the body aspect of *cit* and *acit* remains in a very subtle form, scarcely to be differentiated. Hence, in subtle state Brahman may be called *nirguṇa* and in gross manifested form He is *saguṇa*. But even in the state of *pralaya*, Brahman really remains nescintly qualified.

The Master has taken many illustrations, but none of them can remove this inconsistency. The distinction for Ramakrishna is a matter of his two different kinds of samādhi. In *savikalpaka* samādhi and also in Prema-bhakti the Reality appears as personal and with attributes. However, the same object of love in *nirvikalpaka* samādhi melts into ineffable ocean which remains without any distinction. In this sense the Master has truly said that Divine Mother is none other than the Absolute. Really even for Ramakrishna Brahman is more important, for only on this basis he has been able to establish harmony of religions. On the whole, the worship of *Saguṇa Brahma* is the primary stage of worship[79] and it matures into *nirguṇa Brahma*. Or, as Rolland puts it:

> Dualism, 'qualified Monism', and absolute Monism, are stages on the way to supreme truth. They are not contradictory, but rather are complementary the one to the other.[80]

5. Taking to Islam or Christianity must not be taken seriously. These were not cases of *true conversion*. Whether a Muslim is a Muslim, or, a Christian is a Christian can be known not only by the whole life lived, but also by one's death. He was fully convinced that every deity ultimately merges into Brahman. Every worshipper at first becomes what he worships and finally merges into Brahman. Hence, by taking to Islam, he himself became a Muslim saint, and, by taking to Christianity, he became Christ himself. But as such he failed to become Brahman himself.

6. Ramakrishna laid down the maxim, jīva is Shiva[81] and regarded the service to man as the worship of God.[82] But he was not interested in the improvement of social life, even though he decried caste.[83] He said once:

> "Suppose God appears before you then will you ask Him to build hospitals and dispensaries for you?
> ...... A lover of God never says that. He would rather ask for a place at His Lotus Feet.[84]

He wanted people to love God and the more one loves God, the less active one becomes.[85] Hence, his message grew more powerful with Vivekananda who lost himself in social service and improvement.

Finally it must be confessed that Ramakrishna's doctrine of 'The Unity of Religion' has been backed by a teacher of rare spiritual attainment, and, is a sacred trust bequeathed to Indians.

Conversion or Proselytization

When one religion comes in contact with another, then a number of results follow. At times there is clash which happened between the Christians and Muslims, between the Parsis and Christians, and so on. But by coming in contact with another religion, a religion may also be deepened and enriched, and there may be cross-fertilization of religions. When Christianity came in contact with Hinduism, then a good deal of reformation took place in Hinduism, as a result of which Brahmo-Samaj, Neo-Vedāntism, Arya Samaj and Prarthana Sabha came into being. At the same time, Paul Tillich, one of the foremost theologians and R. Otto included much in their theory the influence of Hinduism. However, in the first phase, missionaries of Christian religion could not fully understand the depth of Shaṅkara and Ramanuja. They thought that it was their religious duty to convert the Hindus into Christianity. Certainly a number of Indians were converted into Christianity. Here two words are used interchangeably, namely, Conversion and proselytization. However, there is a subtle distinction between them.

Conversion means change from an irreligious to a holy life; change on account of a spiritual experience, from one spiritual life to another. But a proselyte is one who has come over from one religion to another. This kind of change may be due to temptation, terrorization and other means. This may not be due to spiritual change of heart and will; for instance, many Shudras were converted into Islam and Christianity to escape from social tyranny and humiliation. Dr. J.N. Sarcar writes that a great many Shudras embraced Islam and welcomed the Muslim conquerors as their liberators.[86] Gandhiji called such Christian converts as 'rice Christians'.

Judaism, Islam and Christianity favour conversion which in many cases are really proselytization. As against these Semitic religions, Hinduism does not favour conversion. There are a number of reasons for Hinduism in not favouring conversion.

1. First reason is that for Hinduism (rather Brahminism) the Vedas are eternal and they contain pure form of religion. Any departure from Vedism is to accept an impure form of religion.

As against this, Semitic religions accept the progressive and gradual revelation of God when the time is ripe for the higher form of religion.[87] Kierkegaard regards that the disciple at the second hand is superior to the older and earlier disciples, because he knows much more about the historical development, needs and enlightenment through the ages. Hence, Semitic religions regard Brahminism as earlier and naturally an incomplete revelation.

Christianity thinks that it has gone through the test of modernity which other religions have not yet faced. So it is in a position to offer better religious insights than either Hindu conservatism or Muslim Fundamentalism. Hence, Christianity is most given to conversion.

2. Brahminism accepts *Karmavāda*, according to which the present state of a Hindu depends on his previous karmas, specially the caste into which he is born. Even the Gītā favours caste-determinism.

> The four-fold caste was made by me, in accordance with guṇas and karmas. (*Gītā* IV.13).

Again,

> Better one's own defective Dharma,
> Than others' Dharma, well-performed;
> Better is death in one's own Dharma;
> Another's Dharma's fraught with fear. (*Gītā* III.55).

Further,

> Better one's Dharma incomplete,
> Than others' Dharma well-performed;
> By acting as our nature calls,
> We do not any sin incur. (*Gītā* 17.47).

The whole caste-system ends in the exploitation of the Shudras in social economics and humiliation in the society. Naturally Christianity has picked up the Adivasis and Scheduled Castes for conversion.

3. Any religion which denounces caste as Buddhism, arouses the anger of Brahmins, for they alone enjoy a very privileged position in social and political life. This has been the case from the time of Chanakya, Peshavas up to the present Indian political life. Hence, conversion and consequent liquidation of the Scheduled Caste would take away a big vote reserve of the Brahmins. We will raise this point again when we come to deal with the political use of religion.

But now we will take up the view of Radhakrishnan who has spoken most vehemently against conversion.

Radhakrishnan on Conversion

1. First, for Radhakrishnan every religion is true for the

person who believes in it, for every form of religion appeals to its devotee with the same inner certitude and devotion.[88]

We have already criticised this subjectivity which is not the essence of religion and Radhakrishnan himself would not subscribe to it. Besides, every form of religion is not equally right, even according to the Gītā (XVII.3-6), for many men of no understanding worship the manifest form, not knowing the Absolute form of Brahman (Gītā 7.24).

2. No individual can live without his personal and traditional memory. If we tear up the individual from his traditional roots, he becomes abstract and aberrant.

> History is something organic, a phase of man's terrestrial destiny as essential for him as memory is for personal identity.........
> To forget our social past is to forget our descent.[89]

Certainly the past history serves as a guide, lesson and at times source of inspiration. But to be wedded to the past is the surest sign of becoming unprogressive. We must not make an idol of the past. Living on the glories of the past, without making efforts to improve our present state of miseries cannot give us consolation for long. Hence, like Radhakrishnan, we must not make fetish of the past. One does not live in the past alone. The present too has to be lived, with its changes and needs, gnawing into the future. Besides, the past has to be living and vibrant in relation to the present. Hence, the past also has to be reviewed and renewed in the light of present and future.

Besides, Radhakrishnan is thinking of the privileges of the Brahmins in the past, and, is quite oblivious of the teeming million Shudras. The Shudras have suffered in the past and even the converted Buddhists from the Shudras, instead of keeping to their past history of exploitation would like to consign it into oblivion.

Again, the world history is moving along, with a view to changing the world picture of the past in the direction of one world, one people one and parliament. Regional histories have to take their place in this world movement.

Further, when one talks about the past history of India, then one is talking about the history of Indo-Aryans, or, the Tamilians, or, the many aboriginal tribes, or, of the Muslims? To ignore all other people, and, to emphasize one single history of Aryan people is neither a way towards making one integrated nation, nor is a way to make India a richer whole for all its variety.

When the Shudras of Bengal were converted into Islam, did they live without their personal and traditional history? Was it not a history of their liberation, of establishing a pan-Islamic brotherhood under the umbrella of One over-arching Allah? It will be too dogmatic to say about Shudras converted into Islam and Christianity that they have become abstract and aberrant. Who can deny the great blessings which Christianity brought to the head-hunters of Khasi and other aboriginal tribes of India? Who can deny the elevation of the Shudras who were converted to Christiantiy? This is a point which has to be kept in view with regard to the next position of Radhakrishnan.

3. As a means of creative religion the native cult has an absolute advantage over any imparted religion

> for a convert to a new religion feels an utter stranger to himself. He feels like an illegitimate child with no heritage, no link with the men who proceeded him........ There is no inner development or natural progress to the new religion.[90]

True, mere copying Western Christianity has not resulted in any new religious upheaval in Indian Christians. Many Western dogmas about Virgin birth of Jesus, Resurrection of Jesus, His Second coming etc., have not pulverized Indian spiritual thinking. As a matter of fact, negligence of Bhakti and advaitic mysticism has resulted in the poverty of Indian Christian theology. But there is no reason why Indian Christianity cannot have an Indian Christian theology. This criticism of Indian Christianity is not true of Indian Islam which even now is contributing much to Islam.

4. Radhakrishnan makes an important plea for the preservation of many religions, for the cross-fertilization of ideas.[91] And it has to be conceded that in most cases missionary zeal for

conversion is based on the depreciation and contempt of other religions.[92]

Radhakrishnan thinks that missionary zeal is based or depreciation and contempt of religions. Is it so? No. At times, missionary zeal based on self-sacrifice is possible with the feeling of sharing a highly valuable spiritual life and experience with others. Here we are reminded of Ramakrishna. Finding a pearl of great price, 'knowing its inestimable worth and not liking to enjoy it alone', missionaries declare the good findings to all people.[93] After reaching religious experience a missionary feels that he has been commissioned by God to preach his gospel throughout the world.[94] Again, the venerable Guru noted:

> There are some who, after eating a mango, will wipe their lips clean, lest others should know, but there are also some who, receiving a mango, will call others to share it with them. So there are some who, realizing the Divine Bliss, cannot rest without seeking to make others also realise it.[95]

Hence, missionary enterprise which at times is not only based on much self-abnegation but also attended with a great deal of risk is really prompted by compassion for others, and also for sharing an experience of bliss of Godly living.

It has to be accepted that men are of different types, and, no one religion will suit all. Even Shaṅkara recommends Karmayoga for the Kshatriyas and *jñānayoga* for the Brahmins or men with Sattvic cast of mind. Hence, different types of religions are bound to flourish. This has been taught by the Gītā and in modern times by C.G. Jung. Why should not a missionary preach a religious creed and practice which may suit some of the types for their acceptance and spiritual benefit? In this connection, Radhakrishnan recommends the worship of one universal religion of the Supreme Spirit.

Yes, in one sense this Supreme Spirit is Brahman to which all religions refer. But this Supreme Spirit can be approached only through some form of theism. Because this common referent of all theistic forms of religion is Supreme Spirit, therefore, it cannot be said that every one worships this Supreme Spirit. Worship is possible only of Brahman with attributes. Only with the ascent to higher forms of the Supreme Spirit one reaches it in the end. But we have already stated that one can reach this differenceless Supreme Spirit by gradually shedding off differences. In this form of the religion of the Supreme Spirit as differenceless Brahman, one does not have to give up one's theistic worship, but one has to keep on refining and purifying his theistic worship. In orther words, people worship the Supreme Spirit ignorantly, and, may also worship it meaningfully and with full recognition as the absolute standard underlying every form of theistic worship. This is implied in the worship of the manifest forms and unmanifest form of Brahman in the Gītā (VII.24). Hence, the universal religion of the Supreme Spirit may be wrongly interpreted, or, rightly interpreted, as has been done under the principle of the unity of religions in this book. In this context, Radhakrishnan makes another important statement.

> Our aim should be not to make converts, Christians into Buddhists or Buddhists into Christians, but enable both Buddhists and Christians to rediscover the basic principle of their own religions and live up to them.[96]

As a matter of fact the discovery of the supreme end of Brahma-realization is known as the point of departure from the ordinary run of life and religious practice. This is really a birth into a new Being. In the real sense this is the valid meaning of conversion in which a religious man is changed into a holy man. This is well illustrated in the life of Balmiki, Tulsidas and some Alvars. In Christianity, Saul was changed into St. Paul, and Peter the fisherman became a fisher of men.

Nobody can really speak against conversion in which there is not only a change *in* will, but *of* will for a New Being or a God-centred Being. But it is proselytization against which Radhakrishnan is so much concerned. A proselyte is one who leaving one religion, adopts another without necessarily a change of heart and will. But proselytization is a historical process from times immemorial, in India, and, all over the world.

Many races have entered India and made India their homes. The Yavanas, the Schythians, the Parthians, the Sakas and

Hunas have entered India and have been absorbed into Hinduism as a result of proselytization. Similarly, when the Buddhists fell on hard times many of them made their way into India and were absorbed into Hinduism, largely as Shudras. Similarly, when the Muslims entered India, they succeeded in proselytizing many Shudras and even the higher castes into Islam. The same thing happened in the case of Christianity when it came as the evangelizing mission in India. Why is Radhakrishnan so much against it? Have not many Buddhists in Bihar, Uttar Pradesh became proselytes in Hinduism? Then why is there hue and cry now? The reason is obvious. It is the political leadership of Brahmins at stake. Hinduism means acceptance of caste and Brahmins as the supreme priestly caste. By virtue of this religious supremacy the Brahmins are ruling India. But is not India a Secular Republic? Does not secularism mean an equal respect for all religions?

Does secularism mean toleration. Hence, we have to deal with secularism and toleration.

SECULARISM

When democracy has to be firmly established in a country with a large number of opposed religions, then it has to define its relation with religion. Usually there are three kinds of relationship in which religion stands in a democratic country.

1. Co-existence of all religions, or, equal respect for all religions.
2. Neutrality with regard to religion.
3. Denial of religions in running the country and its preservation, progress and future aspirations.

Of course, there can be a democracy with one religion as its centre. For example, Pakistan is said to be an Islamic State, and, the same is said to be about Bangladesh. This kind of theocentric democratic government has not been recognized in the West, even though in most of the Western States Christianity is the ruling religion. Why?

The reason is that by making a State a theocratic State, the religious priests or the ecclesiastic authorities begin to interfere in the matter of Government decisions and law-making. What is wrong with it? Well, most of the religions have arisen in a pre-scientific age, and, the modern States are given to science and technology and international relationships. For this reason the Government comes in clash with religion even when it is professed by a vast majority of the citizens. For example, when a government finds that it cannot provide food, jobs and other necessities of life, then it legislates birth-control. This is not liked by Roman Catholic Christians. Hence, this gives rise to conflict between the Government and religion. Hence, purely as a result of historical development, in the Western States religion has not been recognized as a partner of democracy. This does not mean that religion is not made as a weapon for winning election. Till John Kennedy no Roman Catholic could ever be elected as the President of the U.S.A. Even now in Germany Christian Democrats form an important political party. But in general a western government is said to be secular. What does Secularism mean in the West?

Secularism in the West means the cultivation of a scientific attitude in life, and specially towards religious claims in the light of scientific world-view. Hence, it means the full exploitation of the resources of one's country with the help of science and technology in utter disregard of super-naturalism. Therefore, secularism is this-worldly and religion is other-worldly. In this sense, secularism is not anti-religious but quite indifferent to religion. Religion is kept apart from all public activities...... social, economic and political. For example, for facing drought, science and techno-craft are used, and, not mass prayers. Religion is relegated to men's personal life only. This is best seen in John Dewey's Naturalism. Can this meaning of secularism be adopted in India?

No, there are many reasons for not adopting this sense of secularism. First, as yet most Indians have not as developed a scientific attitude to life. Even a scientist thinks of bathing in a sacred river when he is asked to observe the solar eclipse. A team of doctors postponed the hour of surgical operation for witnessing Mahabharat scene on the T.V. (dated 27.11.1988). Most of the Hindu ministers in the morning do not see visitors because of their hour of *Pūjā.* And one can see the vast mass of men on the occasion of *Kumbha* and other melās. Hence, in

India secularism means respect for all types of prevailing religions. Even the Prime Minister of India makes it a point to visit as many temples, shrines, gurdwaras, mosques as possible. Religious orthodoxy in its dazzling colour is maintained on the T.V. for winning elections. Religious holidays have been declared public holidays. Hence, secularism in the preamble of Indian Constitution means 'co-existence of all religions', or, 'equal respect for all religions'. This is what Gandhiji has an maintained.

> I believe in the Bible as I believe in the Gītā. I regard all the great faiths of the world as equally true with my own. It hurts me to see any one of them caricatured as they are today by their own followers.

Thus, in India secularism is a religious and not a political concept. One should remember that for Gandhiji, political activity was taken as a religious activity. Unfortunately people do not also record the view of Mahatma about the kind of religion he had in mind.

> This religion transcends Hinduism, Islam, Christianity etc. It does not supersede them. It harmonises them and gives them reality.[97]

But can this kind of concept work on the Indian scene?

Nehru was a western man. No doubt in his mind 'secularism' meant this-worldly pursuit with the help of science and technology, for taking India forward from her backwardness. Why did he succumb to the confused view of secularism as equal respects for all religions? Nehru advised people not to mix up religion and politics in the government of the State, but encouraged respect for all religions. Thus, Indian secularist partly took from the Mahatma his very *personal way of* taking political life as a form of religious activity, and, Nehru supported the Mahatma's view of having equal respects for all religions. Indian politicians have disregarded the very special meaning of religion which Mahatma had in his mind, and, Nehru's advice not to mix up politics and religion in the affairs of the State. Thus, the confused meaning of secularism has been on the Indian scene, in spite of Mahatmaji and Nehru. But Nehru realized that Hindus and Muslims are religious people and their wishes in favour of religion have to be respected. Secondly, partition of India was followed by a great deal of Hindu-Muslim riots. Both Muslims and Hindus have to be persuaded to live together in peace by securing for them religious co-existence. Nehru granted this concession as a political weapon for restoring Hindu-Muslim peaceful existence in Indian democracy. He hoped that in the long run the Indian politicians will outgrow their religious passion with the growth of industrialisation and spread of science-education. There is little doubt that Nehru laid down the foundation for scientific pursuits and industrial development. Hence, Nehru allowed 'Secular State' to respect all religions equally. Has it worked on the Indian scene?

1. The result of the interpretation of Secularism as equal respect for all religions has made Muslim more fundamentalist and the Hindu intolerant. The Kashmiri Muslims pelt stones on the Indian team when it wins against the Pakistan team. A Hindu is as keen to pit against the Muslim. Hindus in most of the States in India have succeeded in banning cow-slaughter. The result is that with the least provocation Hindu-Muslim riots take place. There can be no peace as long as religions lay exclusive claim for spiritual excellence. Religions make opposite claims. For example, Christians claim that God is Jesus which for the Muslims is blasphemy. A Hindu every morning turns to the rising Sun and most non-Hindu religionists regard this to be an idolatry. Jains and Buddhists in principle are atheistic and, in contrast, the prophetic religions are theistic. How can people live in peace, when they profess opposed religious ideologies.

As a matter of fact, a fairly large number of Indians are Hindus. In cinema shows, T.V. programmes there is bound to be far greater weightage given to Hinduism, than to other religions. How can then religious neutrality be maintained? On the basis of Indian secularism certain problems are bound to create a good deal of headache to Indian government. The problem of Babri Masjid is a case of this nature.

It is altogether false to say that Hindus have remained most tolerant in religious matters. Shivites have killed the Jainas and have always fought against the Vaiṣṇavas. The Hindus never developed that cohesiveness which Muslims have. Caste is a divisive factor. For this reason, the Hindus could never succeed against the external invaders. No doubt, Marathas and Rajputs as local Hindu forces did rise against Muslims. But in Bengal, a large number of Shudras became Muslims and welcomed the Muslim conquerors as their great liberators.[98] Even now the Hindus are divided into the untouchables or scheduled castes, backward Hindus and Hindus of the higher order. All India Hindu Movement has not caught the fire. Once all Hindus become one, there will be more intolerance and riots. Thus, the theory of co-existence of all religions has not worked and is not likely to work.

2. The interpretation of secularism as equal respect for all religions has worked well with Congress political party. It has granted as much latitude and protection to the Muslims as is possible. Muslim vote bank has favoured the Congress. Again, the Brahmin leadership of the party succeeds in catching the Hindu votes too. And the Harijans with their reservations have made them insensitive to the humiliation and atrocities in their everyday life. But has this worked for nationalism?

Some Indian leaders think that 1857 revolt against the Britishers was really the first beginning of Indian nationalism. When even after fortythree years of Independence Indians have not become nationalist, then how can it be hoped that in the past in 1858 they were really nationalist? Because the leaders have to get votes, so most of the political leaders of the Hindus are really caste leaders. Hindus are really not Hindus, but are Brahmins, Rajputs, Bhumiharas, Kayasthas and so on. Because Hinduism means acceptance of caste with Brahmins as the supreme caste, so Hindu religion in political election simply means the acceptance of Hindu fundamentalism.

The same is true of the Muslims. As political party consisting of Hindus works on the basis of caste, so it also works on the basis of Muslim voters. As there are only a few pockets of full Muslim majority, so the Muslim leaders choose that Muslim constituency where political alliance with the Hindus will help them to be elected. This is true for most of the Congress Muslim leaders. But these Congress Muslim leaders can get their Muslim votes for owing full allegiance to Islamic fundamentalism.

Hence, Indian secularism makes a Hindu more of a Hindu, and, a Muslim more of a fundamentalist Muslim. The result? There is no political fight on any principle. Even the communists in Bihar are dominated by the privileged Hindu caste people. For lack of any principle, there is brain drain, unemployment, over-population, no post and no award is possible without the caste and communal backing. Every form of corruption is protected by the caste leadership of the party. Every politician knows that family-planning by legislation is a must. But it is not legislated because of losing Muslim votes.

By defining secularism as 'respect for all religions', religion has entered into the political life of the country as a cancerous growth within it. The sooner this definition of secularism is given up, the better it is. Secularism need not be anti-religion as it was in Russia at the beginning of Communist revolution. The reason is that religion is also a force and many an Indian will do his duty towards his country as God's command. But the Government should remain religion-neutral. Secularism means exploitation of the natural resources of one's country with the help of science and technology with a view to even distribution of resources and jobs for all its citizens. No religion can be higher than the service, defence and furtherance of its future good. Man was not made for religion, but religion was made for man. The ideal man and God are one and the same. The urge to be an ideal citizen by developing one's capacities and abilities to the full in active co-operation with the rest, is most sacred and most in line with the evolutionary *nisus* within man. What man has been in the past is nothing in comparison with what man can be in the future, with the help of science, technology and other modern equipment of mankind. No religion has any right to curtail the happiness of other fellowmen.

Hence, we conclude that secularism can mean that the State should remain indifferent to religion in its drive to make the State industrialized and fully self-sufficient. In the State, religion can be allowed as a private affair of an individual. The West has reached this conclusion after a good deal of experience.

Toleration

It is doubtful to maintain that there is one universal religion of the Supreme Spirit. However, it can be stated that there is one common referent involved in every religion and that there is an absolute standard of reaching a state of differenceless in the final practice of every form of religion. But along this absolute standard of reaching the goal in which all differences are blurred and lost, all forms of religion are infected with relativity, even though there are degrees of being higher and lower. The higher form of relative religions is that which consciously and deliberately adopts this standard of differencelessness. The lower forms of relative religions are those which are not aware of the absolute standard of reaching the state of differencelessness. Besides, the lower forms suffer more from anthropomorphism than the higher forms that keep on refining and purifying their religious concepts to escape from gross anthropomorphism. But one has to realise that every form of religion is relative and as such cannot claim the sole monopoly of religious insight. As such each form of religion should exercise toleration. Toleration means refraining from persecuting the followers of religions other than one's own. It means intellectual breadth and charity which comes not only from a humanitarian consideration, but from the realization that every form of religion is relative. As such we should try to learn from other religions and deepen our own religious sensitivity by appropriating some thing and some insight valuable in other religions. Hence, the most important point to realize is that every form of religion is relative, including one's own. This realization logically would entail toleration. Let us summarise the reasons for holding all religions to be relative.

I. First, we have maintained that the Supreme Reality cannot but be unknown and unknowable (*Bṛhadāraṇyaka Up*. II. 4. 14; Maitri VI. 7; Kant's theory of synthetic unity of apperception; Wittgenstein's theory of keeping silence about God).

But we have also maintained that religion is psychologically embedded in our mental constitution. So we must search after our highest concern of Brahma-realization. Thus, man is condemned to know the unknowable, what can man do?

II. He draws a picture of the unknowable Brahman, according to one's intellectual reaches and world-view. In the primitive stage the picture is most anthropomorphic and with the progress of knowledge and a higher form of world-view the picture gets more refined. For instance, the God of the Jews at first demanded animal sacrifice and later as a result of increase in religious sensitivity, the same God demanded a contrite heart, humbly following the commands of the Lord. Thus the picture in any religion whatsoever cannot but be relative, for it is bound to change in the light of increase in knowledge, world-view and deeper sensitivity towards the unknown reality.

III. Thirdly, we have already drawn attention to the fact that in the growth of personality, everyone has a notion of an ideal self which he projects on the wider screen in the form of one's god. As men differ in their types, function and mental constitution, so their ideal self and god is bound to differ with persons in their cultural upbringing.

IV. The same point has been raised in Indian systems. Men differ in their temperamental constitution, depending on the proportion of *Sattva*, *rajas* and *tamas*, and past Karmas. Hence, as men are, so are their gods (Gītā 17. 4-6). Hence, religions are bound to differ and be relative.

Therefore, from the viewpoint of religious philosophy there is no room for religious intolerance. Further, one should realize that in India there has been a history of religious toleration.

Asoka's edict engraved on the rocks advises us to honour every form of religious faith. The root of this toleration is to reverence one's own faith and never to revile that of others. It rebounds to the glory of India that a parliament of religions was held by the most enlightened Akbar. He allowed free discussions of all faiths and established an eclectic religion of Din-Ilahi. In our own day Mahatma Gandhi has clearly stated:

> I belive in the Bible as I believe in the Gītā. I regard all the great faiths of the world as equally true with my own. It hurts me to see any one of them caricatured as they are today by their own followers.[99]

The Greeks on account of their intellectual breadth and syncretism had held wide toleration. But even Islam advises toleration.

> Unto each nation have We given sacred rites which they are to perform; so let them not dispute with thee of the matter, but summon thou unto the Lord. (*Surah* XXII. 67).
> Allah will judge between you on the Day of Resurrection concerning that wherein ye used to differ. (*Surah* XXII. 69).

Again,

> Let there be no compulsion in religion.

Hence, forcible conversion has been condemned in Islam.

In modern India every faith is allowed to exist and to practise, and even to propagate its own faith. But why is the country not free from caste and religious tumult and tension? The reason is the political use of religion.

Religion and Politics

Secularism as a form of philosophy means a revolt against a theo-centric State, and, separates religion from political life. Nehru has advised us not to mix up politics and religion in the affairs of the State. However, he hoped that people professing different religions will co-operate with the government and will not disturb the peace of the citizens. So he advised people to respect all religions. However, in practice the Prime Ministers of India on various occasions have been visiting shrines, mosques, gurudwaras, thereby encouraging religions. Many religious festivals have been converted into national holidays. Hence, the political practice is to encourage religion, whereas it is the duty of the Secular State of India to weaken the hold of religion. What is wrong with the Secular State of India to encourage religions for obtaining the votes of the masses?

The reason is that the State and religion are opposed in their nature, aims and methodology. Religion is other-worldly, and, the State is this-worldly. Religion relies on *revelation*, largely stored up in scriptures in conducting the lives of its followers. As against this the State relies on science and technology for exploiting the natural resources and even distribution of goods and services to its citizens. There is no limit to the progress of science and technology. Hence, the State seeks control over nature for making progress in lengthening life, good health and prosperity of its citizens. The State honours the scientists, technocraft and all those citizens who make this-worldly life as happy and prosperous as is possible. As against this aim and the claim of progressiveness, religion is conservative. Religions had their rise before the rise of science. Naturally they hearken back to the past. Hinduism believes in the eternity of the Vedas, the Christians in the Bible which was written over two thousand years ago. Thus, religion accepts that all that people are required to know is to have faith in what was taught in the ancient past. Most of the religions believe that this world is only a temporary abode of men and their eternal life is in the heaven. Hence, religions are conservative and other-worldly.

If religion and the State are so much opposed to each other, then how can they co-operate? Well, by respecting each other. Religion has to be relegated to the claim of the private life of each citizen, and, the State has not to interfere with the personal faith of the people. In like manner, the State is not to recognize the claim of religion in its activities and affairs of the State. Religion as a private affair and the State as the public affair of the people should not interfere, since the Ten Commandments of the Bible, and, the *pañca-Mahāvrata* of Indian religion are the oldest laws of the State. Religion as the private faith of citizens will help them in due discharge of their duties in the State, and, the State will ensure freedom to its citizens in the practice of their religion. However, this happy division of religion and the State often comes to be disturbed.

Very often religion claims this-worldly power in the furtherance of its practice. Judaism, Islam and Sikhism claim a share in the affairs of the State in the interest of their religion. According to both Judaism and Islam, religion makes the nation. This seriously collides with the State of India. In India there are two major religions, namely, Hinduism and Islam. Hence, according to Islamic claim, India is the home of two nationalities, namely, the Hindus and Muslims. But it does not require any deep knowledge of history that this is an untenable claim. Many of the Muslims of India were once Hindus. So the two are not separate races and people. Besides, it is not true even in Islamic countries, namely, there are Arabs, Turks, Iranians and many other nationalities. In the same manner Jews may be religious minority, but they owe their citizen rights of the country which they own as their home land. Hence, religion cannot make a nation, even though on the basis of religion, the Indian sub-continent has been partitioned into Pakistan and Hindustan. But what about Sikhism?

Sikhism is a purely Indian religion and in the beginning it was just a sect of Hinduism like Kabir panth, Gorakhnath panth. For Guru Nanak three vows were necessary for a Sikh, namely,

> *Kirt Karna* to earn one's livelihood through hard, honest labour *wand chhakana* (to share one's earning with others) and *nam japna* (muttering the name of Guru).

However, Guru Hargobind assumed two swords called *piri* and *Miri*. *Miri* was there to defend and pursue political end, *piri* was to be used for safeguarding spiritual end. But it was Guru Gobind Singh (1675-1708) who changed the whole complexion of Sikhism. He transformed the peace-loving Sikhs, into soldiers. Bhakti and shakti were interfused and a Sikh now is a saint-soldier, rolled into one. Guru Hargobind emphasized the primacy of allegiance to truth and moral virtues, and, not to submit to the exclusive claims of a secular State. Guru Gobind Singh conferred spiritual power to Guru Granth Saheb which has been installed in the Golden Temple. The temporal sovereignty lay in Akal Takht, and, these two were expected to work in co-ordination. Thus religion and politics are inseparablyblended in Sikhism. How did this kind of religion work in the British time?

True, Guru Gobind Singh had established the identity of the Sikhs by introducing the observances of five *Kakars* (i.e., Kanghā, Kesh, Kaṛā, kirpan, kachha). But these five Kakars were inseparably blended with the politico-spiritual pursuits of the purest of Sikhs, known as *Khalsa*. Britishers fully used the Khalsa by including and recruiting them in the Indian army. The Khalsa Sikhs were not only distinguished from the Hindus, but also from Sahajdhari, Namdari Sikhs and the Udasis. Being called the military class of India, the Khalsa Sikhs sought an independent Khalistan at the the time of handing over the power to the Indians. But the number of Khalsa Sikhs did not justify the creation of an independent Khalistan. What happened then?

The Indian Government continued the policy of recruiting the Sikhs in the army out of all proportion, with the result that they form the sword of India. Indeed it worked well in 1967 and 1971 in war with Pakistan. Why do the Sikhs want an independent Khalistan is not very clear, seeing that they have transformed Punjab into the granary of India, and, into an industrial State of India? Per capita income of a Sikh is higher than that of any Indian in any other part of India. Three points are relevant in this context.

1. Religion and Politics came to be mixed up in the religion of the Khalsa.
2. Secondly, their great prosperity, both at home and abroad gave them the feeling to be the superior class of men. And yet they could hardly dominate Indian Government.
3. Thirdly, the inimical foreign powers could instigate the Indian Sikhs through Sikh settlers. Certainly, Pakistan has been training and arming the Sikhs, may be through the direct or indirect connivance of powers unfriendly to India.

What can India do? Should it use superior force to overcome the Khalistanis by helping other Sikhs loyal to India? But the great lesson which the Government of India has to learn that religious hold over the people has to be weakened by becoming really secular. Secondly, Akal Takht has to be used for political purpose under the democratic set-up of the Government of India. Are the Sikhs really anti-Hindu?

Personally we do not think so. We have already held that Sikhs are Hindus, in the wider sense of 'the Hindus', though Guru Granth Saheb does not favour Brahminism with its caste and idol-worship. Sikhs are killing more Sikhs than Hindus. This shows that their political motivation is against anybody who does not support Khalistan. In any case, the secular government of India has to give up the slogan, 'Equal respect for all religions'. If it be accepted at all, then it should be counted with those religions which do not have politics in their in-built system. Let us take up the case of the Muslims.

Muslims came to India about a thousand years ago and ruled over the vast part of the country for over five and half hundred of years. Muslims never combined as a whole against the Hindus, and, Hindus too never combined against the Muslims. In certain pockets Marathas, Rajputs and Sikhs established themselves against the Muslim rule. But the Hindus never combined themselves against the Muslims during pre-British days. However, under the subjugation of India under one British rule, there could be the possibility of Hindus unifying themselves under one umbrella, and, in like manner the Muslims could have combined. But the British rulers were too shrewed. They introduced the principle of 'divide and rule' and adhered to it very carefully. Sikhs were separated from the Hindus and the Rajputs and Marathas from one another. Yet they could use the Hindus against the Muslims, and, the Muslims against the Hindus.

Under Mahatma Gandhi's leadership to a great extent Hindus and Muslims joined to fight the Britishers. But somehow due to mutual suspicion of each other, Muslims and Hindus separated with the result that Pakistan was created out of India. The years 1946 and 1947 saw great killings, of Hindus by the Muslims, and, of Muslims by the Hindus. Till today the Hindus and Muslims maintain their separate existence, tolerating each other as a matter of convenience. Least points of disagreement lead to communal riots between the two communities. The tension between the two communities is largely political and not religious. Take the instance of Babri Masjid. Muslim leaders raise hue and cry to catch Muslim votes, and, the Hindu leaders do the same to secure Hindu votes. Cannot the Government solve the issue?

Surprisingly enough the nationalist Muslims have no place either amongst the Congress or the Muslims League. The more communal you are, the more popular you are in the community to which you belong. With this communal tendency, how can we afford to escape from communal riots? The Congress Government and party has very great advantage in this regard.

First, under the leadership of Mahatma Gandhi some outstanding Muslim leaders worked on the platform of the Congress. Secondly, Mahatma Gandhi himself met his martyrdom in protecting the lives of the Muslims. Naturally the Congress Party has been siding with the Muslims and championing the cause of their security, religious worship and even Urdu and some employment. In the State of Bihar Urdu in some parts of it is a second language. The Congress Government has established 'Minority Cell' which is really 'Muslim Cell' for redressing some of their outstanding grievances. Yes, so far the Congress Government has succeeded in winning the Muslim votes. But is it a step towards secularism where religions have to be weakened?

Muslims are more fundamentalists in India than even what they are in Pakistan, Egypt, Iran and Turkey with regard to the matter of divorce, or, some such personal law of the Muslims. One must not ignore the fact that the Congress Party lost at the poll because the Muslims did not vote for the Congress in 1977. The issue was one of family planning. But can India become a welfare state with regard to food, employment, health-services and so on, in the situation of our present population explosion? And no community in India is prepared for family planning. Here we are making a political issue under the guise of religion. In a democracy votes count, and, smaller the number of votes fewer are the chances that the community will get its due at the hands of the majority.

Here by making political use of religion, the country is made poor and backward, and religion too gets vulgarised. By assuming religious liberty, retaining Urdu, and, by encouraging the Muslims to retain their personal law regarding divorce, and full freedom not to observe family planning, the Muslims are segregated from the rest of the Indian nationals. Segregation keeps the tension between the Hindus and Muslims alive, resulting at times in communal riots. But it suits the Congress Party, for segregation from the other Indian nationals and by the promise of extending all kinds of security for the Muslims, the Congress Party gets the support of the Muslim mass. The political use of Hinduism is most direct and this again keeps the country disunited, weak and backward.

The Hindus are divided into castes. The political leaders are really caste leaders. This is as much true of the Congress Party as of any political party. Each candidate at the time of election appeals to his caste men and may make pact with other castes for the purpose of election. Hence, Hindu nationalism has not grown up even now. Thus, there is really caste-federation in the legislative assemblies. The result?

Formerly, the slogan used to be socialism and secularism for election purposes. Now at present (1988) 'socialism' remains only in the Constitution on paper; it is not even mentioned in the speeches of political leaders. Thus, the economic exploitation of the poorer castes goes unchecked. In spite of repeated assurances to the poor sections, the programme of raising their economic standard remains unimplemented. Rising inflation, population explosion and corrupt practices add to the woe of the poor castes. Thus, the country remains poor by making direct use of caste-religion for the Hindus.

Secondly, in the British days, there were hardly any caste riots. But by making caste as the basis of election, castes remain in tension, and, in the State of Bihar at present there are caste riots. The reason for this is both economic and political. In the oppression of the scheduled castes by the zamindars belonging to the higher caste, the economic consideration plays its part as political factor. Thus, the political use of caste results in caste riots.

Thirdly, corruption in the States goes unchecked. There are several causes of corruption, but one cause is certainly caste leadership. Any person belonging to the higher caste may indulge in corrupt practices. He can always rely on his caste-leadership in the political field if he gets into trouble for committing economic and other crimes.

Political parties try to enforce and perpetuate reservation for the scheduled castes and tribes. True, a few people have profited from reservation in the services, legislative assemblies and councils, admission into educational institutions. But reservation has not raised the scheduled castes as a whole either socially, economically or politically. Even now after 43 years of Independence they continue to be the object of humiliation, exploitation and mass violence.

Thus, the political use of religion neither serves the State nor religion. The State remains economically, socially and politically poor and backward. Religion gets polluted because of constant riots in the name of religion. Politically the country becomes unstable on account of the separatist tendency based on religion. The political use of religion by the communalist and casteist is highly dishonest and politically unethical and unpatriotic.

But alas! in near future there is no hope to get out of caste or communal consideration.

Religion may not teach to hate one's fellowmen, but politics does. Political use of religion is not in the service of democracy. But will the political leaders learn this lesson?

References

1. Paul Tillich, 'Dynamics of Faith'. George Allen 1957. pp. 45, 50,75 ,77, 1-1, 106, 114.
2. Paul Tillich, *Systematic Theology*, Vol. I, Chicago, 1967, p. 12, also see page 14.
3. Dynamics of Faith, p. 45.
4. *Ibid*., pp. 45-46.
5. Dynamics, p. 18.
6. Dynamics, p. 50.
7. Dynamics, p. 62-63.
8. Systematic Theology I, p. 14.
9. *Beyond the Pleasure Principle*., pp. 50-51.
   Of course, Freud was not without religion. He entertained Jewish Messianic hope of a Millennium in *Future of an Illusion*, pp. 85-86, 93. Then again, a religion of Stoic resignation or Buddhist *Upeksa* (Letters of S. Freud, p. 276) coupled with the ideals of brotherly love, inner freedom and truth (Erich Fromm, *Psychoanalysis and Religion*, p. 21) was taught by Freud. Hence, even Freud was not without a religion.
10. R.S. Bhatnagar, *Dimensions of Classical Sufi Thought*, p. 139.
11. *Bṛhadāraṇyaka Up*. II. 3,6; III. 9.26; IV. 2.4; Taittirīya Up. II. 4; Maitri Up. VI. 7 etc.
12. *Tractatus Logico-Philosophicus* 6.41.
13. *Ibid*., 6.4, 312.
14. *Bṛhadāraṇyaka Up*. III. 7.2-23.
15. *Chhandogya Up* 6.9-16.
16. Space, Time and Deity, Vol. II. p. 365.
17. The Philosophy of Sarvepalli Radhȧkrishnan, p. 78.
18. Paul Tillich, Systematic Theology, Vol. II, p. 100.
19. Paul Tillich, S.T., Vol. I, p. 134.
20. Patrick Sherry, '*Religion, Truth and Language Games*, London 1977, p. 1.
21. P. Sherry, *Religisn, Truth and Language Games*, Macmillan 1977, p. 175.
22. S. Radhakrishnan, *Eastern Religion and Western Thought*, p. 327; Vide p. 338.
23. Paul Tillich, *The Courage to be*, p. 182.
24. *Srībhāṣya*, I, 1.1, pp. 58, 72. Eng. try. by G. Thibaut.
25. Friedich Heiler, *How can Christian and non-Christian Religions Co-operate*? Hibbert Journal, Vol. 52, 1953-54, p. 109.

26. *Ibid.*, p. 111.
27. Bhagwan Das, *The Essential Unity of All Religions*, p. 56.
28. *Contemporary Indian Philosophy*, p. 258 (London 1950).
29. *Eastern Religion and Western Thought*, p. 327.
30. *Ibid.*, p. 238. (italics mine).
31. *Contemporary Indian Philosophy*, p. 275; See also p. 177.
32. *Fragments of a Confession*, p. 66; Eastern Religion, p. 76.
33. *The Gospel of Sri Ramakrishna* by M. Page, reference will be described as M. 104, 273, 331.
34. M. 39.
35 Romain Rolland, *The life of Ramakrishna*, p. 206, Almorah 1930.
36. *Ibid.*, p. 247.
37. M. 134-135. This is the tenor of Ramakrishna's view about Brahman. This is largely Viśiṣṭādvaitic, for Ramanuja regards Brahman in the subtle state of *pralaya* as *nirguṇa* and in manifest form as *saguṇa*.
38. *Teachings of Sri Ramakrishna*, Calcutta 1985. Henceforth it is abbreviated as T. 184.
39. T. 126-127.
40. T. 691.
41. T. 687.
42. M. 135.
43. M. 104.
44. M. 123.
45. Romain Rolland, *Ibid.*, p. 229.
46. Romain Rolland, *Ibid.*, p. 101.
47. Romain Rolland, *Ibid.*, p. 279.
48. M. 236.
49. M. 319, 320, 342.
50. M. 321.
51. M. 320.
52. M. 181.
53. Romain Rolland, *Ibid.*, p. 198.
54. Romain Rolland, *Ibid.*, p. 182.
55. M. 111.
56. M. 93.
57. M. 304-305.
58. M. 289.
59. M. 306.
60. *Teachings* T 696.
61. M. 188-189.
62. M. 211.
63. M. 184.
64. F. Max Müller, *Ramakrishna*, all references to this will be called '*Sayings*'. Here refer to sayings 250, 251.
65. *Teachings* T. 697.
66. *Teachings* T. 17.

67. *Teachings* T. 13.
68. *Teachings* T. 698.
69. *Teachings* T. 695.
70. *Sayings* 247; *Vide Sayings* 250, 251, 272.
71. M.p. 223; *Vide Teachings* T. 683 where respect towards others religions, has been recommended.
72. M. p. 128.
73. M. p. 129.
74. Romain Rolland, *Ibid.*, p. 87; also M. p. 34.
75. M. p. 45.
76. M. p. 98.
77. M. pp. 107-108.
78. M. p. 134.
79. M. p. 127.
80. Romain Rolland, *Ibid.*, p. 198.
81. M. p. 315.
82. M. p. 36.
83. M. pp. 243-244, 309, 336.
84. M. p. 143.
85. M. pp. 108, 114, 138, 151-152, 308, 314, 315, 335.
86. J.N. Sarcar, *Islam in Bengal*, Calcutta 1972, p. 23.
87. Even Mahayana form of Buddhism favours this progressive form of revelation from the Buddha.
88. *Eastern Religion*, p. 327; Vide 328, 329, 345.
89. *Ibid.*, p. 328.
90. *Ibid.*, p. 328.
91. *Ibid.*, p. 330.
92. *Fragments of a Confession*, p. 74.
93. *Teachings of Sri Ramakrishna*, Verse 149.
94. *Teachings*, T. 172; also T. 715.
95. T. 714.
96. *Fragments of a Confession*, p. 74.
97. *Harijan*, p. 10.2.1940.
98. J.C. Sarcar, *Islam in Bengal*, Calcutta, 1972, p. 23.
99. S. Radhakrshnan, *Eastern Religions*, p. 313.

SUMMARY AND CONCLUSIONS

In the light our study of the living religions of the world, a certain metaphysical scheme is suggested to us. We do not think that metaphysics is a scientific enterprise, even though it may be deeply indebted to science. For example, the metaphysics of A.N. Whitehead and Samuel Alexander is based on physics and mathematics of their day. But their metaphysics is not an enterprise of science. The function of metaphysics is to widen the horizon of knowledge and to increase our sensitivity to higher dimensions of reality. This was strongly suggested by Kant, and, this is what we understand as the function of metaphysics.

We had to clarify our stand with regard to metaphysics, because religious theologies are so many instances of metaphysics. Both religious metaphysics and theology do not provide us with scientific knowledge for predicting and guiding the adjustive behaviour of men. They are pleas for intellectual insight or *bodhi* (enlightenment) in the direction of *making of higher men.* Metaphysics is more of an intellectual construction and religious theologies are practical guides towards making men 'fit for heaven'. The element of knowing is subordinate to the end of *becoming*. This is well illustrated in the enlightenment of Lord Buddha and later in achieving *nirvāṇa.* With this introduction let us summarise our main findings of the comparative study of religions.

I. The first important postulate of religion is that the supreme object of religious adoration is unknown and unknowable. Why?

(a) According to Kant, the noumenon behind the phenomena is at the basis of knowing, remembering and perceiving all objects. Hence this *Synthetic Unity of Apperception* is the very condition of knowing, so it cannot be itself an *object* of thought.

> Now it is, indeed, very evident that I cannot know as an object that I must presuppose in order to known any object ....[1]

(b) There is little doubt that the Upanishads are the most profound and respected religious writings of the Hindus. Not only Shaṅkara, Ramaṇuja have devoted their attention to the Upanishads, but even in the modern times, Rammohun Roy, Rabindranath Tagore and Aurobindo cannot be understood without the Upanishads.

For the Upanishads, according to *Advaitism*, Brahman is the sole reality which is to be meditated upon and realised. But this Brahman is pure consciousness, without any object whatsoever. This objectless consciousness is at the basis of any knowledge of any object whatsoever. But it cannot be an object to itself.

> You could not see the seer of seeing.
> You could not hear the hearer of hearing.
> You could not think the thinker of thinking.
> You could not understand the understander of understanding.[2]

(c) That God, the supreme reality of religious worship is unknowable is also supported by Ludwig Wittgenstein who is said to be *the* philosopher of the 20th century. According to this abstruse philosopher God is the meaning of the universe. Perhaps Wittgenstein thinks of God as the Creator of the universe with some end of the universe, and, this end is the meaning of the world. The meaning and the creator God are external to the world. But, according to Wittgenstein, we can know the world and all the objects comprised within it. This is also supported by the fact that according to Judaism God is not immanent in the world but is transcendent of the Universe. Hence, the statement of the Jew Wittgenstein in relation to the unknowable God are:

> It is logically impossible for the sense of the world to be itself a part of the world, since the meaning of anything cannot be a part of that of which it is the meaning.[3]

Further,

> God does not manifest Himself in the World.[4]

Again,

> The solution of the riddle of life in space and time lies outside of space and time.[5]

(d) Certainly the evolutionary scheme of the universe, presented by A.N. Whitehead and Samuel Alexander, is not a scientific construction, but is an imaginative structure in relation to a world-view.

According to the evolutionary scheme of things, the supreme reality is Creative Current which in due course has given rise to Matter, Life, Mind and Self-consciousness. On viewing this scheme we find that there are two major tendencies evolved in things, namely, *conatus* and *nisus*. By virtue of *conatus* each being remains preserved in its being. For many millions of years, things and living species, more or less, have contained to be in the self-same being. Man too has remained physically unchanged in his own nature. But apart from *conatus*, there is also *nisus* by virtue of which man tends to grow higher, psychically and spiritually. By virtue of this *nisus* within man, he makes an ideal picture of his higher being. He projects this picture on the wider canvas of the universe in the form of his creator and determinator of his highest destiny. By virtue of the worship of this projected image of a creator, man feels to be an entire and perfect self.

This *nisus* within each man is said to be an inpingement of the creative reality. This immanence of the transcendent reality has been advanced by Hindu theology all through its entire duration. The Upanishads inform us that the supreme Brahman which is in the sun, sky and all things, is found most articulate in man and in his thinking. *Bṛhadāraṇyaka Upanishad* twentytwo times tells us that the transcendent Brahman is the soul, the inner controller and immortal Self of every man.[6] Again,

> Both he who is here is a person and he who is yonder in the Sun......he is one.[7]

The presence of the transcendent as immanent to some extent is also supported by the doctrine of *holism*.

(e) 'Holism' was first propounded by Aristotle and was raised to the status of *quasi*-scientific explanation by Hans Driesch. The theory of holism was raised to an ontology in J.C. Smuts, A.N. Whitehead and Samuel Alexander. But it received special attention by the Gostaltists in psychology. This theory of holism need not be taken to be fully scientific, but it can be used speculatively to throw light on religious concepts.

According to the psychology of 'Personality', it was thought that there are two tendencies within man, namely, *autonomy* and *homonomy*. By virtue of autonomy, each individual actualizes its potentialities within the organism itself. But by virtue of *homonomy* an individual expands and enriches its personality by appropriating things and values in his social sphere. Not only this, but it also tends to have an ideal self or a symbolic self. It is this self which gives rise to the formation of one's deity. By worshipping his deity, the individual gets the sense of his being a complete and perfect Self. For example, the advaitin maintains that a knower of Brahman himself becomes Brahman. Sri Ramakrishna says,

> If you meditate on an ideal you will acquire its nature. If you think of God day and night, you will acquire the nature of God. (*M* 657, The Gospel of Sri Ramakrishna 1986).[8]

Similarly, the Bible says,

> You must be perfect.....just as your Father in heaven is perfect! (*Mt.* 5.48)

Is this ideal Self in the form of one's deity mere fiction?

II. The picture or the symbolic self is not mere fiction, for it wells up from the very depth of one's being, where there is the *nisus* of the evolutionary current, or, where Brahman dwells as the inner controller. Hence, the ideal Self in the form of deity grips not only an individual, but all the members of a community participating in a common world-view. On account of this holistic homonomy and *nisus* within man, man cannot live without some deity. This is what is known as religion *a priori* i.e., man cannot live without some religion. Hence, the oft-quoted lines of St. Augustine:

> Thou has created us for thyself and our heart knows no rest until it may repose in thee.

What is the nature of this ideal self, projected in the form of one's deity?

III. God, as the picture of what is felt as the inmost being of the individual and shared collectively by the larger community having more or less the same world-view. In this, God remains external and objective for all believers. Besides, this deity in some sense outlines the nature of the supreme reality called Brahman in the Upanishads, and, creative current in the evolutionary scheme of things.

Secondly, the deity as the ideal Self must be various. As the individuals are said to have different Saṁskāras, so their deity also must be relative to the kind of persons they are (Gītā XVII. 3-6). Similarly, C.G. Jung holds that each individual differs from others by virtue of his *type*, *mental structure* and *function*. In his doctrine of individuation he outlines the four kinds of deity, according to the development of an individual, namely, *shadow*, *anima-animus*, *mana-personality* and *maṇḍala-experience*. Thus, the worshipful deity will differ with various believing communities, sharing in different world-views. As a matter of fact in each believing community, some believers may oppose or protest against the prevailing deity due to change in their intellectual climate, yielding different world-views. Can one say that his religious view is better or truer than those of others?

Whatever form of deity we have is of that Supreme reality which has no shape or form. It is said to be the Supreme Spirit. How can anybody claim the monopoly of his form of the Supreme Spirit? But a little more will be added towards the end of this short summary.

IV. We find that the Supreme Reality by itself is unknown and unknowable. Yet again by virtue of the *nisus* and the holistic tendency in man, he is compelled to know the unknowable. This is the great predicament of man. Man has to talk about God in relation to whom he should remain silent. The Upanishads hold that Brahman is inexpressible.

> Wherefrom words turn back,
> Together with the mind, not having attained. (*Taitt. Up.* 2.4)

Similarly, Kabir states that by talking about God, we distort His essence. The more we talk, the greater is distortion.[9] However, communicability about God, specially amongst believers, is necessary. Here Kabir tells us that no God-talk is literally true, but a talk which gives us assurance about Him and yields us peace, then we should talk in that kind of appropriate language.[10] However, towards the end of the 20th century, in the west and in India, religions hold is being loosened. Why?

V. In the west, traditional form of Christianity has lost much of its hold on the masses. Reason? The West fought two devastating wars, bringing ruin and dissolution and much suffering. And the combatants were all Christians. From this the west came to the conclusion that God is not concerned with man. Secondly, with the spread of science and technology, the presence of God is not involved in most cases. For fighting out drought, famine and other natural calamities, not God but the technical skill is most sought. Hence, God has been edged out from almost all walks of life. For this reason, Dietrich Bonhoeffer has popularised secular Christianity. This simply means that God is to be found in the midst of secular activities rather than beyond the clouds. Thus, secular activities have become sanctified. Some of the best Muslims and Christians pray to God before undertaking their secular activities. But this grand spectacle is seen only in a few good devotees. In general however churches have become emptier.

In India the same scene is present though in a different form. Due to over-population, unemployment and run-away inflation, Indian people have become far more this-worldly than ever before. The sole function of religion survives in the form of casteism and communalism. In other words, political election thrives on casteism and communalism. Hence, the politicians trade on the religious sentiments of the people. No doubt certain religious festivals are observed by people in great strength. Hardwar, Kumbh melas, as also Gaṅgā bathing at Sonepur are very big draw. Does this mean that the people have become very religious? Let us look at 'Ashwini Bhatnagar reports' under the caption 'Kumbh Kaleidoscope' presented in 'The Times of India, dated February 19, 1989'.

> A good-looking widow Sharmila of 22, was shaved in spite of her cries and pleadings. Again, the Kumbh was the biggest gathering of religious heads. Three out of four Shankara-

caryas were present and also Deoraha Baba. What were they doing here? They showered their blessings on all the VIPs who cared to come to their Ashrams.
Blessing Rajiv Gandhi here and cursing the National Front there.
They spoke on politics and Ram Janmabhoomi but not on Sati or dowry. The issues were left to torment society.

The people in general do not fully realise the depth of tirade of saint poets against external ritualism. External ritualism robs the people of observing morality. But, religious observances without morality rob the devotees of their spiritualism. This is the real meaning underlying the criticism of external ritualism by the saints. With the loss of spiritual values, corruption has become rampant in all walks of life. There is hardly a day when the reports of such corruption are not made in Indian dailies. However, unless the society improves with a view to supporting religious spiritualism, religious values will be completely ruined. What will be left of the contributions of sages and seers, of Sufism and of Ramakrishna, Vivekananda and Aurobindo?

VI. True, so far great religious insights have been won only by individuals. For example, sages meditating in a forest, a Buddha meditating under the Bunyan tree at Bodh-Gaya, a prophet Muhammed meditating in the cave of Mt. Hira, a Christ praying alone in a desert place, are so many illustrations of religious insights won by religious stalwarts. But the society too, ideal or actual has to serve as a vale of soul-making. When Alexander came to India, he marvelled at the renunciates who had conquered their lower passions. But the then society too held these men and their ideals in great esteem and reverence. Thus, the society has to change as much as the individuals for a higher spiritual attainment.

Pt. Nehru spoke of making India a Welfare State and we can think about it in terms of five sheaths mentioned by Taittiriya Upanishad (2.2.4). The doctrine of five sheaths has been mentioned in relation to an individual. But this doctrine can be more appropriately applied to society which has many times taken as an organism.

The first sheath is called *annamaya* i.e., the basic social order is one in which all the members of a society are provided with food and suitable employment. The second order is said to be *prāṇamaya* i.e., in this order members are given opportunities for health, vigour and virility. Thirdly, there is the *manomaya* order in which members are provided with opportunities of cultivating science, technology and other means of a civilized State. Then, there is the *Vijñānamaya* order in which everybody works according to his abilities and gets according to his need. This is the order in which the State encourages its citizens for higher pursuits for the health of one's Soul. In the last order the society inspires its members to have the vision of bliss and supreme contentment. Each and every order has to be run in accordance with the principle contained in the doctrine of differenceless Brahman i.e., in a spirit of justice and egalitarianism.

VII. (a) Fundamentalism and conservatism maintain that the best religious insight has already been made once for all in the past. Present and future can only distort this insight, but cannot improve upon it. On the contrary reformists and progressives take their stand on Scientism. According to them science is progressive and adds real knowledge about the world. Many things said by religions in pre-scientific age concerning this world and man cannot be accepted if they collide with scientific knowledge.

Even when one cannot set aside the claims of science and the application of scientific methodology to religions, one cannot go all along with science. But religions must get deepened and enriched by mutual religious dialogue and also by the findings of science.

(b) Supreme Reality is unknown and unknowable.

(c) The holistic tendency in each man to become whole and perfect, and, the *nisus* in each man according to the evolutionary scheme of things, compel man to have the image of a worshipful deity, which may be called the divine image in him.

(i) Each deity depends on the hereditary tendencies and environmental upbringing, and also the world-view of each age. All these constituents together are known as one's *Saṁskāra*.

(ii) Naturally as *saṁskāras* differ, so will be the difference with regard to deity.

(iii) No monopolistic claim can be made in favour of any one deity.

(iv) Quite naturally no one has any right to participate in any religious warfare. Any such fight destroys the divine image in him.

(v) No one has any right to blaspheme any religion whether of one's own or of others.

(vi) Each deity has to be worshipped according to the absolute standard of differenceless Brahman. In other words, each form of theistic worship should lead to the attainment of that mental state in which all differences of caste, creed, colour etc., are dissolved.

(vii) Further, each form of religion should try to establish a higher social order which will ultimately lead to the emergence of higher humanity with the prospect of richer and greater spiritual attainments.

References

1. *Critique of Pure Reason*, Eng. tr. N.K. Smith (abridged), p. 201.
2. *Bṛhadāraṇyaka Vpa* 3.4.2.
3. *Tractatus Logico—Philosophicus* 6.41.
4. *Tractatus* 6.432.
5. *Tractatus* 6.4.312.
6. *Bṛhadāraṇyaka* Up. 3.7.2-23.
7. *Taittiriya* Up. 2.8; 3.10.4.
8. M 657. The Gospel of Sri Ramakrishna 1986,
9. *Kabir Granthavali*, pada 67.
10. *Granthavali*, Ramaini 34.

INDEX